THE

OLD FARMER'S ALMANAC

Calculated on a new and improved plan
for the year of our Lord

1991

Being 3rd after LEAP YEAR and (until July 4)
215th year of American Independence

FITTED FOR BOSTON, AND THE NEW ENGLAND STATES, WITH SPECIAL
CORRECTIONS AND CALCULATIONS TO ANSWER FOR ALL THE UNITED STATES.

Containing, besides the large number of Astronomical Calculations
and the Farmer's Calendar for every month in the year, a variety of

NEW, USEFUL, AND ENTERTAINING MATTER.

ESTABLISHED IN 1792

BY ROBERT B. THOMAS

The doubts we vainly seek to solve,
The truths we know, are one;
The known and nameless stars revolve
Around the Central Sun.

– JOHN GREENLEAF WHITTIER

Address all editorial correspondence to

THE OLD FARMER'S ALMANAC, DUBLIN, NH 03444

For advertising information for next year's 200th anniversary edition, call 617-723-4309.

To Patrons

You are holding in your hands the 199th annual edition of the oldest continuously published periodical on the North American continent. How proud our founder, Robert B. Thomas, would be if he knew his creation continued to appear on newsstands every fall so many, many years after he departed this life in 1846.

He'd be irritated, too. With not a little irony, he'd be bothered by the ever-increasing number of brand-new "ye olde" almanacs competing on the newsstands these days, outraged at the clever ways some of them design their covers to look like the real *Old Farmer's Almanac.*

The irony lies in the fact that when Robert B. Thomas first began publishing this almanac, *he* was the one being accused of being an imitator. "A new author has endeavoured to copy our shape, size, and arrangement," wrote a popular almanac maker of the time, Isaiah Thomas (no relation), in 1793.

In reply, Robert B. Thomas utilized this page in 1794 to write, "A selfish editor, who appears to be much chagrined at our success, has not only privately endeavoured to injure us, but publickly attacked our reputation."

Indeed, success was immediate for Robert B. Thomas. His first edition, patterned after Isaiah's and other so-called "farmer's almanacs" of the time, sold 3,000 copies (distributed by peddlers); his second, 9,000. By 1803 he was outselling Isaiah's and everyone else's, too. Suddenly the imitator had become the one most imitated. And there were literally hundreds of competitors — 19 in Boston alone.

In perusing Thomas's annual "To Patrons" pages, one notices how often he utilized this spot each year to vent his frustration at rival almanacs. "Some have even assumed our title," he wrote here in 1820, "which will make it necessary for our friends and patrons to enquire for the 'Farmer's Almanack by R. B. Thomas' to prevent any mistake." (Incidentally, we would offer the very same advice today!)

In 1832 he inserted the word "Old" on the title page to differentiate this almanac from all other "farmer's almanacs," and in 1848 it became a permanent part of the copyrighted title. By that time there were even almanacs not specifically aimed at farmers — i.e., temperance almanacs, political almanacs, health almanacs ("Constipation Leads to Death" is a title in one), comic almanacs, and others. But like rival farmer's almanacs, each would come and go. None endured. None, that is, except the "imitation" created by Robert B. Thomas. Long before the end of the century, it was recognized not only as America's best-loved publication but also as an integral part of American history and culture. As it remains to this day. No other almanac can say it was read by George Washington, utilized by Abraham Lincoln in a murder trial, and parodied by humorist Josh Billings. No other American almanac begun in the 18th century has survived. Except this one.

Now, as this the 199th edition goes to press, we're looking forward to the most exciting milestone in this publication's long history: the 200th! Oh, what a celebration! Please see pages 6 and 170 for ways you can participate. And, please, let's all prepare to celebrate together — from coast to coast. Ol' Robert B. would ask no less.

And today's imitators? Well, God bless 'em. They follow a tradition without which we, ourselves, would not have been created back in 1792. And we certainly feel fortunate we're now the one being imitated — rather than vice versa. From this time forward, all we must do to continue "enduring" is to humbly keep in mind what Robert B. Thomas told his readers in 1829. "Our main endeavour," he wrote on this page, "must be to be useful, but with a pleasant degree of humour." Surely those are words we might all, as individuals, do well to live by ourselves. Thank you, Robert B. Thomas. – J.D.H.

* * *

However, it is by our works and not our words that we would be judged. These, we hope, will sustain us in the humble though proud station we have so long held in the name of   Your ob'd servant,

CONTENTS

FEATURES

40 The Earthshaking Theories of James Berkland

44 How to Have a Baby

76 The President Who Had a Cold ...

88 Can We or Can't We Predict the Tides?

160

94 The Consumer's Guide to 1991

102 The Miracle at Coogan's Bluff

108 Offbeat Museums

164

114 "Turn Over, Dear, for God's Sake, Turn Over!"

124 The Whole Scary Truth About Fire Ants

160 Facts and Stories About Our Foster Mother, the Dairy Cow

164 Following the Lilac's Lead

168 How to Grow the Tastiest Tomatoes

174 On Behalf of Bulldog Gravy

177 America's Love Affair with Pot Pie

184 Praise the Lard and Pass the Flaky Pie Crust

188 Catching the Bass of a Lifetime

194 Go West, Young Man — and See the Elephant

206 The Birth of Basketball

215 The Chemistry of Music

224 Buying by the Pound

184

INDEX OF CHARTS, TABLES, FORECASTS, AND DEPARTMENTS

Anecdotes and Pleasantries..... 218
Aphelion, Earth at...................... 31
Calendar Pages....................... 48-75
Chronological Cycles................. 30
Church Holy Days........... 30, 49-75
Classified Ads............................ 210
Conjunctions, Astronomical............. 31, 49-75
Dawn and Dark........................... 29
Day, Length of............................ 29
Earthquakes.......................... 30, 41
Eclipses 38
Eras.. 30
Essay Contest 171
Fishing...................................... 188
   Best Days for....................... 192
Foreword, To Patrons 4
Frosts and Growing Seasons 84
Gardening 84, 164, 166, 168, 180, 181
Gestation & Mating Table 167
Glossary 34
Holidays 32
How to Use This Almanac 28
Key Letters 28, 80

Meteor Showers 38
Moon: Astrological Place 181
   Astronomical Place 28, 48-74
   Full 1991-1995 38
   Gardening by 180, 181
   Phases of 48-74
   Rise and Set................... 28, 48-74
Perihelion, Earth at 31
Planets: Rise and Set 29, 36
   Symbols for 31
Planting Tables 180, 181
   Plant Hardiness Zones 166
Puzzles...................................... 198
   Answers to 120
Recipe Contest 170
Recipes 170, 174, 177, 184
Seasons, 1991 30
Stars, Bright.............................. 39
Sun: Declination 48-74
   Rise and Set................... 28, 48-74
Sun Fast.............................. 28, 48-74
Sundials.................................... 29
Tidal Glossary 87
Tide Correction Table 86
Time Correction Table 80
Twilight, Length of.................... 29

Weather:
Forecast Methods 32
General U.S. Forecast, 1991 132
Map of U.S. Regions 133
Regional Forecasts 134-158
1. New England 134
2. Greater N.Y.-N.J. 136
3. Middle Atlantic Coast.......... 138
4. Piedmont & S.E. Coast 140
5. Florida 142
6. Upstate N.Y.-Toronto-Montreal 144
7. Greater Ohio Valley............. 146
8. Deep South 148
9. Chicago-S. Great Lakes 150
10. N. Great Plains-Great Lakes 152
11. Central Great Plains 153
12. Texas-Oklahoma................. 154
13. Rocky Mountains................ 155
14. Southwest Desert................ 156
15. Pacific Northwest............... 157
16. California 158
Weights & Measures................. 121
Zodiac...................... 181, 202, 204

CAN YOU RECYCLE
The Old Farmer's Almanac?
(Or should you keep it forever?)

The answer is yes — please keep it forever. However, *if* for some reason you must part with your copy of our Almanac (perhaps to make room for next year's edition), please note that **the newsstand edition of the Almanac may be recycled with your newspapers.** If you have the **bookstore edition (with shiny covers),** tear off the covers and recycle them with magazines and other paper using coated stock; the inside pages can be recycled with newspapers.

We support recycling and buy recycled paper for production purposes when it is available. A portion of the paper used in the Almanac and in packing and shipping materials comes from recycled fiber.

How You Can Be a Part of Our
200TH ANNIVERSARY IN 1992
(WE NEED YOUR HELP!)

Over the last 200 years, ever since Robert B. Thomas brought out the very first edition, the best and most memorable material in *The Old Farmer's Almanac* has come from you, the reader. How else would we find out about feather crowns, arcane uses for herbs, and how to cure hiccups? Now, on the eve of our 200th anniversary, we are soliciting you for material to be published in the special 1992 edition. We especially ask you to address these two topics:

1. *How* **The Old Farmer's Almanac** *has influenced my life.* (Maximum 200 words per entry. The four best entries will receive $100 each.) *Deadline*: March 1, 1991.

2. *Sure-Fire Tips for Successful Gardening,* from anywhere in the United States and Canada. (Maximum 50 words per tip. We will pay $25 for each tip we publish.)*Deadline*: March 1, 1991.

Please address all editorial correspondence to *The Old Farmer's Almanac,* Dublin, NH 03444. All entries become the property of Yankee Publishing Incorporated, which reserves all rights to the materials submitted.

The 1991 Edition of
THE OLD FARMER'S ALMANAC
Established in 1792 and published
every year thereafter

ROBERT B. THOMAS (1766-1846) — FOUNDER

Editor (12th since 1792) —
JUDSON D. HALE

Managing Editor — SUSAN PEERY

Executive Editor — TIM CLARK

Art Director — MARGO LETOURNEAU

Business Manager, Editorial — ANN GROW

Weather Prognosticator —
DR. RICHARD HEAD

Astronomer — DR. GEORGE GREENSTEIN

Copy Editor — LIDA STINCHFIELD

Assistant Editors — ANNA LARSON,
JODY SAVILLE, MARY SHELDON,
DEBRA WALSH, MARTHA WHITE

Research Editor — JAMIE KAGELEIRY

Contributing Editors —
CASTLE FREEMAN, JR., Farmer's Calendar
FRED SCHAAF, Astronomy

Production Manager —
JAMIE TROWBRIDGE

Typesetting Production — LUCILLE RINES

Production Consultant — STEVE MUSKIE

Asst. Production Manager — PAUL BELLIVEAU

* * * * *

Publisher (22nd since 1792) — JOHN PIERCE

Advertising Director — KEVIN SCULLY

Director of Marketing Services —
STEPHEN M. FULLER

Advertising Production Manager —
MARCIA BROOKS

Advertising office: 33 Union St.,
Boston, MA 02108 • Phone 617-723-4309

Newsstand Circulation —
JAMES BINGHAM

Budget Manager — SHERIN WIGHT

YANKEE PUBLISHING INC., DUBLIN, NH 03444
Joseph B. Meagher, *President;* Judson D. Hale, *Senior Vice President;* Brian Piani, *Vice President and Chief Financial Officer;* James H. Fishman, David Noonan, John Pierce, and Joe Timko, *Vice Presidents.*

The Old Farmer's Almanac cannot accept responsibility for unsolicited manuscripts and will not return any manuscripts that do not include a stamped and addressed return envelope.

REWARD $3,000.00 FOR A 1943 COPPER PENNY

OUR COIN CATALOGUE TELLS YOU HOW TO SHIP COINS TO US AND QUICKLY GET THE MOST MONEY WE PAY FOR COINS! SEND FOR IT TODAY! SEE SPECIAL SECTION ON CANADIAN COINS.

We'll Pay You $3,000.00
For A 1943 Copper Penny
Like this One;

FOR CERTAIN COINS WE PAY UP TO:	CERTAIN
Gold Coins Before 1939	$89,000.00
Nickels Before 1969	$16,000.00
Silver Dollars Before 1964	$76,000.00
Half Dollars Before 1967	$ 5,000.00
Pennies Before 1970	$ 4,800.00
Dimes Before 1966	$20,900.00
Quarters Before 1967	$ 5,000.00
Half Cents Before 1910	$ 3,700.00
Lincoln Pennies Before 1973	$ 250.00

Stop spending valuable coins worth hundreds of dollars. New 1991 catalogue with NEW HIGHER PRICES, lists hundreds of coins we want to buy and gives the price range we will pay for these United States Coins. Certain half-cent coins are worth up to $3,500.00 for Canadian Coins. Our valuable Coin Book may reward you many thousands of dollars. Coins do not have to be old to be valuable. Thousands of dollars have been paid for coins dated as recently as 1940 to 1956. Now you too can learn the rare dates and how to identify rare coins in your possession with our new 1991 catalogue. A fortune may be waiting for you. Millions of Dollars have been paid for rare coins. Send your order for this valuable coin catalogue now. Hold on to your coins until you obtain our catalogue. Send $5.00 plus $2.00 postage and handling for 1991 Coin Catalogue to:

Best Values Co., C.M.O. D638
P.O. Box 802, E. Orange, N.J. 07019

$500,000 SEARCH FOR RARE COINS!
OLD and NEW!
MAIL MONEY-SAVING NO-RISK FREE TRIAL COUPON NOW!

Best Values, C.M.O. D638
P.O. Box 802, E. Orange, N.J. 07019
Rush your latest 1990 catalogue listing the actual price range you will pay for United States Coins listed in the catalogue. I enclose $5.00 plus $2.00 postage and handling.

NAME _____

ADDRESS _____

CITY _____ STATE ____ ZIP _____

*Your Money Will Be Refunded in Full
If You Are Not Satisfied With This Catalogue*

Park Seed
Flowers and Vegetables
1991

Your FREE!

The Big New Park Seed Catalog

"With color so real you can almost smell the beautiful flowers and taste the luscious vegetables!"
Our big, 132 page catalog is chock-full of delights for your garden . . . artichokes to zucchini — ageratum to zinnia — from the most advanced new varieties and the rare, to your long-time favorites. Here in one big color catalog you'll find over **2,100 quality products:** flower and vegetable seed, bulbs, plants and garden supplies — many available only from Park. We back each and every one with a solid guarantee of complete satisfaction.

Have more fun gardening this year with **Park High Performer® varieties** — flowers more beautiful and easier to grow, vegetables with better taste and higher yield. Park tests thousands each year to make sure you get only the best. Send for your copy today and let Park Help You Grow!

Complete Satisfaction Guaranteed
"Home Garden Seed Specialists Since 1868"

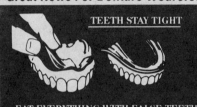

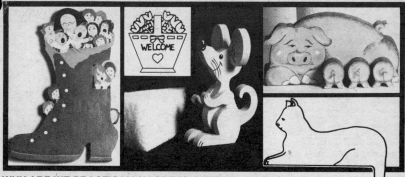

WHY ARE WE PRACTICALLY "GIVING AWAY"

"347 WOODWORKING PATTERNS FOR ONLY 2¢ EACH!"

IF YOU LIKE TO CUT PATTERNS OUT OF WOOD, THIS IS THE BOOK FOR YOU! YOU'LL FIND A TREASURE HOUSE OF IDEAS INSIDE. 347 BEAUTIFUL WOODWORKING PATTERNS AND DESIGNS.

(By Frank K. Wood)

FC&A, a Peachtree City, Georgia, publisher, announced today that it is practically "giving away" an all new book, *"Encyclopedia of 347 Woodworking Patterns"*, for only 2¢ per pattern in a campaign to gain new customers.

LOOK AT WHAT YOU WILL FIND IN THIS NEW BOOK

- Curvy curios, charming country cats.
- Sturdy shelves, shadow boxes, showy plaques.
- Victorian ladies and stylish gents.
- Rack up your spices, spice up your den.
- Holders for candles, napkins and canes.
- Folk art, Shaker art, modern art too.
- Gaggles of geese, or a goose all alone.
- Hanging hearts, huggable bears.
- Doorstop decorations, welcome signs.
- Whizzing whirligigs, models of planes.
- Take flights of fancy with fairies and gnomes.
- Birthday surprises, decorations for major events.
- Dancing bear, prancing pony, soaring eagles.
- Circus animals and barnyard critters.
- Childhood favorites, Noah and the Ark.
- Tulips, bluebirds, springtime motifs.
- Comic cartoons, comfy coat rack.
- Summer garden helpers, lawn deco art.
- Tick-tock clock, chug-along train.
- And much, much more!

IT'S EASY TO ORDER

Just return this notice with your name and address and a check for $5.99 plus $2.00 shipping and handling, and we will send you a copy of *"Encyclopedia of 347 Woodworking Patterns"* right away. Or, for only $9.99 plus $3.00 shipping and handling, you can get both the book and an extra 100 large patterns too big to fit into the book.

Plus, every $9.99 order will receive a free trial membership in the *FC&A Woodworking and Scroll Saw Pattern Club.* About every other month thereafter, you'll get 100 new patterns for only $9.99 plus $3.00 shipping and handling. Pay only for those sets you decide to keep. Cancel anytime you want.

Send your check along with your name and address to: **FC&A, Dept. NOF-91**, 103 Clover Green, Peachtree City, GA, 30269.

You get a no-time-limit guarantee of satisfaction or your money back.

You must cut out and return this notice with your order. Copies will not be accepted!

IMPORTANT — FREE GIFT OFFER EXPIRES IN 30 DAYS.

All orders mailed within 30 days will receive 50 special, seasonal, woodworking patterns as a free gift. Order right away!

Unexplained Weight Loss Puzzles Scientists

FINLAND—The unexpected weight loss experienced by members of a test group has puzzled medical researchers at a leading Finnish university. Scientists were testing a naturally-occurring compound for its ability to lower blood cholesterol levels when, to their surprise, they found that every person who took the formula had lost a significant amount of weight.

The formula was then tested at another prestigious European university hospital. Again, all patients lost weight even though they did not change their eating habits. The report detailing this study, published in the British Journal of Nutrition, stated: "Body weight was significantly reduced even though the patients were specifically asked not to alter their dietary habits".

This woman reportedly lost 134 pounds while on the formula.

While it is still not entirely clear how the formula induces weight loss, some scientists believe this compound actually alters the way the body digests food: when taken before mealtime it bonds with food and suppresses calorie absorption. Unabsorbed calories would pass through and out of the digestive system.

The formula is marketed in capsule form in the United States under the trade name Cal-Ban 3000. A firm located in Tampa, Florida has exclusive North American distribution rights to Cal-Ban 3000. A company spokesman reported that the formula is 100% natural and has been clinically tested for safety. Review of the customer files of this company revealed the names of hundreds of people who have lost as much as 20, 40 or 80 or more pounds overall with Cal-Ban 3000. This appears to be a golden opportunity for people who are plagued by fat and cellulite that they can't seem to lose by conventional methods.

Cal-Ban 3000 is reasonably priced at $19.95 for a 3-week supply and $38.95 for a 6-week supply. Postage and handling is $3. VISA, M/C, AMEX and COD orders are accepted. To order call TOLL-FREE 1-800-635-7529. Canadian orders call 1-800-231-4700. Offer not available in Iowa.

Call today to begin the pleasant transformation from fat and flab to the slender firm body you want! If you fail to achieve a major weight loss you may return the empty bottle within 30 days for a 100% refund.

How to Drill a Backyard Water Well

by Bill Harrington

☐ I had been drilling water wells in Oklahoma for about 15 years when I saw the ad that claimed a man could drill his own water well with a Hydra-Drill. I was skeptical, 'how can that be? It takes a big rig to drill a water well'. But my curiosity kept nagging me, so I sent for the information.

We were having the worst drought since the "dustbowl". It's hard on a lot of people, but business is good for well drillers. I'd been thinking about buying another drill and putting my son, Robert, in business. He's 18 years old, and he'd never worked on a drill before. I decided he could learn with a Hydra-Drill.

Now when I started out, I had a big drill that just about worked me to death. You can't imagine how I felt when they delivered our Hydra-Drill. It was so compact and simple. Robert and a young friend took it out and set it up in just a few minutes.

The day we went out to drill our first well with the Hydra-Drill, I was ready to work with the boys and give them plenty of advice. However, it was hot — about 100 degrees — and once they got started drilling, I could see they didn't need me, so I sat down in the shade. In about an hour, they came over to take a break. They had finished drilling the well!

It was amazing. They had drilled down forty seven feet and hit a layer of beautiful, coarse sand — the kind that produces good water and lots of it. They had drilled that well in less time than it takes me to set up my big drill.

The Hydra-Drill really takes the hard work out of it. It's fast and economical. That's what it takes to make money drill-

"I didn't believe a man could drill his own water well..."

ing wells. It's so portable, we can set up and drill anywhere. I'm just grateful to have this Hydra-Drill. I've got my son started in a good business.

I believe anyone can drill a well with the Hydra-Drill. It's simple and easy if they just read the instructions. And the best part is that you get good, pure water for, say, 5 cents for a thousands gallons. You certainly can't buy city water for that. It's a great feeling to have all the water you want even when the city is rationing water to everyone else.

The man who invented the Hydra-Drill really knew what he was doing. Modern technology is a wonderful thing, isn't it?

For a FREE Information Package, call today TOLL-FREE 1-800-333-7762, Ext. 7229 or mail coupon on the accompanying advertisement to DeepRock, Opelika, AL 36803-0001. Learn how over 100,000 water wells have been drilled this easy, low-cost way since 1962. ☐ ☐

Now I have all the water I need!

Say Goodbye to Expensive Water Bills

--with Your Own Easy-to-Install Water Well System*

Don't use expensive city water on your garden and lawn! Use low-cost well water -- pumped from a well you drill yourself with the amazing Hydra-Drill.

Let me send you a FREE 24-page booklet on **"How To Drill Your Own Well"**, and a recording of some home-owners like yourself who have drilled their own wells! Say you might need some help? There is

Expert Help Available

Suppose you're in your yard drilling your well, and you need some advice -- *call the special toll-free number* and talk to one of our drilling consultants. He will help you with handy on-the-spot tips.

Then you're ready to install the pump. Just watch the FREE video tape on **"How to Install Your Well Pump"** that comes with every pump. It's that easy.

Be Water Independent with your own water well system you install yourself! Request your FREE INFORMATION PACKAGE *today!*

Yours FREE:
* "How To..." booklet
* 33 rpm record
* Complete info & prices

FOR FREE INFORMATION PACKAGE
Call Toll-Free
1-800-333-7762
(Ask for Operator 7228)
Or Clip Coupon and Mail Today!

DeepRock
FACTORY DIRECT
7228 Anderson Road
Opelika, AL 36802

❏ **YES!** I may want to drill on my property. Rush the **FREE INFORMATION PACKAGE** including the booklet, record and prices.

❏ Also, send information and prices on your well pumps and tanks. No obligation!

Print Name

Address

City/State/Zip

Phone

See Why...
Where There's A Will

Canton, OH (Special)
You can spend money for a Will

Heirs Pay

only to have a substantial part of your assets needlessly taken by lawyers, courts and executors through the probate process.

Why should you avoid probate? Simple. It costs too much and takes too long. Probate also creates an "invasion of your family's financial privacy!"

Probate alone can slice up to 10% from an estate and take months or years for settlement.

In fact, the only thing worse than a Will for the average wage earner is the nightmare created by no Will at all. Because then the State decides who gets everything you own.

Now there's a far better way to protect your estate than having only a Will. A new study reveals that a Living Trust is a low-cost alternative to probating a will, even for an average sized estate.

Today you can eliminate costly, time-consuming probate and legal fees by using a simple legal paper called a revocable Living Trust. It avoids probate attorney, managerial and court fees because there is no Will to probate. Your family suffers no expense or settlement delays. And since a Living Trust is revocable, you can change your mind at any time about trustees and who gets your assets. Unlike a Will the estate goes at once to whomever you name -- in complete secrecy.

The many advantages of a Living Trust for the average-sized estate has

been praised by estate planners and reported in financial publications like The Wall Street Journal, Business Week, Money, to name a few. You simply transfer all your assets into a Living Trust and name yourself or anyone you want as trustees.

Lawyers can charge an average of $60 for writing a Will -- and then can get up to 10% for probate. It's smart to set up a Living Trust.

Working with a team of legal scholars, DSA Financial Publishing Corp. of Canton, Ohio has prepared a Living Trust Kit designed so you can easily set up your own Living Trust. You'll get complete instructions written in easy-to understand, step-by-step simple language. You'll also get complete guidelines on how to custom tailor your personal Living Trust so that any special wishes you may have for your estate are carried out.

It's easy to get your Living Trust Kit. All you have to do is send a check or money order in the amount of $19.95 plus $2 postage and handling or charge to your VISA/Mastercard by including account number and expiration date to: DSA Financial Publishing Corp., 708 - 12th Street N.W., Dept. W919, Canton, Ohio 44703. For even faster service, VISA/Mastercard only, call toll free 1-800-321-0888, Ext. W919. A 90 day money back guarantee is naturally offered. Do it now . . . while there is still time to protect your loved ones. © 1990 DSA DW520-5

What You Should Know About Making $1,000 a Week in Your Spare Time.

Be your own boss

We'll show you how to be a Professional Chimney Sweep! You can join thousands of men and women in this fast growing service business. And you can do it in your spare time!

With August West's state-of-the-art equipment and proven techniques, you'll quickly learn how to clean a chimney in less than an hour and walk away with an average of $65 every time.

You could be earning as much as $1000 a week working part-time. Many August West sweeps earn twice that each week when they work full-time.

Keep All You Earn

With August West there are no franchise fees, no commission payments.

For an investment of under $2,500 you get the tools and equipment you need to start earning money immediately.

That includes the famous, high-powered SOOTSWEEPER®, the dust collector Mother Earth News calls "The Height of Technology".

Most important of all, August West backs you up with:
- training and support
- workshops and newsletters
- technical and marketing advice
- advertising and promotion manuals

You have all the advantages of a franchise without any of the drawbacks!

Free Information Kit

Join the many thousands who have found personal freedom, success and the time to do the important things.

Learn more about this extraordinary business. Write for our Free Information Kit today.

Better still, pick up the phone and call us at this Toll-Free number:

1-800-225-4016

SINCE 1976

Ask for Extension 825
(In MA: 508-753-5544)

Send to: August West Systems, 38 Austin St., Box 658, Dept. 4499, Worcester, MA 01601

Yes, please rush me your FREE Information Kit.

Name _____

Address _____

City _____

State/Zip _____

Phone ( ) _____

SHOP AT HOME

MODEL-T WEATHERVANE

Watch the little driver crank up the old Model T with every breeze!

FASCINATING ACTION

Even the slightest breeze starts the fun! As the propellers capture the wind — the little driver cranks up the Old Model T. The more the breeze... the faster he goes. Good cheerful fun for lawn, garden, yard and home. This delightful Weathervane will attract young and old with its continuous action. Brightly HANDPAINTED and WEATHERPROOF. **Measures 1 foot long and comes complete with mounting hardware.** Ready to enjoy in seconds!

No. 8141—Model T Weathervane $6.96
SAVE: TWO ONLY $12

- Roof
- Porch
- Mail Box
- Garden
- Fence
- House

"Classic" ROOSTER WEATHERVANE

Almost 3' High Full-Color

No. 8147 Schooner

A "Country Classic" ... the Rooster Weathervane. Our full color version stands **almost 3 FEET TALL** and measures 17½" across. Specially crafted for us with heavy-duty metal mounting hardware and **weatherproof** hi-impact materials. Easy to assemble hardware adapts to any angle roof. Attaches to porch, fence or mail box too. Can be mounted on pole (included) for your yard or garden ... **It makes a charming garden accent!** And it really does work ... tells which way the wind is blowing. Look at the price — now, that is a good **old fashioned bargain!**

No. 8143D—Rooster Weathervane $14.95
No. 8147—Schooner Weathervane $14.95

LEGENDARY
Copper Bracelets

Pure Copper Bracelets have been cherished for centuries and now they're worn by thousands: athletes, celebrities and people everywhere who want the **latest** in distinctive accessories. We make no claims concerning the "mystical" powers or healing properties often attributed to Copper Bracelets, but we believe you'll want them because they're so NEW ... so beautifully styled! The solid Bracelets are made of thick, natural copper and adjust to any wrist size.

No. 5083—Ladies Link Chain Bracelet $4.98
No. 5082—Men's Heavy Link Chain Bracelet $5.98

SUPER CONTROL THAT REALLY SLIMS YOU!

ZIP AWAY STOMACH BULGE & SUPPORT BACK!

Before | After

Full 4" elastic top eliminates roll

DELUXE No.2190
ONLY 17.97
2 FOR 31.88

SIZES AT WAIST
SMALL 30-32,
MEDIUM 34-36,
LARGE 38-40,
X LARGE 42-44,
XX LARGE 46-48

Mail Order with check, cash or money order. Include $2.95 postage & handling fee (non-refundable). Allow 4 - 6 weeks delivery. All merchandise shipped under no risk, 30 day home trial. Money back guarantee. N.Y.S. residents must include local sales tax. Send order to:

FOSTER-TRENT INC., DEPT.(304·AB), 29 BEECHWOOD AVE., NEW ROCHELLE, N.Y. 10801

INTRODUCTION
Including How to Use This Almanac Anywhere in the U.S.A.
THE LEFT-HAND CALENDAR PAGES
(Pages 48-74)

T HESE PAGES will provide you with the phases of the Moon; the hour and minute of the Sun's rising and setting for each day of the year and month; the length of each day; the times of high tides in Boston in the morning and evening ("11¼" under "Full Sea Boston, A.M." means that the high tide that morning will be at 11:15 A.M. — with the number of feet of high tide shown for some of the dates on the right-hand calendar pages); the hour and minute of the Moon's rising and setting; the declination of the Sun in degrees and minutes (angular distance from the celestial equator); the Moon's place in the heavens; and finally, in the far right column, the Moon's age. The Moon's place and age apply, without correction, throughout the United States.

The Moon's place given on the left-hand pages is its *astronomical* place in the heavens. (*All* calculations in this Almanac, except for the astrological information on pages 181 and 202-205, are based on astronomy, not astrology.) As well as the 12 constellations of the Zodiac, five other abbreviations appear in this column: Ophiuchus (OPH) is a constellation primarily north of the Zodiac, but with a small corner between Scorpio and Sagittarius. Orion (ORI) is a constellation whose northern limit just reaches the Zodiac between Taurus and Gemini. Auriga (AUR) lies just northeast of Taurus. Sextans (SEX) lies south of the Zodiac except for a corner that just touches it near Leo. Cetus (CET) lies south of the Zodiac, just south of Pisces and Aries.

Eastern Standard Time is used throughout this Almanac. (Be sure to add one hour for Daylight Saving Time between April 7 and October 27.) **All of the times on the left-hand calendar pages are calculated for Boston.** Key Letters accompany much of the data; they are provided for the correction of Boston times to other localities. Here's how . . .

SUNRISE, SUNSET

☞ Note the Key Letter to the right of each time for sunrise and sunset in the column entitled "Key." To find the time of sunrise or sunset for your area, consult the Time Correction Tables (pages 80-84). Find your city or the city nearest you and locate the figure, expressed in minutes, in the appropriate Key Letter column. Add, or subtract, that figure to the time given for Boston. The result will be accurate to within 5 minutes for latitudes north of 35°, 10 minutes for latitudes 30°-35°, and 15 minutes for latitudes 25°-30°.

Example: March 31 (Easter) sunrise in Boston is 5:29 A.M., EST, with Key Letter B (p. 56). To find the time of sunrise in San Antonio, Texas, look on page 83. Key Letter B for San Antonio is +66 minutes, so sunrise in San Antonio is 6:35 A.M., CST. Use the same process for sunset. (For dates between April 7 and October 27, add one hour for Daylight Saving Time.)

MOONRISE, MOONSET

☞ Moonrise and moonset are figured the same way except that an additional correction factor (see table below) based on longitude should be used. For the longitude of your city, consult pages 80-84.

Longitude of city	Correction minutes
58°- 76°	0
77°- 89°	+1
90°-102°	+2
103°-115°	+3
116°-127°	+4
128°-141°	+5
142°-155°	+6

Example: To determine moonrise in Minneapolis, Minnesota, for November 21, 1991, see page 72. Moonrise in Boston is 3:52 P.M.,

...ST, with Key Letter B. For Minneapolis, Key Letter B (page 82) is +24 minutes, moving moonrise to 4:16 P.M. The longitude of Minneapolis is 93° 16', so the additional correction is +2 minutes. Moonrise in Minneapolis is therefore 4:18 P.M., CST. (Add one hour for Daylight Saving Time between April 7 and October 27.) Follow the same procedure to determine moonset.

SUNDIALS

☞ Also in the left-hand calendar pages is a column headed "Sun Fast." This is for changing sundial time into local clock time. A sundial reads natural, or Sun, time which is neither Standard nor Daylight time except by coincidence. Simply *subtract* Sun Fast time to get local clock time and use Key Letter C (pages 80-84) to correct the time for your city. (Add one hour for Daylight Saving Time April 7-October 27.)

Example:	Boston
Sundial reading, March 1	12:00
Subtract Sun Fast	–4
Clock Time	11:56 EST

Example:	Memphis
Sundial reading, March 1	12:00
Subtract Sun Fast	–4
Add Key C (for Memphis)	+16
Clock Time	12:12 CST

RISING AND SETTING OF THE PLANETS

☞ The times of rising and setting of visible planets, with the exception of Mercury, are given for Boston on pages 36-37. To convert these times to those of other localities (pages 80-84), follow the same procedure as that given for finding the times of sunrise and sunset.

LENGTH OF DAY

☞ The "Length of Day" column for Boston (pages 48-74) tells how long the Sun will be above the horizon. Use the Time Correction Tables (pages 80-84) to determine sunrise and sunset times for your city. Add 12 hours to the time of sunset, subtract the time of sunrise, and you will have the length of day.

LENGTH OF TWILIGHT

☞ Subtract from time of sunrise for dawn. Add to time of sunset for dark.

Latitude	25°N to 30°N	31°N to 36°N	37°N to 42°N
	h m	h m	h m
Jan. 1 to Apr. 10	1 20	1 26	1 33
Apr. 11 to May 2	1 23	1 28	1 39
May 3 to May 14	1 26	1 34	1 47
May 15 to May 25	1 29	1 38	1 52
May 26 to July 22	1 32	1 43	1 59
July 23 to Aug. 3	1 29	1 38	1 52
Aug. 4 to Aug. 14	1 26	1 34	1 47
Aug. 15 to Sept. 5	1 23	1 28	1 39
Sept. 6 to Dec. 31	1 20	1 26	1 33

Latitude	43°N to 47°N	48°N to 49°N
	h m	h m
Jan. 1 to Apr. 10	1 42	1 50
Apr. 11 to May 2	1 51	2 04
May 3 to May 14	2 02	2 22
May 15 to May 25	2 13	2 42
May 26 to July 22	2 27	—
July 23 to Aug. 3	2 13	2 42
Aug. 4 to Aug. 14	2 02	2 22
Aug. 15 to Sept. 5	1 51	2 04
Sept. 6 to Dec. 31	1 42	1 50

DAWN AND DARK

☞ The approximate times dawn will break and dark descend are found by applying the length of twilight taken from the table above to the times of sunrise and sunset at any specific place. The latitude of the place (see pages 80-84) determines the column from which the length of twilight is to be selected.

Boston (latitude 42° 22')

Sunrise March 1	6:20 A.M.
Length of twilight	–1:33
Dawn breaks	4:47 A.M.
Sunset March 1	5:34 P.M.
Length of twilight	+1:33
Dark descends	7:07 P.M.

Atlanta (latitude 33° 45')

Sunrise March 1	7:00 A.M.
Length of twilight	–1:26
Dawn breaks	5:34 A.M.
Sunset March 1	6:39 P.M.
Length of twilight	+1:26
Dark descends	8:05 P.M.

THE RIGHT-HAND CALENDAR PAGES

(Pages 49-75)

THESE PAGES are a combination of astronomical data; specific dates in mainly the Anglican church calendar, inclusion of which has always been traditional in American and English almanacs (though we also include some other religious dates); tide heights at Boston (the left-hand calendar pages include the daily times of high tides; the corrections for your locality are on pages 86-87); quotations; anniversary dates; appropriate seasonal activities; and a rhyming version of the weather forecasts for New England. (Detailed forecasts for the entire country are presented on pages 134-158.)

The following is a summary of the highlights from this year's right-hand calendar pages, the signs used, and a sample (the first part of December 1990) of a calendar page explained. . . .

MOVABLE FEASTS AND FASTS FOR 1991

Septuagesima Sunday	Jan. 27
Shrove Tuesday	Feb. 12
Ash Wednesday	Feb. 13
Palm Sunday	Mar. 24
Good Friday	Mar. 29
Easter Day	Mar. 31
Low Sunday	Apr. 7
Rogation Sunday	May 5
Ascension Day	May 9
Whit Sunday-Pentecost	May 19
Trinity Sunday	May 26
Corpus Christi	May 30
1st Sunday in Advent	Dec. 1

THE SEASONS OF 1991

Winter 1990	Dec. 21 10:07 P.M., EST (Sun enters Capricorn)
Spring 1991	Mar. 20 10:02 P.M., EST (Sun enters Aries)
Summer 1991	June 21 4:19 P.M., EST (Sun enters Cancer)
Fall 1991	Sept. 23 7:48 A.M., EST (Sun enters Libra)
Winter 1991	Dec. 22 3:54 A.M., EST (Sun enters Capricorn)

CHRONOLOGICAL CYCLES FOR 1991

Golden Number (Lunar Cycle)	16
Epact	14
Solar Cycle	12
Dominical Letter	F
Roman Indiction	14
Year of Julian Period	6704

ERA	Year	Begins
Byzantine	7500	Sept. 14
Jewish (A.M.)*	5752	Sept. 8
Roman (A.U.C.)	2744	Jan. 14
Nabonassar	2740	Apr. 26
Japanese	2651	Jan. 1
Grecian	2303	Sept. 14
(Seleucidae)		(or Oct. 14)
Indian (Saka)	1913	Mar. 22
Diocletian	1708	Sept. 12
Islamic (Hegira)*	1412	July 12
Chinese (Lunar)	4628	Feb. 15
(Sheep/Goat)		

*Year begins at sunset

DETERMINATION OF EARTHQUAKES

☞ Note, on right-hand pages 49-75, the dates when the Moon (☾) "rides high" or "runs low." The date of the high begins the most likely five-day period of earthquakes in the northern hemisphere; the date of the low indicates a similar five-day period in the southern hemisphere. You will also find on these pages a notation for Moon on the Equa-

for (☾ on Eq.) twice each month. At this time, in both hemispheres, is a two-day earthquake period.

NAMES AND CHARACTERS OF THE PRINCIPAL PLANETS AND ASPECTS

☞ Every now and again on these right-hand calendar pages, you will see symbols conjoined in groups to tell you what is happening in the heavens. For example, ♂ ☿ ♅ opposite December 10, 1990, on page 51 means that Mercury ☿ and Uranus ♅ are on that date in conjunction ♂ or apparently near each other.

Here are the symbols used . . .

☉ The Sun ○●☾ The Moon

☿ Mercury ♄ Saturn
♀ Venus ♅ Uranus
⊕ The Earth ♆ Neptune
♂ Mars ♇ Pluto
♃ Jupiter

♂ Conjunction, or in the same degree
☍ Opposition, or 180 degrees
☊ Ascending Node
☋ Descending Node

EARTH AT APHELION AND PERIHELION 1991

☞ The Earth will be at Perihelion on January 2, 1991, when it will be 91,400,005 miles from the Sun. The Earth will be at Aphelion on July 6, 1991, when it will be 94,512,258 miles from the Sun.

SAMPLE PAGE
(from December 1990 — page 51)

Day of the month. Day of the week.

For detailed regional forecasts, see pages 134-158.

Conjunction — closest approach — of Mars and the Moon.

First Sunday in Advent. (Events in the church calendar generally appear in this typeface.)

The Dominical Letter for 1990 was G because the first Sunday of the year fell on the seventh day of January. The letter for 1991 is F.

St. Nicholas, the 4th-century Archbishop of Myra, is regarded as the patron saint of children. (Certain religious feasts and civil holidays appear in this typeface.)

Morning tide at Boston, shown to be at 6:45 A.M. on the left-hand page, will be 9.6 feet. Evening tide, at 7:15 P.M., will be 8.7 feet.

The Moon is at apogee, the point in its orbit farthest from the Earth.

D.M.	D.W.	Dates, Feasts, Fasts, Aspects, Tide Heights	Weather ↓
1	Sa.	♂☾☉ Rosa Parks refused to give up bus seat, Montgomery, Ala., 1955	{11.9 {10.2 Cold
2	G	1ˢᵗ Sun. in Advent • Full ○ • ☾ at peri. Cold	as
3	M.	☾ runs high • Drive thy Business, let it not drive thee. • Tides {12.3 {—	the
4	Tu.	83 m.p.h. winds, Atlantic City, N.J., 1898 • Tides {10.3 {12.2	Dickens!
5	W.	☾ at ☋ • Bus boycott began, Montgomery, Ala., 1955	{10.2 {11.8 Then
6	Th.	St. Nicholas • ☿ Gr. Elong. E. (21°) • ♂♃☾	milder.
7	Fr.	Earthquake killed 25,000, Armenia, 1988 • Tides {9.9 {10.6	Twist
8	Sa.	Concep. of V.M. • John Lennon killed, 1980	beforrit
9	G	2ⁿᵈ S. in Adv. • ☾ on Eq. • John Milton born, 1608	snows
10	M.	♂☿♅ • First Nobel prizes awarded, 1901 • Tides {9.6 {9.0	so
11	Tu.	Make the most of yourself, for that is all there is of you • Tides {9.6 {8.7	hard
12	W.	Chanukah • Jascha Heifetz died, 1987 • Tides {9.7 {8.6	we can
13	Th.	St. Lucy • Brevity is the soul of wit. • Tides {9.8 {8.6	little
14	Fr.	☿ stat. • Beware the pogonip. • Alabama statehood, 1819	enDorrit.
15	Sa.	Occult. Antares by ☾ • ☾ at apo.	{10.0 {8.6 Great
16	G	3ʳᵈ S. in Adv. • New ●	Expectations
17	M.	☾ runs low • Politics makes strange postmasters. • Tides {10.1 {8.7	of
18	Tu.	♂♅☿ • ♂♃☾ • ♂☿♅ • {10.1 {—	mixed

NOTE: The values of Key Letters are given in the Time Correction Tables. (See pages 80-84.)

HOLIDAYS, 1991

(*) Are recommended as holidays with pay
   for all employees
(**) State observances only

Jan. 1 (*) New Year's Day
Jan. 19 (**) Robert E. Lee's Birthday (Ala.,
   Ark., Miss., S.C., Tenn.)
Jan. 21 (*) Martin Luther King Jr.'s Birthday
   (observed)
Feb. 2 Groundhog Day
Feb. 12 (**) Abraham Lincoln's Birthday;
   (**) Mardi Gras (Ala., La.)
Feb. 13 Ash Wednesday
Feb. 14 Valentine's Day
Feb. 18 (*) George Washington's Birthday
   (Presidents' Day) observed
Mar. 2 (**) Texas Independence Day
Mar. 15 (**) Andrew Jackson Day (Tenn.)
Mar. 17 (**) St. Patrick's Day; Evacuation
   Day (Boston and Suffolk Co., Mass.)
Mar. 24 Palm Sunday
Mar. 25 (**) Seward's Day (Alaska)
Mar. 29 Good Friday
Mar. 30 Passover
Mar. 31 Easter
Apr. 7 Greek Orthodox Easter
Apr. 13 (**) Thomas Jefferson's Birthday
   (Ala., Okla.)
Apr. 15 (**) Patriots Day (Maine, Mass.)
Apr. 21 (**) San Jacinto Day (Texas)
Apr. 22 (**) Fast Day (N.H.)
Apr. 26 Arbor Day (except Alaska, Nebraska,
   Wyoming, and Georgia)
May 1 May Day
May 4 (**) Rhode Island Independence Day
May 12 Mother's Day
May 18 Armed Forces Day
May 20 Victoria Day (Canada)

May 27 (*) Memorial Day (observed)
June 5 World Environment Day
June 11 (**) King Kamehameha Day
   (Hawaii)
June 14 Flag Day
June 16 Father's Day
June 17 (**) Bunker Hill Day (Boston and
   Suffolk Co., Mass.)
June 19 Juneteenth (Texas)
July 1 Canada Day (observed)
July 4 (*) Independence Day
July 24 (**) Pioneer Day (Utah)
Aug. 16 (**) Bennington Battle Day (Vt.)
Aug. 26 Women's Equality Day
Aug. 27 (**) Lyndon B. Johnson's Birthday
   (Tex.)
Sept. 2 (*) Labor Day
Sept. 8 Grandparents' Day
Sept. 9 Rosh Hashanah; Admissions Day
   (Calif.)
Sept. 12 (**) Defenders' Day (Md.)
Sept. 18 Yom Kippur
Sept. 27 Native American Day
Sept. 28 (**) Frances Willard Day (Minn., Wis.)
Oct. 14 (*) Columbus Day (observed);
   Thanksgiving (Canada)
Oct. 18 (**) Alaska Day
Oct. 24 United Nations Day
Oct. 31 Halloween
Nov. 4 Will Rogers Day (Okla.)
Nov. 5 Election Day
Nov. 11 (*) Veterans Day (Armistice Day)
Nov. 24 John F. Kennedy Day (Mass.)
Nov. 28 (*) Thanksgiving Day
Dec. 2 Chanukah
Dec. 15 Bill of Rights Day
Dec. 25 (*) Christmas Day
Dec. 26 Boxing Day (Canada)

HOW THE ALMANAC WEATHER FORECASTS ARE MADE

O ur weather forecasts are determined both by the use of a secret
formula devised by the founder of this
almanac in 1792 and by the most modern scientific calculations based on solar
activity. We believe nothing in the universe occurs haphazardly; there is a
cause-and-effect pattern to all phenomena, including weather. It follows, therefore, that we believe weather is predictable. It is obvious, however, that neither we nor anyone else has as yet
gained sufficient insight into the mysteries of the universe to predict weather
with anything resembling total accuracy.

GLOSSARY

Aph. — Aphelion: Planet reaches point in its orbit farthest from the Sun.

Apo. — Apogee: Moon reaches point in its orbit farthest from the Earth.

Celestial Equator: The plane of the Earth's equator projected out into space.

Conj. — Conjunction: Time of apparent closest approach to each other of any two heavenly bodies.

Declination: Measure of angular distance any celestial object lies perpendicularly north or south of celestial equator; analogous to terrestrial latitude. The Almanac gives the Sun's declination at noon E.S.T.

Dominical Letter: Used for the ecclesiastical calendar and determined by the date on which the first Sunday of the year falls. If Jan. 1 is a Sunday, the Letter is A; if Jan. 2 is a Sunday, the Letter is B; and so to G when the first Sunday is Jan. 7. In leap year the Letter applies through February and then takes the Letter before.

Eclipse, Annular: An eclipse in which sunlight shows around the Moon.

Eclipse, Lunar: Opposition of the Sun and Moon with the Moon at or near node.

Eclipse, Solar: Conjunction of Sun and Moon with the Moon at or near node.

Epact: A number from 1 to 30 to harmonize the lunar year with the solar year, used for the ecclesiastical calendar. Indicates the Moon's age at the instant Jan. 1 begins at the meridian of Greenwich, England.

Eq. — Equator: A great circle of the Earth equidistant from the two poles.

Equinox, Fall: Sun passes from northern to southern hemisphere: Sun enters Libra. **Spring:** Sun passes from southern to northern hemisphere: Sun enters Aries.

Evening Star: A planet that is above the horizon at sunset and less than 180° east of the Sun.

Golden Number: The year in the 19-year cycle of the Moon. The Moon phases occur on the same dates every 19 years.

Greatest Elongation (Gr. El.): Greatest apparent angular distance of a planet from the Sun as seen from the Earth.

Inf. — Inferior: Conjunction in which the planet is between the Sun and the Earth.

Julian Period: A period of 7,980 Julian years, being a period of agreement of solar and lunar cycles. Add 4,713 to year to find Julian year.

Moon's Age: The number of days since the previous new Moon. **First Quarter:** Right half of Moon illuminated. **Full Moon:** Moon reaches opposition. **Last Quarter:** Left half of Moon illuminated. **New Moon:** Sun and Moon in conjunction.

Moon Rides High or Runs Low: Day of month Moon is highest or lowest above the south point of the observer's horizon.

Morning Star: A planet that is above the horizon at sunrise and less than 180° west of the Sun in right ascension.

Node: Either of the two points where the Moon's orbit intersects the ecliptic.

Occultations: Eclipses of stars by the Moon.

Opposition: Time when the Sun and Moon or planet appear on opposite sides of the sky (El. 180°).

Perig. — Perigee: Moon reaches point in its orbit closest to the Earth.

Perih. — Perihelion: Planet reaches point in its orbit closest to the Sun.

R.A. — Right Ascension: The coordinate on the celestial sphere analogous to longitude on the Earth.

Roman Indiction: A cycle of 15 years established Jan. 1, A.D. 313, as a fiscal term. Add 3 to the number of years in the Christian era and divide by 15. The remainder of the year is Roman Indiction — no remainder is 15.

Solar Cycle: A period of 28 years, at the end of which the days of the month return to the same days of the week.

Solstice, Summer: Point at which the Sun is farthest north of the celestial equator: Sun enters Cancer. **Winter:** Point at which the Sun is farthest south of the celestial equator: Sun enters Capricorn.

Stat. — Stationary: Halt in the apparent movement of a planet against the background of the stars just before the planet comes to opposition.

Sun Fast: Subtract times given in this column from your sundial to arrive at the correct Standard Time.

Sunrise & Sunset: Visible rising and setting of the Sun's upper limb across the unobstructed horizon of an observer whose eyes are 15' above ground level.

Sup. — Superior: Superior Conjunction; indicates that the Sun is between the planet and the Earth.

Twilight: Begins or ends when stars of the sixth magnitude disappear or appear at the zenith; or when the Sun is about 18 degrees below the horizon.

EVERY MONTH THREE MILLION READERS
JOIN *YANKEE* FOR A NEW ENGLAND EXPERIENCE
. . . AND YOU CAN TOO!

Each issue of *Yankee* is packed with a rich assortment of photo-filled articles . . . taste-tempting recipes . . . fascinating fiction . . . historic happenings . . . intriguing personalities . . . and good old-fashioned Yankee warmth, wisdom, and humor.

Return the attached coupon to reserve a 12-month subscription for yourself or as a gift, and receive absolutely *FREE* a copy of *Yankee's Main Dish Church Supper Cookbook* . . . 64 pages of traditional New England recipes.

THE VISIBLE PLANETS, 1991

The times of rising or setting of the planets Venus, Mars, Jupiter, and Saturn on the 1st, 11th, and 21st of each month are given below. The approximate time of rising or setting of these planets on other days may be found with sufficient accuracy by interpolation. For an explanation of Key Letters (used in adjusting the times given here for Boston to the time in your town), see page 28 and pages 80-84. Key Letters appear as capital letters beside the time of rising or setting. (For definitions of morning and evening stars, see page 34.)

VENUS is brilliant in the evening sky from January until mid-August, when it becomes too close to the Sun for observation, and in the morning sky from late August until the end of the year. Venus is in conjunction with Saturn on January 1, with Jupiter on June 17 and October 17, with Mars on June 23 and July 22, and with Mercury on August 7 and 29.

Boldface — P.M. Lightface — A.M.

Jan. 1	set 5:28	A	May 1	set 10:18	E	Sept. 1	rise 4:13	B
Jan. 11	" 5:53	A	May 11	" 10:31	E	Sept. 11	" 3:18	B
Jan. 21	" 6:19	B	May 21	" 10:37	E	Sept. 21	" 2:40	B
Feb. 1	set 6:47	B	June 1	set 10:35	E	Oct. 1	rise 2:19	B
Feb. 11	" 7:13	B	June 11	" 10:25	E	Oct. 11	" 2:10	B
Feb. 21	" 7:37	C	June 21	" 10:09	D	Oct. 21	" 2:10	B
Mar. 1	set 7:57	C	July 1	set 9:47	D	Nov. 1	rise 2:18	B
Mar. 11	" 8:21	D	July 11	" 9:19	D	Nov. 11	" 2:30	C
Mar. 21	" 8:45	D	July 21	" 8:42	D	Nov. 21	" 2:45	C
Apr. 1	set 9:13	D	Aug. 1	set 7:53	D	Dec. 1	rise 3:02	D
Apr. 11	" 9:37	E	Aug. 11	" 6:58	C	Dec. 11	" 3:22	D
Apr. 21	" 9:59	E	Aug. 21	" 5:58	C	Dec. 21	" 3:43	D
						Dec. 31	rise 4:04	D

MARS is visible in January for more than half the night in Taurus, its eastward elongation decreasing until it can only be seen in the evening sky passing from Taurus through Gemini, Cancer, Leo, and into Virgo where, by the end of September, it becomes too close to the Sun for observation. It reappears in the morning sky in Ophiuchus in late December. Mars is in conjunction with Jupiter on June 14, with Venus on June 23 and July 22.

Jan. 1	set 4:11	E	May 1	set 11:55	E	Sept. 1	set 7:09	C
Jan. 11	" 3:35	E	May 11	" 11:37	E	Sept. 11	" 6:44	C
Jan. 21	" 3:05	E	May 21	" 11:17	E	Sept. 21	" 6:18	B
Feb. 1	set 2:37	E	June 1	set 10:54	E	Oct. 1	set 5:54	B
Feb. 11	" 2:15	E	June 11	" 10:32	E	Oct. 11	" 5:30	B
Feb. 21	" 1:55	E	June 21	" 10:09	D	Oct. 21	" 5:07	B
Mar. 1	set 1:41	E	July 1	set 9:45	D	Nov. 1	set 4:42	B
Mar. 11	" 1:24	E	July 11	" 9:21	D	Nov. 11	rise 6:26	D
Mar. 21	" 1:07	E	July 21	" 8:56	D	Nov. 21	" 6:23	D
Apr. 1	set 12:50	E	Aug. 1	set 8:28	D	Dec. 1	rise 6:20	E
Apr. 11	" 12:33	E	Aug. 11	" 8:03	D	Dec. 11	" 6:17	E
Apr. 21	" 12:16	E	Aug. 21	" 7:37	C	Dec. 21	" 6:13	E
						Dec. 31	rise 6:08	E

JUPITER is visible in Cancer, its westward elongation increasing until it is at opposition January 29. In mid-July it passes into Leo, where it can be seen only in the evening sky. By early August it becomes too close to the Sun for observation. It reappears early September in the morning sky in Leo, where it remains for the rest of the year. Jupiter is in conjunction with Mars on June 14, with Venus on June 17 and October 17, and with Mercury on July 15 and September 10.

IVPITER

Jan. 1	rise 6:46	A	May 1	set 1:00	E	Sept. 1	rise 4:12	B
Jan. 11	" 6:01	A	May 11	" 12:23	E	Sept. 11	" 3:44	B
Jan. 21	" 5:15	A	May 21	set 11:44	D	Sept. 21	" 3:16	B
Feb. 1	set 6:59	E	June 1	set 11:06	D	Oct. 1	rise 2:47	B
Feb. 11	" 6:16	E	June 11	" 10:31	D	Oct. 11	" 2:17	B
Feb. 21	" 5:33	E	June 21	" 9:57	D	Oct. 21	" 1:47	B
Mar. 1	set 4:59	E	July 1	set 9:23	D	Nov. 1	rise 1:14	B
Mar. 11	" 4:17	E	July 11	" 8:50	D	Nov. 11	" 12:42	B
Mar. 21	" 3:37	E	July 21	" 8:16	D	Nov. 21	" 12:09	B
Apr. 1	set 2:53	E	Aug. 1	set 7:39	D	Dec. 1	rise 11:31	A
Apr. 11	" 2:14	E	Aug. 11	" 7:05	D	Dec. 11	" 10:56	B
Apr. 21	" 1:37	E	Aug. 21	rise 4:43	B	Dec. 21	" 10:18	B
						Dec. 31	rise 9:40	B

SATURN is visible on January 1 in the evening sky in Sagittarius, then it becomes too close to the Sun for observation. It reappears in the morning sky in early February in Capricorn, where it remains for the rest of the year. Its westward elongation increases until it is at opposition on July 27, when it is visible all night. From late October, it can only be seen in the evening sky. Saturn is in conjunction with Venus on January 1 and with Mercury on February 5.

SATVRN

Jan. 1	set 5:32	A	May 1	rise 12:55	D	Sept. 1	set 2:02	A
Jan. 11	" 4:58	A	May 11	" 12:16	D	Sept. 11	" 1:20	A
Jan. 21	rise 7:00	E	May 21	rise 11:33	D	Sept. 21	" 12:39	A
Feb. 1	rise 6:22	E	June 1	rise 10:50	D	Oct. 1	set 11:55	A
Feb. 11	" 5:46	E	June 11	" 10:09	D	Oct. 11	" 11:16	A
Feb. 21	" 5:10	E	June 21	" 9:29	D	Oct. 21	" 10:38	A
Mar. 1	rise 4:42	E	July 1	rise 8:48	E	Nov. 1	set 9:57	A
Mar. 11	" 4:05	E	July 11	" 8:07	E	Nov. 11	" 9:20	A
Mar. 21	" 3:29	E	July 21	" 7:25	E	Nov. 21	" 8:44	A
Apr. 1	rise 2:48	D	Aug. 1	set 4:14	A	Dec. 1	set 8:09	A
Apr. 11	" 2:11	D	Aug. 11	" 3:31	A	Dec. 11	" 7:34	A
Apr. 21	" 1:33	D	Aug. 21	" 2:48	A	Dec. 21	" 7:00	A
						Dec. 31	set 6:26	A

MERCURY can only be seen low in the east before sunrise or low in the west after sunset. It is visible mornings between these approximate dates: January 1-February 18, April 23-June 10, August 30-September 23, and December 14-31. The planet is brighter at the end of each period (best viewing conditions in northern latitudes occur the second week in September). It is visible evenings between these approximate dates: March 12-April 6, June 25-August 15, and October 18-December 3. The planet is brighter at the end of each period (best viewing conditions in northern latitudes occur the last two weeks of March).

DO NOT CONFUSE 1) Venus with Saturn January 1; with Mars from mid-June until late July; with Jupiter the last half of June and the second and third weeks of October; and with Mercury late July until mid-August. On all occasions Venus is the brighter object. 2) Mercury with Saturn in early February; Mercury is the brighter object. 3) Jupiter with Mars for most of June; and with Mercury mid-July and early September. On all occasions, Jupiter is the brighter object.

Eclipses for 1991

There will be six eclipses in 1991, two of the Sun and four of the Moon. Lunar eclipses technically are visible from the entire night side of the Earth; solar eclipses are visible only in certain areas. One of the solar and one of the lunar eclipses will not be seen in the United States or Canada; the other four will be visible in certain locations.

1. Annular eclipse of the Sun, January 15. This eclipse will be visible only from southeast Asia, Australia, New Zealand, and Polynesia (but not Hawaii).

2. Penumbral eclipse of the Moon, January 30. This eclipse will be seen throughout North America. The Moon enters penumbra at 10:58 P.M., EST, January 29; the middle occurs at 12:59 A.M., EST, January 30. The Moon leaves penumbra at 2:59 A.M., EST.

3. Penumbral eclipse of the Moon, June 26. The beginning will be visible from eastern North America; the end from North America except Alaska and northwestern Canada. The Moon enters penumbra at 8:46 P.M., EST; the middle occurs at 10:15 P.M., EST; the Moon leaves penumbra at 11:43 P.M., EST.

4. Total eclipse of the Sun, July 11. The partial eclipse will be visible from all of North America except Alaska; the total only from the island of Hawaii, the southern coast of Maui, and the Baja peninsula. The partial eclipse begins in Boston at 2 P.M., EST, and ends at 3:15 P.M., EST; in San Francisco it begins at 9:20 A.M., PST, and ends at 11:20 A.M., PST. It begins in Hawaii at 6:30 A.M., and ends at 8:40 A.M., Hawaii-Aleutian Standard Time. The total eclipse will occur at 7:29 A.M. (HALST).

5. Penumbral eclipse of the Moon, July 26. This eclipse will not be seen in North America or the Hawaiian Islands.

6. Partial eclipse of the Moon, December 21. The eclipse, while slight, will be visible throughout North America. The Moon enters penumbra at 3:25 A.M., EST; enters umbra at 5 A.M., EST; the middle occurs at 5:33 A.M., EST. The Moon leaves umbra at 6:06 A.M., EST, and penumbra at 7:41 A.M., EST.

Full Moon Days

	1991	1992	1993	1994	1995
Jan.	30	19	8	27	16
Feb.	28	18	6	25	15
Mar.	30	18	8	27	16
Apr.	28	16	6	25	15
May	28	16	5	24	14
June	26	14	4	23	12
July	26	14	3	22	12
Aug.	25	13	2/31	21	10
Sept.	23	11	30	19	8
Oct.	23	11	30	19	8
Nov.	21	10	29	18	7
Dec.	21	9	28	17	6

Principal Meteor Showers

Shower	Best Hour (EST)	Radiant Direction*	Date of Maximum**	Approx. Peak Rate (/hr.)	Associated Comet
Quadrantid	5 A.M.	N.	Jan. 4	40-150	—
Lyrid	4 A.M.	S.	Apr. 21	10-15	1861 I
Eta Aquarid	4 A.M.	S.E.	May 4	10-40	Halley
Delta Aquarid	2 A.M.	S.	July 30	10-35	—
Perseid	4 A.M.	N.	Aug. 11-13	50-100	1862 III
Draconid	9 P.M.	N.W.	Oct. 9	10	Giacobini-Zinner
Orionid	4 A.M.	S.	Oct. 20	10-70	Halley
Taurid	midnight	S.	Nov. 9	5-15	Encke
Leonid	5 A.M.	S.	Nov. 16	5-20	1866 I
Andromedid	10 P.M.	S.	Nov. 25-27	10	Biela
Geminid	2 A.M.	S.	Dec.13	50-80	—
Ursid	5 A.M.	N.	Dec. 22	10-15	—

 * Direction from which the meteors appear to come.
** Date of actual maximum occurrence may vary by one or two days in either direction.

BRIGHT STARS, 1991

The upper table shows the Eastern Standard Time when each star transits the meridian of Boston (i.e., lies directly above the horizon's south point there) and its altitude above that point at transit on the dates shown. The time of transit on any other date differs from that on the nearest date listed by approximately four minutes of time for each day. For a place outside Boston the local time of the star's transit is found by correcting the time at Boston by the value of Key Letter "C" for the place. (See footnote.)

Time of Transit (E.S.T.)

Boldface—P.M. Lightface—A.M.

Star	Constellation	Magni-tude	Jan. 1	Mar. 1	May 1	July 1	Sept. 1	Nov. 1	Alt.
Altair	Aquila	0.8	**12 51**	8 59	4 59	12 59	**8 51**	**4 52**	56.3
Deneb	Cygnus	1.3	**1 42**	9 50	**5 50**	**1 50**	**9 42**	**5 42**	87.5
Fomalhaut	Psc. Austr.	1.2	**3 56**	**12 04**	8 04	4 05	12 01	**7 57**	17.8
Algol	Perseus	2.2	**8 07**	**4 15**	**12 15**	8 15	4 11	12 12	88.5
Aldebaran	Taurus	0.9	**9 34**	**5 42**	**1 42**	9 43	5 39	1 39	64.1
Rigel	Orion	0.1	**10 13**	**6 21**	**2 21**	10 21	6 17	2 17	39.4
Capella	Auriga	0.1	**10 14**	**6 22**	**2 23**	10 23	6 19	2 19	85.4
Bellatrix	Orion	1.6	**10 23**	**6 31**	**2 32**	10 32	6 28	2 28	54.0
Betelgeuse	Orion	0.7	**10 53**	**7 01**	**3 01**	11 02	6 58	2 58	55.0
Sirius	Can. Maj.	-1.4	**11 43**	**7 51**	**3 51**	11 51	7 47	3 48	31.0
Procyon	Can. Min.	0.4	12 41	**8 45**	**4 45**	**12 45**	8 41	4 42	52.9
Pollux	Gemini	1.2	12 47	**8 51**	**4 51**	**12 51**	8 47	4 47	75.7
Regulus	Leo	1.4	3 10	**11 14**	**7 14**	**3 14**	11 10	7 11	59.7
Spica	Virgo	1.0	6 26	2 34	**10 30**	**6 30**	**2 27**	10 27	36.6
Arcturus	Bootes	-0.1	7 17	3 25	**11 21**	**7 21**	**3 17**	11 18	66.9
Antares	Scorpius	var.09	9 30	5 38	1 38	**9 34**	**5 30**	**1 30**	21.3
Vega	Lyra	0.0	11 37	7 45	3 45	**11 42**	**7 38**	**3 38**	86.4

RISINGS AND SETTINGS

The times of the star's rising and setting at Boston on any date are found by applying the interval shown to the time of the star's transit on that date. Subtract the interval for the star's rising; add it for its setting. The times for a place outside Boston are found by correcting the times found for Boston by the values of the Key Letters shown. (See footnote.) The directions in which the star rises and sets shown for Boston are generally useful throughout the United States. Deneb, Algol, Capella, and Vega are circumpolar stars — this means that they do not appear to rise or set, but are above the horizon.

Star	Int. hr.m.	Rising Key	Dir.	Setting Key	Dir.
Altair	6 36	B	EbN	D	WbN
Fomalhaut	3 59	E	SE	A	SW
Aldebaran	7 06	B	ENE	D	WNW
Rigel	5 33	D	EbS	B	WbS
Bellatrix	6 27	B	EbN	D	WbN
Betelgeuse	6 31	B	EbN	D	WbN
Sirius	5 00	D	ESE	B	WSW
Procyon	6 23	B	EbN	D	WbN
Pollux	8 01	A	NE	E	NW
Regulus	6 49	B	EbN	D	WbN
Spica	5 23	D	EbS	B	WbS
Arcturus	7 19	A	ENE	E	WNW
Antares	4 17	E	SEbE	A	SWbW

NOTE: The values of Key Letters are given in the Time Correction Tables (pages 80-84).

- illustration by Virginia Peck

The Earthshaking Theories of James Berkland

BY RIC BUCHER

A California geologist predicts earthquakes – not by fancy seismic monitoring, but by counting the number of lost pets in the classified ads!

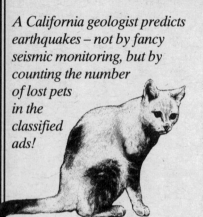

James Berkland, a county geologist with the U.S. Geological Survey in the San Francisco area, has anticipated more earthquakes and how big they'll be than anyone inside or outside the scientific community, and he's not about to stop. He stands on his record: 270 predictions over the last 15 years, and in no one year did he miss more than 1 out of 4.

How does he do it? To the dismay of the established scientific community, which is still struggling with the "seismic gap" theory developed by a Japanese scientist early in this century, Berkland does it by counting the number of missing pets in the classified ads and measuring ocean tides. He also classifies such uncharacteristic animal behavior as elephants refusing to have their nails manicured, homing pigeons losing their way during races, worms wriggling up out of the soil, snakes deserting their dens, and confused swarms of bees flying into churches as harbingers of earthquakes.

When the Loma Prieta fault near San Francisco yawned on October 17, 1989,

it measured 7.1 on the Richter scale and killed 67 people. Berkland was ready. In September, while most people within driving distance of Candlestick Park, site of the World Series, had been scrambling for tickets, he had been scanning the classified ads. "Someone asked me, 'What numbers of animals advertised as lost would scare you?' " he related. "I told them, 'Oh, about 25 or 26 cats and 60 dogs.' " On September 22, cats listed as missing peaked at 27; dogs reported lost numbered 57.

Berkland warned the people in his office to be ready for a 5-plus magnitude quake before the end of the month. The end of September came and went; the ground remained quiet. Berkland said that at that point he realized he had been fooled, that what he had taken as foreshadowing an impending medium-sized tremor was actually the early signs of a larger jolt. In situations where a record earthquake had struck, the first indication had come about one month in advance.

He checked the tide tables and found that on October 14 the highest tidal forces in three years would batter the northern California coast. He felt he was on the right track. After noting a second rise in missing cats developing in mid-October, Berkland was convinced. When the number of AWOL cats hit 21, along with 58 missing canines, on Friday, the 13th of October, he convinced the *Gilroy Dispatch* to print his prediction of an earthquake of a magnitude between 6.5 and 7.0 to strike between October 14 and 21.

Most people did not pay heed, but some did. A USGS colleague who lives in a San Jose suburb known as Los

Gatos (the Cats) strapped down his water heater the night of October 16. When it, unlike those of his neighbors, survived the October 17 earthquake, he sent Berkland a note of thanks. Another family thanked him for his advice, which had led them to safeguard $6,000 worth of china and crystal.

Berkland's belief that unusual animal behavior can serve as alerts to upcoming seismographic disturbances is illustrated by this example: A woman who owns a well-behaved dog reported to Berkland that her dog had disappeared a few days before the October 17 earthquake. The dog returned a few hours after the quake caked with mud and choking on a willow stick. Willow bark, Berkland explained, contains an ingredient that Indians used to cure headaches. He deduced that the dog had developed a whopping headache from the impending quake and attempted to use the same remedy.

Even as recovery drives were being launched to restore order after the October earthquake, Berkland warned publicly that a second serious vibration would assault the Bay area in November. The *Oakland Tribune* contributed to the panic by stating that Berkland expected the November quake to register 8-plus on the Richter scale. Although the paper later ran a correction stating that Berkland's prediction was for a tremor between 3.5 and 5.5 (which actually occurred), Berkland was in trouble with his superiors at the USGS; he was suspended from his job for more than two months for causing undue panic. He was reinstated with the understanding that he would not make predictions while on the job.

In any event, catastrophic or otherwise, Berkland will continue to read the classifieds and the tide tables,

collect data and documented episodes of bizarre animal behavior, and use that information to predict the time, place, and severity of future earthquakes. □ □

SHORT-TERM SIGNALS OF EARTHQUAKES

Although many scientists are concentrating on the ability to make accurate long-term predictions of earthquakes, the following phenomena have been observed to signal imminent quakes:

☞ Release of radon, a mildly radioactive gas, from wells.

☞ An increase in creep, the slow movement along a fault or gentle tilting of land near a fault.

☞ Flashes of bright lights in the sky, possibly related to gas release and dust.

☞ A rise or drop in the level of well water.

☞ Earthquakes may be more likely when the Moon "rides high" or "runs low" during each lunar cycle or when the Moon is on the Equator (see page 30, "Determination of Earthquakes").

☞ Increased intensity of low-frequency electromagnetic waves.

☞ Cattle may bellow and plant their feet widely apart for support.

☞ Certain weather is thought to presage and accompany earthquakes: fog, mists, darkness, and lurid vapors.

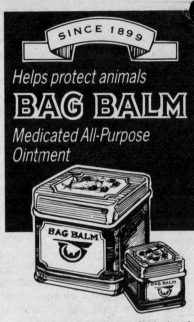

...enting...

The DR™ FIELD and BRUSH MOWER

-the amazing walk-behind brush hog that-

- **CLEARS & MAINTAINS** meadows, pastures, roadsides, fences, wooded and rough non-lawn areas with ease. Mows over 1/2 acre per hour!
- **CUTS** tall grass, weeds, brush, brambles, sumac - even *hardwood saplings up to 1" thick!*
- **Plus CHOPS and MULCHES** most everything it cuts; leaves NO TANGLE of material to trip over or to pick up like hand-held brush cutters and sicklebar mowers.
- **POWERFUL** 8HP Briggs & Stratton engine with BIG 20" SELF-PROPELLED WHEELS! Rolls through ditches, furrows, over bumps and logs with ease.
- **Perfect for low-maintenance wildflower meadows...** European-style woodlots free of undergrowth...walking paths...or any area that you only want to mow once-a-month, or once-a-season!

©1990 CHP, Inc.

So WHY MESS with hand-held brush cutters that are so dangerous, slow and tiring to use...OR with sicklebar mowers that shake unmercifully and leave such a tangled mess?

TOLL FREE 1(800)637-6886

PLEASE MAIL COUPON for Complete Details of the **DR™ FIELD and BRUSH MOWER!**

YES! Please rush complete FREE DETAILS of the DR™ FIELD and BRUSH MOWER including specifications, prices, and "Off-Season" Savings now in effect.

Name_____

Address_____

City_____ State_____ ZIP_____

To: COUNTRY HOME PRODUCTS, Dept. A7709F
Ferry Road, Box 89, Charlotte, VT 05445

OWN YOUR OWN
Retail Apparel or Shoe Store
WE
OFFER YOU

Gain the advantages of business ownership. All profits are yours. Your choice of store size and merchandise...**ladies, mens or mens big and tall shop, infant/preteen, jean/sportswear, large sizes, petite, dance-wear/aerobic, bridal, accessories, lingerie store, sock shop add color analysis.** $19,900 to $29,900 includes beginning inventory from over 2000 first quality national name brands, fixtures (Redwood, Firwood, Brass or Chrome), training, grand opening and more. A proven way to success and independence. 3000 stores sold nationwide. We also offer a **discount ladies, mens and childrens apparel stores and a multi-tier pricing discount or family shoe stores.**
The first step is up to you.
STEPHEN C. LOUGHLIN (612) 888-6555
America's Largest & Oldest Store Opening Service

High Country Fashions, Inc.
Since 1977

How to Have a Baby

Anyone with the brains of a bunny can raise a happy, healthy, successful child by following a few simple rules.

BY TIM CLARK

Let's face it: these are tough times to have a baby. There are so many authorities offering so much conflicting advice on how to raise children. Fortunately, people have managed to do it for thousands of years, even without Japanese-language flash cards or crib mobiles that teach particle physics. The following bits of folk wisdom have been collected from all over the United States and will help anxious parents to determine the sex of the child, to care for the baby, and to predict its future career.

CONCEPTION

— A couple who go to a picture show within three days of getting married will have twins.

— Blow a dandelion seedball, and the number of seeds left on it will be the number of children you will have.

— If you dream of your mother giving birth, you will soon have a child.

— If a woman lays her hat or coat on a strange bed, she will have a child.

— Give away old baby clothes, and you'll soon need them again.

— Attach your wedding ring to a string and dangle it inside a glass tumbler, asking, "How many children shall I have?" Count the number of times the ring strikes the side of the glass.

— If a woman leaves a diaper under a bed in another's house, a baby will soon be born in that house.

— Holding a child on your first visit to the mother will help you conceive.

BOY OR GIRL?

— To have a boy, a woman should hold a nickel in her mouth at the time of conception.

— A baby conceived in the light of the Moon (from new Moon to full Moon) will be a boy.

— A baby conceived in the dark of the Moon (full Moon to new Moon) will be a girl.

— If the woman has no morning sickness, she is carrying a boy.

— If her stomach comes to a point, she is to have a girl.

— Add the mother's age at conception to the number of the month of conception; if it is even, a girl will be born. If odd, it's a boy.

— If the mother eats grapefruit just before conceiving, the child will be a girl.

— If the mother eats vinegar just before conceiving, it will be a boy.

— Suspend a needle from a thread held just above the mother's wrist. If it swings back and forth in a straight line, she will have a boy. If it swings in circles, she will have a girl.

— A baby carried high is a boy; low, a girl.

— During the last three months of pregnancy, count the baby's heartbeats. If it beats from 120 to 140 times per minute, it's a boy; from 140 to 160 times a minute, it's a girl.

— If the father is sick during the first three months of pregnancy, the child will be male.

— If the mother sleeps with her right hand under her head during pregnancy, she will have a girl. If she sleeps with her left hand under her head, she'll have a boy.

— If the mother craves sweets during

pregnancy, her child is female. If she craves sour things, she's carrying a boy.

AT BIRTH

— Labor pains can be eased by putting an axe under the bed.
— If a laboring woman wears her husband's hat, her pain will be lessened.

LOOKS

— Pretty babies become ugly adults, and vice versa.
— Call a child "Piggy" to make her grow.
— To make a child grow tall, put manure inside the baby's shoes.
— To make a child grow faster, sweep his feet with a broom.
— Washing babies in urine makes them handsome.
— A woman frightened by fire during pregnancy will have a red-haired child.
— Heartburn during pregnancy signifies a child with lots of hair.

PERSONALITY

— The child will grow up with a disposition just like that of the first person who takes her outdoors.
— If the baby's fists are tightly clenched at birth, he will be stingy.
— A baby who cries during baptism likes her name.
— March babies make fickle adults.
— A child born in the light of the Moon will be intelligent.
— A child born on a stormy night will be nervous.
— A baby born with a cowlick will be stubborn; but a baby with two cowlicks will be bright.

— A baby who never falls out of bed during his first year will grow up a fool.
— Feed the baby right out of the pot or skillet, and she'll never run away from home.

PROSPECTS

— On your first visit to a new baby, kiss the soles of her feet for luck.
— Carry a new baby upstairs before going downstairs, so that he will rise in the world. If born on the top floor, hold his head near the ceiling.
— Don't take the baby downhill on her first trip away from home. Her fortunes will sink.
— Rub the baby's tongue with a slice of apple immediately after birth, and he will have a good singing voice.
— Crack the first louse you find in your baby's hair on a Bible, and the child will become a preacher.
— A child born foot foremost can't be kept in jail.
— A child born with a caul will be able to tell fortunes.

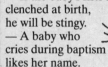

— A baby born with teeth will suffer ill luck.

— A baby born on the 26th of the month will get rich.

— The child will grow up to be wealthy if the initials of her full name spell a word.

— A child born around four o'clock in the afternoon will get rich.

— A child born on Christmas Day can understand the speech of animals.

SICKNESS AND HEALTH

— Burn the first dirty diaper, and the child will have no stomach aches.

— If the child is croupy, mix a lock of her hair with the mortar in a new house.

— For croup, feed the baby jaybird soup.

— Lay a grunting child in the pig pen to make him stop.

— Letting a puppy lick the baby's face after eating prevents illness.

THINGS TO AVOID

— The first time you dress your baby, use old clothes. New clothes will bring bad luck.

— Rain falling on a child's face before its first birthday will cause freckles.

— Frightening a baby will make him knock-kneed.

— Tickling a baby's feet will cause her to stutter (this can be cured by drinking out of a bell).

— Cutting a baby's toenails in the first year of life will cause the child to become pigeon-toed.

— Putting a baby on an ironing board is bad luck.

— Don't cut the baby's hair in the first year, or the child will be tongue-tied.

— Washing the inside of a baby's hand washes all the luck away.

— Never hand a baby over a fence or through a window; it brings bad luck.

— Never keep the baby's shoes above his head.

LEARNING TO WALK

— Set the baby behind the front door for nine mornings, and she will learn to walk sooner.

— If the baby is slow to walk, bury him naked in earth up to his waist with a string tied around his ankle.

— Run up and down stairs with an infant to make it spry.

— Tie a quail's toenail to a baby's ankle, and he will be quick on his feet.

TEETHING

— To ease teething, rub the baby's gums with fresh rabbit brains.

— Cut a sprig of greenery, name it after the baby, and hang it in a corner. When teething hurts the baby, point at the greenery, and the pain will stop.

— Don't let the baby wear his father's hat before he's a year old; it will make teething difficult.

— Hang a mole's paw around the baby's neck to ease teething pains.

— If a baby slobbers, draw a live minnow through his mouth three times, then throw the minnow back in a stream.

GOING TO SLEEP

— A fretful child can be calmed by holding her out in the rain for a few minutes.

— Blow smoke in a baby's ear to put him to sleep.

— Put a crying child in the doorway and sweep dust over her to calm her.

— A baby who smiles in his sleep is listening to angels. □□

1990 NOVEMBER, THE ELEVENTH MONTH

Though Mars was dramatically closer and brighter (and appeared almost 33% wider in telescopes) in its banner year of 1988, its encounter with us this month is excellent and not surpassed again until 2001. This golden-orange planet lies near the waning gibbous Moon on the 4th and six degrees north of Aldebaran on the 13th. Mars is at opposition on the 27th, but closest on the night of November 19th-20th, a "mere" 48.7 million miles away. Jupiter, rising in Cancer several hours after Mars, is only slightly brighter than Mars now. Before dawn on the 16th watch for possibly greater than usual numbers of Leonid meteors streaking from the south. High in the east is brilliant Perseus and small Aries the Ram. Below them are Capella in Auriga and Aldebaran in Taurus, with the V-shaped Hyades cluster and lovely Pleiades or Seven Sisters cluster. The Milky Way runs from east to west now, arching high in the north. Pegasus and Cassiopeia are overhead.

ASTRONOMICAL CALCULATIONS

○	Full Moon	2nd day	16th hour	48th min.
☾	Last Quarter	9th day	8th hour	2nd min.
●	New Moon	17th day	4th hour	5th min.
☽	First Quarter	25th day	8th hour	11th min.

FOR POINTS OUTSIDE BOSTON SEE KEY LETTER CORRECTIONS — PAGES 80-84

Day of Year	Day of Month	Day of Week	☉ Rises h. m.	Key	☉ Sets h. m.	Key	Length of Days h. m.	Sun Fast m.	Full Sea Boston A.M.	Full Sea Boston P.M.	☽ Rises h. m.	Key	☽ Sets h. m.	Key	Declination of sun ° '	☽ Place	☽ Age
305	1	Th.	6 17	D	4 38	B	10 21	32	9¼	9¾	3 P.M. 32	B	4 A.M. 42	E	14 S.30	PSC	14
306	2	Fr.	6 19	D	4 37	B	10 18	32	10	10½	4 06	B	6 01	E	14 49	ARI	15
307	3	Sa.	6 20	D	4 35	B	10 15	32	10¾	11¼	4 48	B	7 22	E	15 07	ARI	16
308	4	**G**	6 21	D	4 34	B	10 13	32	11½	—	5 41	A	8 41	E	15 26	TAU	17
309	5	M.	6 22	D	4 33	B	10 11	32	12¼	12½	6 45	A	9 52	E	15 44	TAU	18
310	6	Tu.	6 24	D	4 32	B	10 08	32	1	1¼	7 56	B	10 51	E	16 02	GEM	19
311	7	W.	6 25	D	4 31	A	10 06	32	2	2¼	9 11	B	11 A.M. 38	E	16 20	GEM	20
312	8	Th.	6 26	D	4 30	A	10 04	32	3	3¼	10 25	B	12 P.M. 15	E	16 38	CAN	21
313	9	Fr.	6 27	D	4 28	A	10 01	32	4	4½	11 P.M. 35	C	12 45	D	16 55	CAN	22
314	10	Sa.	6 29	D	4 27	A	9 58	32	5¼	5½	— —	–	1 10	D	17 12	LEO	23
315	11	**G**	6 30	D	4 26	A	9 56	32	6¼	6½	12 A.M. 43	D	1 33	C	17 29	SEX	24
316	12	M.	6 31	D	4 25	A	9 54	32	7¼	7½	1 49	D	1 54	C	17 45	LEO	25
317	13	Tu.	6 32	D	4 24	A	9 52	32	8	8½	2 53	D	2 16	B	18 01	VIR	26
318	14	W.	6 34	D	4 23	A	9 49	32	8¾	9¼	3 56	E	2 39	B	18 17	VIR	27
319	15	Th.	6 35	D	4 23	A	9 48	31	9½	10	5 00	E	3 04	B	18 32	VIR	28
320	16	Fr.	6 36	D	4 22	A	9 46	31	10¼	10¾	6 03	E	3 34	A	18 47	LIB	29
321	17	Sa.	6 37	D	4 21	A	9 44	31	10¾	11½	7 05	E	4 10	A	19 02	LIB	0
322	18	**G**	6 38	D	4 20	A	9 42	31	11½	—	8 04	E	4 51	A	19 16	SCO	1
323	19	M.	6 40	D	4 19	A	9 39	31	12	12	8 58	E	5 41	A	19 30	OPH	2
324	20	Tu.	6 41	D	4 19	A	9 38	30	12¾	12¾	9 45	E	6 37	A	19 44	SAG	3
325	21	W.	6 42	D	4 18	A	9 36	30	1½	1½	10 25	E	7 37	B	19 57	SAG	4
326	22	Th.	6 43	D	4 17	A	9 34	30	2	2¼	10 59	E	8 40	B	20 11	SAG	5
327	23	Fr.	6 45	D	4 17	A	9 32	30	2¾	3	11 27	E	9 44	B	20 23	CAP	6
328	24	Sa.	6 46	D	4 16	A	9 30	29	3¾	3¾	11 A.M. 53	D	10 50	C	20 35	CAP	7
329	25	**G**	6 47	D	4 15	A	9 28	29	4½	4¾	12 P.M. 16	D	11 P.M. 56	D	20 47	AQU	8
330	26	M.	6 48	E	4 15	A	9 27	29	5¼	5½	12 39	C	— —	–	20 58	AQU	9
331	27	Tu.	6 49	E	4 14	A	9 25	28	6¼	6½	1 02	C	1 A.M. 04	D	21 09	PSC	10
332	28	W.	6 50	E	4 14	A	9 24	28	7	7½	1 28	B	2 16	E	21 20	PSC	11
333	29	Th.	6 51	E	4 14	A	9 23	28	7¾	8½	1 59	B	3 31	E	21 31	PSC	12
334	30	Fr.	6 52	E	4 13	A	9 21	27	8¾	9¼	2 P.M. 36	A	4 A.M. 51	E	21 S.41	ARI	13

NOVEMBER hath 30 days. 1990

Keen, fitful gusts are whisp'ring here and there
Among the bushes half leafless, and dry;
The stars look very cold about the sky,
And I have many miles on foot to fare.
— *John Keats*

D.M.	D.W.	Dates, Feasts, Fasts, Aspects, Tide Heights	Weather ↓
1	Th.	**All Saints** • ♀ in sup. ☌ • Earthquake, Lisbon, 1755 •	*Rain*
2	Fr.	**All Souls** • Full Hunter's ○ • Tides {11.7 10.6 •	*pocks*
3	Sa.	☾ at peri. • Detroit-Windsor auto tunnel opened, 1930 • {12.1 10.7 •	*the*
4	G	**22nd S. af. P.** • ☌♂☾ • Tides {12.2 — •	*lake;*
5	M.	☾ runs high • *Love is the reward of love.* • Tides {10.5 12.1 •	*this*
6	Tu.	**St. Leonard** • 98 m.p.h. winds, Block Island, R.I., 1953 •	*"summer"*
7	W.	Last person publicly burned by Spanish Inquisition, Seville, 1783 • {9.9 11.3	*is fake.*
8	Th.	☾ at ☋ • Kingman Brewster died, 1988 • {9.6 10.7 •	*Clouds*
9	Fr.	☌♃☾ • John Mitchell died, 1988 •	*congregate*
10	Sa.	☌♇☉ • Blackout, Eastern Seaboard, 1965 • Tides {9.3 9.8 •	*and*
11	G	**23rd S. af. P. Veterans Day • St. Martin** ☾ on Eq.	
12	M.	NFL record: Detroit Lions fumbled 11 times, 1967 • {9.7 9.4 •	*dump their*
13	Tu.	*Double Eagle V* completed first transpacific balloon flight, 1981 •	*freight.*
14	W.	Birthday of the Prince of Wales • Dow Jones first topped 1000, 1972 •	*Drowned*
15	Th.	*An idea isn't responsible for the people who believe in it.* • Tides {10.2 9.2 •	*or*
16	Fr.	Oklahoma admitted to Union, 1907 • W.C. Handy born, 1873 •	*buried,*
17	Sa.	New ● • American Theosophical Society founded, 1875 •	*take*
18	G	**24th S. af. P.** • ☌☿☾ • ☾ at apo. •	*your*
19	M.	☾ runs low • ♂ closest approach • Tides {8.9 10.1 •	*pick!*
20	Tu.	**St. Edmund** • ☌♂☾ • Tides {8.8 10.0 •	*Highways*
21	W.	☌♆☾ • ☌♄☾ • Stan Musial born, 1920 •	*slick.*
22	Th.	**Thanksgiving Day** • **St. Cecilia** • ☾ at ☊ •	*Let*
23	Fr.	**St. Clement** • Food rationing ended, 1945 • Tides {8.4 9.3 •	*us*
24	Sa.	Scott Joplin born, 1868 • First national Thanksgiving celebration, 1863 •	*all*
25	G	**25th S. af. P.** • **St. Catherine** • {8.7 9.1 •	*give*
26	M.	☾ on Eq. • *Rotten wood cannot be carved.* • Tides {9.0 9.1 •	*thanks,*
27	Tu.	♂ at ☍ • Jimi Hendrix born, 1942 • Tides {9.5 9.2 •	*digging*
28	W.	Picasso's *Acrobat* sold for $38.45 million, 1988 • William Blake born, 1757 •	*out*
29	Th.	First Army-Navy football game, 1890 (Navy 24, Army 0) • Tides {10.8 9.7 •	*of*
30	Fr.	**St. Andrew** • ♃ stat. • Tides {11.4 10.0 •	*snowbanks!*

A hero is no braver than an ordinary man, but he is braver five minutes longer.

Farmer's Calendar

Well, the wood is in: the shed is full. The long stacks are built, filled, and braced. The axe, the maul, the steel wedges, and the heavy hammer are put away in their corner. The yard is picked up and raked. And inevitably, standing around the woodshed in no order, in silent reproach, are a couple of dozen chunks that could not be made to see the light: the unsplittables.

Unsplittables are crotch-bottom pieces, mostly, or they are pieces where a branch started or where the wood to be split was twisted or where it grew in a curve. Not all such pieces are unsplittable, however, and so a rebellious chunk is apt to announce itself only in that arresting moment when you strike the billet a mighty blow and your axe or maul bounces off the wood like a tennis ball dropped on a granite step. At that point you may hit a couple of more licks, possibly turning the piece over. You can bring out the sledgehammer and wedges, but beware: unsplittables swallow steel wedges the way quicksand swallows dachshunds — without effect from the point of view of the quicksand and with utter finality from the point of view of the dachshund.

At this point you are best advised to apply to your unsplittables the Way of the East: struggle no more, accept, embrace. That incorrigible block is not a useless unsplittable; it is a Yule Log, which will light your hearth next Christmas. I myself have a supply of yule logs that will take me through Christmas 2011. You may not need that many, but there are other paths out of the frustrating battlefield where you and the unsplittables vainly contend. Unsplittables make step stools and doorstops. You can paint them white and use them to mark your driveway. You can furtively lose them beside back roads late at night. What you cannot do is split them.

1990 DECEMBER, THE TWELFTH MONTH

Two full Moons this month, the first (on December 2nd) causes very high tides because it occurs just three hours before the Moon's closest approach in many years. The Moon's center is then just 221,545 miles from Earth's center. By late evening on December 12th, dozens of Geminid meteors per hour should glide from high in the east (moonrise disturbs them later in the night). Mars lies near the Moon on the eves of the 1st and the 28th. Jupiter continues brightening, rising ever earlier in the evening. Observers with a telescope might be able to pick out the Andromeda Nebula, our closest neighbor galaxy; it is overhead, lying between Cassiopeia and the square of Pegasus. On the 15th the crescent Moon is at apogee: its occultation of Antares is visible from the west coast of North America. Solstice is on the 21st at 10:07 P.M. EST. New Year's eve sports a full Moon.

ASTRONOMICAL CALCULATIONS

○	Full Moon	2nd day	2nd hour	50th min.
☾	Last Quarter	8th day	21st hour	4th min.
●	New Moon	16th day	23rd hour	22nd min.
☽	First Quarter	24th day	22nd hour	16th min.
○	Full Moon	31st day	13th hour	35th min.

FOR POINTS OUTSIDE BOSTON SEE KEY LETTER CORRECTIONS — PAGES 80-84

Day of Year	Day of Month	Day of Week	☉ Rises h. m.	Key	☉ Sets h. m.	Key	Length of Days h. m.	Sun Fast m.	Full Sea Boston A.M.	Full Sea Boston P.M.	☽ Rises h. m.	Key	☽ Sets h. m.	Key	Declination of sun ° ′	☽ Place	☽ Age
335	1	Sa.	6 54	E	4 13	A	9 19	27	9½	10¼	3 P.M. 23	A	6 A.M. 11	E	21s.50	ARI	14
336	2	**G**	6 55	E	4 13	A	9 18	27	10¼	11	4 22	A	7 28	E	21 59	TAU	15
337	3	M.	6 56	E	4 12	A	9 16	26	11¼	—	5 33	A	8 34	E	22 07	TAU	16
338	4	Tu.	6 57	E	4 12	A	9 15	26	12	12¼	6 49	B	9 29	E	22 15	GEM	17
339	5	W.	6 58	E	4 12	A	9 14	25	1	1	8 07	B	10 11	E	22 23	GEM	18
340	6	Th.	6 59	E	4 12	A	9 13	25	1¾	2	9 22	C	10 45	E	22 30	CAN	19
341	7	Fr.	7 00	E	4 12	A	9 12	25	2¾	3	10 33	C	11 13	D	22 37	LEO	20
342	8	Sa.	7 01	E	4 12	A	9 11	24	3¾	4	11 P.M. 40	D	11 36	C	22 44	SEX	21
343	9	**G**	7 01	E	4 12	A	9 11	24	4¾	5	— —	–	11 A.M. 58	C	22 50	LEO	22
344	10	M.	7 02	E	4 12	A	9 10	23	5¾	6	12 A.M. 45	D	12 P.M. 20	C	22 56	VIR	23
345	11	Tu.	7 03	E	4 12	A	9 09	23	6¾	7¼	1 49	E	12 43	B	23 00	VIR	24
346	12	W.	7 04	E	4 12	A	9 08	22	7½	8	2 53	E	1 07	B	23 05	VIR	25
347	13	Th.	7 05	E	4 12	A	9 07	22	8¼	9	3 56	E	1 36	B	23 09	VIR	26
348	14	Fr.	7 06	E	4 12	A	9 06	21	9	9¾	4 58	E	2 10	A	23 13	LIB	27
349	15	Sa.	7 06	E	4 12	A	9 06	21	9¾	10½	5 58	E	2 50	A	23 17	SCO	28
350	16	**G**	7 07	E	4 13	A	9 06	20	10½	11	6 53	E	3 37	A	23 19	OPH	0
351	17	M.	7 08	E	4 13	A	9 05	20	11	11¾	7 43	E	4 31	A	23 21	SAG	1
352	18	Tu.	7 08	E	4 13	A	9 05	19	11¾	—	8 25	E	5 30	B	23 23	SAG	2
353	19	W.	7 09	E	4 14	A	9 05	19	12¼	12½	9 01	E	6 33	B	23 24	SAG	3
354	20	Th.	7 09	E	4 14	A	9 05	18	1	1	9 31	E	7 36	B	23 25	CAP	4
355	21	Fr.	7 10	E	4 15	A	9 05	18	1¾	1¾	9 57	D	8 41	C	23 26	CAP	5
356	22	Sa.	7 10	E	4 15	A	9 05	17	2¼	2½	10 20	D	9 46	C	23 26	CAP	6
357	23	**G**	7 11	E	4 16	A	9 05	17	3	3¼	10 42	C	10 P.M. 52	D	23 26	AQU	7
358	24	M.	7 11	E	4 16	A	9 05	17	3¾	4	11 05	C	— —	–	23 25	PSC	8
359	25	Tu.	7 12	E	4 17	A	9 05	16	4½	5	11 28	B	12 A.M. 00	D	23 23	PSC	9
360	26	W.	7 12	E	4 18	A	9 06	16	5½	6	11 A.M. 55	B	1 10	E	23 21	PSC	10
361	27	Th.	7 12	E	4 18	A	9 06	15	6¼	7	12 P.M. 27	B	2 25	E	23 18	ARI	11
362	28	Fr.	7 13	E	4 19	A	9 06	15	7¼	8	1 08	A	3 42	E	23 15	ARI	12
363	29	Sa.	7 13	E	4 20	A	9 07	14	8¼	9	2 00	A	4 58	E	23 12	TAU	13
364	30	**G**	7 13	E	4 20	A	9 07	14	9¼	10	3 04	A	6 10	E	23 09	TAU	14
365	31	M.	7 13	E	4 21	A	9 08	13	10	10¾	4 P.M. 19	B	7 A.M. 11	E	23s.05	GEM	15

Thank God who seasons thus the year,
And sometimes kindly slants his rays;
For in his winter he's most near
And plainest seen upon the shortest days.
— Henry David Thoreau

D.M.	D.W.	Dates, Feasts, Fasts, Aspects, Tide Heights	*Weather* ↓
1	Sa.	☌♅☾ Rosa Parks refused to give up bus seat, Montgomery, Ala., 1955 • {11.9 10.2	*Cold*
2	G	**1st Sun. in Advent** • Full Cold ○ • ☾ at peri.	*as*
3	M.	☾ runs high • *Drive thy Business, let it not drive thee.* • Tides {12.3 — •	*the*
4	Tu.	83 m.p.h. winds, Atlantic City, N.J., 1898 • Tides {10.3 12.2 •	*Dickens!*
5	W.	☾ at ☋ • Bus boycott began, Montgomery, Ala., 1955 • {10.2 11.8 •	*Then*
6	Th.	**St. Nicholas** • ☿ Gr. Elong. E. (21°) • ☌♃☾ •	*milder.*
7	Fr.	Earthquake killed 25,000, Armenia, 1988 • Tides {9.9 10.6 •	*Twist*
8	Sa.	**Concept. of V.M.** • John Lennon killed, 1980 •	*beforrit*
9	G	**2nd S. in Adv.** • ☾ on Eq. • John Milton born, 1608	*snows*
10	M.	☌☿♅ • First Nobel prizes awarded, 1901 • Tides {9.6 9.0 •	*so*
11	Tu.	*Make the most of yourself, for that is all there is of you.* • Tides {9.6 8.7 •	*hard*
12	W.	**Chanukah** • Jascha Heifetz died, 1987 • Tides {9.7 8.6 •	*we can*
13	Th.	**St. Lucy** • *Brevity is the soul of wit.* • Tides {9.8 8.6 •	*little*
14	Fr.	☿ stat. • Beware the pogonip. • Alabama statehood, 1819 •	*enDorrit.*
15	Sa.	Occult. Antares by ☾ • ☾ at apo. • {10.0 8.6 •	*Great*
16	G	**3rd S. in Adv.** • New ● •	*Expectations*
17	M.	☾ runs low • *Politics makes strange postmasters.* • Tides {10.1 8.7 •	*of*
18	Tu.	☌☿♅ • ☌♆☾ • ☌☿♀ • {10.1 — •	*mixed*
19	W.	**St. Timothy** • ☌♀♅ • ☌♄☾ • ☾ at ☊	*precip-*
20	Th.	Halcyon days. • *A humorist is a man who feels bad but who feels good about it.* •	*itations.*
21	Fr.	**St. Thomas** • Winter Solstice • Pilgrims landed, 1620 •	*Colder*
22	Sa.	☌♀♆ • Giacomo Puccini born, 1858 • {8.9 9.5 •	*air'll*
23	G	**4th S. in Adv.** • ☾ on Eq. • {9.0 9.4 •	*chill our*
24	M.	☿ in inf. ☌ • A green Christmas brings a white Easter. •	*Christmas*
25	Tu.	**Christmas Day** • Humphrey Bogart born, 1899	*Carol.*
26	W.	**St. Stephen** • 26″ snow, New York City, 1947 • {9.9 9.0 •	*Hard*
27	Th.	**St. John** • First "Howdy Doody" telecast, 1947 •	*Times*
28	Fr.	**Holy Innocents** • ☌♅☾ • Tides {10.8 9.2 •	*below;*
29	Sa.	*Genius may have its limitations; stupidity is not thus handicapped.* • {11.3 9.5 •	*Heeps*
30	G	**1st S. af. Chr.** • ☾ runs high • ☾ at peri. •	*of*
31	M.	**St. Sylvester** • ☌♅☉ • Full Snow ○ •	*snow!*

Farmer's Calendar

A big storm is blowing in from the north. The wind rises and bears down on this house, which is not much protected on the north. It's an old house, and as it takes the weight of the wind, its boards and timbers creak and crack as if it were one of the clipper ships that were making news when the house was even then not new, but not yet old.

This house was built a little more than 200 years ago by a race of frontier farmer-artisans, a people whose skill, strength, and sheer capacity for hard work I can imagine only imperfectly. Those who built the house knew exactly what they were about. They put up a simple rectangle 40 feet by 30 perched on an enormous rock pile in the cellar, the chimney foundation. It's a convenient house, it even has a kind of plain beauty, but 200 years is a long time. There is not a right angle anyplace in the house. Each door is a parallelogram, and the tilting floors roll like a gentle sea. The entire structure, in fact, is no longer a box but rather a shallow pyramid, the apex held aloft by the massive chimney foundation at the center of the house while the corners settle inexorably into the ground. The ground has been pulling on this house for a long time, pulling on its footings, on its sills, on its roof, drawing it down farther into its destined entropy. With jacks and braces, posts and paint its owners have resisted time, and they will go on doing so. But the contest never ends. And so if I were to decorate the lintel of this house I would do so not with the date of its rearing, but with this: $S^2 - S^1 = q/T$. Engineers will recognize a statement of the Second Law of Thermodynamics, which, if I understand it rightly, says that everything goes to hell unless you prop it up, and which is all the physics an owner of this house will ever need to know.

Low in the southwest dusk on New Year's Day, Saturn is just north of far brighter Venus. On the 2nd, when Earth is closest to the Sun for 1991, the Moon appears near to Jupiter. Moonlight drowns out the sight of Quadrantid meteors before dawn on the 3rd and 4th. The evening sky is resplendent with bright planets and stars, but Mars fades rapidly near the Pleiades cluster. Jupiter reaches opposition (closest and brightest) on the evening of the 28th. In the early hours of the 30th the Moon is near Jupiter a second time this month. Even more dramatically, at around 1:00 A.M. EST, January 30, Earth's penumbral shadow extends almost across the Moon, noticeably darkening the Moon's upper half. This month's annular solar eclipse on the 15th is not visible from the United States, but make reservations now for July's great Hawaiian total solar eclipse.

ASTRONOMICAL CALCULATIONS

☾	Last Quarter	7th day	13th hour	37th min.
●	New Moon	15th day	18th hour	51st min.
☽	First Quarter	23rd day	9th hour	23rd min.
○	Full Moon	30th day	1st hour	10th min.

FOR POINTS OUTSIDE BOSTON SEE KEY LETTER CORRECTIONS — PAGES 80-84

Day of Year	Day of Month	Day of Week	☉ Rises h. m.	Key	☉ Sets h. m.	Key	Length of Days h. m.	Sun Fast m.	Full Sea Boston A.M.	Full Sea Boston P.M.	☽ Rises h. m.	Key	☽ Sets h. m.	Key	Declination of Sun ° '	☽ Place	☽ Age
1	1	Tu.	7 14	E	4 22	A	9 08	13	11	11¾	5 ᴾ₍ₘ₎ 38	B	8 ᴬ₍ₘ₎ 01	E	23s.00	GEM	16
2	2	W.	7 14	E	4 23	A	9 09	12	—	12	6 57	C	8 40	E	22 54	CAN	17
3	3	Th.	7 14	E	4 24	A	9 10	12	12½	12¾	8 12	C	9 11	D	22 49	CAN	18
4	4	Fr.	7 14	E	4 25	A	9 11	11	1½	1¾	9 24	D	9 37	D	22 43	LEO	19
5	5	Sa.	7 14	E	4 26	A	9 12	11	2¼	2½	10 33	D	10 01	C	22 37	LEO	20
6	6	F	7 14	E	4 27	A	9 13	10	3¼	3½	11 ᴾ₍ₘ₎ 39	E	10 23	C	22 30	VIR	21
7	7	M.	7 13	E	4 28	A	9 15	10	4	4½	—	—	10 46	B	22 22	VIR	22
8	8	Tu.	7 13	E	4 29	A	9 16	9	5	5½	12 ᴬ₍ₘ₎ 43	E	11 10	B	22 14	VIR	23
9	9	W.	7 13	E	4 30	A	9 17	9	6	6½	1 47	E	11 ᴬ₍ₘ₎ 37	B	22 06	VIR	24
10	10	Th.	7 13	E	4 31	A	9 18	9	6¾	7½	2 50	E	12 ᴾ₍ₘ₎ 09	A	21 57	LIB	25
11	11	Fr.	7 13	E	4 32	A	9 19	8	7¾	8½	3 50	E	12 47	A	21 48	LIB	26
12	12	Sa.	7 12	E	4 33	A	9 21	8	8½	9¼	4 47	E	1 32	A	21 38	SCO	27
13	13	F	7 12	E	4 34	A	9 22	7	9¼	10	5 39	E	2 24	A	21 28	OPH	28
14	14	M.	7 12	E	4 36	A	9 24	7	10	10¾	6 24	E	3 22	B	21 18	SAG	29
15	15	Tu.	7 11	E	4 37	A	9 26	7	10¾	11¼	7 01	E	4 24	B	21 07	SAG	0
16	16	W.	7 11	E	4 38	A	9 27	6	11¼	—	7 34	E	5 28	B	20 56	SAG	1
17	17	Th.	7 10	E	4 39	A	9 29	6	12	12	8 01	E	6 34	C	20 44	CAP	2
18	18	Fr.	7 10	E	4 40	A	9 30	6	12½	12½	8 25	D	7 39	C	20 32	CAP	3
19	19	Sa.	7 09	E	4 42	A	9 33	5	1	1¼	8 48	D	8 44	D	20 20	AQU	4
20	20	F	7 08	E	4 43	A	9 35	5	1¾	2	9 10	C	9 50	D	20 07	PSC	5
21	21	M.	7 08	E	4 44	A	9 36	5	2½	2¾	9 33	B	10 ᴾ₍ₘ₎ 59	E	19 54	PSC	6
22	22	Tu.	7 07	D	4 45	A	9 38	4	3¼	3½	9 57	B	—	—	19 40	PSC	7
23	23	W.	7 06	D	4 47	A	9 41	4	4	4½	10 26	B	12 ᴬ₍ₘ₎ 10	E	19 27	PSC	8
24	24	Th.	7 05	D	4 48	A	9 43	4	5	5½	11 02	A	1 24	E	19 12	ARI	9
25	25	Fr.	7 05	D	4 49	A	9 44	4	5¾	6½	11 ᴾ₍ₘ₎ 47	A	2 38	E	18 58	TAU	10
26	26	Sa.	7 04	D	4 50	A	9 46	4	7	7¾	12 ᴾ₍ₘ₎ 43	A	3 50	E	18 42	TAU	11
27	27	F	7 03	D	4 52	A	9 49	3	8	8¾	1 51	B	4 54	E	18 27	TAU	12
28	28	M.	7 02	D	4 53	A	9 51	3	9	9¾	3 07	B	5 48	E	18 11	GEM	13
29	29	Tu.	7 01	D	4 54	A	9 53	3	10	10½	4 26	B	6 32	E	17 55	GEM	14
30	30	W.	7 00	D	4 56	A	9 56	3	10¾	11½	5 45	C	7 06	E	17 39	CAN	15
31	31	Th.	6 59	D	4 57	A	9 58	3	11¾	—	6 ᴾ₍ₘ₎ 59	D	7 ᴬ₍ₘ₎ 35	D	17s.22	LEO	16

JANUARY hath 31 days. 1991

> Chill airs and wintry winds! My ear
> Has grown familiar with your song;
> I hear it in the opening year—
> I listen and it cheers me long.
> — *Henry Wadsworth Longfellow*

D.M.	D.W.	Dates, Feasts, Fasts, Aspects, Tide Heights	*Weather* ↓
1	Tu.	**New Year's Day** • **Circumcision** • ☾ at ☋ • ☌♀♄	
2	W.	☌♃☾ • ⊕ at aphelion • Tides — / 12.0	*Gray day*
3	Th.	☿ stat. • Barometer 28.20", Canton, N.Y., 1913 • Tides 10.5 / 11.7 •	*in the*
4	Fr.	☌♆☉ • Washington delivered 1st address to Congress, 1790 • 10.4 / 11.2	*morning.*
5	Sa.	Twelfth Night • ☾ on Eq. • Zebulon Montgomery Pike born, 1779 •	*Storm*
6	**F**	**Epiphany** • 76" snow accum., Seattle, 1880 • Tides 10.1 / 9.8	*warning!*
7	M.	Emperor Hirohito of Japan died, 1989 • DDT banned, 1971 • Tides 9.9 / 9.1	*Still*
8	Tu.	Terry-Thomas died, 1990 • *"They say" is half a lie.* •	*spittin';*
9	W.	Snow and cold across N. Europe, 1982 (-43° F, Sweden) • Tides 9.5 / 8.2 •	*little*
10	Th.	18" snow, Savannah, Georgia, 1800 • Ethan Allen born, 1738 •	*kittens*
11	Fr.	*No snowflake in an avalanche ever feels responsible.* • Tides 9.4 / 8.1 •	*better*
12	Sa.	☾ at apo. • Willamette Univ. estab., 1st on West Coast, 1853 • Tides 9.5 / 8.2	• *wear*
13	**F**	**1st S. af. Epiph.** • ☾ runs low • ☌☿☾ •	*mittens.*
14	M.	☿ Gr. Elong. (24° W.) • Propitious day for birth of women. Tides 9.9 / 8.6	*Mercury*
15	Tu.	New ● • Eclipse ☉ • Tides 10.1 / 8.8 •	*lowers,*
16	W.	☾ at ☊ • Gold $760 per ounce, London, 1980 •	*start*
17	Th.	☌♀☾ • 253.1 million shares traded, N.Y.S.E., 1987 • Tides 9.0 / 10.2 •	*those*
18	Fr.	☌♄☉ • Cary Grant born, 1904 • Tides 9.2 / 10.2 •	*snow-*
19	Sa.	1st transatlantic radio program broadcast, Cape Cod, 1903 • 9.4 / 10.1	*blowers!*
20	**F**	**2nd S. af. Epiph.** • ☾ on Eq. • Tides 9.6 / 9.9 •	*Bright*
21	M.	Martin Luther King Jr.'s Birthday (ob.) • **St. Agnes** • 9.7 / 9.6 •	*out;*
22	Tu.	Sun today foretells much wind. • Queen Victoria died, 1901 •	*white-*
23	W.	☌☿♅ • Salvador Dali died, 1989 • Tides 10.0 / 9.0 •	*out!*
24	Th.	"Esquimo Pie" patented, 1922 • Winston Churchill died, 1965 • Tides 10.1 / 8.7	*Skiers*
25	Fr.	**Conv. of Paul** • *If clear, betides a happy year.* • ☌♂☾ •	*are*
26	Sa.	☌☿♆ • Earthquake, Lisbon, 1531, killed 30,000 • Tides 10.5 / 8.8 •	*due*
27	**F**	**Septuagesima** • ☾ rides high • Jerome Kern born, 1885 •	*for a*
28	M.	☾ at peri. • ♃ at ☍ • Ceasefire, Vietnam, 1973 • Tides 11.2 / 9.6 •	*lift:*
29	Tu.	*Once uttered, words run faster than horses.* • Tides 11.5 / 10.1 •	*get*
30	W.	Charles I beheaded, 1649 • ☾ at ☋ • ☌♃☾ • Full Wolf ○ •	*my*
31	Th.	Record warm month in Midwest, 1987 • Franz Schubert born, 1797 • Tides 11.6 / —	*drift?*

Farmer's Calendar

A foot of snow or maybe a little more fell last night, but then the sky cleared quickly, and now, midmorning, the sun lies over the perfect new snow as smooth and even as a beach. In a minute I'll start shoveling out.

The task of shoveling out at my house consists of making two main lines: the New York Central, a straight shot from the house to the woodshed of about 50 feet; and the Grand Trunk, an 80-foot path to the compost and ash piles that jogs around a big old tree and a picnic table. There are also spur lines connecting those lines to other doors. Total distance is less than 150 feet. Shoveling out, done right, might take half an hour, given good snow.

Today the snow is good. It's not so dry that it fills in behind you like the sands of the trackless Sahara, and it's not so wet that you feel as though you're shoveling concrete; rather, it's snow that cuts like a wedding cake, yielding sharp, clean blocks. In a few minutes the Central is finished, and I embark upon the Grand Trunk.

From the back door I sight upon the ash pile and begin to shovel. Slip the blade under the snow, lift, toss, step, slip the blade again. Presently I stop, straighten up, feel my pulse. It is probably no faster than the pulse of a hummingbird who is about to be presented at the Court of St. James. I slow down a bit, but I keep at it. Up ahead, I see, the ash pile I'm aiming for has veered several points to starboard. I correct course passing the picnic table. How strangely difficult it is to make a true straight line over land, and what a feat for those old Roman engineers who laid paved roads straight as a rule across all Europe. They didn't have to shovel snow, though, did they? Well, I'll soon be done.

FEBRUARY, THE SECOND MONTH

Evenings blaze even after Venus sets. Eastward, Jupiter beams in Cancer, passing in front of the south edge of the Beehive star cluster around the 7th. In the southwest, deep-orange Mars drifts a full 8 degrees north of Taurus the Bull's eye (the light-orange star Aldebaran) later in the month. During February, compare the fading brightness of Mars with that of other stars: yellow Capella (nearly overhead in Auriga the Charioteer); blue Rigel and orange-colored Betelgeuse (in Orion the Hunter); almost-white Procyon (in Canis Minor, the Little Dog). Much brighter than Mars is Sirius, the most brilliant of all stars; much dimmer are Castor and Pollux, the twin bright stars of Gemini. On the 5th, Saturn is near brighter Mercury, low in the southeast before dawn. The occultation of the bright star Antares by the Moon will be visible in southeastern North America just before dawn on the 8th. On the 12th, a telescope shows Saturn passing near the Moon (in a few places, like Hawaii, right behind the Moon) in daylight.

ASTRONOMICAL CALCULATIONS

☾ Last Quarter	6th day	8th hour	53rd min.
● New Moon	14th day	12th hour	33rd min.
☽ First Quarter	21st day	17th hour	59th min.
○ Full Moon	28th day	13th hour	26th min.

FOR POINTS OUTSIDE BOSTON SEE KEY LETTER CORRECTIONS — PAGES 80-84

Day of Year	Day of Month	Day of Week	☉ Rises h. m.	Key	☉ Sets h. m.	Key	Length of Days h. m.	Sun Fast m.	Full Sea Boston A.M.	Full Sea Boston P.M.	☽ Rises h. m.	Key	☽ Sets h. m.	Key	Declination of Sun ° '	☽ Place	☽ Age
32	1	Fr.	6 58	D	4 58	A	10 00	2	12¼	12½	8 P.M. 11	D	8 A.M. 01	D	17s.05	SEX	17
33	2	Sa.	6 57	D	4 59	A	10 02	2	1	1¼	9 20	E	8 24	C	16 48	LEO	18
34	3	**F**	6 56	D	5 01	A	10 05	2	1¾	2¼	10 27	E	8 48	B	16 31	VIR	19
35	4	M.	6 55	D	5 02	A	10 07	2	2½	3	11 P.M. 33	E	9 12	B	16 13	VIR	20
36	5	Tu.	6 54	D	5 03	A	10 09	2	3½	4	— —	–	9 38	B	15 55	VIR	21
37	6	W.	6 53	D	5 05	A	10 12	2	4¼	4¾	12 A.M. 38	E	10 09	A	15 37	LIB	22
38	7	Th.	6 52	D	5 06	B	10 14	2	5	5¾	1 40	E	10 45	A	15 18	LIB	23
39	8	Fr.	6 50	D	5 07	B	10 17	2	6	6¾	2 39	E	11 A.M. 27	A	14 59	SCO	24
40	9	Sa.	6 49	D	5 09	B	10 20	2	7	7¾	3 33	E	12 P.M. 16	A	14 40	OPH	25
41	10	**F**	6 48	D	5 10	B	10 22	2	8	8¾	4 20	E	1 12	B	14 21	SAG	26
42	11	M.	6 47	D	5 11	B	10 24	2	8¾	9½	5 01	E	2 13	B	14 01	SAG	27
43	12	Tu.	6 45	D	5 12	B	10 27	2	9½	10¼	5 35	E	3 16	B	13 41	SAG	28
44	13	W.	6 44	D	5 14	B	10 30	2	10¼	10¾	6 04	E	4 22	C	13 21	CAP	29
45	14	Th.	6 43	D	5 15	B	10 32	2	11	11½	6 30	D	5 28	C	13 01	CAP	0
46	15	Fr.	6 41	D	5 16	B	10 35	2	11½	—	6 53	D	6 34	D	12 40	AQU	1
47	16	Sa.	6 40	D	5 18	B	10 38	2	12	12¼	7 16	C	7 42	D	12 20	PSC	2
48	17	**F**	6 38	D	5 19	B	10 41	2	12½	1	7 38	C	8 51	E	11 59	PSC	3
49	18	M.	6 37	D	5 20	B	10 43	2	1¼	1½	8 02	B	10 01	E	11 38	PSC	4
50	19	Tu.	6 36	D	5 21	B	10 45	2	2	2¼	8 31	B	11 P.M. 14	E	11 17	PSC	5
51	20	W.	6 34	D	5 23	B	10 49	2	2¾	3¼	9 04	B	— —	–	10 55	ARI	6
52	21	Th.	6 33	D	5 24	B	10 51	2	3½	4¼	9 44	A	12 A.M. 27	E	10 33	ARI	7
53	22	Fr.	6 31	D	5 25	B	10 54	2	4½	5¼	10 35	A	1 38	E	10 12	TAU	8
54	23	Sa.	6 30	D	5 26	B	10 56	3	5½	6¼	11 A.M. 36	A	2 43	E	9 50	TAU	9
55	24	**F**	6 28	D	5 28	B	11 00	3	6¾	7½	12 P.M. 47	B	3 39	E	9 27	GEM	10
56	25	M.	6 26	D	5 29	B	11 03	3	7¾	8½	2 03	B	4 25	E	9 05	GEM	11
57	26	Tu.	6 25	D	5 30	B	11 05	3	8¾	9½	3 19	C	5 03	E	8 43	CAN	12
58	27	W.	6 23	D	5 31	B	11 08	3	9¾	10¼	4 34	C	5 34	D	8 20	LEO	13
59	28	Th.	6 22	D	5 33	B	11 11	3	10½	11¼	5 P.M. 47	D	6 A.M. 01	D	7s.58	LEO	14

There was never a leaf on bush or tree;
The bare boughs rattled shudderingly;
The river was dumb, and could not speak,
For the weaver, Winter, his shroud had spun.
— *James Russell Lowell*

Farmer's Calendar

February is the month of power failures. The snow flies, the wind blows, something gives. The lights go out, go on, go out, go on, go out — stay out. Immediately a vast silence descends upon the house. How noisy the place normally is, you realize, how full of sound the condition you ordinarily accept as quiet: refrigerator, furnace, even lights all contribute to a subliminal domestic hum that has now stopped and plunged you into a preindustrial stillness that is exactly as charming as it is brief. A power failure is like a walk in the rain or a performance by a coloratura soprano: for a little while it's fun, but before too long it becomes a bore and at length an ordeal.

If your power failure occurs at night, as fully three quarters of them seem to, your first need is for light. Here we have a couple of drawers in which we keep candles that are used for nothing else. They're a motley assortment: votive candles, plumber's candles, sloppy red Christmas candles, scented candles, candles in the shape of vegetables, of rabbits, busted candles from other occasions. A dozen of them assembled on the kitchen table enable you, with effort, to read a newspaper.

Having provided yourself with light, you are apt to feel some complacency — until you discover that you have no running water. Even then, you may reflect, the very snow that caused the problem will solve it. What is snow after all, you ask, but water? Well, it's a case of "Yes, but . . ." In a power failure early in my own career, I smugly put on the wood stove a bushel basket's worth of snow to melt, to find later (much later) at the bottom of the pot about half a cup of liquid. Snow, you will find, converts to water at a ratio that does not favor the powerless.

D.M.	D.W.	Dates, Feasts, Fasts, Aspects, Tide Heights	Weather ↓
1	Fr.	**St. Bridget** • ℂ on Eq. • Tides {10.6 {11.4	*No*
2	Sa.	**Purif. of Mary** • Candlemas • {10.7 {10.9	*shadows;*
3	**F**	*Sexagesima* • Four Chaplains • Woodrow Wilson died, 1924	*no*
4	M.	Auspicious for marriage and repair of ships. • Tides {10.3 {9.6	*spring,*
5	Tu.	**St. Agatha** • ♂♀♄ • Sir Robert Peel born, 1788 • {9.9 {8.9	*either.*
6	W.	Severe blizzard, Iowa, 1936 • Ronald Reagan born, 1911 • {9.5 {8.3	*Brrr!*
7	Th.	Laura Ingalls Wilder born, 1867 • Tides {9.2 {7.9	*Then a*
8	Fr.	Occultation Antares by ℂ • ℂ apo. • {9.0 {7.7	*breather.*
9	Sa.	ℂ runs low • *Compare your griefs with other men's, and they will seem less.*	*Below*
10	**F**	*Quinquagesima* • ♂♂ℂ • Tides {9.1 {8.3	*zero*
11	M.	♂♃ℂ • Nelson Mandela freed, 1990 • Tides {9.4 {8.3	*degrees;*
12	Tu.	**Shrove Tues.** • Abraham Lincoln born, 1809 • ℂ at ☊ • ♂♄ℂ	
13	W.	**Ash Wed.** • *If you walk on snow, you cannot hide your footprints.*	*Give your*
14	Th.	**St. Valentine** • New ● • Tides {10.2 {9.4	*sweetie*
15	Fr.	Battleship *Maine* exploded, Havana harbor, Cuba, 1898 • Tides {10.3 {—	*antifreeze.*
16	Sa.	ℂ on Eq. • ♂♀ℂ • Winter's back breaks. • Tides {9.8 {10.3	*Mild*
17	**F**	**1st S. in Lent** • 25" snow, Maine, 1955 • Tides {10.1 {10.3	*spell*
18	M.	Presidents' Day • February fog means frost in May.	*brings*
19	Tu.	Kansas enacted alcohol prohibition law, 1891 • Intense aurorae, 1852 • Tides {10.4 {9.7	*us*
20	W.	Ember Day • Alice Roosevelt Longworth died, 1980 • 30" snow, Racine, Wis., 1898	*days*
21	Th.	W. H. Auden born, 1907 • *Better be alone than in bad company.* • Tides {10.4 {8.9	*that*
22	Fr.	Ember Day • ♂♂ℂ • Indians introduced popcorn to English colonists, 1630	*are*
23	Sa.	Ember Day • ℂ rides high • G. F. Handel born, 1635 • {10.2 {8.6	*glorious;*
24	**F**	**2nd S. in Lent** • **St. Matthias** • ℂ at peri.	*more*
25	M.	ℂ at ☊ • ℞ stat. • Clay beat Liston, 1964 • Tides {10.5 {9.2	*like*
26	Tu.	♂♃ℂ • *Valor lies just halfway between rashness and cowardice.*	*that*
27	W.	Cold month closed all harbors, New York City to Eastport, Me., 1875 • {11.0 {10.2	*wouldn't*
28	Th.	Full Snow ○ • Bright and clear brings a good year. • Tides {11.2 {10.6	*Boreas!*

*"Outside of a dog, a book is man's best friend.
Inside of a dog, it's too dark to read."*
– Groucho Marx

MARCH, THE THIRD MONTH

Spring begins at 10:02 P.M. EST on the 20th. For many weeks around the equinoxes this year, displays of the Northern Lights are much more likely than usual. Late in the month Mercury puts in its best evening appearance of 1991, shining low in the west shortly after sunset — especially around the time of its greatest eastern elongation (19 degrees from the Sun) on the 27th. Venus is much higher and brighter in the west; Jupiter, high in the southeast at nightfall, is second brightest. Sirius, the Dog Star, glitters to the left of Orion. Compare the color and brightness of fading Mars with that of Orion's star Betelgeuse (and other stars) in the south. The Big Dipper climbs the northeast evening sky and Leo the Lion, with his heart-star Regulus, ascends in the east.

ASTRONOMICAL CALCULATIONS

☾ Last Quarter	8th day	5th hour	33rd min.
● New Moon	16th day	3rd hour	11th min.
☽ First Quarter	23rd day	1st hour	3rd min.
○ Full Moon	30th day	2nd hour	18th min.

FOR POINTS OUTSIDE BOSTON SEE KEY LETTER CORRECTIONS — PAGES 80-84

Day of Year	Day of Month	Day of Week	☉ Rises h. m.	Key	☉ Sets h. m.	Key	Length of Days h. m.	Sun Fast m.	Full Sea Boston A.M.	Full Sea Boston P.M.	☽ Rises h. m.	Key	☽ Sets h. m.	Key	Declination of Sun ° '	☽ Place	☽ Age
60	1	Fr.	6 20	D	5 34	B	11 14	4	11½	—	6 P.M. 58	D	6 A.M. 25	C	7 s.35	LEO	15
61	2	Sa.	6 19	D	5 35	B	11 16	4	12	12¼	8 07	E	6 49	B	7 12	VIR	16
62	3	**F**	6 17	D	5 36	B	11 19	4	12¼	1	9 14	E	7 13	B	6 49	VIR	17
63	4	M.	6 15	D	5 38	B	11 23	4	1¼	1¾	10 21	E	7 38	B	6 26	VIR	18
64	5	Tu.	6 14	D	5 39	B	11 25	4	2	2½	11 P.M. 26	E	8 08	B	6 03	VIR	19
65	6	W.	6 12	D	5 40	B	11 28	5	2¾	3¼	— —	–	8 42	A	5 39	LIB	20
66	7	Th.	6 10	D	5 41	B	11 31	5	3½	4¼	12 A.M. 26	E	9 22	A	5 16	SCO	21
67	8	Fr.	6 09	D	5 42	B	11 33	5	4¼	5	1 23	E	10 08	A	4 53	OPH	22
68	9	Sa.	6 07	D	5 43	B	11 36	5	5¼	6	2 13	E	11 A.M. 01	A	4 30	SAG	23
69	10	**F**	6 05	D	5 45	B	11 40	6	6¼	7	2 56	E	12 P.M. 00	B	4 06	SAG	24
70	11	M.	6 04	C	5 46	B	11 42	6	7¼	8	3 33	E	1 02	B	3 43	SAG	25
71	12	Tu.	6 02	C	5 47	B	11 45	6	8¼	8¾	4 04	E	2 07	B	3 19	CAP	26
72	13	W.	6 00	C	5 48	B	11 48	6	9	9½	4 31	D	3 13	C	2 56	CAP	27
73	14	Th.	5 58	C	5 49	B	11 51	7	9¾	10¼	4 56	D	4 19	C	2 31	AQU	28
74	15	Fr.	5 57	C	5 50	B	11 53	7	10½	10¾	5 19	C	5 27	D	2 08	AQU	29
75	16	Sa.	5 55	C	5 52	B	11 57	7	11	11½	5 42	C	6 36	D	1 45	PSC	0
76	17	**F**	5 53	C	5 53	B	12 00	8	11¾	—	6 06	B	7 47	E	1 21	PSC	1
77	18	M.	5 52	C	5 54	B	12 02	8	12	12½	6 34	B	9 01	E	0 57	PSC	2
78	19	Tu.	5 50	C	5 55	C	12 05	8	12¾	1¼	7 06	B	10 16	E	0 33	ARI	3
79	20	W.	5 48	C	5 56	C	12 08	8	1½	2	7 45	B	11 P.M. 29	E	0 s.09	ARI	4
80	21	Th.	5 46	C	5 57	C	12 11	9	2¼	3	8 33	A	— —	–	0 N.14	TAU	5
81	22	Fr.	5 45	C	5 59	C	12 14	9	3¼	4	9 31	A	12 A.M. 37	E	0 37	TAU	6
82	23	Sa.	5 43	C	6 00	C	12 17	9	4¼	5	10 38	A	1 35	E	1 01	GEM	7
83	24	**F**	5 41	C	6 01	C	12 20	10	5¼	6¼	11 A.M. 50	B	2 24	E	1 25	GEM	8
84	25	M.	5 39	C	6 02	C	12 23	10	6½	7¼	1 P.M. 05	B	3 02	E	1 48	CAN	9
85	26	Tu.	5 38	C	6 03	C	12 25	10	7½	8¼	2 18	C	3 35	D	2 12	CAN	10
86	27	W.	5 36	C	6 04	C	12 28	10	8½	9¼	3 30	D	4 02	D	2 35	LEO	11
87	28	Th.	5 34	C	6 05	C	12 31	11	9½	10	4 40	D	4 27	D	2 59	LEO	12
88	29	Fr.	5 32	C	6 06	C	12 34	11	10½	10¾	5 49	D	4 50	C	3 22	VIR	13
89	30	Sa.	5 31	C	6 08	C	12 37	11	11¼	11½	6 56	E	5 14	B	3 45	VIR	14
90	31	**F**	5 29	B	6 09	C	12 40	12	—	12	8 P.M. 03	E	5 A.M. 39	B	4 N.08	VIR	15

MARCH hath 31 days. 1991

As welcome as sunshine in every place,
  Is the beaming approach of a good-natured face;
As genial as sunshine, like warmth to impart,
  Is a good-natured word from a good-natured heart.
— *Unknown*

D.M.	D.W.	Dates, Feasts, Fasts, Aspects, Tide Heights	Weather ↓
1	Fr.	**St. David** • ☾ on Eq. • ☿ in sup. ☌ •	*Just*
2	Sa.	Blackthorn winds blow. • Canada geese arrive. • Tides {10.8 10.9 •	*a*
3	**F**	**3rd S. in Lent** • Crocuses up, Edgartown, Mass., 1941 •	*pinch,*
4	M.	Marlon Brando born, 1924 • Blizzard, Cape Cod, 1960 • {10.6 9.9 •	*then a*
5	Tu.	Town Meeting Day, Vermont • Stalin died, 1953 • {10.3 9.3 •	*pounding!*
6	W.	*Time is nature's way of keeping everything from happening all at once.* • {9.9 8.7 •	*Cold*
7	Th.	**St. Perpetua** • Luther Burbank born, 1849 •	*enough*
8	Fr.	☾ at apo. • Skunks mate. • King William III died after riding accident, 1702 {9.1 7.8	*to*
9	Sa.	**Sts. Cyril and Methodius** • ☾ runs low •	*make*
10	**F**	**4th S. in Lent** • ☌♅☾ • ☌♆☾ • {8.8 7.7 •	*you*
11	M.	☾ at ☊ • Blizzard, Eastern Seaboard, 1888 • Woodchucks emerge.	*flinch,*
12	Tu.	**St. Gregory** • ☌♄☾ • Tides {9.2 8.5 •	*watch*
13	W.	So many mists in March we see, so many frosts in May will be. • Tides {9.5 9.0 •	*snow*
14	Th.	*Stick to your winter flannels until your flannels stick to you.* •	*mounding*
15	Fr.	☾ on Eq. • Beware the Ides of March. • Tides {10.1 10.0 •	*inch by*
16	Sa.	New ● • Aubrey Beardsley died at age 25, 1898 • Tides {10.3 10.4 •	*inch!*
17	**F**	**Passion** • **St. Patrick** • ☌☿☾ • Tides {10.4 —	*Bitter*
18	M.	☌♀☾ • Thunder in March means a fruitful but sorrowful year. •	*and*
19	Tu.	Swallows arrive, San Juan Capistrano, Calif. • Tides {11.0 10.2 •	*wetter*
20	W.	Vernal Equinox • *Full cups must be held steady.* • Tides {11.1 9.9 •	*before*
21	Th.	Thomas Jefferson named Secretary of State, 1790 • J. S. Bach born, 1685 • Tides {10.9 9.4	*it*
22	Fr.	☾ rides high • ☾ at peri. • ☌♂☾ • N.E. gale, 1977 •	*gets*
23	Sa.	*Messiah* first performed in London, 1743 • Tides {10.3 8.8 •	*better.*
24	**F**	**Palm Sunday** • ☾ at ☋ • Tides {10.1 8.8	*Jeepers,*
25	M.	**Annunciation** • ☌♃☾ • *Well begun is half done.* •	*creepers,*
26	Tu.	Sarah Bernhardt died, 1923 • 19" snow, Chicago, 1930 • Tides {10.1 9.5 •	*did*
27	W.	☿ Gr. Elong. (19° E.) • Earthquake, Alaska, 1964 • Tides {10.3 10.0 •	*you*
28	Th.	☾ on Eq. • *If you can't bite, don't show your teeth.* • Tides {10.5 10.4 •	*hear*
29	Fr.	**Good Friday** • Jack Benny's radio debut, 1932 •	*those*
30	Sa.	**Passover** • Full Sap ○ • ♃ stat. • Tides {10.5 10.8	*spring*
31	**F**	**Easter** • Knute Rockne died, 1931 • Tides {— 10.3	*peepers?*

Farmer's Calendar

At the bird feeder just beyond the window, a nuthatch has arrived, and instantly the indoor cats go on Full Alert, rigid, staring, even making excited little cackling noises in the backs of their throats. They are avid bird-watchers, although perhaps less in the spirit of the Audubon Society than in that of its great eponym, the wandering artist, who regularly watched his birds from behind the barrels of a shotgun. The cats, like J. J. Audubon, would like to, ah, *secure* that nuthatch so as to render an exact likeness.

The curious thing is that the nuthatch is oblivious to the cats, although they are in plain sight a few feet away. Even when one of the cats leaps up to stand on its hind legs, forepaws on the window, for a better view, the nuthatch continues placidly feeding. A cool bird indeed. Had the bird at the feeder been a blue jay, it would have flown off as soon as the first cat showed its longest whisker's end. Why should it be, as it certainly seems, that among birds at the winter feeder boldness and grace under pressure are in inverse proportion to size?

The smaller winter birds — chickadees, nuthatches, downy woodpeckers — come freely to the feeders near the house and forage there confidently. Of course they fly if you go out and approach them, but movements inside the house, including those of quivering, hyperattentive cats, don't seem to frighten the little birds. The bigger winter birds like jays and hairy woodpeckers are much more skittish. The slightest movement, and they are off. Why? Perhaps they're simply smarter. Certainly it is never blue feathers that are scattered on the ground whenever one of those scientific cats succeeds in adding to its Life List.

APRIL, THE FOURTH MONTH

Clocks must be set ahead an hour on the 7th, making a longer daily wait for the stars. Mercury soon drops from the evening sky. The Moon is fairly near Venus on the 17th and Jupiter on the 21st, while both Uranus and Neptune are stationary on the 18th. At nightfall on the 19th, the Moon lies very close to Mars, and Mars even closer to the star Mebsuta on the 20th. (The planet passed right in front of Mebsuta back in April 1976.) After middle-night moonset on the 21st-22nd, look for Lyrid meteors coming from almost overhead. Venus shines 7 degrees north of Aldebaran on the 22nd and well to the upper left of Venus is Gemini (the Twins). The Big Dipper is at its evening highest in the north; Leo (with its pattern called the Sickle) at its evening highest in the south. Arcturus is brilliant in the northeast. As dawn brightens, Saturn is due south.

ASTRONOMICAL CALCULATIONS

☾ Last Quarter	7th day	1st hour	47th min.
● New Moon	14th day	14th hour	38th min.
☽ First Quarter	21st day	7th hour	40th min.
○ Full Moon	28th day	16th hour	0 min.

ADD 1 hour for Daylight Saving Time after 2 A.M. April 7.

FOR POINTS OUTSIDE BOSTON SEE KEY LETTER CORRECTIONS — PAGES 80-84

Day of Year	Day of Month	Day of Week	☉ Rises h. m.	Key	☉ Sets h. m.	Key	Length of Days h. m.	Sun Fast m.	Full Sea Boston A.M.	Full Sea Boston P.M.	☽ Rises h. m.	Key	☽ Sets h. m.	Key	Declination of Sun ° '	☽ Place	☽ Age
91	1	M.	5 27	B	6 10	C	12 43	12	12	12½	9 P.M. 09	E	6 A.M. 08	B	4 N.32	VIR	16
92	2	Tu.	5 26	B	6 11	C	12 45	12	12¾	1¼	10 13	E	6 40	B	4 55	LIB	17
93	3	W.	5 24	B	6 12	C	12 48	13	1½	2	11 P.M. 12	E	7 18	A	5 18	LIB	18
94	4	Th.	5 22	B	6 13	D	12 51	13	2	2¾	— —	–	8 02	A	5 41	SCO	19
95	5	Fr.	5 20	B	6 14	D	12 54	13	2¾	3½	12 A.M. 04	E	8 53	A	6 04	OPH	20
96	6	Sa.	5 19	B	6 15	D	12 56	13	3¾	4½	12 50	E	9 49	A	6 26	SAG	21
97	7	**F**	5 17	B	6 17	D	13 00	14	4¾	5½	1 29	E	10 49	B	6 49	SAG	22
98	8	M.	5 15	B	6 18	D	13 03	14	5¾	6¼	2 02	E	11 A.M. 52	B	7 11	SAG	23
99	9	Tu.	5 14	B	6 19	D	13 05	14	6½	7¼	2 30	E	12 P.M. 56	C	7 34	CAP	24
100	10	W.	5 12	B	6 20	D	13 08	15	7½	8	2 56	D	2 01	C	7 56	CAP	25
101	11	Th.	5 10	B	6 21	D	13 11	15	8¼	8¾	3 19	D	3 08	D	8 18	AQU	26
102	12	Fr.	5 09	B	6 22	D	13 13	15	9¼	9½	3 43	C	4 16	D	8 40	PSC	27
103	13	Sa.	5 07	B	6 23	D	13 16	15	10	10¼	4 07	B	5 27	E	9 02	PSC	28
104	14	**F**	5 05	B	6 24	D	13 19	16	10¾	10¾	4 34	B	6 41	E	9 23	PSC	0
105	15	M.	5 04	B	6 26	D	13 22	16	11½	11½	5 05	B	7 58	E	9 45	ARI	1
106	16	Tu.	5 02	B	6 27	D	13 25	16	—	12¼	5 42	A	9 14	E	10 06	ARI	2
107	17	W.	5 01	B	6 28	D	13 27	16	12¼	1	6 28	A	10 26	E	10 27	TAU	3
108	18	Th.	4 59	B	6 29	D	13 30	17	1¼	1¾	7 24	A	11 P.M. 29	E	10 48	TAU	4
109	19	Fr.	4 57	B	6 30	D	13 33	17	2	2¾	8 30	B	— —	–	11 09	GEM	5
110	20	Sa.	4 56	B	6 31	D	13 35	17	3	3¾	9 42	B	12 A.M. 21	E	11 30	GEM	6
111	21	**F**	4 54	B	6 32	D	13 38	17	4	4¾	10 A.M. 56	B	1 03	E	11 51	CAN	7
112	22	M.	4 53	B	6 33	D	13 40	17	5¼	6	12 P.M. 10	B	1 37	E	12 11	CAN	8
113	23	Tu.	4 51	B	6 35	D	13 44	18	6¼	7	1 21	C	2 06	D	12 31	LEO	9
114	24	W.	4 50	B	6 36	D	13 46	18	7½	8	2 30	D	2 30	D	12 51	SEX	10
115	25	Th.	4 48	B	6 37	D	13 49	18	8¼	8¾	3 37	D	2 54	C	13 11	LEO	11
116	26	Fr.	4 47	B	6 38	D	13 51	18	9¼	9½	4 44	E	3 18	B	13 30	VIR	12
117	27	Sa.	4 45	B	6 39	D	13 54	18	10	10¼	5 50	E	3 42	B	13 49	VIR	13
118	28	**F**	4 44	B	6 40	D	13 56	18	10¾	11	6 56	E	4 09	B	14 08	VIR	14
119	29	M.	4 43	B	6 41	D	13 58	19	11½	11½	8 00	E	4 39	B	14 27	LIB	15
120	30	Tu.	4 41	B	6 42	D	14 01	19	—	12¼	9 P.M. 00	E	5 A.M. 15	A	14 N.45	LIB	16

APRIL hath 30 days. 1991

We have trod from the threshold of turbulent March,
Till the green scarf of April is hung on the larch,
And down the bright hillsides that welcome the day,
We hear the warm panting of beautiful May.
— Oliver Wendell Holmes

D.M.	D.W.	Dates, Feasts, Fasts, Aspects, Tide Heights	Weather ↓
1	M.	Easter Monday holiday (Canada) • All Fools • Tides {10.8 10.0 •	*Splishes,*
2	Tu.	The voice of the turtle is heard in the land. • Tides {10.6 9.6 •	*sploshes,*
3	W.	Tornadoes in 12 states, Alabama to Ohio, 1974 • Tides {10.3 9.1 •	*wear*
4	Th.	☿ stat. • Sarah Vaughan died, 1990 • El Chichón erupted, Mexico, 1982	*your*
5	Fr.	☾ runs low • ☾ at apo. • Plato died 347 B.C. • {9.6 8.3 •	*galoshes.*
6	Sa.	☌♅☾ • Adm. Robert Peary reached North Pole, 1909 • {9.2 8.0 •	*Chillier,*
7	**F**	Low Sun. • D.S.T. begins • ☾ at ☊ • ☌♆☾	*but*
8	M.	☌♄☾ • Ponce de León landed in Florida, 1513 • Tides {8.8 8.0 •	*daffo-*
9	Tu.	*Three will keep a secret, but only if two are dead.* • Dust storm, Texas, 1956 •	*dillier.*
10	W.	Peepers, Bangor, Maine, 1846 • Tides {9.0 8.8 •	*The*
11	Th.	Jackie Robinson played exhibition game with Dodgers, 1947 • Tides {9.3 9.4 •	*rain*
12	Fr.	☾ on Eq. • A cold April the barn will fill. • *Only the young die good.* •	*in*
13	Sa.	16 lb. 6 oz. baby born, Tom's River, N.J., 1983 • Tides {10.0 10.6 •	*Maine*
14	**F**	2nd S. af. Easter • New ● • ☿ in inf. ☌ •	*is*
15	M.	Hepatica in flower, Lexington, Mass., 1960 • Greta Garbo died, 1990 {10.4 11.4	*plainly*
16	Tu.	*Taxation: plucking the goose to get the most feathers with the least hissing.* •	*on*
17	W.	☌♀☾ • ☾ at peri. • Miss. River in flood, 1947 • Tides {11.6 10.2 •	*the*
18	Th.	☾ rides high • ♅ stat. • ♆ stat. • Einstein died, 1955 •	*gain.*
19	Fr.	☌♂☾ • Daphne du Maurier died, Cornwall, 1989 • Tides {11.3 9.7 •	*Peek*
20	Sa.	☾ at ☋ • Fidel Castro got red-carpet welcome, N.Y.C., 1959 {10.9 9.4	*of sun,*
21	**F**	3rd S. af. Easter • Canadian Capt. R. Brown shot down Red Baron, 1918	*then*
22	M.	☌♃☾ • R.I. raised 1,500 troops, 1775 • Tides {10.1 9.3	*skedaddle!*
23	Tu.	**St. George** • If rye grass can hide a crow, expect a good harvest. •	*We're*
24	W.	☾ on Eq. • Otto Preminger died, 1986 • Tides {9.8 9.9 •	*up the*
25	Th.	**St. Mark** • Red trillium in bloom, New England • 16" rain, Miami, 1979	*creek*
26	Fr.	*God gives the milk, but not the pail.* • Tides {9.9 10.5 •	*without*
27	Sa.	☿ stat. • Wild shad in bloom. • Tides {9.8 10.7 •	*a paddle.*
28	**F**	4th S. af. Easter • Full Pink ○ {9.8 10.7	*Jubilation!*
29	M.	Alfred Hitchcock died, 1980 • Eclipse of Sun terrified people, England, 1652 •	*No*
30	Tu.	Casey Jones killed, 1900 • George Balanchine died, 1983 •	*precipitation!*

An idler is a watch that wants both hands;
As useless when it goes as when it stands.

Farmer's Calendar

All gardening is an act of faith, but in no work in the garden is the chasm that faith must leap wider or deeper than in planting peas. In the North, where peas grow best, they are planted in April, which is called a spring month only out of courtesy to the equinox, much as you might call a mean, stingy, and detested family acquaintance "Uncle" Adolf. Shoving peas into the ground in that season implies powers of belief that would do credit to the sailor shipwrecked in the Andaman Sea who dropped into the surf a bottle containing a note to the First Lord of the Admiralty, London, arguing that his pay should be continued for the time he was marooned.

I have laid out my rows and set up my pea fences in a brisk snowstorm, and I have cleared the row itself through snow. Peas are always planted in half-frozen mud that makes your fingers ache as you poke the holes for planting. Then after the job is done, say in midmonth, a late snowstorm will transform the patch into an arctic desert once more.

The peas themselves test the gardener's belief. They do not leap immediately from the clammy mud; rather they hang back, often for a couple of weeks or more. Then, when they do appear, they are about the frailest, most unpromising young plants in the garden: spindly, weak-kneed infants of hardship. But let them once get a start, and the peas explode, surging up their fences, topping them, flopping over, rising again, and everywhere popping out in a cascade of flowers and pods. Following their poor beginnings, the peas produce an abundance that is little short of miraculous — but then, to justify the faith that dropped them into April's icy mire, nothing less than a miracle was required.

MAY, THE FIFTH MONTH

Early in the month, predawn moonlight hides Eta Aquarid meteors. On the 12th, Mercury is in conjunction with the Moon and has its greatest western elongation of the year; it is barely visible just before dawn in the east. The Moon is between Venus and Mars on the 17th, between Mars and Jupiter on the 18th, and left of Jupiter on the 19th. Watch the three planets slowly converging towards their great conjunction due next month. Mars is 5 degrees south of brighter Pollux on the evening of the 15th. Jupiter goes back through the Beehive star cluster on the 20th, but binoculars are needed. A line through the outside stars of the Big Dipper's bowl extends to the North Star; taking the arc of its handle outward brings you to spring's brightest star, orange Arcturus. Then, drive a straight line to Spica, Virgo's bright star, and to kite-shaped Corvus the Crow near Spica.

ASTRONOMICAL CALCULATIONS

☾ Last Quarter	6th day	19th hour	48th min.
● New Moon	13th day	23rd hour	37th min.
☽ First Quarter	20th day	14th hour	47th min.
○ Full Moon	28th day	6th hour	38th min.

ADD 1 hour for Daylight Saving Time.

FOR POINTS OUTSIDE BOSTON SEE KEY LETTER CORRECTIONS — PAGES 80-84

Day of Year	Day of Month	Day of Week	☉ Rises h. m.	Key	☉ Sets h. m.	Key	Length of Days h. m.	Sun Fast m.	Full Sea Boston A.M.	Full Sea Boston P.M.	☽ Rises h. m.	Key	☽ Sets h. m.	Key	Declination of Sun ° '	☽ Place	☽ Age
121	1	W.	4 40	B	6 44	D	14 04	19	12¼	1	9 P.M. 56	E	5 A.M. 57	A	15N.04	OPH	17
122	2	Th.	4 39	B	6 45	D	14 06	19	1	1½	10 44	E	6 45	A	15 22	SCO	18
123	3	Fr.	4 37	A	6 46	D	14 09	19	1¾	2¼	11 P.M. 25	E	7 39	A	15 40	SAG	19
124	4	Sa.	4 36	A	6 47	D	14 11	19	2½	3	— —	–	8 38	B	15 57	SAG	20
125	5	**F**	4 35	A	6 48	D	14 13	19	3¼	4	12 A.M. 01	E	9 39	B	16 15	SAG	21
126	6	M.	4 33	A	6 49	D	14 16	19	4	4¾	12 30	E	10 42	B	16 32	CAP	22
127	7	Tu.	4 32	A	6 50	D	14 18	19	5	5½	12 56	D	11 A.M. 46	C	16 48	AQU	23
128	8	W.	4 31	A	6 51	D	14 20	20	5¾	6½	1 20	D	12 P.M. 50	D	17 05	AQU	24
129	9	Th.	4 30	A	6 52	D	14 22	20	6¾	7¼	1 43	D	1 56	D	17 21	PSC	25
130	10	Fr.	4 29	A	6 53	D	14 24	20	7¾	8	2 06	C	3 05	D	17 37	PSC	26
131	11	Sa.	4 27	A	6 54	D	14 27	20	8½	8¾	2 31	B	4 17	E	17 52	PSC	27
132	12	**F**	4 26	A	6 55	D	14 29	20	9¼	9½	3 00	B	5 32	E	18 07	PSC	28
133	13	M.	4 25	A	6 57	D	14 32	20	10¼	10¼	3 35	B	6 50	E	18 22	ARI	0
134	14	Tu.	4 24	A	6 58	E	14 34	20	11	11¼	4 17	B	8 06	E	18 37	TAU	1
135	15	W.	4 23	A	6 59	E	14 36	20	11¾	—	5 10	A	9 15	E	18 51	TAU	2
136	16	Th.	4 22	A	7 00	E	14 38	20	12	12¾	6 15	B	10 13	E	19 05	TAU	3
137	17	Fr.	4 21	A	7 01	E	14 40	20	1	1½	7 27	B	11 00	E	19 19	GEM	4
138	18	Sa.	4 20	A	7 02	E	14 42	20	1¾	2½	8 43	B	11 P.M. 38	E	19 32	GEM	5
139	19	**F**	4 19	A	7 03	E	14 44	20	2¾	3½	9 59	C	— —	–	19 46	CAN	6
140	20	M.	4 18	A	7 04	E	14 46	20	3¾	4½	11 A.M. 12	C	12 A.M. 08	D	19 58	LEO	7
141	21	Tu.	4 17	A	7 05	E	14 48	19	4¾	5½	12 P.M. 22	D	12 35	D	20 11	SEX	8
142	22	W.	4 17	A	7 06	E	14 49	19	6	6½	1 30	D	12 59	C	20 22	LEO	9
143	23	Th.	4 16	A	7 07	E	14 51	19	7	7½	2 36	E	1 22	C	20 34	VIR	10
144	24	Fr.	4 15	A	7 07	E	14 52	19	8	8¼	3 42	E	1 46	B	20 45	COR	11
145	25	Sa.	4 14	A	7 08	E	14 54	19	9	9¼	4 46	E	2 11	B	20 56	VIR	12
146	26	**F**	4 14	A	7 09	E	14 55	19	9¾	10	5 51	E	2 41	B	21 07	VIR	13
147	27	M.	4 13	A	7 10	E	14 57	19	10½	10½	6 52	E	3 15	A	21 17	LIB	14
148	28	Tu.	4 12	A	7 11	E	14 59	19	11¼	11¼	7 49	E	3 54	A	21 27	SCO	15
149	29	W.	4 12	A	7 12	E	15 00	19	11¾	—	8 40	E	4 40	A	21 37	OPH	16
150	30	Th.	4 11	A	7 13	E	15 02	19	12	12½	9 23	E	5 32	A	21 46	SAG	17
151	31	Fr.	4 11	A	7 14	E	15 03	18	12½	1¼	10 P.M. 00	E	6 A.M. 30	B	21N.54	SAG	18

MAY hath 31 days. 1991

Violet, violet, sparkling with dew,
Down in the meadow land wild, where you grew,
How did you come by the beautiful blue,
With which your soft petals unfold?
— Hannah F. Gould

D.M.	D.W.	Dates, Feasts, Fasts, Aspects, Tide Heights	Weather ↓
1	W.	**Sts. Philip and James** • Beltane bonfires. •	*A-tisket,*
2	Th.	☾ runs low • 2" snow, Pa., 1841 • Tides {10.3 9.0 •	*a-tasket,*
3	Fr.	**Invention of Cross** • ☾ at apo. • Tides {10.0 8.7	*a water-*
4	Sa.	☾ at ☊ • ☌♅☾ • ☌♆☾ • 19 tornadoes, Okla., 1961 •	*logged*
5	**F**	**Rogation S.** • Karl Marx born, 1818 • {9.4 8.4 •	*May basket.*
6	M.	☌♄☾ • *Love and scandal are the best sweeteners of tea.* •	*Sunny*
7	Tu.	Haiti destroyed by earthquake, 1842 • Gary Cooper born, 1901 • {9.0 8.5 •	*relief*
8	W.	*In baiting a mousetrap with cheese, always leave room for the mouse.* • 28° F, Asheville, N.C., 1989 •	*is*
9	Th.	**Ascension** • ☾ on Eq. • ♇ at ☍ • Tides {9.0 9.3 •	*brief.*
10	Fr.	Skunks are born. • Centennial Exposition opened, Philadelphia, 1876 •	*Rain*
11	Sa.	Apple trees blossom, New England • **Three** • Tides {9.5 10.5 •	*ebbs*
12	**F**	**1st S. af. Asc.** • **Chilly** • ☌☿☾ • ☿ Gr. Elong. (26° W.).	*and*
13	M.	Plant corn now (Midwest). • **Saints** • Tides {10.0 11.6 •	*flows;*
14	Tu.	New ● • Lewis and Clark left St. Louis for West, 1804 • Tides {10.2 11.9	*we're*
15	W.	☾ at peri. • *The largest room in the world is the room for improvement.* •	*growing*
16	Th.	☾ rides high • Jim Henson died, 1990 • Tides {12.0 10.3 •	*webs*
17	Fr.	☾ at ☋ • ☌♀☾ • ♄ stat. • Tides {11.9 10.2 •	*between*
18	Sa.	☌♂☾ • Compulsory-education law (ages 8-14) passed, Mass., 1852 • {11.6 10.0 •	*our*
19	**F**	**Whit Sun.** • **Pentecost** • **Shavuot** • ☌♃☾ •	*toes.*
20	M.	Victoria Day (Canada) • 18 percent of tornadoes occur this month. • {10.6 9.8 •	*We*
21	Tu.	*Money is like manure – it does no good until it's spread around.* •	*demand*
22	W.	Ember Day • ☾ on Eq. • Earthquake, Turkey, 1971 • Tides {9.7 9.9 •	*an*
23	Th.	Capt. Wm. Kidd executed for piracy, London, 1701 • 6" snow, Iowa, 1882 •	*investi-*
24	Fr.	Ember Day • First auto garage opened, Boston, 1899 • Tides {9.3 10.2 •	*gation*
25	Sa.	Ember Day • *Everything has an end except a sausage, which has two.* •	*of*
26	**F**	**Trinity** • B-29s firebombed Tokyo, 1945 • Tides {9.2 10.4 •	*this*
27	M.	**St. Bede** • **Memorial Day** • Tides {9.1 10.4	*constant*
28	Tu.	Full Flower ○ • Lilacs in bloom, N.H. • 100° F, Portland, Ore., 1983	*Niagara-*
29	W.	☾ runs low • *Go out on a limb – That's where the fruit is.* • {9.0 — •	*vation!*
30	Th.	**Corpus Christi** • ☾ at apo. • Tides {10.3 9.0 •	*Cold*
31	Fr.	☾ at ☊ • ☌♅☾ • ☌♆☾ • 25° F, Burlington, Vt., 1961	*mold.*

Farmer's Calendar

Several years ago when the snow went out, I found that a portion of one of the old stone walls near the house had fallen badly. The wall in that section wasn't more than waist high, and only a few of the stones were big, so I decided that repairing the fallen part was a job I could take on. Not that I expected the work to be easy, mind you, or the end result as good as new. Making the round, knobby granite cobbles of my hill form up and hold their places in a good wall takes more art than I will ever have, I know well. Still, I thought, I didn't have to build a wall here, only rebuild one. The hard work had already been done: the stones had been laid up so as to stay put — until now. It only remained for me to put them back more or less where they'd been.

I set to it. A Vermont field rock the size of a footstool is the stubbornest, heaviest object in the universe. The idea that millions of these things are floating around in space, as light as thistledown, is absolutely untenable. I shoved the stones into place, wrestled them about so they lay quiet, wedged them in place with smaller stones. Presently the wall was back up.

But I was puzzled. I had six or seven stones left over. The wall looked, not great, but pretty thrifty, I thought. Why, then, were there still unused stones? I was reminded of when I was little and used to take cheap pocket watches apart. I'd reassemble the scores of pieces, but always there would be a wheel, a pin, a spring too many. As many times as I'd dismantle a watch and put it together again, I'd have excess pieces. My new wall was the same: it was whole, but it wasn't complete. Of course, I reflected, my new wall worked; my new watches, never.

The most stupendous three-planet gathering of the decade is tightest on the 18th in the west, after nightfall, when Venus, Jupiter, and Mars all fit within a circle just 1.8 degrees across! The component conjunctions are: 13th-14th, Mars 0.6 degrees north of Jupiter; 17th, Venus 1.2 degrees north of Jupiter; 23rd, Venus just 0.3 degrees north of Mars. All this happens just after Venus reaches greatest elongation east (45 degrees) on the 13th and is further livened by the Moon passing a bit south of all three planets on the 15th. Earlier in the month, on the 7th, Mars goes right through the midst of the Beehive star cluster. Around new Moon, 12th-13th, tides are especially high. On the 26th, the year's most distant Moon is full, its upper edge darkened imperceptibly by a penumbral eclipse around 10:00 P.M. EST. Summer begins at 4:19 P.M. EST on the 21st.

ASTRONOMICAL CALCULATIONS

☾ Last Quarter	5th day	10th hour	31st min.
● New Moon	12th day	7th hour	7th min.
☽ First Quarter	18th day	23rd hour	20th min.
○ Full Moon	26th day	22nd hour	0 min.

ADD 1 hour for Daylight Saving Time.

FOR POINTS OUTSIDE BOSTON SEE KEY LETTER CORRECTIONS — PAGES 80-84

Day of Year	Day of Month	Day of Week	☉ Rises h. m.	Key	☉ Sets h. m.	Key	Length of Days h. m.	Sun Fast m.	Full Sea Boston A.M.	Full Sea Boston P.M.	☽ Rises h. m.	Key	☽ Sets h. m.	Key	Declination of Sun ° '	☽ Place	☽ Age
152	1	Sa.	4 10	A	7 14	E	15 04	18	1¼	2	10 P.M. 31	E	7 A.M. 30	B	22N.03	SAG	19
153	2	**F**	4 10	A	7 15	E	15 05	18	2	2½	10 58	E	8 32	B	22 10	CAP	20
154	3	M.	4 09	A	7 16	E	15 07	18	2¾	3¼	11 22	D	9 34	C	22 18	AQU	21
155	4	Tu.	4 09	A	7 17	E	15 08	18	3½	4	11 P.M. 45	D	10 37	C	22 25	CAP	22
156	5	W.	4 08	A	7 17	E	15 09	18	4¼	4¾	— —	–	11 A.M. 41	D	22 32	AQU	23
157	6	Th.	4 08	A	7 18	E	15 10	17	5¼	5¾	12 A.M. 08	C	12 P.M. 47	D	22 39	PSC	24
158	7	Fr.	4 08	A	7 18	E	15 10	17	6	6½	12 31	B	1 55	E	22 45	PSC	25
159	8	Sa.	4 08	A	7 19	E	15 11	17	7	7¼	12 57	B	3 07	E	22 50	PSC	26
160	9	**F**	4 08	A	7 20	E	15 12	17	8	8¼	1 28	B	4 22	E	22 55	ARI	27
161	10	M.	4 07	A	7 20	E	15 13	17	8¾	9	2 05	B	5 39	E	23 00	ARI	28
162	11	Tu.	4 07	A	7 21	E	15 14	17	9¾	10	2 54	B	6 52	E	23 04	TAU	29
163	12	W.	4 07	A	7 21	E	15 14	16	10¾	10¾	3 53	A	7 57	E	23 08	TAU	0
164	13	Th.	4 07	A	7 22	E	15 15	16	11½	11¾	5 04	B	8 51	E	23 12	GEM	1
165	14	Fr.	4 07	A	7 22	E	15 15	16	—	12½	6 22	B	9 34	E	23 16	GEM	2
166	15	Sa.	4 07	A	7 23	E	15 16	16	12¾	1¼	7 41	B	10 08	D	23 18	CAN	3
167	16	**F**	4 07	A	7 23	E	15 16	15	1½	2¼	8 57	C	10 37	D	23 21	CAN	4
168	17	M.	4 07	A	7 23	E	15 16	15	2½	3¼	10 10	D	11 02	D	23 22	LEO	5
169	18	Tu.	4 07	A	7 24	E	15 17	15	3½	4¼	11 A.M. 20	D	11 26	C	23 24	LEO	6
170	19	W.	4 07	A	7 24	E	15 17	15	4½	5	12 P.M. 28	E	11 P.M. 50	C	23 25	VIR	7
171	20	Th.	4 07	A	7 24	E	15 17	15	5½	6	1 34	E	— —	–	23 26	VIR	8
172	21	Fr.	4 07	A	7 24	E	15 17	14	6½	7	2 39	E	12 A.M. 15	B	23 26	VIR	9
173	22	Sa.	4 08	A	7 25	E	15 17	14	7½	7¾	3 44	E	12 44	B	23 26	VIR	10
174	23	**F**	4 08	A	7 25	E	15 17	14	8½	8¾	4 45	E	1 15	A	23 26	LIB	11
175	24	M.	4 08	A	7 25	E	15 17	14	9½	9½	5 44	E	1 53	A	23 24	SCO	12
176	25	Tu.	4 08	A	7 25	E	15 17	14	10¼	10¼	6 36	E	2 37	A	23 23	SCO	13
177	26	W.	4 09	A	7 25	E	15 16	13	10¾	10¾	7 22	E	3 27	A	23 21	SAG	14
178	27	Th.	4 09	A	7 25	E	15 16	13	11½	11½	8 01	E	4 23	B	23 19	SAG	15
179	28	Fr.	4 10	A	7 25	E	15 15	13	—	12¼	8 34	E	5 23	B	23 16	SAG	16
180	29	Sa.	4 10	A	7 25	E	15 15	13	12¼	12¾	9 02	E	6 25	B	23 13	CAP	17
181	30	**F**	4 10	A	7 25	E	15 15	12	12¾	1½	9 P.M. 27	D	7 A.M. 27	B	23N.10	CAP	18

The oldest and youngest
Are at work with the strongest;
The cattle are grazing,
Their heads never raising;
They are forty feeding like one.
— *William Wordsworth*

Farmer's Calendar

June 18. Drove to Marlboro over the back road that runs for several miles along the branch. A fine summer day of high, soft clouds and bright sun. Past the old Branch Schoolhouse the road goes through woods, and there the sunlight gleaming through the thick leaf cover overhead and flashing on the water in the branch created a chaos of glare and shadow in which I could hardly see where I was going. On a narrow road in the woods where the trees meet overhead, bright sun produces the effect of one of those festivals known to the 1960s as Happenings: a great darkened room, cavelike, with spotlights playing randomly over the crowded revelers and reflecting off moving mirrors and other lights. Imagine driving a car through a Happening, and you have this unvisited country road on a June morning.

Driving through the woods, we flushed scores of butterflies that had been sitting in the road. They were the white admiral (*Limenitis arthemis*), about the size of a large matchbook, dark purple with a broad white band running vertically down the wings. They were alight in the center of the shadowy road or on the shoulder. Why? Many butterflies like mud puddles, but the road these frequented wasn't mud, only slightly damp earth. In the open stretches of road the white admiral never appeared, only in the shaded woodland sections. Perhaps they sought those parts to hide. Certainly the butterflies' highly contrasting purple-and-white wings, in the dazzling, flashing bright-and-dark of the lane, offered admirable camouflage. It was practically impossible to follow a butterfly with your eye once one flew off into the shifting, sparkling middle distance.

D.M.	D.W.	Dates, Feasts, Fasts, Aspects, Tide Heights	Weather ↓
1	Sa.	Snow, Cleveland, Buffalo, Rochester, 1843 • Tides {10.0 / 8.8	*Warm and*
2	F	2nd S. af. P. • ♂♅☾ Edward Elgar born, 1857 •	*lazy,*
3	M.	*Love is only for the young, the middle-aged, and the old.* • Tides {9.6 / 8.8	*rains*
4	Tu.	Pierre L'Enfant born, 1755 • White House completed, 1800 • Tides {9.4 / 8.9	*like*
5	W.	**St. Boniface** • ☾ on Eq. • Robert Kennedy shot, 1968 •	*crazy!*
6	Th.	Rainy season, Calcutta • Partly cloudy on D-Day, Normandy, 1944 • {9.0 / 9.4	*Watch*
7	Fr.	*If you're dog-tired at night, it might be that you've been growling all day.*	*those*
8	Sa.	Killing frost, Fargo, N.D., 1885 • Satchel Paige died, 1982 • {9.1 / 10.3	*ultraviolet*
9	F	3rd S. af. P. • Laurel in bloom, N.H. • Tides {9.3 / 10.9	*raysies.*
10	M.	Louis L'Amour died, 1988 • Severe earthquakes, Afghanistan, 1956 •	*Cue*
11	Tu.	**St. Barnabas** • John Wayne died, 1979 • Tides {9.8 / 11.8	*the*
12	W.	☾ rides high • New ● • ☾ at peri. • {10.0 / 12.1	*cumulus —*
13	Th.	♀ Gr. Elong. (45° E.) • Year's highest P.M. tide • Tides {10.3 / 12.2	*this*
14	Fr.	☾ at ☊ • ♂♃ Yellow "paint" (pine pollen) rained, Hopkinton, Mass., 1961 •	*week*
15	Sa.	♂♀☾ • ♂♃☾ • ♂♂☾ • Tides {12.0 / 10.4	*will*
16	F	4th S. af. P. • Leland Stanford died, 1893 • Tides {11.7 / 10.4	*be*
17	M.	**St. Alban** • ♀ in sup. ♂ • ♂♃	*gloomulus.*
18	Tu.	☾ on Eq. • I. F. Stone died, 1989 • Tides {10.6 / 10.3	*Holy*
19	W.	*Don't brew when beans are in blossom.* • Earthquake, New York City, 1871 •	*Moly,*
20	Th.	*Enthusiasm is the breath of genius.* • U.S. Great Seal adopted, 1782 •	*gladioli!*
21	Fr.	Summer Solstice • Killing frost, Taunton, Mass., 1918 • Tides {9.0 / 10.0	*No*
22	Sa.	*Any fool can criticize, and most fools do.* • Machiavelli died, 1527 •	*more*
23	F	5th S. af. P. • ♂♀♂ • {8.6 / 10.0	*pencils,*
24	M.	**Nativ. John Baptist** • Rain today means a wet harvest.	*no*
25	Tu.	*Speak kind words and you'll hear kind echoes.* • Tides {8.7 / 10.1	*more*
26	W.	☾ runs low • Eclipse ☾ • Full Strawberry ○ • {8.7 / 10.2	*bells,*
27	Th.	☾ at apo. • ♂☾☾ • ♂♆☾ • Oswald Jacoby died, 1984 •	*summer*
28	Fr.	☾ at ☋ • Widespread drought, Plains-Midwest, 1988 • {— / 8.9	*downpours*
29	Sa.	**St. Peter** • ♂♅☾ • Rubens born, 1577 • {10.2 / 9.0	*fill the*
30	F	5th S. af. P. • **St. Paul** • 26th Amendment ratified, 1971. •	*wells.*

If you want to know what God thinks of money, just look at those he gave it to.

1991 JULY, THE SEVENTH MONTH

A second great month! On the 11th, the longest total eclipse of the Sun until after 2050 visits Hawaii (almost 5 minutes of totality in the morning) and the Baja (almost 7 minutes at midday). The contiguous states, except the extreme northeast, have a partial eclipse. The total eclipse is so long because the Moon is at perigee just a few hours before; watch for very high tides. On the 14th, low in the west at dusk, Jupiter and Mercury almost merge. Higher, Venus is very near Regulus (11th), most brilliant (17th), 4 degrees from Mars (21st). On the 24th, Mercury reaches its greatest elongation east of the Sun for the year: 27 degrees. On the 26th, the Moon has another (unviewable) slight penumbral eclipse, this time near Saturn with the planet at opposition. Telescopes show dim Uranus and Neptune at opposition on the 4th and 7th, while Earth is at aphelion at 10:00 A.M. EST on the 6th. Moonlight hides late July's Delta Aquarid meteors.

ASTRONOMICAL CALCULATIONS

☾ Last Quarter	4th day	21st hour	51st min.
● New Moon	11th day	14th hour	7th min.
☽ First Quarter	18th day	10th hour	12th min.
○ Full Moon	26th day	13th hour	25th min.

ADD 1 hour for Daylight Saving Time.

FOR POINTS OUTSIDE BOSTON SEE KEY LETTER CORRECTIONS — PAGES 80-84

Day of Year	Day of Month	Day of Week	☉ Rises h. m.	Key	☉ Sets h. m.	Key	Length of Days h. m.	Sun Fast m.	Full Sea Boston A.M.	Full Sea Boston P.M.	☽ Rises h. m.	Key	☽ Sets h. m.	Key	Declination of Sun ° '	☽ Place	☽ Age
182	1	M.	4 11	A	7 25	E	15 14	12	$1\frac{1}{2}$	2	9 P.M. 50	D	8 A.M. 29	C	23N.06	CAP	19
183	2	Tu.	4 12	A	7 25	E	15 13	12	$2\frac{1}{4}$	$2\frac{3}{4}$	10 12	C	9 32	D	23 02	AQU	20
184	3	W.	4 12	A	7 24	E	15 12	12	3	$3\frac{1}{2}$	10 34	C	10 35	D	22 57	PSC	21
185	4	Th.	4 13	A	7 24	E	15 11	12	$3\frac{3}{4}$	$4\frac{1}{4}$	10 58	B	11 A.M. 41	D	22 52	PSC	22
186	5	Fr.	4 13	A	7 24	E	15 11	12	$4\frac{1}{2}$	5	11 P.M. 25	B	12 P.M. 49	E	22 47	PSC	23
187	6	Sa.	4 14	A	7 24	E	15 10	11	$5\frac{1}{2}$	$5\frac{3}{4}$	— —	–	2 01	E	22 41	PSC	24
188	7	**F**	4 14	A	7 23	E	15 09	11	$6\frac{1}{2}$	$6\frac{3}{4}$	12 A.M. 00	B	3 14	E	22 35	ARI	25
189	8	M.	4 15	A	7 23	E	15 08	11	$7\frac{1}{2}$	$7\frac{3}{4}$	12 40	B	4 28	E	22 28	TAU	26
190	9	Tu.	4 16	A	7 23	E	15 07	11	$8\frac{1}{2}$	$8\frac{3}{4}$	1 33	A	5 37	E	22 22	TAU	27
191	10	W.	4 16	A	7 22	E	15 06	11	$9\frac{1}{2}$	$9\frac{1}{2}$	2 37	B	6 36	E	22 14	TAU	28
192	11	Th.	4 17	A	7 22	E	15 05	11	$10\frac{1}{4}$	$10\frac{1}{2}$	3 52	B	7 25	E	22 06	GEM	0
193	12	Fr.	4 18	A	7 21	E	15 03	10	$11\frac{1}{4}$	$11\frac{1}{2}$	5 12	B	8 04	E	21 58	GEM	1
194	13	Sa.	4 19	A	7 21	E	15 02	10	—	$12\frac{1}{4}$	6 32	C	8 36	D	21 49	CAN	2
195	14	**F**	4 20	A	7 20	E	15 00	10	$12\frac{1}{2}$	1	7 50	C	9 03	D	21 40	LEO	3
196	15	M.	4 20	A	7 19	E	14 59	10	$1\frac{1}{4}$	2	9 03	D	9 28	C	21 31	SEX	4
197	16	Tu.	4 21	A	7 19	E	14 58	10	$2\frac{1}{4}$	$2\frac{3}{4}$	10 14	D	9 53	C	21 21	LEO	5
198	17	W.	4 22	A	7 18	E	14 56	10	$3\frac{1}{4}$	$3\frac{3}{4}$	11 A.M. 23	E	10 18	B	21 11	VIR	6
199	18	Th.	4 23	A	7 17	E	14 54	10	4	$4\frac{1}{2}$	12 P.M. 29	E	10 46	B	21 01	VIR	7
200	19	Fr.	4 24	A	7 17	E	14 53	10	5	$5\frac{1}{2}$	1 35	E	11 16	B	20 51	VIR	8
201	20	Sa.	4 25	A	7 16	E	14 51	10	6	$6\frac{1}{2}$	2 38	E	11 P.M. 52	B	20 40	LIB	9
202	21	**F**	4 26	A	7 15	E	14 49	10	7	$7\frac{1}{4}$	3 38	E	— —	–	20 28	LIB	10
203	22	M.	4 27	A	7 14	E	14 47	10	8	$8\frac{1}{4}$	4 33	E	12 A.M. 34	A	20 16	SCO	11
204	23	Tu.	4 28	A	7 13	E	14 45	10	9	9	5 20	E	1 22	A	20 04	OPH	12
205	24	W.	4 28	A	7 12	E	14 44	10	$9\frac{3}{4}$	$9\frac{3}{4}$	6 02	E	2 16	A	19 52	SAG	13
206	25	Th.	4 29	A	7 11	D	14 42	10	$10\frac{1}{2}$	$10\frac{1}{2}$	6 36	E	3 15	B	19 39	SAG	14
207	26	Fr.	4 30	A	7 10	D	14 40	10	11	$11\frac{1}{4}$	7 06	E	4 17	B	19 26	SAG	15
208	27	Sa.	4 31	A	7 09	D	14 38	10	$11\frac{3}{4}$	$11\frac{3}{4}$	7 32	D	5 19	C	19 13	CAP	16
209	28	**F**	4 32	A	7 08	D	14 36	10	—	$12\frac{1}{4}$	7 55	D	6 22	C	18 59	CAP	17
210	29	M.	4 33	A	7 07	D	14 34	10	$12\frac{1}{2}$	1	8 18	C	7 25	D	18 45	AQU	18
211	30	Tu.	4 34	A	7 06	D	14 32	10	1	$1\frac{1}{2}$	8 40	C	8 28	D	18 31	PSC	19
212	31	W.	4 35	A	7 05	D	14 30	10	$1\frac{3}{4}$	$2\frac{1}{4}$	9 P.M. 03	B	9 A.M. 32	D	18N.16	PSC	20

On a glorious July day,
The meadows were ripe and sweet with hay,
And the purple mountains, erect and bold,
Propped pyramid clouds of ruffled gold.
— A.C. Bristol

Farmer's Calendar

Gliding off the edge of an old stone wellhead with the bewildering motion peculiar to its kind, the garter snake pours itself into the grass and disappears. It is gone in the same instant that it is seen. And for that instant, however well I know the innocence of the harmless creature, however many of them I have myself kept and handled, I pull back. The irreducible creepiness of the snake is not in its crawling over the ground or in the evil reputation of some of its tribe, but in the uncanniness of its way of going: the snake moves without moving.

Our familiar snake is *Thamnophis sirtalis sirtalis*, the Eastern Garter. It lives among the stone walls, by the house foundations, beside the gardens. A big one is a foot and a half long. One summer we kept a little one in a dry fish tank. Every week or so it ate an earthworm. The great American herpetologist Ditmars had several garter snakes that he kept in his study. "They seemed to have real affection," he wrote, "and enjoyed being handled." I can't say I ever felt burdened by the affection of our little snake, whom the children named Slithers (Slith for short). At the end of the summer we let him go because we weren't sure we could keep him healthy over winter. If Slithers's affectionate nature was injured by our releasing him, he didn't let his feelings show much at all.

A garter snake can live for ten years and more. Today when I spot one and can catch him, I examine him closely and wonder if it's old Slith. Sometimes I think I detect in the snake an answering nod, a faint smile of old affection. But I'm never sure: it's been too many years, and the fact is, all those snakes smile about the same.

D.M.	D.W.	Dates, Feasts, Fasts, Aspects, Tide Heights	Weather ↓
1	M.	Canada Day • *Fish and visitors smell in three days.* • Tides {10.0 / 9.2	*Wet*
2	Tu.	**Visit. of Mary** • Betty Grable died, 1973 •	*tendency*
3	W.	☾ on Eq. • Dog Days begin • Corn should be knee high. • Tides {9.5 / 9.4	*for*
4	Th.	**Independence Day** • ♂ at ☍ •	*Independency.*
5	Fr.	Trace of snow, Newton, N.J., 1881 • Tides {9.1 / 9.9	*Get*
6	Sa.	⊕ at aphelion • *Indecision is the key to flexibility.* • Tides {9.0 / 10.2	*thee*
7	**F**	7ᵗʰ ☉. af. ℗. • ♥ Ψ at ☍ • 121° F, Steele, N.D., 1936	*to the*
8	M.	American premiere of Mozart's "Lost" Symphony in F, 1981 • Tides {9.0 / 10.9	*links,*
9	Tu.	*How silent the woods would be if only the best birds sang.* • Tides {9.3 / 11.8	*methinks.*
10	W.	☾ rides high • Mel Blanc died, 1989 • Tides {9.6 / 11.8	*Over-*
11	Th.	☾ at ☊ • ☾ at peri. • New • Eclipse ☉ • {10.0 / 12.0	*flowing gutta;*
12	Fr.	Hudson first saw North American continent, 1609 • Tides {10.3 / 12.1	*you'd*
13	Sa.	♂♂☾ • ♂♃☾ • Wordsworth wrote "Tintern Abbey," 1798 •	*think*
14	**F**	8ᵗʰ ☉. af. ℗. • ♂♂☾ • ♂♃☾ • {12.0 / 10.8	*it was*
15	M.	**St. Swithin** • ☾ on Eq. • ♂♃♃ •	*Calcutta!*
16	Tu.	Cornscateous air now. • Herbert von Karajan died, 1989 • Tides {11.1 / 10.7	
17	W.	♀ Greatest Brilliancy • 104° F, San Francisco, 1988 • James Cagney born, 1899 •	*It's*
18	Th.	Man punishes the action; God, the intention. • Tides {9.7 / 10.2	*no*
19	Fr.	**St. Vincent de Paul** • Rain ceases, wind increases. •	*quiddity*
20	Sa.	**St. Margaret** • Petrarch born, 1304 • Tides {8.6 / 9.7	*to*
21	**F**	9ᵗʰ ☉. af. ℗. • Neil Armstrong walked on Moon, 1969 •	*complain*
22	M.	**St. Mary Magdalene** • ♂♂♂ • {8.2 / 9.6	*about*
23	Tu.	☾ runs low • Birdie May Vogt died, age 112, 1989 • Kay Kyser died, 1985 •	*the*
24	W.	☾ at apo. • ♂♂☾ • ♀ Gr. Elong. (27° E.) • {8.4 / 9.9	*humidity.*
25	Th.	**St. James** • **St. Christopher** • ☾ at ☋ • ♂Ψ☾ •	
26	Fr.	**St. Anne** • Buck Full ○ • Eclipse ☾ • ♂♭☾ • ♭ at ☍ •	
27	Sa.	Now the state of the crops is known. • Hurricane, Jacksonville, Fla., 1926 • {9.1 / 10.2	*Don't*
28	**F**	10ᵗʰ ☉. af. ℗. • Earthquake, Tientsin, China, 1976 •	*sit*
29	M.	**St. Martha** • ♀ stat. • 8' high jump by J. Sotomayor, 1989	*still, phew!*
30	Tu.	☾ on Eq. • *Great estates may venture more; Little boats must keep near shore.* • {10.0 / 9.6	*You'll*
31	W.	**St. Ignatius of Loyola** • 12" hail, Scituate, Mass., 1769 •	*mildew!*

After midnight on the 12th and 13th, the Perseid meteors zoom across moonless skies at rates of up to 60 per hour. Mercury and Venus race to follow Jupiter out of the evening sky; the Moon is near Saturn on the 22nd. A telescope shows the asteroid Vesta passing through the Beehive star cluster in the predawn sky on the 24th. Otherwise, a lack of special events allows us to catch up with summer constellations: S-shaped Scorpius (with its ruddy heart-star Antares) low in the south; Lyra, Cygnus, and Aquila high in the east. Lyra's bright star Vega now shines almost overhead in the early evening. The Milky Way arches through the huge Summer Triangle, which blue Vega forms with Deneb in Cygnus and Altair in Aquila. Arcturus lowers in the west. Draco the Dragon coils in the north.

ASTRONOMICAL CALCULATIONS

☾	Last Quarter	3rd day	6th hour	27th min.
●	New Moon	9th day	21st hour	28th min.
☽	First Quarter	17th day	0 hour	2nd min.
○	Full Moon	25th day	4th hour	8th min.

ADD 1 hour for Daylight Saving Time.

FOR POINTS OUTSIDE BOSTON SEE KEY LETTER CORRECTIONS — PAGES 80-84

Day of Year	Day of Month	Day of Week	☉ Rises h. m.	Key	☉ Sets h. m.	Key	Length of Days h. m.	Sun Fast m.	Full Sea Boston A.M.	Full Sea Boston P.M.	☽ Rises h. m.	Key	☽ Sets h. m.	Key	Declination of Sun ° '	☽ Place	☽ Age
213	1	Th.	4 36	A	7 04	D	14 28	10	2½	2¾	9 28 ᵖₘ	B	10 38 ᴬₘ	E	18 N.01	PSC	21
214	2	Fr.	4 37	A	7 03	D	14 26	10	3¼	3½	9 58	B	11 47 ᴬₘ	E	17 46	PSC	22
215	3	Sa.	4 38	A	7 02	D	14 24	10	4	4½	10 35	B	12 59 ᵖₘ	E	17 30	ARI	23
216	4	**F**	4 39	A	7 00	D	14 21	10	5	5¼	11 21 ᵖₘ	B	2 10	E	17 14	ARI	24
217	5	M.	4 40	A	6 59	D	14 19	10	6	6¼	— —	–	3 19	E	16 58	TAU	25
218	6	Tu.	4 42	A	6 58	D	14 16	10	7	7¼	12 18 ᴬₘ	B	4 21	E	16 41	TAU	26
219	7	W.	4 43	A	6 57	D	14 14	10	8	8½	1 27	B	5 14	E	16 25	GEM	27
220	8	Th.	4 44	A	6 55	D	14 11	10	9	9½	2 43	B	5 57	E	16 08	GEM	28
221	9	Fr.	4 45	A	6 54	D	14 09	10	10	10¼	4 03	B	6 32	D	15 51	CAN	0
222	10	Sa.	4 46	A	6 53	D	14 07	11	11	11¼	5 22	C	7 02	D	15 33	CAN	1
223	11	**F**	4 47	A	6 51	D	14 04	11	11¾		6 39	D	7 29	D	15 16	SEX	2
224	12	M.	4 48	A	6 50	D	14 02	11	12	12¾	7 53	D	7 54	C	14 58	LEO	3
225	13	Tu.	4 49	A	6 49	D	14 00	11	1	1½	9 04	D	8 20	B	14 40	VIR	4
226	14	W.	4 50	B	6 47	D	13 57	11	1¾	2¼	10 14	E	8 47	B	14 22	VIR	5
227	15	Th.	4 51	B	6 46	D	13 55	11	2¾	3	11 21 ᴬₘ	E	9 17	B	14 03	VIR	6
228	16	Fr.	4 52	B	6 44	D	13 52	12	3½	4	12 27 ᵖₘ	E	9 52	A	13 44	LIB	7
229	17	Sa.	4 53	B	6 43	D	13 50	12	4½	4¾	1 29	E	10 31	A	13 25	LIB	8
230	18	**F**	4 54	B	6 41	D	13 47	12	5½	5¾	2 26	E	11 18 ᵖₘ	A	13 06	SCO	9
231	19	M.	4 55	B	6 40	D	13 45	12	6½	6¾	3 16	E	— —	–	12 46	OPH	10
232	20	Tu.	4 56	B	6 38	D	13 42	13	7½	7¾	4 00	E	12 10 ᴬₘ	A	12 26	SAG	11
233	21	W.	4 57	B	6 37	D	13 40	13	8½	8½	4 37	E	1 07	B	12 06	SAG	12
234	22	Th.	4 58	B	6 35	D	13 37	13	9¼	9¼	5 09	E	2 08	B	11 46	SAG	13
235	23	Fr.	4 59	B	6 33	D	13 34	13	10	10	5 36	D	3 10	B	11 26	CAP	14
236	24	Sa.	5 01	B	6 32	D	13 31	14	10½	10¾	6 00	D	4 13	C	11 06	AQU	15
237	25	**F**	5 02	B	6 30	D	13 28	14	11¼	11¼	6 23	D	5 16	C	10 45	AQU	16
238	26	M.	5 03	B	6 29	D	13 26	14	11¾	—	6 45	C	6 20	D	10 25	PSC	17
239	27	Tu.	5 04	B	6 27	D	13 23	14	12	12¼	7 08	C	7 24	D	10 04	PSC	18
240	28	W.	5 05	B	6 25	D	13 20	15	12½	1	7 33	B	8 30	E	9 43	PSC	19
241	29	Th.	5 06	B	6 24	D	13 18	15	1¼	1½	8 02	B	9 39	E	9 22	PSC	20
242	30	Fr.	5 07	B	6 22	D	13 15	15	2	2¼	8 36	B	10 49	E	9 00	ARI	21
243	31	Sa.	5 08	B	6 20	D	13 12	16	2¾	3	9 18 ᵖₘ	A	11 59 ᴬₘ	E	8 N.39	ARI	22

AUGUST hath 31 days. 1991

And thanks that from our daily need
The joy of simple faith is born;
That he who smites the summer weed
May trust thee for the autumn corn.
— John Greenleaf Whittier

D.M.	D.W.	Dates, Feasts, Fasts, Aspects, Tide Heights	Weather ↓
1	Th.	**Lammas Day** • "Handfast" marriages, Scotland. • {9.6 / 9.9	*Damp*
2	Fr.	♇ stat. • Warren G. Harding died in office, 1923 • Tides {9.4 / 10.0 •	*Yankees.*
3	Sa.	Freezing rain, New England, 1816 • *Nautilus* at North Pole, 1958 • {9.1 / 10.2	*Escape*
4	**F**	**11th S. af. P.** • Borden murders, Fall River, Mass., 1892 • {8.9 / 10.3	*to the*
5	M.	Civic holiday, much of Canada. • *The narrower the mind, the broader the statement.* •	*Cape*
6	Tu.	**Transfiguration** • ☾ rides high • ☿ stat. • Tides {8.9 / 10.8	*for*
7	W.	☌☿♀ • **Name of Jesus** • Titov orbited Earth 17 times, 1961 •	*beacha-*
8	Th.	☾ at ☋ • ☾ at peri. • Bulfinch born, 1763 • Tides {9.6 / 11.6	*holic's*
9	Fr.	New ● • Nixon resigned, Ford sworn in, 1974 • {10.1 / 11.8 •	*frolics.*
10	Sa.	**St. Laurence** • Herbert Hoover born, 1874 • Tides {10.6 / 11.9	*Hold*
11	**F**	**12th S. af. P.** • Dog Days end. • ☌♀☾ • ☌☿☾ •	*the*
12	M.	☾ on Eq. • ☌♂☾ • **St. Clare** • Tides {11.7 / 11.1	*maillot!*
13	Tu.	*As much of heaven is visible as we have eyes to see.* • Tides {11.3 / 11.0 •	*Stay*
14	W.	Electric meter patented, 1888 • First Esperanto convention, 1910 •	*overnight,*
15	Th.	**Assumption** • 50,000-acre fire, N. Idaho, 1967 • {10.1 / 11.0	*stargazer's*
16	Fr.	**St. Hyacinth** • *The hole and the patch should be commensurate.* •	*delight*
17	Sa.	☌♃☉ • Cat nights begin. • Davy Crockett born, 1786 • {8.8 / 9.6 •	*Son*
18	**F**	**13th S. af. P.** • **St. Helena** • Tides {8.3 / 9.4 •	*et*
19	M.	☾ runs low • ☾ at apo. • Discovery Day (Yukon) •	*lumière,*
20	Tu.	☌♅☾ • **St. Bernard** • Tornado, St. Paul, 1904 • {8.1 / 9.3	*then*
21	W.	☾ at ☊ • ☌♆☾ • ☿ in inf. ☌ • U.N. bldg. opened, 1950 •	*it's*
22	Th.	♀ in inf. ☌ • ☌♄☾ • Debussy born, 1862 • {8.5 / 9.8 •	*gloomier.*
23	Fr.	First graduation at a women's college, Mount Holyoke Seminary, Mass., 1838 •	*Clams*
24	Sa.	**St. Bartholomew** • If fair and clear, a prosperous autumn. •	*aren't*
25	**F**	**14th S. af. P.** • Full Sturgeon ○ • Tides {9.5 / 10.2 •	*all*
26	M.	☾ on Eq. • Fog in August indicates a cold, snowy winter. • Cloudburst, Kansas, 1876	*that's*
27	Tu.	First arrest for automobile speeding, Newport, R.I., 1904 • Tides {10.2 / 10.0	*baking;*
28	W.	**St. Augustine** • *A dog house is no place to keep a sausage.*	*temperature*
29	Th.	John the Baptist beheaded. • ☌☿♀ • Tides {9.9 / 10.3 •	*records*
30	Fr.	☿ stat. • First college music department established, Harvard U., 1875 •	*are*
31	Sa.	110° F, Los Angeles, 1955 • First lawn tennis nat'l championships, 1881 {9.4 / 10.4	*breaking.*

Farmer's Calendar

Now blooming profusely in orange, red, and yellow on dark, bushy foliage and covering the garden with its strange perfume, the marigold comes into its own. It's not the most prettily scented flower, I know, but still the marigold is a favorite of mine precisely for its odor, a heavy, smoky, autumnal reek that is unique in nature as far as I know, and that is as much a part of fall in the garden as pumpkins and nodding sunflowers.

The pungent marigold I'm describing (*Tagetes*), an annual member of the daisy family, is a classic study in the naming of familiar plants, being called the African or French marigold when it is neither African nor French nor a marigold. The true marigold is *Calendula*, an old Eurasian medicinal sometimes called pot marigold. *Tagetes* is a New World plant that came to Europe around 1520 when Cortez, the conqueror of Mexico, sent its seeds back to Spain. The Aztecs had held the flower sacred and had even succeeded in producing hybrid plants with outsized flower heads. *Tagetes* came to North America in the 1780s from nurseries in England and the Netherlands and must today be one of the commonest flowers we have.

Not everybody likes the marigold's musky scent. W. A. Burpee (1858-1915) set out to develop an odorless strain, finally succeeding by growing hybrids of a wild marigold from China. These are curiosities, however. The marigold's scent is an important part of its role in the garden as a repellent of insects. For my part, I plant marigolds because it's so easy — the seeds like little porcupine quills spring up in a couple of days — and because of that unmistakable scent that comes just before the first Vs of geese overhead to tell of the turning of the year.

1991 SEPTEMBER, THE NINTH MONTH

Autumn begins at 7:48 A.M. EST on the 23rd — about 10 hours before that night's Harvest Moon is exactly full (and rising as seen from the East Coast). Venus, Mercury, Jupiter, and the star Regulus climb rapidly higher in the east before dawn each day. Venus soars above the others and reaches greatest brilliancy as Morning Star on the 28th; the other three are a low but spectacular sight before daybreak on the 10th. As in July, Mercury (again near greatest elongation) and Jupiter almost merge as seen with the naked eye — and Regulus now twinkles less than half a degree from them. The Milky Way is magnificent in its stretch from Cygnus (overhead) to Sagittarius (in the southwest). Capella rises in the northeast, Fomalhaut in the southeast after dusk.

ASTRONOMICAL CALCULATIONS

☾ Last Quarter	1st day	13th hour	17th min.
● New Moon	8th day	6th hour	2nd min.
☽ First Quarter	15th day	17th hour	2nd min.
○ Full Moon	23rd day	17th hour	41st min.
☾ Last Quarter	30th day	19th hour	31st min.

ADD 1 hour for Daylight Saving Time.

FOR POINTS OUTSIDE BOSTON SEE KEY LETTER CORRECTIONS — PAGES 80-84

Day of Year	Day of Month	Day of Week	☉ Rises h. m.	Key	☉ Sets h. m.	Key	Length of Days h. m.	Sun Fast m.	Full Sea Boston A.M.	Full Sea Boston P.M.	☽ Rises h. m.	Key	☽ Sets h. m.	Key	Declination of Sun ° '	☽ Place	☽ Age
244	1	**F**	5 09	B	6 19	D	13 10	16	3¾	4	10 P.M. 10	A	1 P.M. 08	E	8N.17	TAU	23
245	2	M.	5 10	B	6 17	D	13 07	16	4¾	5	11 P.M. 12	B	2 10	E	7 55	TAU	24
246	3	Tu.	5 11	B	6 15	D	13 04	17	5¾	6	— —	–	3 05	E	7 33	GEM	25
247	4	W.	5 12	B	6 14	D	13 02	17	6¾	7¼	12 A.M. 23	B	3 50	E	7 11	GEM	26
248	5	Th.	5 13	B	6 12	D	12 59	17	8	8¼	1 39	B	4 28	E	6 49	CAN	27
249	6	Fr.	5 14	B	6 10	D	12 56	18	9	9¼	2 57	C	5 00	D	6 26	CAN	28
250	7	Sa.	5 15	B	6 08	D	12 53	18	9¾	10	4 13	D	5 28	D	6 04	LEO	29
251	8	**F**	5 16	B	6 07	C	12 51	18	10½	11	5 28	D	5 53	C	5 41	LEO	0
252	9	M.	5 17	B	6 05	C	12 48	19	11½	11¾	6 41	D	6 19	C	5 19	VIR	1
253	10	Tu.	5 19	B	6 03	C	12 44	19	—	12¼	7 53	E	6 47	B	4 56	VIR	2
254	11	W.	5 20	B	6 01	C	12 41	19	12½	1	9 03	E	7 16	B	4 33	VIR	3
255	12	Th.	5 21	B	6 00	C	12 39	20	1¼	1¾	10 10	E	7 49	A	4 10	VIR	4
256	13	Fr.	5 22	B	5 58	C	12 36	20	2¼	2½	11 A.M. 15	E	8 28	A	3 47	LIB	5
257	14	Sa.	5 23	B	5 56	C	12 33	20	3	3¼	12 P.M. 15	E	9 12	A	3 24	SCO	6
258	15	**F**	5 24	B	5 54	C	12 30	21	4	4¼	1 08	E	10 02	A	3 01	OPH	7
259	16	M.	5 25	B	5 53	C	12 28	21	5	5¼	1 55	E	10 58	A	2 38	SAG	8
260	17	Tu.	5 26	B	5 51	C	12 25	21	6	6¼	2 35	E	11 P.M. 57	B	2 15	SAG	9
261	18	W.	5 27	B	5 49	C	12 22	22	7	7	3 08	E	— —	–	1 52	SAG	10
262	19	Th.	5 28	C	5 47	C	12 19	22	7¾	8	3 37	E	12 A.M. 58	B	1 29	CAP	11
263	20	Fr.	5 29	C	5 46	C	12 17	22	8½	8¾	4 03	D	2 01	B	1 05	AQU	12
264	21	Sa.	5 30	C	5 44	C	12 14	23	9¼	9½	4 26	D	3 04	C	0 42	CAP	13
265	22	**F**	5 31	C	5 42	C	12 11	23	10	10¼	4 49	D	4 08	D	0N.19	AQU	14
266	23	M.	5 32	C	5 40	C	12 08	23	10½	10¾	5 13	C	5 13	D	0S.04	PSC	15
267	24	Tu.	5 33	C	5 39	C	12 06	24	11	11½	5 37	B	6 19	E	0 27	PSC	16
268	25	W.	5 34	C	5 37	C	12 03	24	11¾	—	6 05	B	7 28	E	0 51	PSC	17
269	26	Th.	5 36	C	5 35	C	11 59	25	12¼	12¼	6 38	B	8 38	E	1 14	ARI	18
270	27	Fr.	5 37	C	5 33	B	11 56	25	1	1	7 18	A	9 50	E	1 37	ARI	19
271	28	Sa.	5 38	C	5 31	B	11 53	25	1¾	1¾	8 07	A	11 A.M. 00	E	2 00	TAU	20
272	29	**F**	5 39	C	5 30	B	11 51	26	2½	2¾	9 06	B	12 P.M. 04	E	2 24	TAU	21
273	30	M.	5 40	C	5 28	B	11 48	26	3½	3¾	10 P.M. 13	B	1 P.M. 00	E	2S.47	TAU	22

SEPTEMBER hath 30 days. 1991

September's slender crescent grows again
Distinct in yonder peaceful evening red,
Clearer the stars are sparkling overhead;
And all the sky is pure without a stain.
— Celia Thaxter

D.M.	D.W.	Dates, Feasts, Fasts, Aspects, Tide Heights	Weather ↓
1	**F**	15th S. af. P. • **St. Giles** • 110° F, L.A., 1955 • {9.1 / 10.3	*If*
2	M.	☾ rides high • **Labor Day** • Tides {8.8 / 10.3 •	*this*
3	Tu.	Cranberry harvest, Cape Cod, Mass. • 4" snow, Denver, 1961 •	*warming's*
4	W.	☾ at ☋ • Tornado hit Minneapolis, 1941 • Los Angeles founded, 1781 •	*global,*
5	Th.	☾ at peri. • Lowell Thomas died, 1981 • *Never too old to yearn.* •	*we're*
6	Fr.	☌♀☾ • Pilgrims left England, 1620 • Tides {9.9 / 11.2 •	*in*
7	Sa.	☌☿☾ • ☌♃☾ • ☿ Gr. Elong. (18° W.) • {10.5 / 11.4 •	*troble.*
8	**F**	16th S. af. P. • ☾ on Eq. • New ● • {10.9 / 11.4	*Flora*
9	M.	☌♂☾ • **Rosh Hashanah** • Tides {11.2 / 11.2 •	*and*
10	Tu.	☌☿♃ • Hard freeze, Duluth, Minn., 1917 • Sewing machine pat., 1846	*fauna*
11	W.	♀ stat. • Pete Rose got 1,493rd base hit, 1985 • Tides {10.8 / 11.1 •	*get*
12	Th.	John Fitzgerald Kennedy married Jacqueline Lee Bouvier, 1953 • Robert Service died, 1958	*a*
13	Fr.	Hurricane Gilbert hit Caribbean, 1988 • Walter Reed born, 1851 • {9.7 / 10.3	*sauna.*
14	Sa.	**Holy Cross** • *Many a man's tongue has broken his nose.* •	*Somewhat*
15	**F**	17th S. af. P. • ☾ runs low • Tides {8.5 / 9.4	*squallish;*
16	M.	Village of Shawmut, Mass. Bay Colony, changed name to Boston, 1630 • {8.2 / 9.1 •	*fine*
17	Tu.	☾ at ☊ • ☌♅☾ • ☾ at apo. • ☌♆☾ • {8.0 / 9.0 •	*and*
18	W.	Ember Day • **Yom Kippur** • *Painting the pump won't clear the well.* •	*fallish.*
19	Th.	♅ stat. • "Dixie" first sung, N.Y.C. minstrel show, 1859 • Tides {8.3 / 9.3	*Here's*
20	Fr.	Ember Day • Radio KDKA, Pittsburgh, Penn., began daily news program, 1921 •	*what*
21	Sa.	Ember Day • **St. Matthew** • South wind means a warm fall.	*Autumn*
22	**F**	18th S. af. P. • ☾ on Eq. • Irving Berlin died, 1989	*taught 'em:*
23	M.	Autumnal Equinox • Full Harvest ○ • Tides {10.0 / 10.1 •	*School's*
24	Tu.	**Harvest Home** • *'Tis hard for an empty sack to stand upright.* •	*not*
25	W.	Yosemite Nat'l Park established, 1890 • Walter Pidgeon died, 1984 •	*so*
26	Th.	♆ stat. • **St. Cyprian** • Clara Bow died, 1965 • {10.1 / 10.8	*terrible*
27	Fr.	Woman in auto arrested for smoking, Fifth Ave., N.Y.C., 1904 • 21" snow, Denver, 1936	*when*
28	Sa.	♀ Greatest Brilliancy • George Greenstein born, 1940 • Tides {9.7 / 10.8	*the*
29	**F**	19th S. af. P. • **St. Michael** •	*heat's*
30	M.	☾ rides high • **St. Jerome** • Hay fever ends. {9.1 / 10.4	*bearable.*

No pain, no palm; no thorns, no throne;
No gall, no glory; no cross, no crown. – John Donne

Farmer's Calendar

We are aware of the weather in more ways than we know. Of course, we are informed about it by the news and by our friends and neighbors, and we observe it immediately when we look out the window. But our senses and minds are alert also to weather signals far more subtle than a local report or the sound of rain on a roof. Perhaps these more obscure clues are most easily observed when they tell of extreme weather, especially extreme weather at some distance.

It will be just two years ago this month that Hurricane Hugo emerged from the Atlantic's great autumnal storm factory below the Tropic of Cancer. It raged over the Leeward Islands and hit the Carolina coast as one of the most powerful and destructive storms in recent years. Hugo didn't have a lot of punch left for New England, but we felt the breeze from the swing he took at South Carolina — not a mighty blast, but a passing flick that was the more ominous for having its full force withheld.

The day Hugo was ripping around down south, the air at my house, a little less than a thousand miles to the north, was full of unease. The sky was a funny purple gray, and there was a wind — never a very strong wind — that was unusual in that it came from the south and east, a rare thing here where the winds are northwesterly. More disquieting, the wind was steady rather than gusting. Hugo's wind leaned into the trees with a constant pressure, steadily bending them like bows rather than making them whip and thrash their tops as an ordinary wind would do. Those gently bending trees and that south wind were what set my senses on edge until the great storm scattered and died out.

OCTOBER, THE TENTH MONTH

The occultation of Venus by the Moon on the 4th is visible in Hawaii just before dawn. Venus passes 3 degrees from Regulus in the early morning hours of the 8th and only 2 degrees from Jupiter on the 16th. The Moon and Saturn are in conjunction on the 16th. On the 20th and 21st, Orionid meteors can be observed for a little while between moonset and dawn. Clocks should be set back one hour on the 27th, bringing nightfall and stars out earlier in the daily schedule. The Summer Triangle is in the west, star Fomalhaut far below the Great Square of Pegasus in the south. Cassiopeia is a bright zigzag of stars in the north. The Pleiades rise around nightfall in late month, an event the Druids apparently used to judge the time for what has since come to be called Halloween.

ASTRONOMICAL CALCULATIONS

● New Moon	7th day	16th hour	39th min.
☽ First Quarter	15th day	12th hour	34th min.
○ Full Moon	23rd day	6th hour	9th min.
☾ Last Quarter	30th day	2nd hour	12th min.

ADD 1 hour for Daylight Saving Time until 2 A.M. October 27th.

FOR POINTS OUTSIDE BOSTON SEE KEY LETTER CORRECTIONS — PAGES 80-84

Day of Year	Day of Month	Day of Week	☉ Rises h. m.	Key	☉ Sets h. m.	Key	Length of Days h. m.	Sun Fast m.	Full Sea Boston A.M.	Full Sea Boston P.M.	☽ Rises h. m.	Key	☽ Sets h. m.	Key	Declination of Sun ° '	☽ Place	☽ Age
274	1	Tu.	5 41	C	5 26	B	11 45	26	4½	4¾	11 P.M. 26	B	1 P.M. 48	E	3s.11	GEM	23
275	2	W.	5 42	C	5 25	B	11 43	27	5½	5¾	— —	–	2 26	E	3 34	GEM	24
276	3	Th.	5 43	C	5 23	B	11 40	27	6¾	7	12 A.M. 40	B	3 00	D	3 57	CAN	25
277	4	Fr.	5 44	C	5 21	B	11 37	27	7¾	8	1 55	C	3 28	D	4 20	LEO	26
278	5	Sa.	5 45	C	5 19	B	11 34	27	8½	9	3 08	D	3 55	D	4 43	SEX	27
279	6	**F**	5 47	C	5 18	B	11 31	28	9½	9¾	4 20	D	4 20	C	5 06	LEO	28
280	7	M.	5 48	C	5 16	B	11 28	28	10¼	10¾	5 32	E	4 46	B	5 29	VIR	0
281	8	Tu.	5 49	C	5 14	B	11 25	28	11	11½	6 42	E	5 15	B	5 52	VIR	1
282	9	W.	5 50	C	5 13	B	11 23	29	11¾	—	7 51	E	5 47	B	6 15	VIR	2
283	10	Th.	5 51	C	5 11	B	11 20	29	12¼	12½	8 58	E	6 23	A	6 38	LIB	3
284	11	Fr.	5 52	C	5 09	B	11 17	29	1	1	10 00	E	7 05	A	7 01	LIB	4
285	12	Sa.	5 53	C	5 08	B	11 15	29	1¾	1¾	10 58	E	7 54	A	7 23	SCO	5
286	13	**F**	5 54	D	5 06	B	11 12	30	2½	2¾	11 A.M. 48	E	8 48	A	7 46	OPH	6
287	14	M.	5 56	D	5 04	B	11 08	30	3½	3½	12 P.M. 30	E	9 46	B	8 08	SAG	7
288	15	Tu.	5 57	D	5 03	B	11 06	30	4¼	4½	1 06	E	10 46	B	8 30	SAG	8
289	16	W.	5 58	D	5 01	B	11 03	30	5¼	5½	1 37	E	11 P.M. 48	B	8 52	SAG	9
290	17	Th.	5 59	D	5 00	B	11 01	31	6¼	6½	2 04	D	— —	–	9 14	CAP	10
291	18	Fr.	6 00	D	4 58	B	10 58	31	7	7¼	2 28	D	12 A.M. 50	C	9 36	CAP	11
292	19	Sa.	6 01	D	4 56	B	10 55	31	7¾	8	2 51	D	1 53	D	9 58	AQU	12
293	20	**F**	6 03	D	4 55	B	10 52	31	8½	8¾	3 14	C	2 56	D	10 19	PSC	13
294	21	M.	6 04	D	4 53	B	10 49	31	9¼	9½	3 38	B	4 02	D	10 41	PSC	14
295	22	Tu.	6 05	D	4 52	B	10 47	31	9¾	10¼	4 06	B	5 11	E	11 02	PSC	15
296	23	W.	6 06	D	4 50	B	10 44	32	10½	11	4 38	B	6 22	E	11 23	PSC	16
297	24	Th.	6 07	D	4 49	B	10 42	32	11¼	11¾	5 16	B	7 35	E	11 44	ARI	17
298	25	Fr.	6 09	D	4 48	B	10 39	32	—	12	6 03	B	8 47	E	12 05	TAU	18
299	26	Sa.	6 10	D	4 46	B	10 36	32	12½	12¾	7 00	A	9 55	E	12 26	TAU	19
300	27	**F**	6 11	D	4 45	B	10 34	32	1¼	1½	8 06	B	10 55	E	12 46	TAU	20
301	28	M.	6 12	D	4 43	B	10 31	32	2¼	2½	9 18	B	11 A.M. 45	E	13 07	GEM	21
302	29	Tu.	6 14	D	4 42	B	10 28	32	3¼	3½	10 31	B	12 P.M. 27	E	13 27	GEM	22
303	30	W.	6 15	D	4 41	B	10 26	32	4¼	4½	11 P.M. 45	C	1 01	E	13 46	CAN	23
304	31	Th.	6 16	D	4 39	B	10 23	32	5¼	5¾	— —	–	1 P.M. 31	D	14s.06	LEO	24

OCTOBER hath 31 days. 1991

I love to wander through the woodlands hoary
In the soft light of an autumnal day,
When Summer gathers up her robes of glory,
And like a dream of beauty glides away.
— Sarah H. Whitman

D.M.	D.W.	Dates, Feasts, Fasts, Aspects, Tide Heights	Weather ↓
1	Tu.	**St. Remigius** • ☾ at ☋ • E. B. White died, 1985 •	*Maples*
2	W.	☾ at peri. • W. H. Vanderbilt said, "The public be damned!" 1882 • {9.0 10.2	*blaze*
3	Th.	☿ in sup. ☌ • Watch for line storms: lash of St. Francis. {9.3 10.3	*like Joseph's*
4	Fr.	**St. Francis of Assisi** • Occult. ♀ by ☾ • ♄ stat. • {9.7 10.5	
5	Sa.	☾ on Eq. • ☌♃☾ • "A mighty tempest," Mass. Bay Colony, 1638 • {10.3 10.7	*coat;*
6	**F**	20th S. af. P. • **St. Faith** • Antioch College opened, 1853	*makes*
7	M.	New ● • *The best way out is always through.* • Tides {11.1 10.7 •	*your*
8	Tu.	Great fire followed a severe drought, Chicago, 1871 • Tides {11.2 10.5 •	*heart*
9	W.	**St. Denis** • 4" snow, Boston, 1703 • Calliope patented by J. Stoddard, 1855 •	*stick*
10	Th.	*Too many people confuse bad management with destiny.* • Tides {10.2 11.0 •	*in*
11	Fr.	Eleanor Roosevelt born, 1884 • D.A.R. founded, 1890 •	*your*
12	Sa.	Barometer 25.69", Typhoon Tip, Philippines, 1979 • "Big Blow," Ore. and Wash., 1962 •	*throat.*
13	**F**	21st S. af. P. • ☾ runs low • Tides {8.9 9.7 •	*Orchards*
14	M.	**Columbus Day** • Thanksgiving Day (Canada) • ☾ at ☊ • ☌♅☾ • ☌♆☾	
15	Tu.	**St. Theresa** • ☾ at apo. • World Poetry Day	*bend with*
16	W.	☌♄☾ • ☌♀♃ • **St. Gallus** • If dry today, a dry spring. •	*apple*
17	Th.	**St. Ethelreda** • Earthquake, San Francisco, 1989 • {8.3 8.9	*bounty;*
18	Fr.	**St. Luke** • St. Luke's Little Summer. • 48" snow, Buffalo, N.Y., 1930	*there's*
19	Sa.	*If you think you have influence, try ordering someone else's dog around.* • {9.0 9.3 •	*a fair*
20	**F**	22nd S. af. P. • ☾ on Eq. • Chipmunks hibernate. {9.5 9.6	*in every*
21	M.	Columbus landed, San Salvador Island, 1492 • Nelson's victory off Cape of Trafalgar, Spain, 1805	*county.*
22	Tu.	104° F, San Diego, 1965 • Pablo Casals died, 1973 • Franz Liszt born, 1811 • {10.5 10.0	*Frosty*
23	W.	Full Hunter's ○ • Swallows leave San Juan Capistrano • Tides {10.9 10.1	*nights*
24	Th.	October always has 19 fine days. • Charles II first tasted cranberries, 1667 • {11.2 10.1	*of*
25	Fr.	**St. Crispin** • *Imitation is the sincerest form of competition.* •	*hooting*
26	Sa.	Rocky Marciano knocked out Joe Louis, 1951 • D.S.T. ends tomorrow. • {10.0 11.4	*owls;*
27	**F**	23rd S. af. P. • ☾ rides high • ☾ at peri. •	*Northeaster*
28	M.	**Sts. Simon and Jude** • ☾ at ☋ • {9.6 10.9 •	*howls!*
29	Tu.	-33° F, Soda Butte, Wyo., 1917 • Pandemonium in N.Y. Stock Exchange, 1929	*Soaking*
30	W.	Rain in October means wind in December. • John Adams born, 1735 {9.3 10.2	*witches'*
31	Th.	**All Hallows Eve** • George Halas died, 1983 • {9.4 10.0	*croaking.*

Farmer's Calendar

For every show that nature puts on spectacularly to an audience of millions, it puts on a hundred little, fleeting exhibitions for one or two who happen to pass by. In this our finest month, the air is like a shot of brandy, the sky is a limitless blue, and the country roads glow like the aisles of a cathedral with the light coming through the turning leaves of the hardwoods. October is a feast for all the senses; people come from around the world to attend at it, and who can blame them? They drive through the hills, or they simply sit and look out at the spectacle laid before them.

No one is suggesting that we should parse our autumn and try to resolve it into its constituent phenomena — so many days of cool, clear air, so many gold-and-copper hillsides — but any who are lucky and alert can also enjoy smaller, momentary shows. Leaf-fall offers one of them. Every one of those billion, trillion leaves must come down. How will they do it? Most days, the leaves seem to fall slowly, by ones and twos, here and there. You'll notice one in the corner of your eye, or you'll pick out another and follow it down. It's as though each leaf had its own moment to fall.

Then on other days all the leaves will briefly fall at once, like a flock of birds that turns suddenly in flight, flashing their wings as one. For a moment the air will be crowded, thronged with falling leaves. I understand a single tree will sometimes lose all its leaves together and in an instant stand bare. You'd expect to see that on a windy day, but often moments of sudden leaf-fall come on still days, when the drifts of leaves slip down through the quiet air like bright coins dropped into a pool.

1991 NOVEMBER, THE ELEVENTH MONTH

On the 2nd of the month, Venus is in conjunction with the Moon and reaches its greatest elongation west (47 degrees) in the southeast predawn sky. The planet passes very near stars in Virgo on the 6th and 13th and 4 degrees north of Virgo's brightest star, Spica, on the 29th. As dawn brightens, Jupiter is in the south in Leo. The Moon is near Saturn on the evening of the 12th. Evenings are Moon-free and allow for good viewing of Taurid meteors early in the month. Taurus the Bull is in the east in mid evening, his face outlined by a V of stars that includes bright Aldebaran. Overhead there shines a fuzzy glow, which is over 10,000 times farther than many of the stars we see: the Great Galaxy in Andromeda. High in the northeast is the constellation Perseus. Moonlight does not impede predawn observation of the Leonid meteors on the 16th.

ASTRONOMICAL CALCULATIONS

●	New Moon	6th day	6th hour	12th min.
☽	First Quarter	14th day	9th hour	2nd min.
○	Full Moon	21st day	17th hour	58th min.
☾	Last Quarter	28th day	10th hour	22nd min.

FOR POINTS OUTSIDE BOSTON SEE KEY LETTER CORRECTIONS — PAGES 80-84

Day of Year	Day of Month	Day of Week	☉ Rises h. m.	Key	☉ Sets h. m.	Key	Length of Days h. m.	Sun Fast m.	Full Sea Boston A.M.	Full Sea Boston P.M.	☽ Rises h. m.	Key	☽ Sets h. m.	Key	Declination of Sun ° '	☽ Place	☽ Age
305	1	Fr.	6 17	D	4 38	B	10 21	32	6½	6¾	12 A.M. 57	D	1 P.M. 57	D	14s.25	LEO	25
306	2	Sa.	6 19	D	4 37	B	10 18	32	7½	7¾	2 08	D	2 22	C	14 44	LEO	26
307	3	**F**	6 20	D	4 35	B	10 15	32	8¼	8¾	3 17	D	2 48	B	15 03	VIR	27
308	4	M.	6 21	D	4 34	B	10 13	32	9	9¾	4 26	E	3 15	B	15 21	VIR	28
309	5	Tu.	6 22	D	4 33	B	10 11	32	9¾	10½	5 35	E	3 45	B	15 40	VIR	29
310	6	W.	6 24	D	4 32	B	10 08	32	10½	11¼	6 42	E	4 20	A	15 58	LIB	0
311	7	Th.	6 25	D	4 31	A	10 06	32	11¼	—	7 47	E	5 00	A	16 16	LIB	1
312	8	Fr.	6 26	D	4 30	A	10 04	32	12	12	8 46	E	5 46	A	16 34	SCO	2
313	9	Sa.	6 27	D	4 28	A	10 01	32	12½	12¾	9 39	E	6 38	A	16 51	OPH	3
314	10	**F**	6 29	D	4 27	A	9 58	32	1¼	1¼	10 25	E	7 35	B	17 08	SAG	4
315	11	M.	6 30	D	4 26	A	9 56	32	2	2	11 03	E	8 34	B	17 25	SAG	5
316	12	Tu.	6 31	D	4 25	A	9 54	32	2¾	3	11 A.M. 36	E	9 35	B	17 41	SAG	6
317	13	W.	6 32	D	4 24	A	9 52	32	3¾	3¾	12 P.M. 03	E	10 37	C	17 57	CAP	7
318	14	Th.	6 34	D	4 23	A	9 49	32	4½	4¾	12 29	D	11 P.M. 38	C	18 13	AQU	8
319	15	Fr.	6 35	D	4 23	A	9 48	31	5½	5¾	12 52	D	— —	–	18 28	AQU	9
320	16	Sa.	6 36	D	4 22	A	9 46	31	6¼	6½	1 14	D	12 A.M. 40	D	18 43	PSC	10
321	17	**F**	6 37	D	4 21	A	9 44	31	7	7½	1 38	C	1 43	D	18 58	PSC	11
322	18	M.	6 38	D	4 20	A	9 42	31	7¾	8¼	2 03	B	2 49	E	19 12	PSC	12
323	19	Tu.	6 40	D	4 19	A	9 39	31	8½	9	2 33	B	3 59	E	19 26	PSC	13
324	20	W.	6 41	D	4 19	A	9 38	30	9¼	9¾	3 09	B	5 11	E	19 40	ARI	14
325	21	Th.	6 42	D	4 18	A	9 36	30	10	10½	3 52	B	6 25	E	19 54	ARI	15
326	22	Fr.	6 43	D	4 17	A	9 34	30	10¾	11½	4 46	A	7 37	E	20 07	TAU	16
327	23	Sa.	6 45	D	4 17	A	9 32	30	11½	—	5 51	B	8 42	E	20 20	TAU	17
328	24	**F**	6 46	D	4 16	A	9 30	29	12¼	12½	7 04	B	9 38	E	20 32	GEM	18
329	25	M.	6 47	D	4 15	A	9 28	29	1	1¼	8 19	B	10 25	E	20 44	GEM	19
330	26	Tu.	6 48	E	4 15	A	9 27	29	2	2¼	9 35	C	11 02	D	20 56	CAN	20
331	27	W.	6 49	E	4 14	A	9 25	29	3	3¼	10 P.M. 49	C	11 A.M. 33	D	21 07	CAN	21
332	28	Th.	6 50	E	4 14	A	9 24	28	4	4¼	— —	–	12 P.M. 01	D	21 18	LEO	22
333	29	Fr.	6 51	E	4 14	A	9 23	28	5	5½	12 A.M. 00	D	12 26	C	21 28	LEO	23
334	30	Sa.	6 52	E	4 13	A	9 21	27	6	6½	1 A.M. 09	D	12 P.M. 51	C	21s.38	VIR	24

When shrieked
The bleak November winds, and smote the woods,
And the brown fields were herbless, and the shades
That met above the merry rivulet were spoiled,
I sought and loved them still.
— *William Cullen Bryant*

D.M.	D.W.	Dates, Feasts, Fasts, Aspects, Tide Heights	Weather ↓
1	Fr.	**All Saints** • ☌♃☾ • Dark day, New England, 1716 •	*Summer*
2	Sa.	☾ on Eq. • ♀ Gr. Elong. (47° W.) • ☌♀☾ • Tides {10.1 / 10.0 •	*sings*
3	**F**	24th S. af. P. • 96° F, Los Angeles, 1890 • Tides {10.5 / 10.0 •	*one*
4	M.	*No one has a good enough memory to make a successful liar.* • Will Rogers born, 1879	*last*
5	Tu.	Fawkes's Plot (Never forgot) • V. Horowitz died, 1989 • Tides {11.0 / 9.9	*refrain,*
6	W.	**St. Leonard** • New ● • Buchan cold spell begins. • {11.0 / 9.8	*then*
7	Th.	Lewis and Clark sighted Pacific at mouth of Columbia River, 1805 • Battle of Tippecanoe, 1811	*exits*
8	Fr.	☌☿☾ • ☌♂☉ • Louvre opened, Paris, 1793 •	*south,*
9	Sa.	☾ runs low • Border opened between East and West Berlin, 1989 • {9.3 / 10.4	*pursued*
10	**F**	25th S. af. P. • ☾ at ☊ • ☌⛢☾ •	*by rain.*
11	M.	Remembrance Day (Canada) • Veterans Day • **Martinmas** • ☌♆☾	
12	Tu.	☾ at apo. • ☌♄☾ • ☌♇☉ • Elizabeth Cady Stanton Day •	*Trees*
13	W.	Buchan cold spell ends. • Alysheba, richest racehorse ever, retired to stud, 1988 • Tides {8.4 / 9.1	*are*
14	Th.	*Moby Dick* published to cool reviews, N.Y.C., 1851 • Prince Charles born, 1948	*stripped,*
15	Fr.	*Don't talk about yourself: it will be done when you leave.* • Lech Walesa addressed Congress, 1989	*peaks*
16	Sa.	☾ on Eq. • Sadie Hawkins Day • 6" snow, Tucson, 1958 • {8.9 / 8.8 •	*white-*
17	**F**	26th S. af. P. • **St. Hugh of Lincoln** •	*tipped.*
18	M.	☿ Gr. Elong. (22° E.) • Female Charitable Society organized, Wiscasset, Me., 1805 • {9.8 / 9.2	*Cool*
19	Tu.	*True love is like a ghost: everyone talks about it but few have seen it.* •	*and*
20	W.	**St. Edmund** • Indian summer ends now. • Tides {10.8 / 9.7	*bracing;*
21	Th.	Full Beaver ○ • Red Grange played last varsity game, U. of Illinois, 1925 {11.3 / 9.9	*you'll*
22	Fr.	**St. Cecilia** • Skunks hibernate. • Prune grapevines. • Tides {11.6 / 10.0 •	*be*
23	Sa.	**St. Clement** • ☾ rides high • ☾ at peri. • {11.8 / —	*chasing*
24	**F**	27th S. af. P. • ☾ at ☋ • Tides {10.1 / 11.8 •	*your*
25	M.	**St. Catharine** • Foul or fair, so next February. •	*turkey*
26	Tu.	Ford roadsters on sale for $260, 1925 • Ice storm, N.E., 1921 • {9.9 / 11.2 •	*through*
27	W.	*If there be ice in November that will bear a duck, There'll be nothing thereafter but sleet & muck.* •	*woods*
28	Th.	**Thanksgiving Day** • ☿ stat. • Tides {9.8 / 10.2	*damp*
29	Fr.	☾ on Eq. • ☌♃☾ • *Lack of pep is often mistaken for patience.* •	*and*
30	Sa.	**St. Andrew** • –45° F, Pokegama Dam, Minn., 1896 • {10.0 / 9.5 •	*murky.*

At given points in a man's life he must take it by the scruff of the neck and shake it. – Moss Hart

Farmer's Calendar

Fifteen years ago, when you couldn't vote in the state of Vermont unless you heated your house with wood, no intelligent adult was without an opinion on what was the best firewood. Oak, beech, hickory, and the rest, each had its legion of proponents: one or another of them burned hotter, burned longer, made less ashes, made more coals. Ash wood, as I recall, was most widely accepted at the time as the philosopher's stone of fuel.

I was never so certain, myself. It seemed to me that the best wood came from the tree that grew closest to the woodshed. In an age of faith where firewood was concerned, I was an agnostic.

Since then the debate on oak versus ash seems sometimes to have become as quaint as that over the relative merits of the barouche and the hansom. I still burn my share, however, and I find, now that conviction is irrelevant, that I have entered upon a certainty with respect to firewood —not as to which is the best wood, but as to which is the worst. The worst firewood is butternut.

It doesn't look like lousy wood. The butternut is a substantial, broad-leaved tree with beautiful, pale brown wood having a silky, close grain and a perfectly respectable weight — when fresh cut, that is. Let that wood dry, though, and the same husky chunk of butternut which you heaved onto the stack when it was green now feels like a piece of stage-prop wood made of foam. In a fire it burns like a match and then disappears utterly, leaving a half cup of cold and worthless powder. You might as well try to heat your house by putting a handful of cigarettes into your stove as burn butternut. Fortunately I have at least a year's supply.

1991 DECEMBER, The Twelfth Month

The partial eclipse of the Moon on the 21st is only a slight one but far more conspicuous than the year's other lunar eclipses. Around mideclipse (5:33 A.M. EST) the darkening will be quite obvious at the Moon's southern edge. The next day, 3:54 A.M. EST, winter begins. After middle-night moonset on the 13th-14th, one Geminid meteor a minute may be seen in country skies. Early and late in the month there are Moon-free evenings for stars: the Northern Cross (main pattern of Cygnus the Swan) stands upright as it sets in the west; Orion the Hunter's famous Belt of three bright stars in a row is vertical as it rises in the east. Saturn, low in the southwest, is the only planet really visible all evening. Jupiter rises in the middle of the night; Venus, Mercury, and Mars rise soon before dawn.

ASTRONOMICAL CALCULATIONS

● New Moon	5th day	22nd hour	57th min.
☽ First Quarter	14th day	4th hour	33rd min.
○ Full Moon	21st day	5th hour	24th min.
☾ Last Quarter	27th day	20th hour	56th min.

FOR POINTS OUTSIDE BOSTON SEE KEY LETTER CORRECTIONS — PAGES 80-84

Day of Year	Day of Month	Day of Week	☉ Rises h. m.	Key	☉ Sets h. m.	Key	Length of Days h. m.	Sun Fast m.	Full Sea Boston A.M.	Full Sea Boston P.M.	☽ Rises h. m.	Key	☽ Sets h. m.	Key	Declination of Sun ° '	Place	☽ Age
335	1	F	6 54	E	4 13	A	9 19	27	7	7½	2 ᴬ 17	E	1 ᴾ 17	B	21s.48	VIR	25
336	2	M.	6 55	E	4 13	A	9 18	27	8	8½	3 24	E	1 46	B	21 57	VIR	26
337	3	Tu.	6 56	E	4 12	A	9 16	26	8¾	9½	4 31	E	2 19	B	22 05	VIR	27
338	4	W.	6 57	E	4 12	A	9 15	26	9½	10¼	5 36	E	2 57	A	22 13	LIB	28
339	5	Th.	6 58	E	4 12	A	9 14	26	10¼	11	6 37	E	3 41	A	22 21	SCO	0
340	6	Fr.	6 59	E	4 12	A	9 13	25	11	11½	7 32	E	4 31	A	22 28	OPH	1
341	7	Sa.	7 00	E	4 12	A	9 12	25	11½	—	8 20	E	5 25	A	22 35	SAG	2
342	8	F	7 01	E	4 12	A	9 11	24	12¼	12¼	9 01	E	6 24	B	22 42	SAG	3
343	9	M.	7 01	E	4 12	A	9 11	24	1	1	9 36	E	7 25	B	22 49	SAG	4
344	10	Tu.	7 02	E	4 12	A	9 10	23	1¾	1¾	10 05	D	8 26	C	22 54	CAP	5
345	11	W.	7 03	E	4 12	A	9 09	23	2¼	2½	10 31	D	9 26	C	22 59	AQU	6
346	12	Th.	7 04	E	4 12	A	9 08	22	3	3¼	10 54	D	10 27	C	23 04	CAP	7
347	13	Fr.	7 05	E	4 12	A	9 07	22	3¾	4	11 16	C	11 ᴾ 29	D	23 08	AQU	8
348	14	Sa.	7 06	E	4 12	A	9 06	22	4½	4¾	11 ᴬ 39	C	— —	–	23 12	PSC	9
349	15	F	7 06	E	4 12	A	9 06	21	5½	5¾	12 ᴾ 02	B	12 ᴬ 31	D	23 16	PSC	10
350	16	M.	7 07	E	4 13	A	9 06	21	6¼	6¾	12 29	B	1 37	E	23 19	PSC	11
351	17	Tu.	7 08	E	4 13	A	9 05	20	7	7½	1 01	B	2 46	E	23 21	PSC	12
352	18	W.	7 08	E	4 13	A	9 05	20	7¾	8½	1 39	B	3 58	E	23 23	ARI	13
353	19	Th.	7 09	E	4 14	A	9 05	19	8¾	9¼	2 28	B	5 11	E	23 24	TAU	14
354	20	Fr.	7 09	E	4 14	A	9 05	19	9½	10¼	3 28	B	6 20	E	23 25	TAU	15
355	21	Sa.	7 10	E	4 15	A	9 05	18	10½	11	4 39	B	7 23	E	23 26	TAU	16
356	22	F	7 10	E	4 15	A	9 05	18	11¼	—	5 56	B	8 15	E	23 26	GEM	17
357	23	M.	7 11	E	4 16	A	9 05	17	12	12¼	7 15	C	8 58	E	23 26	GEM	18
358	24	Tu.	7 11	E	4 16	A	9 05	17	12¾	1	8 33	C	9 33	D	23 25	CAN	19
359	25	W.	7 12	E	4 17	A	9 05	16	1¾	2	9 47	D	10 03	D	23 23	LEO	20
360	26	Th.	7 12	E	4 18	A	9 06	16	2¾	3	10 ᴹ 59	D	10 30	D	23 21	SEX	21
361	27	Fr.	7 12	E	4 18	A	9 06	15	3½	4	— —	–	10 55	C	23 19	LEO	22
362	28	Sa.	7 13	E	4 19	A	9 06	15	4½	5	12 ᴬ 09	E	11 21	B	23 16	VIR	23
363	29	F	7 13	E	4 20	A	9 07	14	5½	6	1 17	E	11 ᴬ 50	B	23 13	VIR	24
364	30	M.	7 13	E	4 20	A	9 07	14	6½	7¼	2 23	E	12 ᴾ 20	B	23 10	VIR	25
365	31	Tu.	7 13	E	4 21	A	9 08	13	7½	8¼	3 ᴬ 29	E	12 ᴾ 56	A	23s.06	LIB	26

DECEMBER hath 31 days. 1991

I heard the bells of Christmas Day
Their old familiar carols play,
And wild and sweet the words repeat
Of peace on earth, good will to men.
— Henry Wadsworth Longfellow

D.M.	D.W.	Dates, Feasts, Fasts, Aspects, Tide Heights	*Weather* ↓
1	F	1st S. in Advent • David Ben Gurion died, 1973 • Tides {10.2 9.3	*A*
2	M.	☌♀☾ • **Chanukah** • Napoleon crowned Emperor of France, 1804	*teaser,*
3	Tu.	Buchan warm spell begins. • *The best mirror is an old friend.* • Tides {10.5 9.2 •	*then*
4	W.	Geo. Washington's farewell to his officers, Fraunces Tavern, N.Y.C., 1783 • 70°F, Boston, 1982	*a*
5	Th.	New ● • Prohibition ended 3:32 P.M. (M.S.T.), 1933 • Tides {10.6 9.1	*freezer!*
6	Fr.	**St. Nicholas** • ☾ runs low • Dave Brubeck born, 1920 •	*Bright*
7	Sa.	**St. Ambrose** • Attack on Pearl Harbor, 1941 • Delaware ratified Constitution, 1787	*and*
8	F	2nd S. in Adv. • ☾ at ☊ • ☌♅☾ • ☿ in inf. ☌ • ☌♆☾	
9	M.	☾ at apo. • *To learn the value of money, borrow some.* • {8.9 10.1	*delightful*
10	Tu.	☌♄☾ • Mississippi admitted as 20th state, 1817 • {8.8 9.8	*followed by*
11	W.	Edward VIII abdicated, 1936 • Big Ben stopped by cold, 12:27 P.M., 1981 •	*frightful.*
12	Th.	Beethoven paid Haydn 19¢ for first music lesson, 1792 • Tides {8.7 9.2 •	*Visit*
13	Fr.	**St. Lucy** • ☾ on Eq. • ☌☿♂ • Grandma Moses died, 1961 •	*the*
14	Sa.	Buchan warm spell ends. • 1st cold wave in "Hard Winter" of 1779. • Tides {8.9 8.7	*mall,*
15	F	3rd S. in Advent • Bill of Rights ratified, 1791 • {9.1 8.6 •	*flakes*
16	M.	Beware the Pogonip. • Beethoven born, 1770 • Tea Party, Boston, 1773 •	*fall.*
17	Tu.	*We may achieve climate, but weather is thrust upon us.* • Tides {9.9 8.8 •	*It's*
18	W.	Ember Day • ☿ stat. • Ty Cobb born, 1886 • 13th Amendment abol. slavery, 1865 •	*mild*
19	Th.	"Piercing cold" at Valley Forge, 1777 • *Poor Richard's Almanac* pub., 1732 • {10.9 9.4	*again;*
20	Fr.	Ember Day • Halcyon Days • *Peg o' My Heart* opened, N.Y.C., 1912 • {11.4 9.7 •	*be-*
21	Sa.	Ember Day • ☾ at ☋ • ☾ rides high • Full Cold ○ • Eclipse ☾ •	
22	F	4th S. in Adv. • ☾ at peri. • Winter Solstice • {12.0 —	*guiled*
23	M.	Boogie-woogie, eight-to-the-bar bass, introduced at Carnegie Hall, 1938 • {10.2 12.0	*again.*
24	Tu.	*No brook is too little to seek the sea.* • Kit Carson born, 1809 • {10.4 11.8	*Christmas*
25	W.	Christmas Day • Green Christmas means a white Easter.	*is white,*
26	Th.	**St. Stephen** • ☾ on Eq. • ☌♃☾ • Boxing Day •	*but lips*
27	Fr.	**St. John** • ☿ Gr. Elong. (22° W.) • "Sweet Adeline" first sung, 1903	*are blue*
28	Sa.	**Holy Innocents** • Creosote bush in Mojave Desert determined to be 11,700 years old, 1984	
29	F	1st S. af. Ch. • Hitler firebombed London, 1940 • {10.1 9.0	*when we*
30	M.	–44° F, N.H. and Vt., 1917 • Dress rehearsal, *Pirates of Penzance*, N.Y.C., 1879 •	*welcome*
31	Tu.	**St. Sylvester** • *Begin the New Year square with every man.* –R. B. Thomas •	*'92!*

Farmer's Calendar

Behind the very tops of the maples that surround the steep meadow across the road, a distant blue mass enters again its winter presence. Mount Monadnock — 50 miles to the east from where I sit. Ten years ago you could see it from here in all seasons, but since then the trees have mostly hidden it in the warm months. Today I can see the mountain's bright summit and a length of one of its northern flanks.

Mount Monadnock is to New England what Mount Olympus was to the ancient Mediterranean: not the highest or the grandest mountain, not the wildest or the most difficult, but still somehow the sovereign mountain. It is middle-sized at 3,166 feet high and stands alone in the middle of a plain in southern New Hampshire like a clipper ship in a parking lot. Virtually all the great New England authors apostrophized Monadnock. Emerson wanted to build a cabin near Concord to get a view of the mountain, and Thoreau hiked to its summit at least four times, not without deploring, on a visit in June 1858, the papers, bottles, and other trash left on the trails by the hordes of unwashed laborers and mechanics who flocked to Monadnock as tourists.

The top of Monadnock is mostly bald. Legend says sheep-raisers in the last century burned it bare to kill off the wolves that came down from the height to raid their flocks. I doubt that's the case, but I don't really know. I have never been to Monadnock, have preferred to enjoy it from a distance and as the seasons reveal it, in the spirit of Rudyard Kipling, who watched the peak from a point near my own spot and wrote that the distant mountain "makes us sane and sober and free from little things, if we trust him."

The President Who Had a Cold ...

Time for a tip of the hat to "Old Tip," the nation's all-but-forgotten ninth president: William Henry Harrison.

BY DAVID A. LORD

His term was the most anticlimactic in American history. After an uproarious campaign, a landslide victory, and a glorious inauguration, William Henry Harrison was overwhelmed by the demands of the presidency. He contracted pneumonia and died in one month flat.

But while his presidency was remarkably insignificant, Harrison's other achievements affected events and issues from the settlement of the West to the way modern political campaigns are run. As we look back 150 years to Harrison's heyday, it is worth examining his life and its impact.

Harrison ran for president as the Whig's "log cabin and hard cider" candidate, but he actually had aristocratic roots. His father, Benjamin Harrison, signed the Declaration of Independence, and William Henry grew up during the 1780s not in a log cabin, but at his family's splendid Berke-

ley plantation near Williamsburg, Virginia. The young Harrison studied medicine under Dr. Benjamin Rush in Philadelphia, but he left school in 1791 to go to war against the Indians.

Harrison represented Indiana Territory in Congress in 1799, where he pushed through the adoption of the Harrison Land Act of 1800, which halved the size of individual settlement tracts (from 640 acres to 320 acres, or a half section) and extended terms of payment — the first significant steps towards a democratized settlement of the American West. At the ripe old age of 27, in 1800 he was appointed governor of Indiana Territory. He became a military hero at the battle of Tippecanoe in 1811. Harrison is said to have killed the great Indian leader Tecumseh at the battle of the Thames in 1813, but Democrats disputed this during the presidential campaign and historians have yet to settle it.

Harrison married Anna Symmes, settled at North Bend, Ohio, and fathered ten children. (Of all American presidents, only Harrison's successor, John Tyler, had more children. Tyler had 14 from two marriages.)

After resigning from the army and helping to negotiate a final peace treaty with the Indians, Harrison returned to Congress, served in the U.S. Senate, and in 1828 was appointed envoy to Colombia.

By 1836 Harrison was widely enough known to run as a regional candidate for president on the Whig ticket. Although he lost to Democrat Martin Van Buren, he gathered enough votes to be remembered when the convention of 1840 convened.

CAMPAIGN OF 1840: THE ART OF SAYING NOTHING, LOUDLY

The financial Panic of 1837 had split the nation, giving the Whigs a shot at the presidency. Whig leaders Henry Clay and Daniel Webster, though formidable, carried too much political baggage to be considered sure winners against Van Buren. (Clay was a two-time loser in presidential politics.)

Instead, the Whigs made two moves that proved brilliant. They nominated Harrison, a noncontroversial war hero, and gave him no platform to stand on (or be judged against). Philadelphia banker Nicholas Biddle advised, "Let [Harrison] say not one single word about his principles or his creed — let him say nothing, promise nothing."

When the *Baltimore Republican* editorialized that Harrison appeared better suited to sitting in a log cabin and drinking hard cider than to winning the presidency, the Whigs got the image they needed — populism — to beat the Jacksonian Democrats at their own game. Harrison the Virginia aristocrat became Harrison the man of the frontier, making New Yorker Van Buren look stuffy by comparison and setting the stage for months of high-spirited hullabaloo.

Harrison became "Old Buckeye" (as in Andrew "Old Hickory" Jackson) and "the Hero of Tippecanoe" (Jackson had been "the Hero of New Orleans"). With running mate John Tyler, it was "Tippecanoe and Tyler, Too." There was Tippecanoe shaving soap, log cabin badges, buttons and handkerchiefs, teacups and tableware. A young man from New York, Horace Greeley, launched his first newspaper, *The Log Cabin*, which quickly had a circulation of 80,000.

There were log cabin glee clubs, songbooks full of Whiggy lyrics:
"Old Tip he wears a homespun coat
He has no ruffled shirt-wirt-wirt
But Mat he has the golden plate
And he's a little squirt-wirt-wirt."
And slogans by the barrel: "Matty's policy is 50¢ a day and French soup. Ours is $2 a day and roast beef."

Rip-roaring rallies of crowds measured by the acre and miles-long coonskin-capped parades marked the campaign. There was free liquor and a bumper crop of populist rhetoric. The word "booze" was coined. Giant balls of twine, paper, leather, and tin were rolled from town to town and became the source of the phrase "keep the ball rolling." We can also thank the campaign of 1840 for the world's most universally understood expression: "OK" — short for Van Buren's home, Old Kinderhook, New York.

Jackson called Harrison "Clay's stool pigeon," but Old Tip had out-foxed the Democrats. In an election that attracted a spectacular 80-percent turnout (of 2.4 million voters), Harrison drew 53 percent of the vote, 19 states, and 234 electoral votes to Van Buren's 47 percent, 7 states, and 60 electoral votes.

The victory has made a big impression on nearly every campaign since, and much of the work of today's party leaders, candidate handlers, and cam-

Harrison ate and drank "enormously" to combat his illness.

---

paign image-makers can be traced to the classic 1840 model of all form and no substance.

HARRISON'S PRESIDENCY, IN SHORT . . .

William Henry Harrison seemed destined for a colorful presidency when he rode coatless on horseback up Pennsylvania Avenue on Inauguration Day, March 4, 1841. But it was bitterly cold and rainy. Harrison stood hatless before the shivering crowd on the east steps of the Capitol and delivered a scholarly address — carefully avoiding stands on controversial issues — that Daniel Webster had edited down to a mere two hours! He caught cold.

Brief histories of the foreshortened Harrison administration imply that the same cold he caught on Inauguration Day was the one that killed him a month later. Not necessarily. Among the few published details of Harrison's presidency is the fact that the chief executive liked to do his own "marketing" (and we don't mean selling ideas — he liked to shop for groceries). Apparently on another brisk, wet day in March, Harrison caught a chill while shopping.

The president had been weakened by the long campaign and by new, overwhelming demands on his time by hundreds of office seekers pestering him for political appointments. The chill became pneumonia. Harrison ate and drank "enormously" to combat the illness. But on April 4 he died, having achieved virtually nothing as chief executive. Emerson said, "He died of the presidency in a month." Tyler, a nominal Whig who had few values in common with Harrison, took office and erased the effects of the election. "The Lord ruleth. Let our nation rejoice," said Andrew Jackson.

Despite Harrison's well-to-do roots, and perhaps because he had devoted his career to public service, the president died a relatively poor man. One report called him penniless. Congress provided Anna Symmes Harrison with the first pension for a president's widow — a one-time payment of $25,000.

William Henry Harrison gave American history several firsts (see accompanying box) and one final curiosity. His sudden passing began a chain of deaths of presidents in office at roughly 20-year intervals: Harrison in 1841; Lincoln in 1865; Garfield in 1881; McKinley in 1901; Harding in 1923; Roosevelt in 1945; and Kennedy in 1963. Ronald Reagan, our oldest president, broke the pattern. □□

ONE PRESIDENT'S PRECEDENTS

William Henry Harrison:

☞ First president to die in office

☞ Second president elected from a state other than his native state

☞ Fifth president born in Virginia

☞ Last president born before the American Revolution

☞ Only president whose father (Benjamin Harrison) signed the Declaration of Independence

☞ First and only president who studied medicine

☞ Served the shortest term

☞ Only president whose grandson (Benjamin Harrison) later became president

☞ First president to lie in state in the White House

TIME CORRECTION TABLES

The times of sunrise, sunset, moonrise, moonset, and the rising and setting of the planets are given for Boston only on pages 48-74 and 36-37. Use the Key Letter shown there and this table to find the number of minutes that should be added to or subtracted from Boston time to give the correct time of your city. The answer will not be as precise as that for Boston, but will be within approximately 5 minutes. If your city is not listed, find the city closest to you in both latitude and longitude and use those figures. **Boston's latitude is 42° 22' and longitude is 71° 03'.** Canadian cities appear at the end of the list. For a more complete explanation see pages 28-29.

Time Zone Code: Atlantic Std. is -1; Eastern Std. is 0; Central Std. is 1; Mountain Std. is 2; Pacific Std. is 3; Alaska Std. is 4; Hawaii-Aleutian Std. is 5.

City	North Latitude ° '		West Longitude ° '		Time Zone Code	Key Letters				
						A min.	B min.	C min.	D min.	E min.
Aberdeen, SD	45	28	98	29	1	+37	+44	+49	+54	+59
Akron, OH	41	5	81	31	0	+46	+43	+41	+39	+37
Albany, NY	42	39	73	45	0	+ 9	+10	+10	+11	+11
Albert Lea, MN	43	39	93	22	1	+24	+26	+28	+31	+33
Albuquerque, NM	35	5	106	39	2	+45	+32	+22	+11	+ 2
Alexandria, LA	31	18	92	27	1	+58	+40	+26	+ 9	– 3
Allentown-Bethlehem, PA	40	3	75	28	0	+25	+20	+17	+13	+10
Amarillo, TX	35	12	101	50	1	+85	+73	+63	+52	+43
Anchorage, AK	61	10	149	59	4	–46	+27	+71	+122	+171
Ardmore, OK	34	10	97	8	1	+69	+55	+44	+32	+22
Asheville, NC	35	36	82	33	0	+67	+55	+46	+35	+27
Atlanta, GA	33	45	84	24	0	+79	+65	+53	+40	+30
Atlantic City, NJ	39	22	74	26	0	+23	+17	+13	+ 8	+ 4
Augusta, GA	33	28	81	58	0	+70	+55	+44	+30	+19
Augusta, ME	44	19	69	46	0	–12	– 8	– 5	– 1	0
Austin, TX	30	16	97	45	1	+82	+62	+47	+29	+15
Bakersfield, CA	35	23	119	1	3	+33	+21	+12	+ 1	– 7
Baltimore, MD	39	17	76	37	0	+32	+26	+22	+17	+13
Bangor, ME	44	48	68	46	0	–18	–13	– 9	– 5	– 1
Barstow, CA	34	54	117	1	3	+27	+14	+ 4	– 7	–16
Baton Rouge, LA	30	27	91	11	1	+55	+36	+21	+ 3	–10
Beaumont, TX	30	5	94	6	1	+67	+48	+32	+14	0
Bellingham, WA	48	45	122	29	3	0	+13	+24	+37	+47
Bemidji, MN	47	28	94	53	1	+14	+26	+34	+44	+52
Berlin, NH	44	28	71	11	0	– 7	– 3	0	+ 3	+ 7
Billings, MT	45	47	108	30	2	+16	+23	+29	+35	+40
Biloxi, MS	30	24	88	53	1	+46	+27	+11	– 5	–19
Binghamton, NY	42	6	75	55	0	+20	+19	+19	+18	+18
Birmingham, AL	33	31	86	49	1	+30	+15	+ 3	–10	–20
Bismarck, ND	46	48	100	47	1	+41	+50	+58	+66	+73
Boise, ID	43	37	116	12	2	+55	+58	+60	+62	+64
Brattleboro, VT	42	51	72	34	0	+ 4	+ 5	+ 5	+ 6	+ 7
Bridgeport, CT	41	11	73	11	0	+12	+10	+ 8	+ 6	+ 4
Brockton, MA	42	5	71	1	0	0	0	0	0	– 1
Buffalo, NY	42	53	78	52	0	+29	+30	+30	+31	+32
Burlington, VT	44	29	73	13	0	0	+ 4	+ 8	+12	+15
Butte, MT	46	1	112	32	2	+31	+39	+45	+52	+57
Cairo, IL	37	0	89	11	1	+29	+20	+12	+ 4	– 2
Camden, NJ	39	57	75	7	0	+24	+19	+16	+12	+ 9
Canton, OH	40	48	81	23	0	+46	+43	+41	+38	+36
Cape May, NJ	38	56	74	56	0	+26	+20	+15	+ 9	+ 5
Carson City–Reno, NV	39	10	119	46	3	+25	+19	+14	+ 9	+ 5
Casper, WY	42	51	106	19	2	+19	+19	+20	+21	+22
Chadron, NE	42	50	103	0	2	+ 5	+ 6	+ 7	+ 8	+ 9
Charleston, SC	32	47	79	56	0	+64	+48	+36	+21	+10
Charleston, WV	38	21	81	38	0	+55	+48	+42	+35	+30
Charlotte, NC	35	14	80	51	0	+61	+49	+39	+28	+19
Charlottesville, VA	38	2	78	30	0	+43	+35	+29	+22	+17
Chattanooga, TN	35	3	85	19	0	+79	+67	+57	+45	+36
Cheboygan, MI	45	39	84	29	0	+40	+47	+53	+59	+64
Cheyenne, WY	41	8	104	49	2	+19	+16	+14	+12	+11

City	North Latitude ° '	West Longitude ° '	Time Zone Code	Key Letters A min.	B min.	C min.	D min.	E min.
Chicago-Oak Park, IL..........	41 52	87 38	1	+ 7	+ 6	+ 6	+ 5	+ 4
Cincinnati-Hamilton, OH....	39 6	84 31	0	+64	+58	+53	+48	+44
Cleveland-Lakewood, OH ..	41 30	81 42	0	+45	+43	+42	+40	+39
Columbia, SC	34 0	81 2	0	+65	+51	+40	+27	+17
Columbus, OH	39 57	83 1	0	+55	+51	+47	+43	+40
Cordova, AK........................	60 33	145 45	4	−55	+13	+55	+103	+149
Corpus Christi, TX	27 48	97 24	1	+86	+64	+46	+25	+ 9
Craig, CO............................	40 31	107 33	2	+32	+28	+25	+22	+20
Dallas-Fort Worth, TX........	32 47	96 48	1	+71	+55	+43	+28	+17
Danville, IL	40 8	87 37	1	+13	+ 9	+ 6	+ 2	0
Danville, VA	36 36	79 23	0	+51	+41	+33	+24	+17
Davenport, IA......................	41 32	90 35	1	+20	+19	+17	+16	+15
Dayton, OH.........................	39 45	84 10	0	+61	+56	+52	+48	+44
Decatur, AL.........................	34 36	86 59	1	+27	+14	+ 4	− 7	−17
Decatur, IL..........................	39 51	88 57	1	+19	+15	+11	+ 7	+ 4
Denver-Boulder, CO	39 44	104 59	2	+24	+19	+15	+11	+ 7
Des Moines, IA....................	41 35	93 37	1	+32	+31	+30	+28	+27
Detroit-Dearborn, MI..........	42 20	83 3	0	+47	+47	+47	+47	+47
Dubuque, IA	42 30	90 41	1	+17	+18	+18	+18	+18
Duluth, MN	46 47	92 6	1	+ 6	+16	+23	+31	+38
Durham, NC	36 0	78 55	0	+51	+40	+31	+21	+13
Eastport, ME.......................	44 54	67 0	0	−26	−20	−16	−11	− 8
Eau Claire, WI	44 49	91 30	1	+12	+17	+21	+25	+29
El Paso, TX	31 45	106 29	2	+53	+35	+22	+ 6	− 6
Elko, NV	40 50	115 46	3	+ 3	0	− 1	− 3	− 5
Ellsworth, ME.....................	44 33	68 25	0	−18	−14	−10	− 6	− 3
Erie, PA	42 7	80 5	0	+36	+36	+35	+35	+35
Eugene, OR.........................	44 3	123 6	3	+21	+24	+27	+30	+33
Fairbanks, AK......................	64 48	147 51	4	−127	+ 2	+61	+131	+205
Fall River– New Bedford, MA	41 42	71 9	0	+ 2	+ 1	0	0	− 1
Fargo, ND...........................	46 53	96 47	1	+24	+34	+42	+50	+57
Flagstaff, AZ	35 12	111 39	2	+64	+52	+42	+31	+22
Flint, MI	43 1	83 41	0	+47	+49	+50	+51	+52
Fort Randall, AK.................	55 10	162 47	4	+62	+99	+124	+153	+179
Fort Scott, KS.....................	37 50	94 42	1	+49	+41	+34	+27	+21
Fort Smith, AR	35 23	94 25	1	+55	+43	+33	+22	+14
Fort Wayne, IN	41 4	85 9	0	+60	+58	+56	+54	+52
Fort Yukon, AK...................	66 34	145 16	4	+30	−18	+50	+131	+227
Fresno, CA	36 44	119 47	3	+32	+22	+15	+ 6	0
Gallup, NM	35 32	108 45	2	+52	+40	+31	+20	+11
Galveston, TX	29 18	94 48	1	+72	+52	+35	+16	+ 1
Gary, IN	41 36	87 20	1	+ 7	+ 6	+ 4	+ 3	+ 2
Glasgow, MT	48 12	106 38	2	− 1	+11	+21	+32	+42
Grand Forks, ND..................	47 55	97 3	1	+21	+33	+43	+53	+62
Grand Island, NE	40 55	98 21	1	+53	+51	+49	+46	+44
Grand Junction, CO	39 4	108 33	2	+40	+34	+29	+24	+20
Great Falls, MT...................	47 30	111 17	2	+20	+31	+39	+49	+58
Green Bay, WI	44 31	88 0	1	0	+ 3	+ 7	+11	+14
Greensboro, NC....................	36 4	79 47	0	+54	+43	+35	+25	+17
Hagerstown, MD	39 39	77 43	0	+35	+30	+26	+22	+18
Harrisburg, PA	40 16	76 53	0	+30	+26	+23	+19	+16
Hartford-New Britain, CT ...	41 46	72 41	0	+ 8	+ 7	+ 6	+ 5	+ 4
Helena, MT	46 36	112 2	2	+27	+36	+43	+51	+57
Hilo, HI	19 44	155 5	5	+94	+62	+37	+ 7	−15
Honolulu, HI	21 18	157 52	5	+102	+72	+48	+19	− 1
Houston, TX........................	29 45	95 22	1	+73	+53	+37	+19	+ 5
Indianapolis, IN	39 46	86 10	0	+69	+64	+60	+56	+52
Ironwood, MI	46 27	90 9	1	0	+ 9	+15	+23	+29
Jackson, MI	42 15	84 24	0	+53	+53	+53	+52	+52
Jackson, MS	32 18	90 11	1	+46	+30	+17	+ 1	−10
Jacksonville, FL	30 20	81 40	0	+77	+58	+43	+25	+11
Jefferson City, MO	38 34	92 10	1	+36	+29	+24	+18	+13
Joplin, MO..........................	37 6	94 30	1	+50	+41	+33	+25	+18
Juneau, AK..........................	58 18	134 25	4	−76	−23	+10	+49	+86
Kalamazoo, MI	42 17	85 35	0	+58	+57	+57	+57	+57
Kanab, UT...........................	37 3	112 32	2	+62	+53	+46	+37	+30

City	North Latitude ° '		West Longitude ° '		Time Zone Code	Key Letters				
						A min.	B min.	C min.	D min.	E min.
Kansas City, MO	39	1	94	20	1	+44	+37	+33	+27	+23
Keene, NH	42	56	72	17	0	+ 2	+ 3	+ 4	+ 5	+ 6
Ketchikan, AK	55	21	131	39	4	−62	−25	0	+29	+56
Knoxville, TN	35	58	83	55	0	+71	+60	+51	+41	+33
Kodiak, AK	57	47	152	24	4	0	+49	+82	+120	+154
LaCrosse, WI	43	48	91	15	1	+15	+18	+20	+22	+25
Lake Charles, LA	30	14	93	13	1	+64	+44	+29	+11	− 2
Lanai City, HI	20	50	156	55	5	+99	+69	+44	+15	− 6
Lancaster, PA	40	2	76	18	0	+28	+24	+20	+17	+13
Lansing, MI	42	44	84	33	0	+52	+53	+53	+54	+54
Las Cruces, NM	32	19	106	47	2	+53	+36	+23	+ 8	− 3
Las Vegas, NV	36	10	115	9	3	+16	+ 4	− 3	−13	−20
Lawrence-Lowell, MA	42	42	71	10	0	0	0	0	0	+ 1
Lewiston, ID	46	25	117	1	3	−12	− 3	+ 2	+10	+17
Lexington-Frankfort, KY	38	3	84	30	0	+67	+59	+53	+46	+41
Liberal, KS	37	3	100	55	1	+76	+66	+59	+51	+44
Lihue, HI	21	59	159	23	5	+107	+77	+54	+26	+ 5
Lincoln, NE	40	49	96	41	1	+47	+44	+42	+39	+37
Little Rock, AR	34	45	92	17	1	+48	+35	+25	+13	+ 4
Los Angeles incl. Pasadena and Santa Monica, CA	34	3	118	14	3	+34	+20	+ 9	− 3	−13
Louisville, KY	38	15	85	46	0	+72	+64	+58	+52	+46
Macon, GA	32	50	83	38	0	+79	+63	+50	+36	+24
Madison, WI	43	4	89	23	1	+10	+11	+12	+14	+15
Manchester-Concord, NH	42	59	71	28	0	0	0	+ 1	+ 2	+ 3
McGrath, AK	62	58	155	36	4	−52	+42	+93	+152	+213
Memphis, TN	35	9	90	3	1	+38	+26	+16	+ 5	− 3
Meridian, MS	32	22	88	42	1	+40	+24	+11	− 4	−15
Miami, FL	25	47	80	12	0	+88	+57	+37	+14	− 3
Miles City, MT	46	25	105	51	2	+ 3	+11	+18	+26	+32
Milwaukee, WI	43	2	87	54	1	+ 4	+ 6	+ 7	+ 8	+ 9
Minneapolis-St. Paul, MN	44	59	93	16	1	+18	+24	+28	+33	+37
Minot, ND	48	14	101	18	1	+36	+50	+59	+71	+81
Moab, UT	38	35	109	33	2	+46	+39	+33	+27	+22
Mobile, AL	30	42	88	3	1	+42	+23	+ 8	− 8	−22
Monroe, LA	32	30	92	7	1	+53	+37	+24	+ 9	− 1
Montgomery, AL	32	23	86	19	1	+31	+14	+ 1	−13	−25
Muncie, IN	40	12	85	23	0	+64	+60	+57	+53	+50
Murdo, SD	43	53	100	43	1	+52	+55	+58	+60	+63
Nashville, TN	36	10	86	47	1	+22	+11	+ 3	− 6	−14
New Haven, CT	41	18	72	56	0	+11	+ 8	+ 7	+ 5	+ 4
New London, CT	41	22	72	6	0	+ 7	+ 5	+ 4	+ 2	+ 1
New Orleans, LA	29	57	90	4	1	+52	+32	+16	− 1	−15
New York, NY	40	45	74	0	0	+17	+14	+11	+ 9	+ 6
Newark–Irvington– East Orange, NJ	40	44	74	10	0	+17	+14	+12	+ 9	+ 7
Nome, AK	64	30	165	25	4	−48	+74	+132	+199	+271
Norfolk, VA	36	51	76	17	0	+38	+28	+21	+12	+ 5
North Platte, NE	41	8	100	46	1	+62	+60	+58	+56	+54
Norwalk-Stamford, CT	41	7	73	22	0	+13	+10	+ 9	+ 7	+ 5
Oakley, KS	39	8	100	51	1	+69	+63	+59	+53	+49
Ogden, UT	41	13	111	58	2	+47	+45	+43	+41	+40
Ogdensburg, NY	44	42	75	30	0	+ 8	+13	+17	+21	+25
Oklahoma City, OK	35	28	97	31	1	+67	+55	+46	+35	+26
Omaha, NE	41	16	95	56	1	+43	+40	+39	+37	+36
Orlando, FL	28	32	81	22	0	+80	+59	+42	+22	+ 6
Ortonville, MN	45	19	96	27	1	+30	+36	+40	+46	+51
Oshkosh, WI	44	1	88	33	1	+ 3	+ 6	+ 9	+12	+15
Parkersburg, WV	39	16	81	34	0	+52	+46	+42	+36	+32
Paterson, NJ	40	55	74	10	0	+17	+14	+12	+ 9	+ 7
Pendleton, OR	45	40	118	47	3	− 1	+ 4	+10	+16	+21
Pensacola, FL	30	25	87	13	1	+39	+20	+ 5	−12	−26
Peoria, IL	40	42	89	36	1	+19	+16	+14	+11	+ 9
Philadelphia-Chester, PA	39	57	75	9	0	+24	+19	+16	+12	+ 9
Phoenix, AZ	33	27	112	4	2	+71	+56	+44	+30	+20
Pierre, SD	44	22	100	21	1	+49	+53	+56	+60	+63
Pittsburgh-McKeesport, PA	40	26	80	0	0	+42	+38	+35	+32	+29

City	North Latitude ° ′		West Longitude ° ′		Time Zone Code	Key Letters				
						A min.	B min.	C min.	D min.	E min.
Pittsfield, MA	42	27	73	15	0	+ 8	+ 8	+ 8	+ 8	+ 8
Pocatello, ID	42	52	112	27	2	+43	+44	+45	+46	+46
Poplar Bluff, MO	36	46	90	24	1	+35	+25	+17	+ 8	+ 1
Portland, ME	43	40	70	15	0	− 8	− 5	− 3	− 1	0
Portland, OR	45	31	122	41	3	+14	+20	+25	+31	+36
Portsmouth, NH	43	5	70	45	0	− 4	− 2	− 1	0	0
Presque Isle, ME	46	41	68	1	0	−29	−19	−12	− 4	+ 2
Providence, RI	41	50	71	25	0	+ 3	+ 2	+ 1	0	0
Pueblo, CO	38	16	104	37	2	+27	+20	+14	+ 7	+ 2
Raleigh, NC	35	47	78	38	0	+51	+39	+30	+20	+12
Rapid City, SD	44	5	103	14	2	+ 2	+ 5	+ 8	+11	+13
Reading, PA	40	20	75	56	0	+26	+22	+19	+16	+13
Redding, CA	40	35	122	24	3	+31	+27	+25	+22	+19
Richmond, VA	37	32	77	26	0	+41	+32	+25	+17	+11
Roanoke, VA	37	16	79	57	0	+51	+42	+35	+27	+21
Roswell, NM	33	24	104	32	2	+41	+26	+14	0	−10
Rutland, VT	43	37	72	58	0	+ 2	+ 5	+ 7	+ 9	+11
Sacramento, CA	38	35	121	30	3	+34	+27	+21	+15	+10
Salem, OR	44	57	123	1	3	+17	+23	+27	+31	+35
Salina, KS	38	50	97	37	1	+57	+51	+46	+40	+35
Salisbury, MD	38	22	75	36	0	+31	+23	+18	+11	+ 6
Salt Lake City, UT	40	45	111	53	2	+48	+45	+43	+40	+38
San Antonio, TX	29	25	98	30	1	+87	+66	+50	+31	+16
San Diego, CA	32	43	117	9	3	+33	+17	+ 4	− 9	−21
San Francisco incl. Oak-land and San Jose, CA	37	47	122	25	3	+40	+31	+25	+18	+12
Santa Fe, NM	35	41	105	56	2	+40	+28	+19	+ 9	0
Savannah, GA	32	5	81	6	0	+70	+54	+40	+25	+13
Scranton–Wilkes Barre, PA.	41	25	75	40	0	+21	+19	+18	+16	+15
Seattle-Tacoma-Olympia, WA	47	37	122	20	3	+ 3	+15	+24	+34	+42
Sheridan, WY	44	48	106	58	2	+14	+19	+23	+27	+31
Shreveport, LA	32	31	93	45	1	+60	+44	+31	+16	+ 4
Sioux Falls, SD	43	33	96	44	1	+38	+40	+42	+44	+46
South Bend, IN	41	41	86	15	0	+62	+61	+60	+59	+58
Spartanburg, SC	34	56	81	57	0	+66	+53	+43	+32	+23
Spokane, WA	47	40	117	24	3	−16	− 4	+ 4	+14	+23
Springfield, IL	39	48	89	39	1	+22	+18	+14	+10	+ 6
Springfield-Holyoke, MA	42	6	72	36	0	+ 6	+ 6	+ 6	+ 5	+ 5
Springfield, MO	37	13	93	18	1	+45	+36	+29	+20	+14
St. Johnsbury, VT	44	25	72	1	0	− 4	0	+ 3	+ 7	+10
St. Joseph, MO	39	46	94	50	1	+43	+38	+35	+30	+27
St. Louis, MO	38	37	90	12	1	+28	+21	+16	+10	+ 5
St. Petersburg, FL	27	46	82	39	0	+87	+65	+47	+26	+10
Syracuse, NY	43	3	76	9	0	+17	+19	+20	+21	+22
Tallahassee, FL	30	27	84	17	0	+87	+68	+53	+35	+22
Tampa, FL	27	57	82	27	0	+86	+64	+46	+25	+ 9
Terre Haute, IN	39	28	87	24	0	+74	+69	+65	+60	+56
Texarkana, AR	33	26	94	3	1	+59	+44	+32	+18	+ 8
Toledo, OH	41	39	83	33	0	+52	+50	+49	+48	+47
Topeka, KS	39	3	95	40	1	+49	+43	+38	+32	+28
Traverse City, MI	44	46	85	38	0	+49	+54	+57	+62	+65
Trenton, NJ	40	13	74	46	0	+21	+17	+14	+11	+ 8
Trinidad, CO	37	10	104	31	2	+30	+21	+13	+ 5	0
Tucson, AZ	32	13	110	58	2	+70	+53	+40	+24	+12
Tulsa, OK	36	9	95	60	1	+59	+48	+40	+30	+22
Tupelo, MS	34	16	88	34	1	+35	+21	+10	− 2	−11
Vernal, UT	40	27	109	32	2	+40	+36	+33	+30	+28
Walla Walla, WA	46	4	118	20	3	− 5	+ 2	+ 8	+15	+21
Washington, DC	38	54	77	1	0	+35	+28	+23	+18	+13
Waterbury-Meriden, CT	41	33	73	3	0	+10	+ 9	+ 7	+ 6	+ 5
Waterloo, IA	42	30	92	20	1	+24	+24	+24	+25	+25
Wausau, WI	44	58	89	38	1	+ 4	+ 9	+13	+18	+22
West Palm Beach, FL	26	43	80	3	0	+79	+55	+36	+14	− 2
Wichita, KS	37	42	97	20	1	+60	+51	+45	+37	+31
Williston, ND	48	9	103	37	1	+46	+59	+69	+80	+90
Wilmington, DE	39	45	75	33	0	+26	+21	+18	+13	+10

City	North Latitude ° '		West Longitude ° '		Time Zone Code	Key Letters A min.	B min.	C min.	D min.	E min.
Wilmington, NC	34	14	77	55	0	+52	+38	+27	+15	+ 5
Winchester, VA	39	11	78	10	0	+38	+33	+28	+23	+19
Worcester, MA	42	16	71	48	0	+ 3	+ 2	+ 2	+ 2	+ 2
York, PA	39	58	76	43	0	+30	+26	+22	+18	+15
Youngstown, OH	41	6	80	39	0	+42	40	+38	+36	+34
Yuma, AZ	32	43	114	37	2	+83	+67	+54	+40	+28
CANADA										
Calgary, AB	51	5	114	5	2	+13	+35	+50	+68	+84
Edmonton, AB	53	34	113	25	2	− 3	+26	+47	+72	+93
Halifax, NS	44	38	63	35	− 1	+21	+26	+29	+33	+37
Montreal, PQ	45	28	73	39	0	− 1	+ 4	+ 9	+15	+20
Ottawa, ON	45	25	75	43	0	+ 6	+13	+18	+23	+28
Saint John, NB	45	16	66	3	− 1	+28	+34	+39	+44	+49
Saskatoon, SK	52	10	106	40	1	+37	+63	+80	+101	+119
Sydney, NS	46	10	60	10	− 1	+ 1	+ 9	+15	+23	+28
Thunder Bay, ON	48	27	89	12	0	+47	+61	+71	+83	+93
Toronto, ON	43	39	79	23	0	+28	+30	+32	+35	+37
Vancouver, BC	49	13	123	6	3	0	+15	+26	+40	+52
Winnipeg, MB	49	53	97	10	1	+12	+30	+43	+58	+71

KILLING FROSTS AND GROWING SEASONS

Courtesy of National Climatic Center

Dates given are averages; local weather and topography may cause considerable variation.

City	Growing Season (Days)	Last Frost Spring	First Frost Fall	City	Growing Season (Days)	Last Frost Spring	First Frost Fall
Montgomery, AL	279	Feb. 27	Dec. 3	St. Louis, MO	220	Apr. 2	Nov. 8
Little Rock, AR	244	Mar. 16	Nov. 15	Helena, MT	134	May 12	Sept. 23
Phoenix, AZ	318	Jan. 27	Dec. 11	Omaha, NE	189	Apr. 14	Oct. 20
Tucson, AZ	262	Mar. 6	Nov. 23	Reno, NV	141	May 14	Oct. 2
Eureka, CA	335	Jan. 24	Dec. 25	Concord, NH	142	May 11	Sept. 30
Los Angeles, CA	*	*	*	Trenton, NJ	211	Apr. 8	Nov. 5
Sacramento, CA	321	Jan. 24	Dec. 11	Albuquerque, NM	196	Apr. 16	Oct. 29
San Diego, CA	*	*	*	Albany, NY	169	Apr. 27	Oct. 13
San Francisco, CA	*	*	*	Raleigh, NC	237	Mar. 24	Nov. 16
Denver, CO	165	May 2	Oct. 14	Bismarck, ND	136	May 11	Sept. 24
Hartford, CT	180	Apr. 22	Oct. 19	Cincinnati, OH	203	Apr. 5	Oct. 25
Washington, DC	201	Apr. 10	Oct. 28	Toledo, OH	184	Apr. 24	Oct. 25
Miami, FL	*	*	*	Oklahoma City, OK	224	Mar. 28	Nov. 7
Macon, GA	252	Mar. 12	Nov. 19	Medford, OR	178	Apr. 25	Oct. 20
Pocatello, ID	145	May 8	Sept. 30	Portland, OR	279	Feb. 25	Dec. 1
Chicago, IL	192	Apr. 19	Oct. 28	Harrisburg, PA	201	Apr. 10	Oct. 28
Evansville, IN	217	Apr. 2	Nov. 4	Scranton, PA	173	Apr. 24	Oct. 14
Fort Wayne, IN	179	Apr. 24	Oct. 20	Columbia, SC	252	Mar. 14	Nov. 21
Des Moines, IA	182	Apr. 20	Oct. 19	Huron, SD	149	May 4	Sept. 30
Wichita, KS	210	Apr. 5	Nov. 1	Chattanooga, TN	229	Mar. 26	Nov. 10
Shreveport, LA	271	Mar. 1	Nov. 27	Del Rio, TX	300	Feb. 12	Dec. 9
New Orleans, LA	302	Feb. 13	Dec. 12	Midland, TX	217	Apr. 3	Nov. 6
Portland, ME	169	Apr. 29	Oct. 15	Salt Lake City, UT	203	Apr. 12	Nov. 1
Boston, MA	192	Apr. 16	Oct. 25	Burlington, VT	148	May 8	Oct. 3
Alpena, MI	156	May 6	Oct. 9	Richmond, VA	220	Apr. 2	Nov. 8
Detroit, MI	181	Apr. 25	Oct. 23	Spokane, WA	175	Apr. 20	Oct. 12
Marquette, MI	156	May 14	Oct. 17	Parkersburg, WV	188	Apr. 16	Oct. 21
Duluth, MN	125	May 22	Sept. 24	Green Bay, WI	160	May 6	Oct. 13
Minneapolis, MN	166	Apr. 30	Oct. 13	Madison, WI	176	Apr. 26	Oct. 19
Jackson, MS	248	Mar. 10	Nov. 13	Lander, WY	128	May 15	Sept. 20
Columbia, MO	198	Apr. 9	Oct. 24	*Frosts do not occur every year			

- Illustration by Virginia Peck

Mantis - the 20-lb. wonder tiller!

The Mantis tiller/cultivator handles like a dream, yet works like a dynamo! It starts with a flick of the wrist, turns on a dime, lifts nimbly over hedges, but never gets out of control. Just pull it back and forth the way you would a hoe...couldn't be simpler!

Best of all, our tough little Mantis does more gardening jobs than any other tiller!

Prepares perfect seedbeds. Its 36 serpentine tine teeth spin at up to 240 rpm — twice the speed of other tillers. That's why Mantis can till down to 8" deep and churn tough clay into soft, loose, crumbly soil for healthy plants.

Weeds your garden in minutes. And, since it works a sensible 6" to 9" wide, it weeds precisely between narrow rows, next to walkways, even right along fences, without disturbing your plants' tender roots.

Does your lawn care and yard work, too! See other side for more details.

Test Mantis *risk-free* for a full month in your own garden and see for yourself!

For more information, call toll-free 1-800-366-6268 ...or mail the coupon below today!

Mantis

TIDE CORRECTIONS

Many factors affect the time and height of the tides: the coastal configuration, the time of the Moon's southing (crossing the meridian) at the place, and the phase of the Moon. This table of tidal corrections is a sufficiently accurate guide to the times and heights of the high water at the places shown. (Low tides occur approximately 6.25 hours before and after high tides.) No figures are shown for the West Coast or the Gulf of Mexico, since the method used in compiling this table does not apply there. For such places and elsewhere where precise accuracy is required, consult the Tide Tables published annually by the National Ocean Service, 6501 Lafayette Ave., Riverdale, MD 20840; telephone 301-436-6990.

The figures for Full Sea on the Left-Hand Calendar Pages 48-74 are the times of high tide at Commonwealth Pier in Boston Harbor. The heights of these tides are given on the Right-Hand Calendar Pages 49-75. The heights are reckoned from Mean Lower Low Water, and each day listed has a set of figures — upper for the morning, lower for the evening. To obtain the time and height of high water at any of the following places, apply the time difference to the daily times of high water at Boston (pages 48-74), and the height difference to the heights at Boston (pages 49-75).

	Time Difference: Hr. Min.	Height Feet
MAINE		
Bar Harbor	−0 34	+0.9
Belfast	−0 20	+0.4
BoothBoothbay Harbor	−0 18	−0.8
Chebeague Island	−0 16	−0.6
Eastport	−0 28	+8.4
Kennebunkport	+0 04	−1.0
Machias	−0 28	+2.8
Monhegan Island	−0 25	−0.8
Old Orchard	0 00	−0.8
Portland	−0 12	−0.6
Rockland	−0 28	+0.1
Stonington	−0 30	+0.1
York	−0 09	−1.0
NEW HAMPSHIRE		
Hampton	+0 02	−1.3
Portsmouth	+0 11	−1.5
Rye Beach	−0 09	−0.9
MASSACHUSETTS		
Annisquam	−0 02	−1.1
Beverly Farms	0 00	−0.5
Boston	0 00	0.0
Cape Cod Canal:		
East Entrance	−0 01	−0.8
West Entrance	−2 16	−5.9
Chatham Outer Coast	+0 30	−2.8
Inside	+1 54	*0.4

	Time Difference: Hr. Min.	Height Feet
Cohasset	+0 02	− 0.07
Cotuit Highlands	+1 15	*0.3
Dennisport	+1 01	*0.4
Duxbury (Gurnet Pt.)	+0 02	− 0.3
Fall River	−3 03	− 5.0
Gloucester	−0 03	−0.8
Hingham	+0 07	0.0
Hull	+0 03	− 0.2
Hyannis Port	+1 01	*0.3
Magnolia (Manchester)	−0 02	−0.7
Marblehead	−0 02	−0.4
Marion	−3 22	−5.4
Monument Beach	−3 08	−5.4
Nahant	−0 01	−0.5
Nantasket	+0 04	−0.1
Nantucket	−0 56	*0.3
Nauset Beach	+0 30	*0.6
New Bedford	−3 24	−5.7
Newburyport	+0 19	−1.8
Oak Bluffs	+0 30	*0.2
Onset (R.R. Bridge)	−2 16	−5.9
Plymouth	+0 05	0.0
Provincetown	+0 14	−0.4
Revere Beach	−0 01	−0.3
Rockport	−0 08	−1.0
Salem	0 00	−0.5
Scituate	−0 05	−0.7
Wareham	−3 09	−5.3
Wellfleet	+0 12	+0.5
West Falmouth	−3 10	−5.4
Westport Harbor	−3 22	−6.4
Woods Hole Little Harbor	−2 50	*0.2
Oceanographic Institute	−3 07	*0.2
RHODE ISLAND		
Bristol	−3 24	−5.3
Sakonnet	−3 44	−5.6
Narragansett Pier	−3 42	−6.2
Newport	−3 34	−5.9
Pt. Judith	−3 41	−6.3
Providence	−3 20	−4.8
Watch Hill	−2 50	−6.8
CONNECTICUT		
Bridgeport	+0 01	−2.6
Madison	−0 22	−2.3
New Haven	−0 11	−3.2
New London	−1 54	−6.7
Norwalk	+0 01	−2.2
Old Lyme (Highway Bridge)	−0 30	−6.2
Stamford	+0 01	−2.2
Stonington	−2 27	−6.6
NEW YORK		
Coney Island	−3 33	−4.9
Fire Island Lt.	−2 43	*0.1
Long Beach	−3 11	−5.7
Montauk Harbor	−2 19	−7.4
New York City (Battery)	−2 43	−5.0
Oyster Bay	+0 04	−1.8
Port Chester	−0 09	−2.2
Port Washington	−0 01	−2.1
Sag Harbor	−0 55	−6.8
Southampton	−4 20	*0.2
(Shinnecock Inlet)		
Willets Point	0 00	−2.3

	Time Difference: Hr. Min.	Height Feet
NEW JERSEY		
Asbury Park	−4 04	−5.3
Atlantic City	−3 56	−5.5
Bay Head (Sea Girt)	−4 04	−5.3
Beach Haven	−1 43	*0.24
Cape May	−3 28	−5.3
Ocean City	−3 06	−5.9
Sandy Hook	−3 30	−5.0
Seaside Park	−4 03	−5.4
PENNSYLVANIA		
Philadelphia	+2 40	−3.5
DELAWARE		
Cape Henlopen	−2 48	−5.3
Rehoboth Beach	−3 37	−5.7
Wilmington	+1 56	−3.8
MARYLAND		
Annapolis	+6 23	−8.5
Baltimore	+7 59	−8.3
Cambridge	+5 05	−7.8
Havre de Grace	+11 21	−7.7
Point No Point	+2 28	−8.1
Prince Frederick	+4 25	−8.5
(Plum Point)		
VIRGINIA		
Cape Charles	−2 20	−7.0
Hampton Roads	−2 02	−6.9
Norfolk	−2 06	−6.6
Virginia Beach	−4 00	−6.0
Yorktown	−2 13	−7.0
NORTH CAROLINA		
Cape Fear	−3 55	−5.0
Cape Lookout	−4 28	−5.7
Currituck	−4 10	−5.8
Hatteras:		
Ocean	−4 26	−6.0
Inlet	−4 03	−7.4
Kitty Hawk	−4 14	−6.2
SOUTH CAROLINA		
Charleston	−3 22	−4.3
Georgetown	−1 48	*0.36
Hilton Head	−3 22	−2.9
Myrtle Beach	−3 49	−4.4
St. Helena		
Harbor Entrance	−3 15	−3.4
GEORGIA		
Jekyll Island	−3 46	−2.9
Saint Simon's Island	−2 50	−2.9
Savannah Beach:		
River Entrance	−3 14	−5.5
Tybee Light	−3 22	−2.7
FLORIDA		
Cape Canaveral	−3 59	−6.0
Daytona Beach	−3 28	−5.3
Fort Lauderdale	−2 50	−7.2
Fort Pierce Inlet	−3 32	−6.9
Jacksonville		
Railroad Bridge	−6 55	*0.10
Miami Harbor Entrance	−3 18	−7.0
St. Augustine	−2 55	−4.9
CANADA		
Alberton, P.E.I.	−5 45**	−7.5
Charlottetown, P.E.I.	−0 45**	−3.5
Halifax, N.S.	−3 23	−4.5
North Sydney, N. S.	−3 15	−6.5
Saint John, N.B.	+0 30	−8.0
St. John's, Nfld.	−4 00	−6.5
Yarmouth, N.S.	−0 40	+3.0

* Where the difference in the "Height/Feet" column is so marked, height at Boston should be multiplied by this ratio.

** Varies widely; accurate only within 1½ hours. Consult local tide tables for precise times and heights.

Example: The conversion of the times and heights of the tides at Boston to those of Rockport, Massachusetts, is given below:

Sample tide calculation July 1, 1991:

High tide Boston (p. 64)	1:30	A.M. EST
Correction for Rockport	−0:08	hrs.
High tide Rockport	1:22	A.M. EST

Tide height Boston (p. 65)	10.0 ft.
Correction for Rockport	−1.0 ft.
Tide height Rockport	9.0 ft.

TIDAL GLOSSARY

Apogean tide: A monthly tide of decreased range that occurs when the Moon is farthest from the Earth (at apogee).

Diurnal: Applies to a location that normally experiences one high water and one low water during a tidal day of approximately 24 hours.

Mean Lower Low Water: The arithmetic mean of the lesser of a daily pair of low waters, observed over a specific 19-year cycle called the National Tidal Datum Epoch.

Neap tide: A tide of decreased range occurring twice a month when the Moon is in quadrature (during the First and Last Quarter Moons, when the Sun and Moon are at right angles to each other relative to the Earth).

Perigean tide: A monthly tide of increased range that occurs when the Moon is closest to the Earth (at perigee).

Semidiurnal: Having a period of half a tidal day. East Coast tides, for example, are semidiurnal, with two highs and two lows in approximately 24 hours.

Spring tide: Named not for the season of spring, but from the German *springen* (to leap up). This tide of increased range occurs at times of syzygy (q.v.) each month. A spring tide also brings a lower low water.

Syzygy: Occurs twice a month when the Sun and Moon are in conjunction (lined up on the same side of the Earth at the New Moon) and when they are in opposition (on opposite sides of the Earth at the Full Moon, though usually not so directly in line as to produce an eclipse). In either case, the gravitational effects of the Sun and Moon reinforce each other and tidal range is increased.

Vanishing tide: A mixed tide of considerable inequality in the two highs or two lows, so that the "high low" may become indistinguishable from the "low high" or vice versa. The result is a vanishing tide, where no significant difference is apparent.

Can We or Can't We Predict the Tides?

Well, depends on the weather, the exact position of the Moon, the shape of the ocean floor, and enough other factors to baffle a clam at high tide – not to mention Aristotle.

BY MARTHA WHITE

Charles Dickens knew the influence of the tides. In *David Copperfield* he wrote, "People can't die, along the coast . . . except when the tide's pretty nigh out. They can't be born, unless it's pretty nigh in — not properly born, till flood. He's going out with the tide."

Walt Whitman noted the effects of these cycles when he visited Civil War hospitals. He remarked that drugs seemed more effective and deaths gentler when they came with the ebb or flood tides.

"Every tide has its ebb," says one familiar adage, preaching patience or acceptance of change. "Time and tide wait for no man," warns another. To be born at flood tide was considered lucky. In sickness the ebb tide was a time of weakness and extra caution, especially for old salts. If a patient survived the ebb, he might improve in strength with the flood. Not surprisingly, the full Moon carried similar lore; it was considered a time of births, but also of increased bleeding and greater susceptibility to sickness.

☞ *Why Do the Tides Rise and Fall?*

Stated simply, tides are the vertical movement of water, specifically the alternate rise (flood) and fall (ebb) of water in the ocean. The word "tide" derives from the Greek for "to divide" and the Middle English for "time." Most of us take the tides for granted, just as we do the changing phases of the Moon or the rising and setting of the Sun, assuming that tides are constant and predictable. But how much do we really know?

One thing is sure: Tides are more influenced by the gravitational effect of the Moon than they are by that of the Sun (the Moon's closeness to us outweighs by far the Sun's greater size), although both affect the cycles. The gravitational effect of the Moon on the tides is about 2½ times greater than that of the Sun. Similarly, the lunar day and the tidal day are both about 50 minutes longer than the solar day, which accounts for the daily variations we notice. High tides occur at an average interval of 12 hours and 25 minutes, so we can expect that "full sea" or high tide will occur a little later each day than the day before.

Two factors combine to create the vertical tidal bulge, or high tide, which in turn creates a low tide elsewhere. One factor is the force of gravity, the other is the centrifugal force of the Earth rotating on its axis. Imagine the Moon over the ocean. Directly below the Moon, where the water is most strongly attracted by the Moon's gravity, a tidal hump or bulge is created. On the opposite side of the Earth, the water is least attracted by the Moon's gravitational pull, but the Earth's land masses are being strongly attracted by the Moon. In effect, the main body of the Earth is being pulled away from the water and toward the Moon. In addition, the centrifugal force is greatest. Instead of a negative bulge (like the inside of a bowl) being created, as you might otherwise guess, another high tide bulge is apparent. As the Earth rotates, any given area, such as Boston Harbor, is brought into proximity with both the bulges (high tides) and bowls (low tides) — resulting, most noticeably, in the semidiurnal character of the tide. So, as long as our world turns and the Moon continues in its orbit, you can count on the rise and fall of the tides.

☞ *What Else Affects the Tides?*

Astronomical variations that affect the tides are also predictable, although it takes an elaborate computer to run the calculations. Times of apogee, quadrature, perigee, conjunctions or oppositions, and maximum declination (angular distance) of the Moon from the celestial equator — and their effect on the tides — can all be calculated. These factors are commonly figured into published tide charts.

With these predictable astronomical variations come names of some of the more noteworthy tides. For example, we have *spring tides*, which you might think happen only in the spring. Actually, the term comes from the German *springen* — to leap up — and they occur twice each month with every new and full Moon, when the Earth, Moon, and Sun are in *syzygy* ('sizz-uh-jee, from the Greek word meaning "yoked") or in a straight line. Spring tides bring both unusually high water and unusually low water.

In contrast, when the Earth, Moon, and Sun are in quadrature, or at right angles, you have a *neap tide* of moderate range — not very high and not very low. These come with equal regularity, at the first and last quarter Moons each month. You may have heard of a ship that is neaped or beneaped. In this case, the ship has gone aground and must wait for the next spring tide to float it free.

In general, tides are highest when the Moon is at perigee (nearest Earth) and less high when the Earth is at perihelion

(nearest the Sun). When the Moon is nearest the celestial equator (the plane of the Earth's equator projected out into space), the two tides of the day are most equal to each other in their heights.

When the Moon "rides high" or "runs low" (and in either

High tides occur simultaneously on opposite sides of the Earth.

case is farthest from the celestial equator), there will be a more noticeable difference in the heights of the two tides. As you might expect, the highest tide will come with a combination of these astronomical factors, such as when the Earth is near perihelion, the Moon is at perigee, its phase is new or full, and it "rides high" or "runs low." You will notice all of these terms listed in our calendar pages, along with occasional tide heights at Boston. For definitions, see the Tidal Glossary accompanying pages 86-87 or the general Glossary on page 34.

Science has enabled us to chart, to a high degree of accuracy, the times and heights of the tides in various locations. Robert Eldridge White's annual *Eldridge Tide and Pilot Book*, established in 1875, is perhaps the best-known publication on tides and currents for the East Coast and is the source of *The Old Farmer's Almanac* tide data for Boston. The Eldridges get their own raw data from the National Oceanic and Atmospheric Administration (NOAA) in Rockville, Maryland. NOAA continually updates the accuracy of these tables by collecting information from a network of paid observers and recording instruments.

☞ *What About Weather?*

Ridge White at the *Eldridge* office gave this considered response: "Of course, the weather adds so many variables that it's almost impossible to predict how the weather is going to affect the tides beyond the mean. A storm may affect the tides significantly at one harbor and negligibly at another harbor very close by. Also, two or three following tides may be affected before they get back to normal, depending upon the severity of the storm."

Lest it all seem more cut and dried than moving water could ever be, here are just a few of the things that can influence the tides, making them unpredictably higher or lower: prolonged onshore or offshore winds, low or high barometric pressure, unusual freshets or droughts, and seasonal variations in sea level. In the Boston area, for example, the rise and fall of the tides averages about 9½ feet. Under the most severe weather conditions, this figure might be as much as 17 or 18 feet. A Cape Cod tide that is usually only a foot or so might go as high as 5 feet. On the other hand, it is unlikely that a tide that is already extreme — such as along the Bay of Fundy, where a large volume of water funnels into a narrow, shallow inlet, causing tides in excess of 50 feet — would double or triple under storm conditions.

☞ *Why West Coast Tides Are Less Predictable Than East Coast Tides*

Coastal configurations and wave patterns add still more variables. The East Coast ocean floor tapers off in a comparatively wide and shallow fashion, while the West Coast edge of the continental shelf is relatively close and steep. Friction caused by these irregular coastlines and sea bottoms modifies tides in ways that are very difficult to predict, although yearly records at various stations can help with this.

Within large bodies of water, such as the Pacific Ocean, there may be several interconnected tidal basins, each with its own wave patterns. There are free waves, forced waves, standing waves, and internal waves, to name just a few. Scientists talk of their oscillation and resonance, and timing of the high or low is everything. Where oceanic basins merge and their wave patterns meet, the result may be a calming of the tide or a dramatic surge, depending on the timing.

The most common tide, globally, is the semidiurnal tide such as that of Boston;

Be Your Own Boss and Make

$18.00 to $30.00 AN HOUR!

Find out how by sending now for your Free Lifetime Security Fact Kit!

Your FREE Lifetime Security Fact Kit tells you how to make $18.00 to $30.00 an hour in your own Foley-Belsaw Full-Service Saw and Tool Sharpening Business. Your FREE Fact Kit explains how you can:

— be your own BOSS!
— work full time or part time, right at home.
— do work you enjoy and take pride in.
— operate a CASH business where 90¢ of every dollar you take in is clear cash profit.

And it is so easy to learn. Foley-Belsaw gives you all the facts and instructions. No previous experience or special training necessary. All you need is the desire and ambition to be your own boss. Foley-Belsaw tells you everything you need to know to be successful. There's plenty of business where you live to keep you busy. It doesn't matter whether you live in a big city, small town or a small farm community.

Earn While You Learn

You'll quickly be able to develop the skills necessary to earn a steady income. You'll be able to sharpen all types of saws, garden and shop tools for home, farm and industry. Profits from your Foley-Belsaw Full-Service Sharpening Business can provide...

... CASH for future security or supplemental income
... CASH for travel, vacations, fishing trips
... CASH for things you've always wanted!

And you'll be able to set your own hours and not have to worry about layoffs and strikes. There are no franchise fees. Best of all — age or physical condition is no barrier — any age person can succeed.

You can be like Steve Taylor of Brookville, Ohio, who told us:
"... the first year I grossed $21,000.00."

Or James B. Jones, of Albuquerque, NM who reported:
"This past summer my sales and service amounted to almost $6,000.00 a month."

But you've got to get the FACTS before you can get started. So WRITE NOW for your FREE Lifetime Security Fact Kit. It's yours to keep with NO OBLIGATION!

FOLEY BELSAW

FREE Lifetime Security FACT KIT

Foley-Belsaw Co.
6301 Equitable Rd.
Dept. 20909
Kansas City, Mo. 64120

LIFETIME SECURITY IN YOUR OWN BUSINESS FULL TIME or PART TIME

Foley-Belsaw Co.
6301 Equitable Rd., Dept. 20909
Kansas City, Mo. 64120

☐ **YES,** I want to know more! Please rush my FREE Lifetime Security Fact Kit. No obligation and no salesman will call.

Name _____

Address _____

City _____ State _____ Zip _____

( ) _____
Area Code Phone

that is, the tide has a cycle of half a tidal day, with two high tides and two low tides (approximately) every 24 hours. On the West Coast, however, where tides may be neither diurnal nor semidiurnal, there may be mixed tides with a large inequality in the high and/or low water heights. Here the language gets interesting, and you have lower high waters and higher low waters, not to mention higher high waters and lower low waters. These are still predictable, although the calculations are more complex. In some areas, however, such as in the Gulf of Mexico, the tides are diurnal; there is just one high water and one low water in 24 hours. Some areas even have "vanishing" tides, which seem to stand still for many hours.

If you've always thought the rhythmic rise and fall of tides happens as reliably as death and taxes, you've thought wrong. Suffice it to say that the confusion to mariners caused by sailing unaware into any of these areas has greatly increased the number of groundings and shipwrecks to the extent that certain precarious coastlines — such as along the north side of Vineyard Sound off Cape Cod, Massachusetts, or near Bodie Island, North Carolina, to name just a couple — have come to be known as watery graveyards.

"Storms burst as the tides turn," reads the weather lore. For centuries, storms have been thought to come in on the high tide — but it may be just the opposite. Scientists today suggest that an advancing storm brings a dramatic drop in the barometric pressure, which then affects the tides. With the drop (and the storm), the tide rises unusually high; when the storm abates and the pressure again increases, the tide ebbs. Strong winds and seasonal freshets may also come with the storms, increasing tide heights even further.

☞ *So, Again, Can We or Can't We Predict the Tides?*

The fact is, there is still much that is unpredictable about the tides, although we know more about them than we ever have before. More often than not, the differences between the actual tides and the predictions are negligible, which is to say that our margin of error is narrowing. Nevertheless, Ridge White is cautious. Attorneys handling a law case on which the tides have some bearing will occasionally call the *Eldridge* and ask for tide charts for a specific date and location, just as they sometimes call *The Old Farmer's Almanac* for a pertinent Moon phase.

"All the *Eldridge* — or any publication — can do," Ridge says, "is to say what the predictions were. We can't tell what the tide actually was. We tell them they'd have to find the weather for that time and location or find someone who was actually recording the tides to get a firm idea."

Even Aristotle was baffled by the tides. So if you're baffled, too, consider yourself in good company. Francis E. Wylie, in his book *Tides and the Pull of the Moon* (now out of print), says, "Aristotle spent the last months of his life on Euboea, an island separated from mainland Greece by the Euripe, a narrow channel through which there is a notoriously dangerous tidal current of nine knots. A legend grew, and persisted for centuries, that Aristotle flung himself into the strait, committing suicide because he could not find the cause of the tides."

We prefer to enjoy the mystery . . . and we hope you do, too. Glad tidings. ☐☐

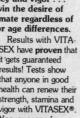

The CONSUMER'S GUIDE to 1991

A professional forecaster analyzes trends, statistics, and human behavior and offers a sketch of what the year ahead may bring.

BY KIM LONG

Congratulations, consumers! We've made it to the 1990s without the world ending. Now we can relax for a few years before the end of the decade and a new millenium. If we choose to be optimistic about the next year, we can look forward to a strong new public awareness of the environment, a new commitment to recycling, powerful new drugs to help the sick, and useful new gadgets to improve our lives. On the other hand, awareness of the environment has yet to yield any improvement, the boom in recycling is leading to thefts of aluminum and copper, many of the new drugs are too expensive for the people they're meant to help, and some of the new gadgets will displace workers who haven't any other skills to exploit.

That's the future in a nutshell — it's either half full or half empty. The way you see it is up to you!

MILESTONES

☞ **200th anniversary:** First excise tax on distilled liquors was enacted by Congress, March 3, 1791.

☞ **100th anniversary:** First correspondence school in the United States. Invention of the zipper. Carnegie Hall opened, New York City, May 5, 1891.

☞ **50th anniversary:** Japanese attacked Pearl Harbor, December 7, 1941.

☞ **35th anniversary:** Beginning of construction of the nation's interstate highway system (scheduled for completion in 1991).

VITAL STATISTICS

	1981	1991 (est.)
Population	230 mil.	252 mil
Births	3.6 mil.	3.9 mil.
Deaths	1.9 mil.	2.2 mil.
Marriages	2.4 mil.	2.3 mil.
Divorces	1.2 mil.	1.1 mil.
Average Family Size	3.28 pers.	3.09 pers.

MOST POPULAR VACATION DESTINATIONS:

● **Eastern Europe:** Behind the old Iron Curtain, 1991 is expected to be a busy year for tour groups, organized travel, and independent adventuring. Accommodations vary widely in accessibility and comfort.

● **In your land yacht:** Motor homes and recreational vehicles will go upscale — RV aficionados are often upscale themselves, earning enough to purchase motor homes costing $500,000 or more.

● **Off the beaten track:** Try Belize, Saba,

Montserrat, and Nevis in the Caribbean, or South American cities of Montevideo, Santiago, Asunción, or Caracas.

- **For safety in numbers:** Try Disneyland, now planning a three-acre expansion to include Tomorrowland, Hollywoodland, and a 3-D Muppets movie. Or go to the new visitors' center at the NASA space center in Houston.

- **Factory tours:** Those jaded by museums and historic sites can check out the assembly lines at flagship industrial operations, including manufacturers of automobiles, food, beer, airplanes, and clothing.

READY TO CLIMB THE WALLS? CALL IT EXERCISE!

- Wall climbing is one of the hottest new exercise fads in athletic clubs across the nation. Some rabid climbers are building their own climbing walls at home.

- Golf is certain to get even more popular as an aging population looks for less strenuous exercise. A new emphasis on golf fashion will feature a retro-Twenties look, à la Bobby Jones.

- Skiing's new lure comes from slopes oriented toward families, including day care, classes for youngsters, activities for single parents, and tough restrictions on reckless skiers and ski speeders.

- Other trends in exercise include increased interest in Ping-Pong, the resurgence of racquetball, and special exercise clubs for overweight women only.

GOOD NEWS IN HEALTH: CURES AND FIXES

- Plastic muscles, which can expand and

- illustrated by Tom Payne

BAD HABITS

☞ **On the wane in 1991:** Smoking, beer drinking (except for imports, specialty brews, and premium brands), cocaine use, dog bite fatalities, and child abuse.

☞ **On the increase in 1991:** snuff use, heroin, speed, marijuana, designer drugs, killer bees, and illegal dumping of toxic materials.

---

contract with electrical signals, are being perfected.

- An inflatable vest can do CPR (cardiopulmonary resuscitation) more efficiently than traditional hands-on massage.

- Surgeons in England have perfected a technique for sewing up stomachs from the inside out, using special tools. So far only cows have benefited from this noninvasive surgery, but look for human applications soon.

- New breast enlargement surgery may use recycled fat from hips and thighs instead of foreign implants. Sterilized peanut oil is another silicon substitute.

- New drugs are being tested for their ability to treat addiction to (what else) drugs, alcohol, tobacco, and even food.

- A special protein that has shown promise in blocking the effects of rheumatoid arthritis is being tested on humans and may be available for sale within five years.

- A new sun block made from seaweed is derived from a natural microorganism that protects coral reefs from ultraviolet rays.

- Prophylactic users with poor night vision can reach for a new invention from Great Britain: the luminous condom. This device is said to be nontoxic and leaves no residual glow.

- Lasers, already widely used as efficient, low-impact surgical tools, will be used by dentists, who are enthusiastic about the advantages of lasers in traditional dental procedures, including drilling. The best part, from the patient's standpoint, is the prospect of pain-free visits to the dentist.

AUTOMOTIVES

from plugging potholes to solving cellular gridlock

• Increased use of "whisper asphalt" (a special mixture to reduce traffic noise) and quick-dry pothole patches will make traveling more pleasant.

• Futuristic "active air" tires featuring pressure detectors and automatic pressure adjustment are being developed.

• Also being perfected is an electronic noise-control system that produces sound waves exactly opposite to those coming from unwanted sources such as tires or wind. The two waves cancel each other, leaving only the sound of silence.

• Sales of minivans among upscale buyers will get a boost when Mercedes introduces its version, expected in the next few years.

• Station wagons — in various new streamlined shapes — are expected to boom in popularity.

• Cellular gridlock — already a problem in cities where the number of car phones exceeds the transmission capability — will be solved by a new network of digital equipment, already being installed in some locations. Until then, mobile callers may be stuck in traffic with no dial tones.

BORN TO SHOP? BORN TO FAX?

• The competition for a share of the market has led to oversaturation of shopping centers and malls in the United States. Fewer malls will be built in the coming decade; many of the ones actually constructed will be smaller than their predecessors. Community objec-

tions to large shopping developments are forcing malls to change their appearance. One change will be the elimination of huge open parking lots, to be replaced by enclosed multilevel parking buildings.

• A new shopping concept being de-

BAD DREAMS

Feeling pessimistic about the future? The next few years could witness these nightmarish changes:

☞ **Organ thefts:** As waiting lists for transplants get longer, it's only a matter of time before someone starts a black market for lifesaving body parts.

☞ **Killer pigs:** Feral porkers are becoming a problem in some wilderness areas. With superior intelligence and skills as ferocious fighters, these runaway domestic pigs can annoy and even threaten hikers and campers.

☞ **Laser speed traps:** No fuzz-buster can warn drivers when these laser-beam speed monitors are in use.

☞ **Ad nauseam:** Sick of commercials? Coming soon will be telephone ads while you're on hold, ads on TV monitors at gasoline pumps and grocery checkout lines, hot dogs with ads printed in edible ink (hold the mustard!), ads printed on eggs, and ads in the bottom of golf course holes.

Treading Water?

I s the cost of living going up faster than your paycheck? In 1991, assuming an annual inflation rate of five percent (an educated guess), expect the following realities.

If you earned this much in 1990 . . .	. . .you'll have to earn this much in 1991 just to keep up with inflation . . .	. . . and if you have the same income in 1991 as in 1990, your "real" income will be . . .
$15,000	$15,750	$14,250
$20,000	$21,000	$19,000
$25,000	$26,250	$23,750
$30,000	$31,500	$28,500
$35,000	$36,750	$33,250
$40,000	$42,000	$38,000

veloped in Canada is the multistore home supermarket, providing everything for the home from construction to decorating. Similar centers are expected to appear in the United States.

- Using a home FAX, TV viewers will be able to request discounts on advertised products and their FAX machines will spit out the appropriate coupons.

- For those who hate to be out of touch while they shop for groceries, supermarkets will install self-service FAX machines.

- Japanese companies are testing an automated teller machine on wheels, able to be driven to locations where people are likely to need cash, such as fairs, flea markets, concerts, and parks.

Food Trends

- Butter may soon be produced with a new process that removes 95 percent of the cholesterol without altering the taste.

- The next development in the campaign to sell yogurt to Americans will be yogurt mousse, already popular in Europe.

- Meat products such as hot dogs may soon include bones, due to a Japanese process that uses acetic acid to soften bones enough to add them to a variety of meat products.

- Corn fungus, or corn smut, causes despair among gardeners, but upscale chefs are seeing it as another exotic delicacy. Look for it on tony menus. (It's not polite to gag, dear.)

- "New wave" pizza includes just about anything except tomato sauce and cheese. Try smoked duck, caviar, black beans, pheasant sausage, Thai chicken, and banana chutney.

- With little improvement to be expected in water quality in the next few years, consumers may turn away from fish. One exception will be fish raised on "farms," including crayfish, catfish, trout, salmon, redfish, sturgeon, striped bass, turbot, and abalone.

- Fast-food chains are experiencing saturation with burger outlets already on virtually every corner of every city street. Advertising battles may produce price wars in the hamburger kingdom. A boom is expected in one to three years, when new fat substitutes appear.

FARM FACTS

	1966	1976	1986	1991 (est.)
Total acres	1.13 bil.	1.08 bil.	1.01 bil.	0.98 bil.
Number of farms	3.3 mil.	2.7 mil.	2.2 mil.	2.0 mil.
Average farm size	348 acres	394 acres	456 acres	476 acres
Average value	$157/acre	$419/acre	$595/acre	$650/acre
Fertilizer used	34 mil. tons	49 mil. tons	20 mil. tons	17 mil. tons
Agricultural exports	$6 bil.	$23 bil.	$26 bil.	$40 bil.
Farm subsidies	$4 bil.	$3 bil.	$30 bil.	$12 bil.

WHAT'S NEW ON THE FARM

● *Compost* is hot. And it's finally getting mainstream respect in the way of composting kits, books, and videos. Commercial composting equipment is being sold to municipalities, now that there's an economic incentive to make organic soil conditioners.

● What else is hot: *Kenaf*, a prolific plant that has the potential to be a major substitute for wood pulp (see the 1990 *Old Farmer's Almanac*, page 98). *Psyllium*, a high-fiber, cholesterol-lowering seed in demand for use in laxatives and cereals (and currently grown almost exclusively in India). *Potato peels and whey from cheese making*, which can be used to make a degradable plastic — meaning more profits for food processors (no need to throw away 10 billion tons of potato peelings a year!).

● High-tech gadgets for farms will include electronic meters for measuring the sweetness of melons, and laser grass zappers, which are beamed at livestock fodder before feeding time to increase its digestibility and boost weight gains in cattle.

TECHNO-TRENDS

☞ **Lightweight concrete** — It floats and has more insulating value.

☞ **Chewing gum** — Its flavor is trapped in microscopic sponges to last longer.

☞ **Smart bricks** — They can respond to changes in the weather, improving energy efficiency.

☞ **"Fuzzy" air conditioners** — They use "fuzzy" logic, a computing program that makes complex decisions constantly to  find optimum operating conditions, thereby saving energy and producing consistent air temperature.

☞ **Fast beer** — A new process has cut brewing time from two months to three days.

OFFICE INNOVATIONS

● Desktop lunching joins desktop publishing, especially in large cities where it takes more than a lunch hour just to travel to and from restaurants. Caterers, restaurants, and groceries will offer FAX orders and delivery services.

● Offices may not get any larger, but they will get quieter, thanks to a new emphasis on sound insulation.

● Tiny cordless phones will connect with multiple-line telephone systems, allowing users to carry the phone from room to room, floor to floor.

● The punch clock is on the way out, replaced by computerized ID systems.

(continued on page 100)

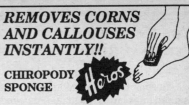

YOU AND YOUR PERSONAL ROBOT

On the verge of availability to the average consumer are new robotic machines that can mow lawns, vacuum rooms, and scrub floors. Another robot, initially available only to clothes manufacturers and cleaners, is the "intelligent iron" that presses clothes without human hands or sweat.

STYLE TRENDS: TIGHTS AND BAGGIES

☞ **Fabrics and fibers:** Mohair, cashmere, and angora will be in vogue as upscale, natural fibers. Cotton will gain new clout from plants that produce stronger fibers. A new generation of synthetic fibers will be able to be woven into fabric almost as thin as silk.

☞ **Colors:** Interior decor will emphasize warmer hues, particularly yellows, browns, and reds, for upholstery fabric, wall paints, wallpaper, and appliances.

☞ **Baggies:** Men's clothing will feature looser-fitting styles in suits, jackets, slacks, and even jeans. Call it a more natural, softer, rounder look — or just call it baggy.

☞ **Tights:** Thanks to the popularity of shorter skirts, sales of pantyhose, stockings, tights, and leggings are booming. Pantyhose from Japan will include skin lotions and perfumes. These therapeutic hose may catch on here, except for one variety that is uniquely Japanese — it contains tiny capsules of seaweed extract.

☞ **Shoe repair shops are back** — most of them in high-traffic areas such as shopping centers and large offices.

WHAT A DIFFERENCE A DECADE CAN MAKE

	1981	1991 (est.)
Asphalt use	280 mil. tons	900 mil. tons
Homes with microwave ovens	15 mil.	70 mil.
Economists employed by Federal government	5,500	8,000
Adults who fish	65 mil.	40 mil.
Credit cards in use	600 mil.	900 mil.
Credit card debt	$90 bil.	$510 bil.
Candy sales	$7 bil.	$14 bil.
Fur sales	$400 mil.	$300 mil.
Breast implants	72,000	150,000
Facelifts	39,000	100,000

Automated ministores with no human employees, except for restocking and cleaning, will sell compact discs. Customers make selections on computer screens and pay an automated teller machine; a robot arm picks out the desired disc and moves it to a check-out slot.

A Canadian company has developed a robotic sow, complete with prewarmed milk, to feed and mother the estimated 15 to 20 percent of newborn piglets who would die in overly large litters.

Finally, for the ultimate in effortless leisure activity, there's a robot fishing rod that senses when a fish bites, sets the hook, reels it in, and weighs the catch. It can land anything up to 66 pounds. But the bragging is still left up to the robot's owner. □ □

Author Kim Long has been researching and writing about consumer trends for the past eight years. He is the author of The American Forecaster Almanac, *an annual book about the future published by Johnson Books, Boulder, Colorado; 800-662-2665.*

The Miracle at Coogan's Bluff

BY MEL R. ALLEN

I
f they had not faced each other on that cold, dark afternoon in the Polo Grounds, if it had not been their fate to be involved in the single most dramatic moment in American sports, perhaps Ralph Branca and Bobby Thomson would have been friends all along.

Branca grew up in a large, close-knit Italian family in Mount Vernon, New York; Thomson in a large, close-knit Scottish clan in Staten Island. Tall, dark, strongly built — physically they might have been brothers. Indeed, at one time both bore the nickname "Hawk" for their wide-spaced eyes, high cheekbones, and prominent noses. But one man was a slugger, and the other was a fireballing pitcher, and 40 years ago one pitch and one swing joined them forever in our memory.

For a few minutes now, go back to that Wednesday afternoon, October 3, 1951, in the Polo Grounds beneath Coogan's Bluff along the Harlem River. Rain threatened, and by two o'clock the lights shone on the field. The old ballpark, home of the New York Giants, held nearly 60,000. But many fans were certain the final game of the National League playoffs between the New York Giants and the Brooklyn Dodgers would be canceled. When the historic game began, only 34,000 seats were filled.

The two teams were the most bitter rivals in baseball. During the season, fights would break out between the opposing players and the rival fans would battle in the stands. The 1951 pennant race had already proved perhaps the most exciting

> *"Now it is done. Now the story ends. And there is no way to tell it. The art of fiction is dead. Reality has strangled invention. Only the utterly impossible, the inexpressibly fantastic, can ever be plausible again...."*
>
> – Red Smith, writing after the "greatest baseball game ever played" between the Brooklyn Dodgers and the New York Giants, October 3, 1951.

in history. Giants manager Leo Durocher had hoped his team would contend, but they began the season miserably, losing 11 in a row during April. In May they brought up a minor-league sensation named Willie Mays to play center field, shifted Bobby Thomson from center to third base, and the Giants started to jell. But in mid-August they still remained 13½ games behind the Dodgers. Then it seemed as if a magic dust had been sprinkled on the team. Suddenly the Giants could not lose. They won 16 straight, and in the season's final week they caught the Dodgers to force the play-off. It had been the greatest comeback in baseball history.

The two teams split the opening two games of the play-offs, the Giants winning the first 3-1 behind Bobby Thomson's first inning home run off Ralph Branca, and the Dodgers the second 10-0.

Now the pitchers on both sides were worn down. Throughout the final, grueling month of the season, they had often pitched on only two days' rest. The Giants' starting pitcher was 23-game winner Sal "The Barber" Maglie. He was opposed by Don Newcombe, winner of 20 and possessor of one of the strongest arms in baseball.

In the first inning Maglie, normally a control pitcher, was wild, walking two. When Jackie Robinson singled, the Dodgers took a 1-0 lead. The Giants threatened in the second when Thomson followed a Whitey Lockman single with a smash to left. The speedy Thomson tried for a double without noticing that

Lockman had stopped on second. Too late, Thomson realized his mistake and was an easy out.

In the seventh a Monte Irvin double, a Lockman bunt, and a Thomson sacrifice fly tied the game. But in the eighth the Dodgers combined four hits, a wild pitch, and some sloppy Thomson fielding at third to take what seemed an insurmountable 4-1 lead. When Thomson came off the field, boos cascaded from the stands. He was clearly the goat in the biggest game of the year.

In the ninth inning the Dodgers and their rooters began releasing the pent-up emotions of a furious pennant race that finally seemed securely in their grasp. The Dodgers hooted at their hated rivals, "Where are you going to play tomorrow?" The Dodgers went out easily, but no matter. Only three more outs to go. And if Newcombe faltered, two-time all-star Ralph Branca and 16-game winner Carl Erskine were firing in the bull pen. Gordon McClendon on the

Liberty Radio Network told America: "Now the Giants, strangling, struggling for breath, three outs away from extinction, come up . . ."

Has there ever been a single inning in baseball to match the drama that built, batter after batter, in the Giants' half of the ninth? Al Dark led off with a single to right. Don Mueller followed with a grounder just beyond the reach of diving first baseman Gil Hodges. Runners on first and second, no outs. The Giants' cleanup hitter, Monte Irvin, at bat.

Charlie Dressen, the Dodgers' manager, considered removing Newcombe, but the big right-hander got Irvin on a pop-up. One out. But Whitey Lockman lined a double down the left field line, scoring Dark, while Mueller slid hard into third. The Polo Grounds erupted. The comeback Giants had the tying runs in scoring position.

Then a disturbing omen silenced the crowd. Don Mueller had caught his ankle sliding into third base, and it was

turning a horrible blue. As the crowd waited for a stretcher to carry Mueller off the field, Charlie Dressen picked up the phone in the dugout and spoke to Clyde Sukeforth, his bull-pen coach.

"How do they look?" Dressen asked.

"Erskine just bounced a curve," Sukeforth replied. "Branca's sharp." So it would be 25-year-old Ralph Branca. No matter that he had pitched eight innings two days before. No matter that when he first warmed up in the sixth inning, his arm had been so stiff he could not throw 50 feet. Now he was ready. "I relished the chance to be the hero," he would say years later. "I wanted the ball."

He wore number 13 and delighted in proving the number held no bad luck for him. He had been a star for five years wearing that number. Once he posed for a photograph with a black cat draped around his shoulder, his "13" jersey turned toward the camera.

He passed the exhausted Newcombe at the edge of the infield grass and they embraced. When he reached the mound, Branca turned to his grim-faced teammates and cracked a joke. "Anybody nervous?" he smiled.

As he warmed up, he thought of how he would pitch to the dangerous Bobby Thomson, who had hit safely in 15 straight games and homered in two of the past three.

Durocher called Thomson over to the third-base coaching box. "Boy, if you ever hit one, hit one now," Durocher said. As he walked to home plate, Thomson thought, "Leo, you're out of your mind."

Setting himself in the batter's box, Thomson repeated, "Be patient. Wait and watch. Wait and watch."

Branca's first pitch, a fastball, cut the heart of the plate for a called strike.

It has always hurt him that despite his years of stardom, his legacy as the man who threw "The Pitch" is all that endures.

Lockman standing at second could not believe that Thomson did not swing.

From his coach's box, Durocher yelled, "He'll come back with another fastball, Bobby. Be ready!"

On deck was a struggling Willie Mays, who already had struck out and hit into a double play. He began to pray, "Don't make me come to bat now, God. Please don't let it be me."

All season pitchers had been getting Thomson out with the high, inside fastball, and Branca's second pitch was a fastball inside, a "waste pitch" designed to move Thomson back off the plate, to set him up for the overhand, sinking curve on the outside corner.

There would never be the sinking curve, only this moment, frozen forever as Thomson took a quick step back and swung. The ball sailed on a line to left field. Branca whirled. "Sink, sink, sink!" he cried. Dodger left fielder Andy Pafko ran to the wall and stopped. The ball barely cleared the wall 315 feet away from home plate. The Giants had won the pennant, 5-4.

McClendon shouted into his microphone, "Wild pandemonium the likes I have never seen.... This is baseball's most amazing finish!" Throughout New York City a wild, frenzied roar erupted from the bowels of office buildings and spilled onto the streets, and for a moment people who had not listened to the game were frightened, thinking the shouts and cries could only mean atomic war.

Thomson leaped and danced around the bases. "Going around those bases, I couldn't believe what was happening to me," Thomson said after the game. "It felt as if I was actually living one of those middle-of-the-night dreams. Everything was hazy. I heard yells, I saw paper flying. I noticed people jumping in the air, but I just kept riding high on that cloud."

As Thomson rounded third, Leo Durocher leaped beside him and spiked his hero's foot. Bobby's widowed mother, with whom he lived in Staten Island, could not bear to watch the game in person and had snapped off the radio after the Dodgers' score in the eighth, too heartbroken to listen. Suddenly she heard a clamor as her neighbor, also a Scot, beat on the door shouting, "Bawbby did it!" In her excitement, Mrs. Thomson would later say, she had to do *something*, so she mopped the basement floor.

And what of Ralph Branca? He trudged off the mound, a figure of despair. In the locker room he sat numbly on a staircase. A photograph of Branca crying into his hands would be seen around the world. "You had to crouch before him and put your face just an inch or two away to hear his brief replies," wrote one reporter. Finally Branca dressed. Outside he saw a priest. "Why me, Father?" he asked.

The next day as Thomson entered Yankee Stadium to begin the World Series, a man hollered. He had the home run ball, he said. Thomson could have it for a World Series ticket. Thomson cornered the clubhouse man. "You've got to get me a ticket," he said. "There's a guy outside with the ball I hit!" The clubhouse man laughed. "He took me to my locker," said Thomson, "and opened it. 'Look, there's a dozen balls in there,' he told me. 'They all came from the guy who caught the ball!' "

The World Series was won by the New York Yankees four games to two,

but there was no doubt that the season belonged to the Giants, who taught a country never to quit.

Three years later Thomson would be traded from the Giants and soon after, in 1958, the Giants traded the Polo Grounds for San Francisco. Bobby Thomson retired in 1960, and the Polo Grounds, scene of baseball's greatest moment, was demolished in 1964.

He goes by Bob Thomson these days and is a businessman living in New Jersey. Now and then someone remarks, "You aren't *Bobby* Thomson, are you?" and he will say he is, and he knows that once again he will be asked to relive the miracle at Coogan's Bluff.

Ralph Branca is an insurance broker, and he still lives close to his boyhood home. The season after he surrendered the home run, the Dodgers tried to make him change his number. Branca refused. But that year he hurt his back and never regained his fastball; in his career he won only 12 more games. It has always hurt him that despite his years of stardom his legacy as the man who threw "The Pitch" is all that endures. "Even a murderer gets pardoned after 25 years," he says. "I've never been pardoned."

There was an uneasiness between Branca and Thomson for many years. Forty years has changed all that, and they find that their names, joined indelibly in baseball history, have become a drawing card of sorts.

Fans today can find Ralph Branca and Bobby Thomson together again, seated beside each other at baseball card shows. Their autographs will appear side by side: the all-star pitcher who is remembered only for a single fastball he did not get quite far enough inside, and the hitter who hit 264 home runs, but is remembered for only one.

And that one he knows was probably a mistake. "If I had been a good hitter," he says, "I never would have swung." □□

"Clean-up

The TROY-BILT® Junior TOMAHAWK® Chipper/Shredder rids your property of unsightly yard debris... and turns it into FREE mulch and compost material!

At last!...there's a FAST, EASY way to clean-up unsightly brush piles and other yard debris from around your property!

The Junior Model Chipper/Shredder is unlike anything previously available to suburban and small property owners.

It's as easy to use as a kitchen garbage disposal...costs less than a good quality mower...and takes up less space in your garage than a trash barrel.

Yet this compost dynamo solves one of the thorniest problems homeowners face in trying to keep their places looking nice ...what to do with all the leaves, brush, branches, prunings and other yard debris that accumulates so quickly.

No more bagging, dumping or accumulating yard debris!

With half the nation's landfills scheduled to close within five years, tossing out our yard debris with the trash could soon become a thing of the past.

But now, with the Junior TOMA-HAWK® Chipper/Shredder, you can easily reduce these yard wastes in bulk and put them to productive use.

Home Property
Machine"

Big, oversized hopper takes leaves, twigs and other loose materials by the armload!

The Junior TOMAHAWK Model beautifies your property this easily:

- ● *Eliminates ugly brush piles*- cleans up fallen branches, winter damage and yard debris after storms.

- ● *Puts Fall leaves to good use*- shreds Fall leaves into a fine, compost-like plant food for feeding your prize roses, your garden and your lawn!

- ● *Makes landscape chips*- turns branches up to 2″ thick into attractive wood chips for smothering weeds around trees and shrubs.

The Junior TOMAHAWK Chipper/Shredder's direct drive and weighted flywheel enable it to chip 2″ thick branches with ease.

Ideal for small or suburban properties!

The Junior Model is lightweight and completely portable...compact for easy storage... much quieter than larger machines...so trouble free it carries a Full No-Time-Limit Warranty... and best of all, so affordable that now suburban and small property homeowners can easily justify the convenience of owning a full performance shredder.

Makes attractive wood chips for landscaping and keeping down the weeds!

Recycles ALL your yard wastes!

Unsightly and hard to manage prunings, branches, weeds, suckers and garden leftovers can now be cleaned up on the spot and put to good use!

For complete information on this remarkable new small property "Clean-up Machine," please call or write TODAY.

Offbeat Museums

Liberace's 175-pound fur coat, a guitar made from an armadillo, and an exhibit devoted to goats are only three of the finds you can come across in funny little museums around the country. BY JAMIE KAGELEIRY

THE LOCK MUSEUM
TERRYVILLE, CONNECTICUT

People must feel very secure in Terryville. There are more locks in their Lock Museum — 18,000 at last count — than there are people in town. Lock history goes back further than you might think: there's a 4,000-year-old Egyptian securing device on display. Examples abound of locks made by the Eagle Lock Company and 40 other companies (earning Terryville the title, "Lock Town of America") that at one time or another busily turned out tumblers, padlocks, mail locks, skeleton keys, even a dog collar lock. For information: 203-589-6359.

R. A. KEMP'S MACK TRUCK MUSEUM
HILLSBORO, NEW HAMPSHIRE

More than 100 trucks and 26 tractors plus shovels, backhoes, and bulldozers have been brought here and fixed up by Mr. Kemp since 1953. "To me it's just a couple of yahds full of stuff," he reports. "I was a driver, back years ago, and always wanted just one Mack truck to fix up. It just got blown all out of hand. ..." Lucky for us — just about every variety of Mack, lots of shiny Mack bulldogs, and other trucks are here, and R.A. will let you wander around during daylight just about any day. 603-464-3386.

PHILLIPS MUSHROOM MUSEUM
KENNETT SQUARE, PENNSYLVANIA

Kennett Square is the mushroom capital of the world, home of Phillips Mushroom Farms, which sends out more than 10,000,000 pounds of fresh mushooms a year! You can learn all about the lore and the mystique of the mushroom at this museum. Did you know that mushrooms can be used as meat substitutes? That there are about 38,000 known species? That ancient Egyptians thought they promoted immortality? Information: 215-388-6082.

DAISY BB GUN PLANT AND AIR GUN MUSEUM
ROGERS, ARKANSAS

Daisy is the world's largest and oldest manufacturer of nonpowder guns and ammo; the plant spits out over

50,000,000 BBs a day! Daisy guns were so popular in the first half of this century that our success in World War II has been attributed in part to the crack shots who'd been practicing their entire childhoods with Daisy guns. Their museum houses guns dating back to the turn of the century, including their famous and still popular "Red Ryder" model, which just celebrated its 50th anniversary and is sure to stir the hearts and trigger fingers of many a grown-up boy and girl. 501-636-1200.

VENT HAVEN VENTRILOQUISM MUSEUM

FORT MITCHELL, KENTUCKY

Call anyone here a "dummy" and you'll get roundly scolded (though you won't know who's doing the screeching). "Figure" is the preferred term among the 500 creatures inhabiting the country's only ventriloquial museum. Permanent residents include replicas of Mortimer Snerd and Charlie McCarthy, who rose to fame (on — figure this one out — the radio) on the lap of "second banana" Edgar Bergen. The museum serves as the site of the annual ventriloquists' convention attracting 1,000 figures and their rides (that's at least 2,000 points of view on everything). 606-341-0461.

McILHENNY TABASCO COMPANY

AVERY ISLAND, NEW IBERIA, LOUISIANA

This is an outdoor museum of sorts, and it's truly a hot one. The McIlhenny Company is the one who spices up your life and your Bloody Mary — they're the originators and the country's largest producer of pepper sauce under their trademarked name, Tabasco. The fiery red stuff comes from pepper plants (you'll see them all over Avery Island), which are crushed with salt taken from an almost-hidden but bustling salt mine right there. 318-365-8173.

NATIONAL ATOMIC MUSEUM

ALBUQUERQUE, NEW MEXICO

At the country's only complete interpretive collection of nuclear weapons (and energy sources), you can learn about their construction, touch the scary things, and see the evolution of bombs. They've gone from looking bulging to bulbous to sleek. Nearby Los Alamos was the site of the country's first bomb test, and Kirtland Field is still the planning site for bombs of the future. 505-845-6670.

- Culver Pictures

THE ANGORA GOAT BREEDERS ASSOCIATION MUSEUM

ROCKSPRINGS, TEXAS

The Rocksprings area is the Mohair Capital of the World, producing 90 percent of U.S. mohair, and this is the only museum in America devoted to goats. There are stuffed goats, breeding charts, old pictures, and memorabilia of the annual Mohair Extravaganza in nearby Kerrville—for which an annual Mohair Queen is chosen (that's a better title than "Goat Queen," we guessed). You can enjoy the museum in under a half hour, and it's a great stop if you're at one of the two nearby state parks—Kickapoo Indian Caverns or Devil's Sinkhole. 512-683-3155.

INDIAN MOTORCYCLE MUSEUM

SPRINGFIELD, MASSACHUSETTS

The world's oldest motorcycle — an 1885 Daimler — is here, as well as an example of every single model Indian motorcycle ever created from 1901 to 1953. And they all work perfectly. That includes the collapsible, portable Indians manufactured for the Second World War and motorcycles with skis attached. "Indians are quiet," states the owner, perhaps explaining the almost cultlike loyalty they inspire. Come hear for yourselves: 413-737-2624.

JOHN DILLINGER HISTORICAL MUSEUM

NASHVILLE, INDIANA

After making off with over $1,000,000 from bank robberies, in 1934 John Dillinger was done in by the two things he said a man should never trust: a woman and an automatic pistol. You can see his blood-soaked death-night trousers here, meet a couple dozen wax replicas of FBI agents, gangsters, even the mysterious "Lady in Red." The gun he whittled to escape from the "escape-proof" Lake County jail and even a re-creation of Dillinger's morgue scene are displayed at this one-of-a-kind place, homage to a Hoosier gone bad. 812-988-7172.

BARBED WIRE MUSEUM

LA CROSSE, KANSAS

It was barbed wire that tamed the West, defining once and for all just whose land and whose cattle were whose. Since LaCrosse is the world's Barbed Wire Capital, it's the perfect spot for this off-the-beaten-path museum that extols the importance (and amazing designs) of barbed wire in our history. Call for hours: 913-222-3116.

LIBERACE MUSEUM

LAS VEGAS (where else?), NEVADA

All, or most, of what glitters is here at the Liberace Museum. That includes the world's finest collection of rare pianos (Chopin owned one of them), dozens of costumes, including a 175-pound Norwegian Blue Shadow Fox coat with a 16-foot train. Mr. Showmanship's cars are here, one of which is a 1962 Rolls (one of only seven made) completely mirrored in thousands of tiny mosaic tiles and etched with designs of galloping horses. 702-798-5595.

THE GRAND GUITAR

BRISTOL, TENNESSEE

This museum houses such musical obscurities as a guitar made from an armadillo (a hollowed out, dead armadillo) and a violin built with matchsticks, but that's not all. This place actually *is* a guitar. Lying on its side, the instrument/museum is 70 feet long, 35 feet high with a curved roof; windows create the "frets"

and the round sound hole. Joe Morrell, curator of the Grand Guitar for the last 25 years, says that, as far as he knows, his is the only guitar-shaped building in the world. Save some time for this place — there's a lot to see, including an old Gibson Electric shaped like the U.S.A., autoharps from the last century, a collection of fiddles shaped like farm tools, and instruments of famous musicians. The oldest radio station between Roanoke and Knoxville will soon be housed right here in the Guitar. 615-968-2277.

W. C. HANDY HOME AND MUSEUM

FLORENCE, ALABAMA

Born in this log cabin in 1873, W.C. left home at 19 and explored the country. He landed in Memphis when he was 36. Ed Crump was running for mayor that year, and W.C. wrote his campaign song for him. The song lasted longer than the mayor and became known as "The Memphis Blues," the first blues number ever preserved in musical notation, earning W. C. Handy the title of "Father of the Blues." The blues will lead you through the museum dedicated to Mr. Handy, where you can see the piano on which he composed his most famous song, "The St. Louis Blues," also his trumpet and his braille music library (he was blind for the last 15 years of his life). 205-760-6434.

HOOVER HISTORICAL CENTER

NORTH CANTON, OHIO

If you've been looking for domestic heaven, search no further, for here you'll find the most extensive collection of antique vacuum cleaners in the world. In one of many rooms filled with all types of cleaners, your eye sweeps from left to right to take in style changes, from the first 1908 Hoover that introduced bristles to the "beater bars" to hand- and foot-operated models. There's no admission fee, and outside are herb gardens around which you might picnic. 216-499-0287.

THE OLD FAN MUSEUM

DALLAS, TEXAS

Kurt House has a lot of fans. So many (almost 1,000), in fact, that he had to build a museum for them in the birthplace of the American Fan Collectors Club. Kurt's got water-powered fans from New England, belt-driven and steam-operated fans, and funeral parlor fans to blow flies away from the corpse. He's got fans that are 70 years old and "good for another 100." If it's a hot day in Texas, go shoot the breeze with the Fan Man. 214-559-4440.

THE POTATO MUSEUM

WASHINGTON, D.C.

When all those institutes, monuments, and memorials begin to taste a bit bland, head for the Potato Museum. Besides singing the sweet praises of spuds, this unique stop displays tools, potato postcards and lithographs, and the largest-ever private library of potato books. Call first: 202-544-1558. □□

FREE BOOKLET

The Energy Efficient LOG HOME

Traditional full log or insulated log kits with up to R-40 roof system. Handcrafted Northern White CEDAR or PINE logs. Complete kits priced from $9,900. Nationwide FREE DELIVERY. Dealership's available at no charge.

Send for the Free Log Home Lovers Design Booklet or order our new color Plan Book of 79 beautiful models.

MasterCard or Visa accepted.
Call TOLL FREE 1-800-558-5812 In Wisconsin Call 1-800-242-1021

Hand crafted

Log Homes Greatwood®

©1986

"Turn Over, Dear, for God's Sake, Turn Over!"

Snoring levels in excess of 80 decibels – equivalent to a pneumatic jackhammer – have been recorded, and an estimated 50 million Americans snore. So … can anything be done?

BY JIM COLLINS

*Till ere the splendid visions close
We snore quartettes of ecstasy in nose.*
　　　– Samuel Taylor Coleridge, 1790

T is said that snoring is the only human frailty that bothers the subject not at all; it merely makes life miserable for those who are forced to endure it. True enough. But one night legendary Texas gunfighter John Wesley Harding made life miserable for the fellow snoring in the adjacent hotel room. He shot a bullet through the wall and killed the snorer in his sleep.

If the incident is isolated (it isn't unique: in December 1983 a Dallas woman calmly pulled a gun from beneath the covers and fired five shots into her bedmate who "snored too loudly"), at least the motive behind such a violent reaction is familiar to many. Countless hours of sleep have been lost over the years in army barracks, dormitories, and bedrooms, causing severe embarrassment, ruining hunting trips, straining relationships, and worse. A 1971 issue of *Eye Ear Nose Throat Monthly* reported that snoring had finally been declared legal grounds for divorce.

Chuckle if you will. Snorers have long been the stuff of humor, from Charles Dickens's character Joe in *The Posthumous Papers of the Pickwick Club* to memorable scenes by Zero Mostel and "The Three Stooges." Over in the medical community, however, no one is laughing. In addition to its social implications, snoring has been linked with elevated blood pressure, cardiovascular stress, headaches, depression, excessive sleepiness, and fatigue. Behind alcohol, excessive sleepiness is the second leading cause of highway fatalities, and fatigue costs American industry an estimated $70 billion each year in lowered productivity and avoidable accidents.

WHO SNORES THE MOST?

As the old adage says, "Laugh and the world laughs with you. Snore and you sleep alone." True, but if you do snore, you aren't alone in your isolation. An estimated 50 million Americans are afflicted with the ailment. And you certainly aren't in poor company. Twenty of the first 32 U.S. presidents were known to snore, including Washington, Lincoln, both Adamses, both Roosevelts, Taft, Hoover, and Grant. So were Mussolini (he was renowned), Hemingway, Lord Chesterfield, and even Beau Brummel, the ladies' man.

Between the ages of 20 and 35, 20 percent of all American men and five percent of all American women snore; by age 60 the percentages rise to 60 and 40, respectively. These statistics don't lie. Men are much more likely to snore than women; old people more likely than young. So there's a good chance you're either already snoring or you will be in the near future. Or you know somebody close to you who does or will. What, then, is there to do?

EXACTLY WHY WE SNORE

Snoring, very simply, is caused by the vibrations of the soft tissues at the back of the throat. The sounds originate from restricted air flowing through the collapsible part of the airway — roughly from the epiglottis to the choanae — where there is no rigid support. The seriousness of the snoring depends entirely on how restricted that airway is.

In general, three factors contribute to the bad vibrations: weak or inadequate musculature, space-occupying masses encroaching on the airway, and obstructed nasal breathing. Different factors influence people to different degrees, sometimes alone and sometimes in combination.

The first factor explains why most snoring occurs during the deep stages of sleep, when the muscles in the back of the throat relax, lose their tone, even fold into each other. The relaxed, limp muscles of the upper throat descend into the airway, and the tongue falls back, causing vibration. Understanding gravity, it's easy to see why snoring often occurs when people sleep on their backs. Understanding aging, it's easy to see how less active, more sedentary people are

'Tis easy to snore,
Hard to ignore.

often afflicted. And since the aging process tends to have a greater impact on men's muscle tone than on women's (men simply have more mass that can atrophy), it's easy to start understanding why men are the more common snorers. There's no truth, then, to the old husbands' tale that primitive men snored to protect their women, their noises frightening away the nightly beasts of prey.

The second factor — things that take up room in the vicinity of the airway — can sometimes be blamed on heredity. In children, for instance, snoring can almost always be traced to enlarged tonsils and adenoids. And while the average-sized uvula (that fleshy, lobe-shaped thing that hangs down in the back of your throat) measures a quarter inch, some poor souls have one that's closer to four times that. Inherited traits can be exacerbated, too. Obese people are three times more likely to snore than thin ones (their bulkiness and lack of muscle tone extend throughout their bodies, not just the visible parts). Smokers irritate their pharynxes daily, causing mucous membranes to swell, narrowing the airway. So if you had to guess who snores and you picked a large, sedentary, male smoker — say, Orson Welles, just to pick a name (he was a first-class snorer) — you'd most probably be right.

The third factor involves obstructed or irregular nasal breathing. Congestion, hay fever, polyps, even a deviated septum from your old boxing days can be the culprit, creating negative pressure during inspiration, which in turn draws together the soft tissues of the collapsible airway. Which in turn causes snoring.

During the most advanced stage of snoring, the passage becomes completely blocked. The sleeper actually

> **The method of choice today is a pocket sewn on the back of a pajama top, containing a marble, golf ball, or tennis ball.**

stops breathing for a period before he is jolted awake — which causes the relaxed muscles to tighten and reopen the airway. Labored breathing may continue for a while before the process is repeated, then repeated again, often accompanied by gasping, choking, and violent body spasms. Known as obstructed sleep apnea (from the Greek *apnea,* "for want of breath"), the social fallout of the condition is obvious, but it's nothing compared with the more serious dangers: apnea has led to severe behavioral, cardiac, and pulmonary problems and in several instances sleep apnea has resulted in cardiac arrest and death. So much for quartets of ecstasy.

OLD-TIME "CURES"

The most popular cure for snoring, historically, can be traced back to the Revolutionary War, when soldiers sewed a small cannonball into a pocket on the back of a snoring comrade's nightshirt. Variations on this device — intended to discourage the sleeper from sleeping on his back, thus keeping the tongue forward and the airway open — have appeared periodically ever since then. Leonidas Wilson applied for a patent in 1900 on a leather harness that strapped a multipronged object between the wearer's shoulder blades. Other antisnoring devices (there are more than 300 registered with the U.S. Patent Office, most of them invented by men) include all manner of straitjackets and restraining harnesses based on the same premise. The method of choice today is a pocket sewn on the back of a pajama top, containing (in lieu of a cannonball)

a marble, golf ball, or tennis ball. Some creative people have been known to use jacks or bottle caps. The message is the same as a sharp elbow from a companion or a shoe thrown across a bunk room: Turn over.

For many mild or infrequent snorers, these methods are successful, even to the point of conditioning the snorer to abandon sleeping on his back. Trouble is, not all snorers are mild or infrequent. Seven

out of ten snore just as well on their sides as on their backs.

Other attempts have focused on extending the snorer's neck or jaw to help keep the airway open, as in Cyrus Johnson's mouth-restraining device patented in 1948 or the ground-breaking experiments of St. Louis physician Robert Elman in the early 1960s. A more common approach has been to force the snorer's mouth shut — thereby forcing him to breathe through his nose. (Francis Pulford's "facial molding device" did that in 1893, as did John Rothenberger's "anti-mouth breathing device" 26 years later.) Apparently proponents of this method overlook the possibility of the nose being obstructed at the same time, leaving the snorer no way to breathe at all. Or maybe they *don't* overlook that possibility....

Still other devices have come and gone and come again. Nasal tubes. Neck collars. Chin straps. Respirators. Even sophisticated electronic gadgets that de-

ARCHEOLOGY PROVES THE BIBLE!

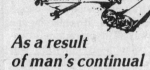

As a result of man's continual search for truth,

archeological discoveries have unearthed many artifacts which establish Biblical records as both reliable and accurate.

• • •

The booklet, "Archeology Proves the Bible" unveils these findings and confirms the validity of Bible truths — historic and prophetic.

• • •

Discover the ancient Bible cities — Ur, Ninevah, Jericho, Babylon. In the past, skeptics questioned the very existence of some of these ancient cities. But the spade and pick of the archeologist have uncovered their ruins in the very locations in which the Bible places them!

• • •

Your confidence in God's Word will be confirmed and strengthened as you read this little booklet. Send for your free copy now, with no obligation.

• • • • • •

Send TODAY for your FREE copy of "Archeology Proves the Bible" **DAWN PUBLICATIONS, Dept. F East Rutherford, NJ 07073**

TURN YOUR TIMBER INTO CASH!

FOLEY-BELSAW ONE-MAN SAWMILL

Goes right to the trees!

FOLEY BELSAW

The only ONE-MAN PORTABLE SAWMILL of its kind in the world!

If you need good, high-quality lumber, don't let inflated lumber prices stop your important building projects. The Foley-Belsaw goes right to the trees and turns out smooth, true-cut lumber... even beginners get excellent results. Just one man (no crew needed) can easily cut enough on weekends to save hundreds of dollars over high lumberyard prices. For power use tractor PTO or other low HP diesel or electric unit. Factory direct selling keeps price low, and convenient time payments may be arranged.

Send for FREE BOOK! Just mail coupon below for *"How To Saw Lumber"* booklet and complete facts on the One-Man Sawmill. There is NO Obligation and NO Salesman Will Call on you. **Do It TODAY!**

HOW TO SAW LUMBER

FREE BOOKLET

ONE-MAN SAWMILL
Foley-Belsaw Co.
6301 Equitable Rd., Dept. 30899
Kansas City, Mo. 64120

Please send all facts and details plus FREE 'How To Saw Lumber' Booklet. There is No Obligation and No Salesman Will Call on me.

Name _____

Address _____

City _____

State _____ Zip _____

---

liver shocks or other startling stimuli to patients when they snore. Mail order catalogs are filled with these "guaranteed" cures and "miracle" treatments. "They all work for some people," says Dr. Martin Scharf, sleep specialist at Cincinnati's Mercy Hospital of Fairfield. "They're all worth a try. But first try nasal spray."

WHAT YOU SHOULD DO NOW

Taking Dr. Scharf's approach, there are some simple, proven methods that snorers may want to try before spending money on expensive gadgetry. All of them come down to this: understand the simple physiology behind snoring, then do things to your body that help reduce or eliminate the contributing factors. For instance:

1. Reduce your weight and tone your muscles. Better eating habits and general exercise will help firm up the flaccid throat tissues causing so much noise.

2. Better still, perform prescribed "mouth exercises" to isolate the particular jaw and throat muscles that affect the air passageway. Learn some from your local sleep disorders clinic.

3. Avoid eating large meals or taking depressants or muscle relaxants before going to bed. This includes alcohol, warm milk, antihistamines, and ironically, sleeping pills. Take instead prescription medications that clear nasal passages, stimulate respiration, or promote wakefulness.

4. Sleep on a firm mattress with a single pillow in a cool, well-ventilated room. Don't use a large pillow or pillows that force you to bend at the waist or neck (which puts pressure on the diaphragm and abdomen). Tilting the entire bed by placing bricks below the bedposts at the head of the bed will help relieve pressure in those same areas and drain congested nasal passages.

5. Consult your allergist — your solution may be as simple as replacing a feather pillow with a synthetic one.

6. Quit smoking.

There are, of course, more drastic solutions. Orthodontic appliances can be fitted. Machines providing "continuous, positive airway pressure" can be prescribed. Routine surgery can remove polyps or straighten septums. Other surgery can trim away some of the excess tissue in the throat cavity, enlarging the air passageway. (The procedure is uvulopharyngopalatoplasty, but you might want to refer to it as UPPP when you inquire about it.) And there are medications that might work in your particular situation. The best advice? Consult your family physician or an ear, throat, and nose specialist, especially if you suspect you suffer from apnea. You'll sleep better for it. And so will your spouse.

A final thought. Snoring levels in excess of 80 decibels have been recorded in the lab — equivalent to a pneumatic jackhammer blasting concrete. (The deep-throated diesel sounds from the back of a Greyhound bus are closer to 40.) Winston Churchill was said to be a 35-decibel man, though he doesn't come close to fellow Brit Melvyn Switzer, the current world record holder. On June 28, 1984, Switzer hit a peak of 87.5 decibels. They say his wife, Julie, is deaf in one ear. □□

WHERE TO TURN

Stop Your Husband from Snoring, Derek S. Lipman, M.D., Rodale Press (1990). Send $8.95 to P.O. Box 4444, Portland, OR 97208.

How to Stop Snoring, Lois Rosenthal, Writer's Digest Books (1986). Send $7.95 plus $2 postage to Writer's Digest Books, 9933 Alliance Road, Cincinnati, OH 45242.

Association of Sleep Disorders Centers 604 2nd St. S.W. Rochester, MN 55902

(There are more than 2,000 sleep disorders centers across the U.S. and Canada.)

Fishing Breakthrough Catches Too Many Fish... Banned In Some States!!!

After years of research and development by a multi-billion dollar corporation, a fishing device has been developed that actually works TOO well. It's called the FISHTECH 2000 and is so effective, that it has actually been granted more than ten worldwide patents. Unlike other fish attractants that may only get the attention of single fish, the incredible FISHTECH 2000 actually draws the ENTIRE SCHOOL of fish to your line!

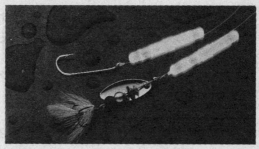

Works equally as well with hooks & lures.

UNBELIEVABLE EXPERIENCE

Here's how it works. FISHTECH 2000 is a slender 1½ inch stick that is attached to any fishing line, approximately 2 inches above your hook or lure. Using a highly sophisticated technology known as "Chemiluminescence", this device shoots an unbelievably brilliant beam of green light piercing through even the murkiest water. Within seconds, the nearest school is surrounding your line fighting to get at your bait or lure. The results are absolutely amazing! Just look at these unbelievable real life experiences:

"One August day I was trolling for King salmon on Lake Huron. A friend of mine gave me a package of [Fishtech devices] to try out. I started trolling one hour before daylight. I trolled with 4 lines. On 2 of these lines I attached the [Fishtech devices]. We landed 8 Kings ranging from 9 to 19 lbs., all on the 2 lines with [Fishtech]. The other 2 lines only had 2 strikes, we missed both fish. Thanks to your product, my son and I had a great fishing trip."

J.B. - Milford, MI

"I've been fishing for more than 35 years. The new [Fishtech 2000] are sure a shot in the arm for the old sport. They're a fisherman's dream. I used them for ice fishing. [Put one Fishtech device on my line.] 16 good eaters in less than one hour. Best was smelting. Tied some [Fishtech] devices to the nets. Dropped the nets into the dark waters... and whamo. Over 900 smelts and 2 salmon in ½ hour.

D.U. - Ciero, IL

Reports are coming in from across the nation of unheard of fishing experiences. What's more, the amazing FISHTECH 2000 is probably the only attractant that can be used on ALL species of fish. From deep sea fishing off the coast of Bermuda, to fresh water fishing for trout and bass, FISHTECH 2000 will catch more fish than you've ever dreamed about!

ENVIRONMENTALLY SAFE

FISHTECH'S incredible brightness is generated by a technologically advanced process in which two non-toxic ingredients interact within a confined hollow 1½ inch tube. This process is activated by flexing the tube and lasts for about 4 hours. It is completely non-toxic and safe to the environment.

FISHTECH 2000 is so effective that it has actually been barred for use in the pursuit of gamefish in some states (Minnesota and Wyoming) and parts of Canada. Some officials feel that the use of this device gives the leisure fisherman too much of an advantage. They are however used regularly for commercial fishing (99.9% of all Swordfish caught in this country are caught using a FISHTECH 2000 type device) and are absolutely LEGAL in most of the country.

BEST FISHING DAY

Try the amazing FISHTECH 2000 for yourself. If you don't have the best fishing day you've ever had in your life, we'll gladly refund your money. Also we'd like you to write to us about your fishing experience with FISHTECH 2000 for use in future ads. Thanks for your order and good fishing!

© *Direct Marketing of Virginia, Inc. 1990, (2331)*

1. Same.

2. Only 3 opening (0), and 12 second (2) moves; all others being rotations or reflections. Never, unless first player errs.

0	2	2
	2	2
		2

0	2	
2	2	
2	2	

	2	2
	0	

3. You can, every time. It is 9 times the original difference.

4. Yes. For example, a baby born in the east at 1:00 A.M., EST, first day of the 1990s is an hour older than a western birth at 11 P.M., PST, last day of the 1980s.

5. They will meet at successively increasing distances from alternate ends of the pool, 29 times.

6. a.) 17 mph.

b.) About 31d, 4h, 40m.

7. a.) Pinch AB in half at H.

b.) Bring D to H and fold flat.

c.) TC = (AC)/3.

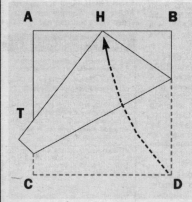

8. He took 1 coin from roll 1, 2 from 2, etc., marked and weighed them together. Against a total of all 10-gram coins, a weight 1 gram less indicated roll 1, 2 grams short meant roll 2, etc.

9. Noncannibal, noncannibal, and cannibal, in order. Key: first man will answer "non," regardless. Therefore, number two's confirmation of the "non" makes him a truth-teller, in view of number three's blanket statement.

10. 120.

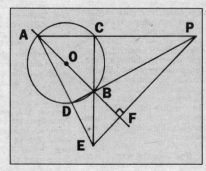

11. At least 2 simple types of construction: 1.) The bisector of an arc about P crossing AB at G + H (not shown), or: 2.) A circle on diameter AB, and the connector of similar right triangles formed with the 4 intersections of 2 lines to the circle.

Details of Puzzle 11, other elaborations, and Prize Set answers to any reader sending $1 and a SASE to:
Puzzle Answers
1991 Old Farmer's Almanac,
Dublin, NH 03444.

12-15. Prize set. See instructions, page 198.

TABLE OF MEASURES

APOTHECARIES'

1 scruple = 20 grains
1 dram = 3 scruples
1 ounce = 8 drams
1 pound = 12 ounces

AVOIRDUPOIS

1 ounce = 16 drams
1 pound = 16 ounces
1 hundredweight = 100 pounds
1 ton = 2000 pounds
1 long ton = 2240 pounds

CUBIC MEASURE

1 cubic foot = 1728 cubic inches
1 cubic yard = 27 cubic feet
1 cord = 128 cubic feet
1 U.S. liquid gallon = 4 quarts = 231 cubic inches
1 Imperial gallon = 1.20 U.S. gallons = 0.16 cubic feet
1 board foot = 144 cubic inches

DRY MEASURE

2 pints = 1 quart
4 quarts = 1 gallon
2 gallons = 1 peck
4 pecks = 1 bushel

LIQUID MEASURE

4 gills = 1 pint
2 pints = 1 quart
4 quarts = 1 gallon
63 gallons = 1 hogshead
2 hogsheads = 1 pipe or butt
2 pipes = 1 tun

LINEAR MEASURE

1 foot = 12 inches
1 yard = 3 feet
1 rod = 5½ yards
1 mile = 320 rods = 1760 yards = 5280 feet
1 Int. nautical mile = 6076.1155 feet
1 knot = 1 nautical mile per hour
1 furlong = ⅛ mile = 660 feet = 220 yards
1 league = 3 miles = 24 furlongs
1 fathom = 2 yards = 6 feet
1 chain = 100 links = 22 yards
1 link = 7.92 inches
1 hand = 4 inches
1 span = 9 inches

SQUARE MEASURE

1 square foot = 144 square inches
1 square yard = 9 square feet
1 square rod = 30¼ square yards = 272¼ square feet

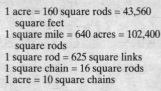

1 acre = 160 square rods = 43,560 square feet
1 square mile = 640 acres = 102,400 square rods
1 square rod = 625 square links
1 square chain = 16 square rods
1 acre = 10 square chains

HOUSEHOLD MEASURES

120 drops of water = 1 teaspoon
60 drops thick fluid = 1 teaspoon
2 teaspoons = 1 dessertspoon
3 teaspoons = 1 tablespoon
16 tablespoons = 1 cup
2 cups = 1 pint
2 pints = 1 quart
4 quarts = 1 gallon
3 tablespoons flour = 1 ounce
2 tablespoons butter = 1 ounce
2 cups granulated sugar = 1 pound
3¾ cups confectioner's sugar = 1 pound
3½ cups wheat flour = 1 pound
5⅓ cups dry coffee = 1 pound
6½ cups dry tea = 1 pound
2 cups shortening = 1 pound
1 stick butter = ½ cup
2 cups cornmeal = 1 pound
2¾ cups brown sugar = 1 pound
2⅜ cups raisins = 1 pound
9 eggs = 1 pound
1 ounce yeast = 1 scant tablespoon

METRIC

1 inch = 2.54 centimeters
1 centimeter = 0.39 inch
1 meter = 39.37 inches
1 yard = 0.914 meters
1 mile = 1609.344 meters = 1.61 kilometers
1 kilometer = .62 mile
1 square inch = 6.45 square centimeters
1 square yard = 0.84 square meter
1 square mile = 2.59 square kilometers
1 square kilometer = 0.386 square mile
1 acre = 0.40 hectare
1 hectare = 2.47 acres
1 cubic yard = 0.76 cubic meter
1 cubic meter = 1.31 cubic yards
1 liter = 1.057 U.S. liquid quarts
1 U.S. liquid quart = 0.946 liter
1 U.S. liquid gallon = 3.78 liters
1 gram = 0.035 ounce
1 ounce = 28.349 grams
1 kilogram = 2.2 pounds
1 pound avoirdupois = 0.45 kilogram

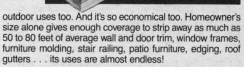

NOW AVAILABLE IN COMMERCIAL PRE-MIX, simply apply—let set—and lift away paint in one single action.

- Ends sanding—scraping—spraying—chipping—steel wool virtually FOREVER!

- Amazing European discovery turns layers of paint into a single sheet, so it LIFTS AWAY INTACT!

- There are NO TOXIC FUMES and NO FLAMMABLE SOLVENTS!

You've seen it on TV's "THIS OLD HOUSE." You've read about it in newspapers and magazines. Now here it is, the amazing wonder formula that starts to penetrate old paint (shellac and varnish, too) IN JUST MINUTES! Transforms it into a soft, plastic-like film. Then simply let set . . . lift, roll, strip up to 30 coats of paint away in a single lift-away action! Years of built-up paint, lift away quick and easy.

"PEEL-AWAY" will also remove painted or unpainted wallpaper.

SIMPLY COAT IT ON—LET SET—SEE IT TURN PAINT TO "PAPER"—AND PEEL IT AWAY IN A SINGLE LIFT-OFF ACTION!

And now it's even easier than ever to apply, because easy to use, "PEEL-AWAY" comes in a NEW READY-MIX formula. Ready to use, just coat onto practically any painted surface, (except on factory baked finishes such as cars, washing machines, etc.) press down special "PEEL-AWAY" magic Liftex Strip away cloth . . . let formula set and adhere to surface and lift away old paint. It is as simple and easy as that!

SO ECONOMICAL TOO! REMOVES YEARS OF BUILT-UP PAINT . . . UP TO 30 LAYERS AT A TIME!

"PEEL-AWAY" is every home-owners dream come true. Ideal for indoors on walls, windows, furniture, etc.—Plus 101
© 1990 Dumond Chemicals, Inc.

outdoor uses too. And it's so economical too. Homeowner's size alone gives enough coverage to strip away as much as 50 to 80 feet of average wall and door trim, window frames, furniture molding, stair railing, patio furniture, edging, roof gutters . . . its uses are almost endless!

SAVES WORK! SAVES TIME! SAVES MONEY! MAKES TAKING OFF PAINT ALMOST AS EASY AS PUTTING IT ON!

So for the new low-cost, super-fast way to lift away old paint . . . lift away old varnish and shellac . . . order your "PEEL-AWAY" today on a full money-back guarantee.

For hardwoods, PEEL-AWAY should only be used when surface is to be repainted. Do not use when you wish to reveal the natural color of the wood. Use PEEL-AWAY Hardwood #6, see coupon.

The Whole Scary Truth About Fire Ants

BY RICHARD CONNIFF

O n May 29, 1945, a United States Department of Agriculture researcher named William F. Buren stopped to examine a large ant nest along U.S. Route 98 near Daphne, Alabama. If this were a period science fiction movie — and it has all the ingredients, including a creepy ending — then the earth would have begun to tremble as Buren crouched down to collect a sample. Ominous organ music would build up on the sound track as he disturbed the nest. And then the maw of the earth would rip open, and what would come seething and lurching up, spattering Buren's shoes and driving him back to his car, first in disbelief, then in terror, would be the source of the next 45 years of blood-curdling headlines: "The Invasion of the Fire Ants ... Red Tide ... Masters of Destruction ... *The Ants from Hell.*"

What Buren had documented, for the first time in this country, was an infestation of red imported fire ants, a small, harmless-looking South American species. They were by no means the first fire ants in North America, which already had several native species as well as an imported black fire ant accidentally introduced in about 1918. But red imported fire ants proved to be far more active, building 40 nests to the acre where their native counterparts built only four, and they were also more aggressive. Over the

> *Their sting isn't as painful as a bee's. They're not as damaging to agriculture as many pests. They even eat boll weevils. And yet most everyone agrees these rapidly advancing little buggers are no less than "fiends from hell."*

next four decades they were to spread from their port of entry, Mobile, Alabama, across 260 million acres in 11 southern states and put themselves in a position to sting (usually more than once) an estimated three to five million outraged Americans a year.

The red imported fire ant was also destined to become a classic object of insect-phobia. Traveling everywhere ahead of its front lines was a coterie of horror stories that were rarely, if ever, documented: fire ants climbing the umbilical cords of newborn calves to attack their eyes and mouths, ultimately killing them, or children who'd fallen on fire ant mounds and died from an allergic reaction to the stings.

These stories together with the headlines that accompanied the fire ant's progress ("Uncontrolled Fire Ants Ravage South," "Texas Losing Ground in War with Killer Ants") were often reminiscent of a nightmarish, mid-20th-century short story, "Leiningen Versus the Ants," read by generations of high school students. In it a Brazilian plantation owner, supremely confident in the power of the human brain, prepares to resist the advance of a 20-square-mile army of "ants, nothing but ants! And every single one of them a fiend from hell; before you can spit three times they'll eat a full-grown buffalo to the bones...."

With moats, an insecticidal spray, and the help of 400 "peons," the plantation battles the sea of "thumb-long" ants for days, eyeball to "brilliant, cold" eyeball, shovels to "razor-sharp mandibles," before Leiningen triumphs, having been chewed to the bone in no more than one or two places.

The trouble with the story is that, in real life, Leiningen lost. For 20 years the U.S. government and the states waged a massive aerial pesticide war on the red imported fire ant, spraying heptachlor and mirex over tens of millions of acres from Florida to Texas. The main effect was to kill wildlife (the heptachlor program figured largely in Rachel Carson's *Silent Spring*) and put dangerous chemicals into the human food chain, while also inadvertently *spreading* imported fire ants. The pesticides knocked back all ant species, and the fire ant, a weedy creature with appalling reproductive potential and few natural enemies outside of South America, quickly took the place of its former competitors. The pesticide campaign, which cost $172 million, entered environmental history as "the Vietnam of entomology."

The good news, if you can call it that, was that real-life fire ants weren't as bad as the diabolical ants that Leiningen faced, nor even as bad as their own advance publicity. Indeed, fire ants might serve as a perfect case study of unreasonable human fears of the natural world, except that nothing about fire ants is clearcut. They are a remarkably changeable creature, and the people who study them are accustomed to shaking their heads in wonder and remarking, "Just when you think you know everything about fire ants, they turn around and make a fool of you." About all one can safely say is that if fire ants aren't quite "sons of hell"

(daughters would be more like it, since the males live only long enough to mate), they aren't real nice either.

Probably nobody hates fire ants worse than farmers, though you wouldn't want to judge a competition on this point. Fire ants sting farm workers and drive them from the fields. Their sun-hardened mounds, up to 18 inches high, require harvesting equipment operators either to raise their cutter bars, losing a substantial chunk of the crop, or risk bending and fouling the hardware. A typical complaint begins, "I put in three elevator chains in one season cutting beans, and they don't cost but $400 a chain," and from there it often escalates into angry plans for nuclear annihilation of fire ants (all other remedies having failed). Fire ants also eat some crops, in one case wiping out half of a Florida farmer's eggplants and causing an estimated loss upwards of $60,000.

The fire ant might easily have replaced that other notorious import, the boll weevil, as the archfiend of southern agriculture, except for one thing — and it is just the sort of thing to tip an enraged farmer with a broken elevator chain right over the edge: Fire ants eat boll weevils, sugar cane borers, and almost every other kind of insect pest, making it possible to argue that they may actually be beneficial to agriculture. Even considering the damage they do, fire ants rank far down on the list of pests, well behind such notorious public enemies as the mole cricket and the green peach aphid.

Fire ants also, of course, do plenty of nonagricultural damage. For reasons no one yet understands, they are attracted to electrical fields, and on his desk at Texas A & M, researcher Brad Vinson has a circuit breaker into which the fire ants appear to have been pressure packed. In 1986 alone, Houston Lighting and Power found that fire ants in transformers caused 28 outages involving 50 to 100 homes each. It is the sort of thing that drives people to dream up ingenious new ways to kill fire ants and, incidentally, make a million dollars. One device, called the Electracat, purported to zap 'em with electricity. During a field test, fire ants used the device as a nest.

But what makes fire ants seem diabolical to humans isn't the material damage they do. It's their abundance and their sting, which they apply liberally to farm workers, to suburbanites, and increasingly, to city dwellers. Fire ant mounds are everywhere in the South, making it difficult for people to stage a backyard barbecue in peace and impossible for their children to lie in the grass and see imaginary shapes in the clouds. Fire ants enter buildings and sometimes sting people in their beds — provoking at least three lawsuits on behalf of incapacitated nursing home patients. Mark Trostle of the Texas Department of Agriculture has found fire ants nesting 14 stories high in the dirt accumulated on a flat roof. He once responded to a case involving a Northern family transferred to Texas by IBM. Their child flipped a light switch in their new home and a fire ant fell out and stung him, causing a severe allergic reaction. When he got out of the hospital, the family grabbed the first plane north, where the winters are too cold for the ghastly tropical profusion of fire ants.

But fire ants, which tend to be as big as a freckle rather than a thumb, by and large don't eat people to the bone, and their sting produces no allergic reaction in an estimated 99 percent of human victims. The sting is less painful than a bee sting, and it passes quickly. Unlike bees, fire ants often sting more than once and usually in large groups. But the most common result is a cluster of yellow pustules, like pimples, which may itch for a week or more.

Hyperallergenic people sometimes die from fire ant stings, as they do from bee stings, but most know enough to seek treatment before the symptoms become life threatening. Unfortunately, no solid statistics exist, in part because deaths from fire ant stings aren't easy to distinguish from routine cases of cardiac arrest. In the absence of such data, what stick in people's minds are the horror stories, the ungodly possibilities rather than the extremely low probabilities. In Bostrop, Texas, last year, for example, police found an elderly man dead in his home, probably from heart attack, but possibly — shades of Leiningen — from the fire ants discovered building a mound on his chest. It is a story against which data, plain facts, and common sense never stand a chance.

Because fire ants have spread so rapidly in this country and behaved so often in unexpected ways, researchers often wonder aloud what they will do next. In truth, no one really knows. Red imported fire ants mate once, in a nuptial flight that takes them to an altitude of 800 feet. The females come back to earth and usually build new nests within a half mile of their starting point, in itself an effective means of colonizing new worlds. But they also like to land in shiny places, perhaps as a built-in way of finding water, and thus they often wind up not just in swimming pools, but on cars and trucks.

Highway inspection stations in New Mexico, Arizona, and California find

> *One device ... purported to zap 'em with electricity. When researchers ran a field test, fire ants used the device as a nest.*

them almost daily holed up in shipments of nursery stock and also amid less predictable merchandise like VCRs. In 1988 imported fire ants established short-lived outposts around Phoenix and Santa Barbara, and in 1989 they turned up in an arboretum in Philadelphia. Richard Paterson, who runs the USDA's fire ant research program in Gainesville, Florida, predicts that imported fire ants will colonize California within the next 10 years and that their territory will ultimately extend up the West Coast almost to the Canadian border and up the East Coast to Long Island. Skeptics dispute this prediction. But others note that red imported fire ants in northern Alabama and Mississippi have begun to hybridize with the black imported fire ants that preceded them. They suggest that the hybrid may yet overcome the traditional impediments of cold or dry climates and spread even farther, if only as an indoor pest. Shopping malls, which carefully shield their customers from nature, may inadvertently provide a perfect fire ant habitat in their planted arboretums.

Another more worrisome change is that, over the last 10 years, a new and even less pleasant form of red imported fire ant has appeared and covered large areas of Texas with 400 mounds per acre, instead of a mere 40.

The old-fashioned imported fire ant mound has a single queen capable of laying eggs. If she succeeds in establishing a colony and building it to maturity, a single queen weighing 24 milligrams will produce up to 800 grams of offspring annually — roughly the equivalent of a 120-pound woman giving birth to 500,000 eight-pound babies a year ("You can do it, honey, just keep panting!"). But the new fire ant mounds may have up to *300* egg-laying queens, producing altogether vastly more offspring. And, whereas single-queen mounds are strictly territorial, quickly killing any intruder, multiple-queen colonies mix freely with their neighbors, forming huge supercolonies over an acre or more in size. Along highways, densities may run as high as 800 mounds per acre, and ambulance crews frequently have to remove fire ants from accident victims.

Most Texans see multiple-queen fire ants as a nuisance, even a damned bad nuisance, but not as a threat to their lives. They are learning that if they can't eradicate fire ants, they can at least knock the populations down to manageable levels with modern baits and mound drenches. (It's a complicated world out there: You don't fight single-queen mounds anymore, if you're smart enough to tell the difference, because they all of a sudden seem like good neighbors compared to the multiple-queen colonies that will take their place.) What worries Texans, though, is the idea that multiple-queen fire ants may be a threat to wildlife.

Because fawns instinctively stand still when they sense danger, they become easy targets for fire ants, which head first for the moist areas around the eyes and mouth. Fire ants also swarm over bird and lizard eggs, sometimes entering the first pip holes. They have killed bluebird, cliff swallow, and brown pelican hatchlings, among other species. No one really knows yet if these cases merely represent horrible deaths for individual animals or, as one researcher put it, "a major devastating blow" to whole populations. In addition to direct predation, multiple-queen fire ants may simply out-eat other animals. In one study the fire ants consumed 100 percent of the available food in a test area. When multiple-queen fire ants entered new territory in another study, the native ant species virtually disappeared.

To some people fire ants thus begin to look like what Leiningen saw as he peered across his defenses: "Over the range of hills, as far as eye could see, crept a darkening hem, ever longer and broader, until the shadow spread across the slope from east to west …"

But this time, unfortunately, there are no moats. □ □

"We're so positive that you'll enjoy eating these delicious, mouth-watering Vidalia Onions that we'll send you a free booklet of Vidalia Onion recipes just for trying them."

"THE AMAZING SECRET OF THE MOUTH-WATERING SWEET VIDALIA ONION"

WHY ONLY FARMERS AROUND VIDALIA, GEORGIA, CAN GROW AN ONION SO SWEET AND JUICY YOU CAN EAT IT LIKE A RAW APPLE WITH NO TEARS

By Gordon Delo

Delo's Vidalia Onion Store, a distributor of farm fresh produce from Vidalia, Georgia, announced today the release of choice, select, sweet Vidalia Onions for delivery in the United States.

HERE'S THE SECRET OF THE AMAZING VIDALIA ONION

The authentic Vidalia Onion grows only in a small area around Vidalia, Georgia. The mouth-watering flavor of the Vidalia Onion can't be reproduced in other areas. The secret of its sweetness isn't just from its special seed stock. Instead, scientists say that the real secret lies in the unique combination of minerals in the soil around Vidalia, Georgia.

All efforts to grow sweet Vidalia Onions elsewhere have failed. In fact, by special act of the Georgia Legislature, only onions grown in this small area of southeast Georgia can bear the "Vidalia" name.

Sweet Vidalia Onions are so succulent . . . so sweet and mild that they can be eaten raw like an apple with no tears. They're always delicious whether eaten sliced on a hamburger, chopped in a salad or cooked with a roast. You can cook them in aluminum foil with a little soy sauce for a juicy side dish that will outshine your entree. You can even make an onion pie with them! We'll send you a recipe. The reputation of the sweet Vidalia Onion is spreading. Ten years ago, the onions were sold mainly within Georgia. But now, the majority are shipped to other states.

We sell farm-fresh, sweet Vidalia Onions specially selected and packed with loving care. We ship right to your door from the Vidalia, Georgia, area.

IT'S EASY TO ORDER

Order your sweet Vidalia Onions now! Cut out and return this notice with your name and a street address and a check for $14.99 plus $5.00 shipping and handling to: **Delo's Vidalia Onion Store, Dept. UOF-91,** P. O. Box 1719, Vidalia, GA, 30474, and we will send you a 10-pound bag of perfect, select, medium-size, sweet Vidalia Onions to be shipped at the peak of the season in late May and early June. (Sorry we cannot ship to Alaska, Hawaii or Canada.)

Or, for only $29.99 + $9.00 shipping and handling, you can get 25 pounds of jumbo-size, sweet Vidalia Onions packed in small bags.

You must cut out and return this notice with your order. Copies not accepted!

FREE VIDALIA ONION RECIPE BOOKLET OFFER EXPIRES IN 30 DAYS

All advance orders mailed within 30 days will receive a free booklet of Vidalia Onion recipes with your onion shipment in May 1991. Order right away!

GENERAL WEATHER FORECAST
1990-1991

(For details see regional forecasts beginning on page 134.)

NOVEMBER THROUGH MARCH is expected to be quite variable, with below-normal temperatures over most of the country. Exceptions to this include

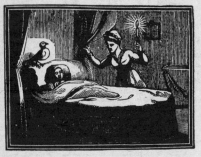

Florida, which should be well above normal, and sections of the Ohio and lower Mississippi River valleys and the far Northwest, where temperatures will be above average. Precipitation is anticipated to be above normal east of the Rocky Mountains with the exception of the eastern Great Lakes through northern New England and portions of the northern Great Plains. The West will have below-normal precipitation, particularly in California, but the higher elevations should have greater than normal snowfall. East of the Rockies, snowfall will be well above normal in the Atlantic states and western Great Lakes, slightly above normal in the northern Great Plains, but slightly below average in the southern Great Plains.

APRIL THROUGH OCTOBER:

SPRING will be generally warmer than normal over the country, except for the Great Lakes through the Northeast and scattered portions of the far West, which will be colder than normal. Precipitation is expected to be well below normal from the Mississippi River valley eastward except for wetter than normal conditions in the eastern Great Lakes through southern New England and the middle Atlantic states. The western Great Plains on through to the Northwest should see progressively greater than normal precipitation, while much of the Southwest across through southern Texas is expected to be drier than normal.

SUMMER over most of the country will be hotter and drier than normal. Exceptions to this include the far Northwest, the southern Atlantic seaboard through Florida, and scattered portions of the lower Great Plains, all of which will be milder and wetter than normal. Watch for possible tropical storms or hurricanes in mid-September in the eastern Gulf and near the end of September and in mid-October over Florida.

EARLY FALL will be cool and wet over much of the country with northern sections having a period of Indian summer-like weather in early October before cold and wet spells close out the month. Inland regions of the middle and south Atlantic states are expected to be quite dry with near drought conditions, while the western part of the country will see cool and wet spells alternating with warm and dry ones.

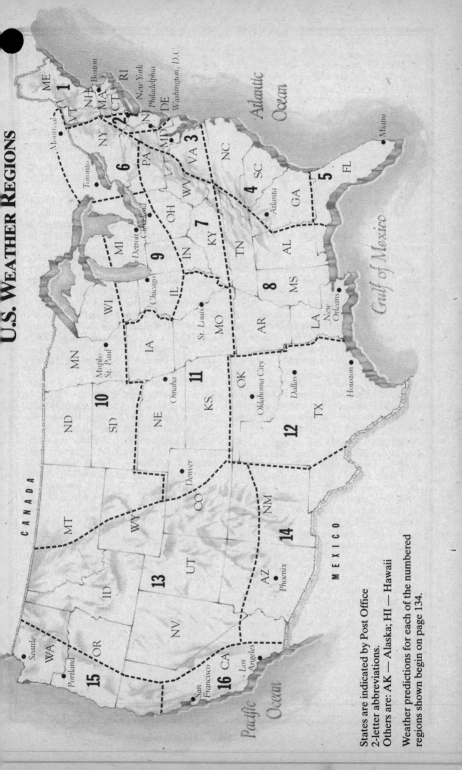

U.S. WEATHER REGIONS

States are indicated by Post Office
2-letter abbreviations.
Others are: AK — Alaska; HI — Hawaii

Weather predictions for each of the numbered
regions shown begin on page 134.

1. NEW ENGLAND

For regional boundaries, see map page 133.

SUMMARY: *November through March is expected to be considerably colder than normal, with slightly above normal precipitation but well above normal snowfall, particularly in central and southern sections. November will be cold and wet with severe storms at the middle and end of the month. December will continue cold except for a few brief mild spells. Severe winter weather is anticipated from Christmas through March, with breaks in the severe cold in mid-January and the latter part of February. Frequent snowstorms, heavy in the south, will occur from New Year's through mid-February when the first break arrives with general rains and thawing. March may come in like a lion with more snowstorms and severe cold.*

April through June is expected to be cold and wet despite starting out mild with frequent warm spells. Most of May and June will be cool, cloudy, and rainy, except for brief sunny spells in mid-May and early June.

July through September is anticipated to be warmer and considerably drier than normal, particularly during the latter half of the period. July through mid-August should see heavy shower activity, with hot spells alternating with milder ones. Generally hot, sunny, and dry weather is expected to last through much of September, including drought conditions. Expect cooler weather at the end of September.

Indian summer-like weather should prevail the first week of October.

Nov. 1990: Temp. 43° (2° below avg.; avg. north); Precip. 6" (2" above avg.; 1" above north). 1-3 Warm; rain. 4-7 Clear, cold nights. 8-10 Rain south. 11-14 Rain, then clearing. 15-16 Northeaster, cold. 17-19 Cloudy & cold. 20-22 Sleet, snow north. 23-26 Clear, cold. 27-29 Freezing rain & snow. 30 Clearing.

Dec. 1990: Temp. 31° (3° below avg.); Precip. 3.5" (1" below avg.). 1-3 Light snow. 4-6 Clear & cold. 7-8 Milder, few showers. 9-11 Snowstorm, cold. 12-15 Flurries. 16-18 Cold snap, clear. 19-21 Rain, snow mountains; milder. 22-25 Clear, very cold. 26-29 Snowstorm, heavy south, then clear & cold. 30-31 Snow.

Jan. 1991: Temp. 25° (4° below avg.) Precip. 5" (1" above avg.; 0.5" below north). 1-4 Cloudy, cold; flurries. 5-7 Snowstorm. 8-9 Flurries. 10-13 Flurries, seasonable. 14-15 Clear, very cold. 16-18 Snowstorm, heavy south. 19-20 Clearing, very cold. 21-24 Snowstorm, then clear & cold. 25-29 Intermittent snow. 30-31 Cold.

Feb. 1991: Temp. 25° (5° below avg.); Precip. 1.5" (1" below avg.). 1-3 Cold; flurries north.

4-7 Cold wave, then seasonable. 8-10 Cold wave; snow. 11-12 Snow, milder. 13-15 Clearing, very cold. 16-18 Rain; snow mountains. 19-21 Mild. 22-24 Sunny, mild days. 25-28 Cold wave, snow south.

March 1991: Temp. 37° (1° below avg.); Precip. 4" (Avg.). 1-3 Seasonable, light snow. 4-6 Snowstorm; then clear, cold. 7-9 Snowstorm, seasonable. 10-11 Severe cold. 12-16 Heavy snow, seasonable. 17-19 Severe cold. 20-23 Showers, snow mountains. 24-27 Rain, mild. 28-31 Cloudy, mild.

Apr. 1991: Temp. 50° (1° above avg.); Precip. 3" (0.5" below avg.). 1-2 Rain, mild. 3-4 Clearing, cold. 5-7 Rainstorm, then cold. 8-10 Sunny & warm. 11-15 Rain then cold. 16-19 Intermittent heavy rain, cold. 20-22 Showers. 23-26 Rain, locally heavy; milder. 27-30 Sunny, warm.

May 1991: Temp. 55° (3° below avg.); Precip. 4.5" (1" above avg.). 1-2 Cloudy, colder. 3-5 Showers, heavy inland; cold. 6-9 Clearing & warm. 10-12 Heavy rain, cold. 13-16 Showers; milder. 17-19 Cold & rainy. 20-22 Heavy rain, cold. 23-25 Cold, drizzly. 26-27 Rain. 28-31 Rain; quite cool.

June 1991: Temp. 65° (3° below avg.); Precip. 5" (2" above avg., avg. north). 1-2 Sunny & warm. 3-5 Showers, rain south; cool. 6-9 Clear, warm. 10-11 Showers, colder. 12-17 Rain, locally heavy; cold. 18-21 Sunny, seasonable. 22-24 Rain, light north. 25-27 Few showers; seasonable. 28-30 Heavy rain, warmer.

July 1991: Temp. 74° (0.5° above avg.). Precip. 4" (1" above avg.). 1-5 Light rain, brief hot spell. 6-9 Sunny; showers inland. 10-12 Heavy rain. 13-16 Clear & hot. 17-18 Showers, seasonable. 19-22 Sunny, few showers. 23-26 Showers. 27-31 Heavy rain, cooler.

Aug. 1991: Temp. 73° (1° above avg.); Precip. 2" (1.5" below avg.; avg. west). 1-2 Rain, warm. 3-6 Few showers. 7-9 Cloudy, cooler. 10-12 Rain. 13-16 Clear, warm. 17-19 Thundershowers, cooler. 20-24 Few showers. 25-27 Showers, warmer. 28-31 Heat wave, light showers.

Sept. 1991: Temp. 66° (1.5° above avg.); Precip. 2" (1.5" below avg.). 1-2 Sunny, hot. 3-5 Showers, seasonable. 6-8 Clearing & warming. 9-13 Sunny, showers; hot. 14-16 Showers. 17-20 Sunny, cool. 21-22 Clear, warm. 23-27 Scattered showers, cool. 28-30 Clearing & warm.

Oct. 1991: Temp. 54.5° (0.5° below avg.); Precip. 4" (0.5" above avg.; 0.5" below inland). 1-4 Clear, Indian summer-like. 5-7 Rain, cool. 8-11 Sunny, warming. 12-17 Rain, seasonable. 18-21 Few showers. 22-24 Cold wave, rain. 25-27 Clearing, cold. 28-31 Northeaster.

Some things cannot be ignored...
Spices & Home Fragrances good enough to be named "The Old Farmer's Almanac."

The Old Farmer's Almanac Spices & Home Fragrances will add a flavorful touch of American tradition to every household. Available at leading retailers across the country.

Spice Market, Inc. • 664 Bergen Street • Brooklyn, NY 11238

2. GREATER NEW YORK-NEW JERSEY

For regional boundaries, see map page 133.

SUMMARY: *Late fall and winter are expected to be considerably colder than normal, with above-normal precipitation and snowfall, particularly in northern sections. November should be cold and wet, with heavy rains during the first half. December should see a few mild spells alternating with cold ones, with a heavy snowstorm expected at the end of the month. January through mid-February will be very cold and wet, with well above normal snowfall, while the latter part of February should see some mild and dry weather. March should be quite variable, with cold, wet, and snowy weather lasting through midmonth before an unseasonably warm period arrives.*

Spring is anticipated to be cooler and wetter than normal, particularly in May and June. April will have cool spells alternating with warm ones, while May and June should be quite cool except for a warm spell in mid-May. Frequent and heavy rains will bring well above normal precipitation.

Summer is expected to be warmer and drier than normal in northern sections, but cooler and wetter in southern ones. Following brief hot spells in early July, temperatures should vary between normal and subnormal, with frequent and heavy showers. A severe heat wave at the end of August ushers in a warm, dry September.

Following a sunny and warm beginning, October is expected to be cloudy and cool, with frequent showers, light in the north.

Nov. 1990: Temp. 46° (1° below avg.); Precip. 6" (2.5" above avg.). 1-5 Rain, turning cold. 6-7 Cloudy, seasonable. 8-11 Heavy rain, then clearing. 12-13 Heavy rain, cool. 14-17 Sunny, cold nights. 18-26 Cold, showers south. 27-29 Seasonable. 30 Turning cold.

Dec. 1990: Temp. 34° (2° below avg.); Precip. 4" (Avg.; 1" below south). 1-4 Cloudy & cold. 5-8 Clear, mild. 9-12 Intermittent rain, snow north. 13-15 Cold snap, snow. 16-18 Cloudy, unseasonably cold. 19-21 Snowstorm. 22-25 Clear, cold nights. 26-29 Snow, then clearing. 30-31 Snowstorm, heavy north; cold.

Jan. 1991: Temp. 28° (3.5° below avg.); Precip. 4" (1" above avg.). 1-4 Snow ending, cold. 5-6 Snowstorm. 7-11 Cloudy, cold; light snow. 12-15 Clearing, milder. 16-17 Snowstorm. 18-21 Cold, then seasonable; sunny. 22-24 Very cold, light snow. 25-29 Snowstorm, seasonable, then cold. 30-31 Cloudy, very cold.

Feb. 1991: Temp. 29° (4° below avg.); Precip. 2" (1" below avg.). 1-3 Cloudy, cold. 4-8 Clear, unseasonably cold. 9-12 Snowstorm, then flurries; cold. 13-15 Partly cloudy, very cold. 16-18 Snowstorm, seasonable. 19-25 Sunny, mild. 26-28 Cold wave, snow.

Mar. 1991: Temp. 41° (Avg.; 2° above south); Precip. 4" (Avg.). 1-4 Rain, heavy north; mild. 5-6 Clear, cold. 7-9 Snowstorm, seasonable. 10-11 Cold snap. 12-16 Intermittent snow, rain south. 17-20 Cold snap, then mild. 21-24 Showers, turning cool. 25-28 Sunny & mild; few showers. 29-31 Seasonable.

Apr. 1991: Temp. 53° (0.5° above avg.); Precip. 3.5" (0.5" below avg.). 1-3 Rain, cold. 4-5 Clear & mild. 6-8 Heavy rain, cold. 9-10 Clear & warm. 11-13 Light rain, cool. 14-15 Clearing, cold nights. 16-20 Rain, very cool. 21-23 Partly cloudy, very cool. 24-26 Sunny & warm. 27-30 Seasonable, then showers.

May 1991: Temp. 59° (2.5° below avg.); Precip. 5.5" (2" above avg.). 1-3 Cold snap, sprinkles. 4-6 Sunny & warm, showers. 7-12 Intermittent heavy rain, cool. 13-16 Clear, warm. 17-22 Rain, locally heavy; cool. 23-25 Clearing, warmer. 26-28 Sunny, few showers, seasonable. 29-31 Rain, cool.

June 1991: Temp. 70° (1° below avg.); Precip. 6" (3" above avg.). 1-2 Partly cloudy, warm. 3-5 Heavy rain, cool. 6-10 Sunny, sprinkles; seasonable. 11-13 Rain, heavy south. 14-16 Clearing & warm. 17-21 Showers, heavy north; cooler. 22-24 Heavy rain; seasonable. 25-28 Rain; sunny south. 29-30 Clear, hot.

July 1991: Temp. 77° (Avg.); Precip. 5" (1" above avg.; 0.5" below south). 1-5 Hot, showers. 6-8 Sunny, seasonable. 9-11 Rain, milder. 12-16 Sunny, warm. 17-19 Heavy rain, milder. 20-24 Showers, seasonable. 25-27 Showers. 28-31 Sunny & warm.

Aug. 1991: Temp. 74° (1° below avg.); Precip. 4" (Avg.; 3" above south). 1-3 Showers, then clearing; hot. 4-6 Rain, heavy south; cooler. 7-10 Thundershowers, cool. 11-14 Seasonable. 15-17 Showers, heavy south. 18-22 Sunny, hot. 23-25 Heavy rain, cooler. 26-28 Showers, warm. 29-31 Clear, heat wave.

Sept. 1991: Temp. 69° (1° above avg.; avg. south); Precip. 2" (1.5" above avg.). 1-3 Heat wave. 4-6 Showers, cooler. 7-10 Sunny, seasonable. 11-13 Showers, warm. 14-15 Rain, mild. 16-18 Clear, warm. 19-21 Cloudy, seasonable. 22-24 Warm, sprinkles. 25-30 Cool.

Oct. 1991: Temp. 56.5° (1° below avg. 2° below south); Precip. 2.5" (0.5" below avg.; 1" above inland). 1-3 Clear. 4-5 Showers, warm. 6-8 Cloudy & cold. 9-11 Rain. 12-16 Showers, seasonable. 17-19 Light rain, cool. 20-21 Sunny, warmer. 22-23 Cold, rain. 24-27 Cloudy & cold. 28-31 Rain, then clearing & warm.

For regional boundaries, see map page 133.

SUMMARY: *Late fall and winter will be colder and wetter than normal, with well above normal snowfall. November is expected to be cold and wet, with greater snowfall than usual, while December should be cold, but sunny and dry, with below-normal snowfall. However, a snowstorm should close out the year. January should be very cold and snowy, with slightly above normal precipitation continuing through mid-February before turning warm, sunny, and drier. March will start out warm, then turn cold for two weeks before warming again. Snowfall and precipitation will be slightly below normal.*

Spring is anticipated to be cooler and wetter than normal except in southwestern sections which will be slightly warmer and drier. April should be warm, very wet in the north, but slightly dry in the south, while May and June will be cool with northern sections getting above-normal rainfall; southern ones will have close to normal.

Summer will be close to normal in temperature, although variable, with northern sections drier than normal, but southern sections wetter. Several hot spells are expected in July, but August will be slightly cool, with frequent showers, until a heat wave arrives at month's end. September will be a fairly dry month with alternating warm and mild spells.

The early fall will be cloudy, cool, and rainy, except for southwestern sections that may have near-drought conditions.

Nov. 1990: Temp. 48° (1° below avg.); Precip. 5" (2" above avg.). 1-3 Rain, turning cold. 4-6 Cloudy, cold. 7-10 Rain, then clearing; milder. 11-13 Rain. 14-16 Sunny then showers, seasonable. 17-18 Clear, cold nights. 19-20 Cold wave; rain. 21-25 Cloudy, cold; rain south. 26-30 Rain, then cloudy & cold.

Dec. 1990: Temp. 37° (2° below avg.); Precip. 2" (1" below avg.). 1-4 Flurries, sprinkles south; turning cold. 5-8 Sunny & mild. 9-12 Rain west, scattered east. 13-15 Cold, snow. 16-18 Cold. 19-21 Rain, snow west; seasonable. 22-27 Sunny, cold. 28-31 Snow, cold.

Jan. 1991: Temp. 32° (3° below avg.); Precip. 4" (1" above avg.; avg. south). 1-4 Snow, then clearing; sunny south. 5-6 Rain & snow, rain south. 7-11 Cloudy, cold; light snow north. 12-15 Sunny, mild. 16-18 Snow, cold. 19-20 Clearing, seasonable. 21-24 Cold wave; snow; then sunny. 25-28 Rain, then snow. 29-31 Sunny, cold.

Feb. 1991: Temp. 34° (3° below avg.); Precip. 2" (1" below avg.). 1-3 Light snow, cold. 4-5 Sunny, very cold; snowstorm south. 6-8 Clear-

ing, seasonable. 9-12 Snow, rain, then snow south. 13-15 Cold snap, snowstorm south. 16-18 Snowstorm, turning to rain south; mild. 19-25 Sunny & mild. 26-28 Cold wave; snow.

Mar. 1991: Temp. 49° (3° above avg.); Precip. 3.5" (Avg.). 1-3 Mild, light rain. 4-5 Sunny, warm. 6-9 Turning cold; snow, rain south. 10-11 Cold. 12-13 Rain, snow north. 14-17 Seasonable, rain; then cold snap. 18-20 Clear, warming. 21-23 Rain, warm. 24-27 Showers, very warm. 28-31 Rain, then clearing.

Apr. 1991: Temp. 58° (1° above avg.); Precip. 2.5" (0.5" below avg.). 1-2 Rain, warm. 3-4 Clear, cold. 5-7 Rain. 8-10 Sunny & warm. 11-13 Light rain, seasonable. 14-15 Cloudy, cool. 16-19 Heavy rain; warm, then cool. 20-23 Sunny, cool. 24-28 Warm, then cool; rain north. 29-30 Warm, rain; sunny south.

May 1991: Temp. 64° (2° below avg.; avg. south); Precip. 6" (2.5" above avg.; avg. south). 1-3 Cold snap; rain. 4-5 Sunny, very warm south. 6-12 Rain, cool. 13-15 Clear, very warm. 16-18 Heavy rain, cooling. 19-22 Cloudy & cool; then rain. 23-28 Sunny & warm, showers. 29-31 Heavy rain, cool.

June 1991: Temp. 73.5° (1° below avg.; 0.5° above south); Precip. 5" (2" above avg.; avg. south). 1-5 Cloudy, intermittent heavy rain; seasonable. 6-9 Cloudy, light rain. 10-13 Heavy rain, seasonable. 14-16 Sunny, warm. 17-21 Showers, cooler. 22-24 Heavy rain. 25-28 Sprinkles, then sunny. 29-30 Clear & hot.

July 1991: Temp. 79° (Avg.; 1° above south); Precip. 3.5" (0.5" below avg.; 2" below south). 1-3 Hot, showers. 4-6 Rain, cooler. 7-10 Clear & hot. 11-12 Showers, cooler. 13-17 Sunny. 18-21 Rain, cooler. 22-26 Cloudy, light rain; sunny & hot south. 27-28 Cloudy, mild; hot south. 29-31 Sunny & hot; then rain north.

Aug. 1991: Temp. 76° (1.5° below avg.); Precip. 8.5" (4" above avg.). 1-4 Rain, then sunny; seasonable. 5-9 Rain, cooler. 10-14 Sunny, showers. 15-17 Heavy showers, warm. 18-21 Cloudy, light rain south; cooler. 22-26 Rain, seasonable. 27-31 Sunny, very hot.

Sept. 1991: Temp. 71° (Avg.); Precip. 2.5" (0.5" below avg.; 1.5" below south). 1-3 Clear & hot. 4-6 Rain, cooler. 7-9 Sunny, seasonable. 10-14 Rain. 15-17 Clear & warm. 18-21 Sunny, warm. 22-24 Clear, very warm. 25-28 Showers, cooler. 29-30 Clearing & warming.

Oct. 1991: Temp. 57° (2° below avg.); Precip. 4" (1" above avg.). 1-2 Clear, warm. 3-5 Rain. 6-8 Cloudy, cold. 9-12 Heavy rain, cool. 13-14 Clear & warm. 15-19 Showers, cooling. 20-21 Clear, warm. 22-23 Rain, cold. 24-26 Cloudy & cold. 27-31 Rain, then sunny & warm.

4. PIEDMONT & SOUTHEAST COAST

For regional boundaries, see map page 133.

SUMMARY: *Late fall and winter will be cooler than normal, also much wetter and snowier than usual. November will be cold and extremely wet, but mild spells in December will bring temperatures close to normal. Precipitation will be below normal in the north and above in the south. January through mid-February will be cold and wet, with heavy snows in the north and mountains before a warm, drier period arrives. Watch for more snow at the close of February.*

Despite a couple of cold snaps, March should be very warm and wet, particularly in southern sections.

Spring is expected to be warmer and drier than normal, with most of April being quite warm, and little rain after midmonth. May and June should be close to normal in temperature, but becoming progressively drier.

Summer is anticipated to have close to normal temperatures and above-normal rainfall in the north, while the south will stay cooler with below-normal rainfall. July may see several heat waves, partially balanced by a milder spell at midmonth, particularly in southern sections, during a mild rainy period. August is expected to be mild much of the time, with thundershowers bringing above-normal rainfall. September may see a brief heat wave at the beginning of the month, but otherwise be milder and drier than normal.

Early fall is expected to be quite cold and wet along the coast, but dry inland with near-drought conditions.

Nov. 1990: Temp. 50° (1° below avg.); Precip. 8" (5" above avg.). 1-4 Sunny & warm. 5-7 Rain, cold. 8-10 Sunny. 11-13 Rain, cool; clearing. 14-15 Heavy rain. 16-17 Clearing; cool. 18-19 Rain, cool. 20-21 Seasonable, showers. 22-24 Rain, heavy west; cold. 25-26 Cold, light rain. 27-30 Rain, heavy east.

Dec. 1990: Temp. 42° (0.5° below avg.); Precip. 2" (1" below avg.; 1.5" above south). 1-5 Sunny, cool. 6-8 Clear & mild. 9-11 Rain. 12-16 Showers, heavy south; cooler. 17-18 Cloudy, cold; snow west. 19-20 Rain, milder. 21-23 Sunny. 24-26 Cloudy, rain south; cool. 27-28 Sunny, mild. 29-31 Snowstorm.

Jan. 1991: Temp. 38.5° (2° below avg.); Precip. 3.5" (0.5" below avg.). 1-4 Sunny & mild. 5-6 Rain, turning cool. 7-9 Showers, some sun. 10-15 Clearing & warming. 16-18 Rain, cold. 19-20 Cold snap, clear. 21-26 Rain east, snow west; cold. 27-29 Heavy rain & snow. 30-31 Sunny, milder.

Feb. 1991: Temp. 41° (2° below avg.); Precip. 5" (1" above avg.). 1-2 Snow, cold. 3-5 Snow-storm. 6-8 Clearing. 9-12 Rain, cooler. 13-15 Snowstorm, cold wave. 16-19 Snow turning to heavy rain. 20-24 Sunny & warm, few showers. 25-28 Cold wave; rain, snow.

Mar. 1991: Temp. 54° (4° above avg.); Precip. 5" (Avg.; 1" above south). 1-5 Sunny, warm; showers. 6-8 Rain. 9-10 Clear & mild. 11-12 Cold wave; rain, snowstorm west. 13-16 Rain, heavy east & south. 17-20 Clear, cold nights. 21-22 Rain, mild. 23-26 Cloudy, warm. 27-28 Rain. 29-31 Sunny, warm.

Apr. 1991: Temp. 62° (2° above avg.); Precip. 2" (1" below avg.; avg. south). 1-2 Rain, heavy west. 3-4 Cold snap. 5-8 Rain, heavy west, clearing. 9-15 Warm; showers. 16-19 Sunny, warm; few showers. 20-25 Clear. 26-27 Cloudy, cool; rain east. 28-30 Clear, hot.

May 1991: Temp. 69° (1° above avg.); Precip. 3.5" (0.5" below avg.). 1-2 Clear & very warm. 3-4 Showers; cool. 5-7 Clear, warm. 8-11 Showers, cool. 12-15 Sunny & warm. 16-18 Rain, heavy east. 19-21 Clear & warm. 22-24 Cloudy, showers east. 25-28 Clear & hot. 29-31 Rain, heavy central; milder.

June 1991: Temp. 76° (1° above avg.); Precip. 3" (0.5" below avg.; 1.5" below south). 1-4 Rain, mild. 5-8 Clearing, showers. 9-10 Clear & warm. 11-13 Showers, rain north; milder. 14-18 Sunny & hot. 19-21 Rain, heavy east. 22-26 Cloudy, showers. 27-30 Sunny, hot; showers east.

July 1991: Temp. 80° (1.5° above avg.; avg. south); Precip. 3" (1" below avg.; 0.5" above south). 1-2 Sunny, hot. 3-6 Rain, heavy west; milder. 7-11 Clear, very hot. 12-16 Cloudy, heavy rain west & south; mild. 17-21 Rain. 22-28 Sunny, hot; showers. 29-31 Clear & hot.

Aug. 1991: Temp. 76° (2° below avg.); Precip. 8" (4" above avg.; avg. south). 1-4 Rain, milder. 5-8 Thundershowers, mild. 9-12 Sunny, cool. 13-15 Cloudy, showers south; seasonable. 16-18 Sunny & hot, showers west. 19-22 Showers, rain south; mild. 23-27 Showers, sun west. 28-31 Sunny & hot.

Sept. 1991: Temp. 71.5° (0.5° below avg.); Precip. 1.5" (2" below avg.). 1-3 Clear, hot. 4-7 Showers, clearing; mild. 8-12 Thundershowers, warming. 13-15 Scattered showers, cooler than normal. 16-21 Partly cloudy; seasonably warm. 22-26 Clear & hot. 27-30 Sprinkles, turning unseasonably cool.

Oct. 1991: Temp. 58° (2.5° below avg.); Precip. 4.5" (1.5" above avg.). 1-4 Rain, cool. 5-7 Cloudy, rain south; seasonable. 8-10 Rain; cool. 11-15 Showers, warm. 16-20 Clear & warm. 21-23 Sprinkles, cold snap. 24-26 Cloudy, cool. 27-29 Showers. 30-31 Clear & warm.

You'd never guess her age within 20 years—

Yet, plastic surgery is not her secret!

What is? A Special Wonder-Food Formula That Actually Helps Skin Grow Younger-Looking While You Sleep...and keeps you younger-looking EVERY DAY FOR THE REST OF YOUR LIFE!

"What a difference in the way I look. Everyone I meet cannot believe my age!"

These are the words of Mrs. Ida Pellegrini of Lake Worth, FL, shown in this completely unretouched photograph...taken when she was 59 years, 11 months and 9 days old!

But can you see a single line, sag or wrinkle in her face? Can you see even the faintest trace of crows' feet, under-eye bags, or age-shouting furrows from nose to mouth?—despite the fact that she has never, ever in her life had a surgical face lift!

Her Secret—A Night-Food For The Skin That Helps Firm Away Age While You Sleep!

Now look at the other 3 women pictured at the right...who are also "living miracle proof" of how this incredible youth-builder food for the skin not only retards the effects of age...but actually encourages your skin to grow younger-looking and more beautiful while you sleep!

 age 37
 age 48
 age 62

LOOK AT THEIR AGES—THEN ASK YOURSELF IF YOU STILL HAVE A SINGLE DOUBT THAT YOU CAN MAKE YOURSELF LOOK 10—15—20 YEARS YOUNGER—WITHOUT PLASTIC SURGERY—JUST AS THE WOMEN YOU SEE PICTURED HERE DID, IN JUST A MATTER OF DAYS!

To learn their secret—which is a unique, natural food extract—read the rest of this page...and see free-trial offer below.

Before You Do Another Single Thing To Your Face—Read This:

Let's talk frankly. The only reason your skin ages is a single, dreaded word called "sag". Sagging support muscles beneath the skin that cause wrinkles ...sagging skin tissue on the surface that causes lines, furrows and crinkles...sagging support fibers that cause droopy chin, under-eye bags and those horrid deep creases in your forehead.

Defeat the most obvious effects of sag and you repel the assault of age. Arrest the march of 'sag' and the eternal look of a glowing, younger-looking skin is YOURS FOREVER! And that is why thousands upon thousands of women both here and in Europe are so excited about a remarkable wonder-development that can make any woman appear 10–15–even 20 years younger in just 14 to 21 days...without plastic surgery!

The Doctor's Alternative To A Lift—Youth-Builder Food For The Skin!

The secret which was discovered by a doctor, is an extract of the nectar and cellulose fibers found in the heart of the cucumber...nature's very own YOUTH-BUILDER FACTOR for the skin...that when concentrated into a super-nutrient creme begins to YOUTHIFY aging surface skin tissues almost on contact! Yes, an amazing natural firm-up wonder-formula for the skin that you simply apply nightly to the problem areas of your face, chin and neck...then, when you awake, look into your mirror and see your complexion ACTUALLY APPEAR YOUNGER-LOOKING OVERNIGHT! Think of it! Medical science's nightime YOUTH TREATMENT that helps smoothe, draw and firm surface skin tissues...helps buoy up your skin...reduce surface slackening as it firms away complexion problems...and restores to your appearance that fresh glow of youth each and every day FOR THE REST OF YOUR LIFE!

Not A Makeup, Not A Cover-Up But An All-Night Facial-Firm That Makes Skin Smoother, Younger-Looking In Just Days!

That's right! Miracle food-extracts that give an ALL-NIGHT "LIFT" to your appearance...youthify the texture of your skin...firm, smoothe, soften those crinkled, sagging areas...so you look 10–15–20 years younger in as little as 14 to 21 days...as this doctor's ANTI-AGE REJUVINATOR called "CUCUMBRE FROST," helps combat the appearance of age these 4 different ways:

ALL NIGHT LONG 8 hours of continuous facial firming action to counteract the aging effects on face, chin and neck.

ALL NIGHT LONG 8 hours of continuous toning and tightening to overcome the harshest effects of surface sag, lines and under-eye crepeiness.

ALL NIGHT LONG 8 hours of continuous deep moisturizing for overall smoothness and suppleness.

ALL NIGHT LONG 8 hours of continuous deep hydration to discourage external dry-up the skin.

But best of all it means that by simply using this "CUCUMBRE FROST" all-night youth-treatment each evening before bed...in just a matter of weeks you not only make yourself look years younger...but, KEEP ON LOOKING YEARS YOUNGER THAN YOU REALLY ARE, EVERY DAY FOR THE REST OF YOUR LIFE!

Prove It Yourself Entirely At Our Risk

But to really experience the full wonder of this chemist's ALL NIGHT FACIAL FIRM UP...we invite you to try 'Cucumbre Frost' entirely at our risk on this special introductory offer.

Simply send the no risk-coupon today. When your ALL NIGHT FACIAL FIRM UP arrives...simply apply to any problem area on your face, chin, or neck that broadcasts your age to the world. Then go to sleep. If after just a few nights of treatment you

do not thrill to the incredible firm-up action on the surface of your skin...if you do not marvel at how your entire complexion starts to firm and grow more youthful looking...if each and every morning you do not look into your mirror and find yourself held absolutely breathless at the gradual night-to-day difference in your appearance...then simply return for a full refund...you have tried 'Cucumbre Frost' entirely at our expense. Could anything possibly be fairer? Remember—thanks to this incredible development by medical science, no woman need ever look her age again...so act NOW!

5. FLORIDA

For regional boundaries, see map page 133.

SUMMARY: Late fall and winter are expected to be warmer than normal, with near-normal precipitation in the south but wetter than normal toward the north. November will be warm and wet, with heavy rains in the north, while December will be warmer than normal with above-normal precipitation in northern and southern sections. January is anticipated to be cold and wet, with a severe cold snap shortly after midmonth, but most of February should be warmer and drier than normal. March will be warm and wet, with heavy rains.

Spring may be quite dry, with temperatures varying from well above normal in the north to slightly below in the south. Central and southern sections may experience below-normal rainfall from April through June, while the north should be quite variable with normal rainfall in April, below in May, and above in June. Temperatures will vary, but will average warmer than normal in the north and slightly below in the south.

Summer temperatures will be near normal, but slightly below in the south. Frequent showers will bring above-normal rainfall, particularly to central sections during August. Watch for heavy rains before mid-September in the northwest due to a possible tropical storm and near the end of the month in the south due to a possible hurricane.

Early fall is expected to be cooler and wetter than normal with the possibility of a hurricane in the south before mid-October.

Nov. 1990: Temp. 70° (3° above avg.); Precip. 3" (1" above avg.; 3" above north). 1-3 Sunny & warm. 4-7 Showers. 8-10 Clear, warm. 11-14 Showers, heavy north; clearing, cold snap. 15-16 Rain, heavy north. 17-18 Clearing, warm. 19-23 Rain. 24-26 Sprinkles, cold snap. 27-28 Sunny, warm. 29-30 Rain, cold.

Dec. 1990: Temp. 63° (1° above avg.); Precip. 1.5" (0.5" above avg.; 1" above north & south). 1-3 Rain, heavy south; cold. 4-6 Cloudy, rain south. 7-12 Clear & warm. 13-15 Sunny & warm; rain north. 16-20 Showers cool. 21-23 Seasonable, some clouds. 24-25 Rain. 26-31 Showers, cool.

Jan. 1991: Temp. 57° (1.5° below avg.; avg. north); Precip. 4" (2" above avg.). 1-3 Cold snap, showers. 4-6 Sunny, warm; showers. 7-10 Cloudy & cool. 11-15 Clear, warm. 16-17 Heavy rain. 18-20 Severe cold wave, hard frost. 21-26 Rain, heavy central; clearing; mild. 27-28 Rain. 29-31 Cloudy, cold north.

Feb. 1991: Temp. 64° (2.5° above avg.); Precip. 2" (1" below avg.). 1-4 Rain. 5-7 Cloudy, cold. 8-11 Sunny & warm, sprinkles. 12-14 Showers, rain north; warm. 15-16 Showers, cool. 17-18 Sunny & warm. 19-21 Rain; cool. 22-25 Sunny, warm. 26-28 Showers, cold.

Mar. 1991: Temp. 71° (4° above avg.); Precip. 4" (1" above avg.; 3" above north & south). 1-4 Clear, warm. 5-7 Showers. 8-10 Rain central & north, cooler. 11-13 Rain, cool. 14-17 Rain; warm. 18-20 Cloudy, cold snap. 21-23 Sunny, warm; rain north. 24-31 Showers.

Apr. 1991: Temp. 73° (1° above avg.; 1° below south); Precip. 1" (1" below avg.; 2" below south; avg. north). 1-4 Rain; then clear & cold. 5-7 Showers, heavy north; warm. 8-9 Cloudy. 10-13 Sunny & hot. 14-18 Cloudy, showers; warm. 19-23 Showers, heavy south; mild. 24-26 Clear & warm. 27-30 Cloudy.

May 1991: Temp. 78° (1° above avg.; 3° above north); Precip. 1" (3" below avg.). 1-3 Clearing, warm; showers south. 4-8 Sunny, hot. 9-11 Clear, hot; showers north. 12-16 Rain, heavy south. 17-21 Sunny & hot; showers. 22-24 Cloudy, rain south; seasonable. 25-31 Sunny & hot.

June 1991: Temp. 82° (1° above avg.; 1° below south); Precip. 4" (3.5" below avg.; 1" above north). 1-4 Rain, warm. 5-7 Showers, heavy south. 8-13 Clear & hot, showers north. 14-19 Thundershowers; milder. 20-25 Showers, heavy north; hot. 26-28 Clear & hot. 29-30 Sprinkles, heavy north.

July 1991: Temp. 82.5° (Avg.; 1° above north); Precip. 8.5" (0.5" above avg.; 1" below south). 1-3 Sprinkles; hot. 4-8 Warm; thundershowers, heavy north. 9-12 Showers. 13-20 Thundershowers; mild. 21-23 Sprinkles, sunny & hot north. 24-29 Thundershowers. 30-31 Showers.

Aug. 1991: Temp. 82° (0.5° below avg.); Precip. 10" (4" above avg.; 1" above north & south). 1-5 Showers, heavy north; warm. 6-10 Thundershowers; milder. 11-15 Showers, heavy central & south; warm. 16-18 Cloudy, rain central. 19-22 Thundershowers. 23-26 Showers, heavy central & south. 27-31 Rain.

Sept. 1991: Temp. 81° (Avg.; 1° below south); Precip. 7.5" (2" above avg.; 2" below north). 1-4 Clear & warm; showers south. 5-7 Mild, thundershowers. 8-15 Showers, tropical storm northwest. 16-19 Rain; mild. 20-22 Rain; cool. 23-24 Clear. 25-27 Hurricane south, heavy rain. 28-30 Clear, warm.

Oct. 1991: Temp. 74° (1° below avg.); Precip. 5" (2.5" above avg.; 5" above south). 1-3 Rain, heavy central & south; cooler. 4-7 Rain. 8-10 Possible hurricane south, mild. 11-13 Sunny, warm. 14-16 Rain. 17-19 Clear & pleasant. 20-23 Showers, heavy south; cool. 24-31 Cloudy & mild.

6. UPSTATE N.Y.-TORONTO AND MONTREAL

For regional boundaries, see map page 133.

SUMMARY: *Late fall and winter are expected to show temperatures well below normal in central and eastern sections, with slightly above normal precipitation and well above normal snowfall. Western sections should be colder than normal, with precipitation and snowfall well below normal. Following a slightly mild beginning, November will turn cold with a heavy snowstorm before midmonth and another at the end. December should see a few brief mild spells interspersed with the cold, with below-normal precipitation but above-normal snowfall. January through mid-February will be quite cold and slightly dry, with above-normal snowfall. February will finish on a milder note, but March will be highly variable with a cold, snowy first half turning warmer after midmonth.*

Despite a mild April, spring overall will be cooler than normal, with May in particular being cold and wet. Precipitation will be above normal in central and eastern sections, but is expected to be slightly below normal in the west.

Summer will be warmer than normal, with late August through September being quite hot and dry, especially in central and eastern sections. Heavy showers in the west during the latter half of September may bring the precipitation close to normal there.

Indian summer-like weather begins October, followed by cold and, in the west, wet weather for the balance of the month.

Nov. 1990: Temp. 38° (1° below avg.; avg. west); Precip. 5" (2" above avg.; 0.5" above west). 1-4 Rain, lighter west; mild. 5-7 Sunny & mild, cold nights. 8-11 Cloudy & rainy. 12-14 Heavy snowstorm; clearing. 15-17 Snowstorm. 18-22 Cold, flurries. 23-26 Sunny. 27-30 Snowstorm, turning cold.

Dec. 1990: Temp. 23.5° (3° below avg.; 1° below west); Precip. 2.5" (0.5" below avg.). 1-4 Cold, flurries. 5-6 Clear & cold. 7-8 Sleet, milder. 9-11 Snowstorm, cold. 12-16 Rain changing to snow. 17-19 Clear, milder. 20-22 Snowstorm. 23-26 Cold, then seasonable. 27-29 Snowstorm, cold. 30-31 Snow, heavy southeast.

Jan. 1991: Temp. 17° (4° below avg.); Precip. 2.5" (Avg.; 1" below west). 1-2 Light snow. 3-5 Cold wave, flurries. 6-7 Snowstorm, heavy south. 8-13 Cloudy, cold; snow. 14-16 Clear, very cold. 17-19 Cloudy. 20-22 Snowstorm. 23-24 Clear, very cold. 25-27 Snow, seasonable. 28-31 Very cold, then snowstorm.

Feb. 1991: Temp. 17° (6° below avg.; 3° below west); Precip. 1.5" (1" below avg.). 1-2 Cloudy, cold; snow central. 3-5 Severe cold. 6-7 Clear. 8-9 Snow, very cold. 10-15 Seasonable, then very cold; light snow. 16-18 Snowstorm & freezing rain. 19-21 Cloudy, warming. 22-24 Sunny & mild. 25-28 Cold wave, flurries.

Mar. 1991: Temp. 32° (1.5° below avg.; 2° above west). Precip. 3" (Avg.; 1" above west). 1-2 Snow, mild. 3-5 Snowstorm. 6-9 Clear, cold; snowstorm. 10-11 Clear, cold nights. 12-15 Cloudy, snow west. 16-18 Severe cold, snow. 19-20 Sunny, mild. 21-23 Rain changing to snow. 24-27 Rain; warm. 28-31 Showers.

Apr. 1991: Temp. 48° (1.5° above avg.); Precip. 3" (Avg.). 1-3 Rain, heavy north, cold. 4-5 Cloudy, milder. 6-8 Rain & snow, cold. 9-10 Sunny & warm. 11-14 Rain, turning cold. 15-16 Clearing. 17-20 Rain, snow mountains; cold. 21-23 Sunny; showers. 24-28 Rain, then clearing; warm. 29-30 Warm, rain central & south.

May 1991: Temp. 55° (2.5° below avg.); Precip. 5" (1.5" above avg.; avg. west). 1-3 Cold, cloudy; showers. 4-6 Rain, warming. 7-9 Clear, warm. 10-12 Showers, turning cold. 13-16 Rainstorm, warming. 17-21 Cold & rainy. 22-24 Partial clearing, cold. 25-28 Rain, heavy east; cold. 29-31 Clearing, very warm.

June 1991: Temp. 66° (1° below avg.); Precip. 3" (0.5" below avg.). 1-4 Showers east, sunny west. 5-8 Clear, very warm. 9-11 Showers, cool. 12-14 Heavy rain. 15-17 Light rain. 18-23 Cloudy, showers; cool. 24-26 Sunny & warm; showers west. 27-30 Rain; clearing & warm.

July 1991: Temp. 72° (0.5° above avg.); Precip. 3.5" (0.5" above avg.). 1-3 Heavy rain, very warm. 4-6 Cloudy, cooler. 7-9 Clear, warm. 10-12 Rain; cooler. 13-16 Clear & hot. 17-19 Rain, seasonable. 20-24 Sunny, scattered showers, cool nights. 25-27 Thundershowers. 28-31 Partly cloudy, milder; showers west.

Aug. 1991: Temp. 70° (1° above avg.); Precip. 1.5" (1.5" below avg.; 2.5" below west). 1-6 Sunny & warm, showers. 7-8 Sunny & pleasant. 9-11 Thundershowers, cool. 12-15 Clear & warm. 16-19 Thundershowers. 20-22 Clear. 23-27 Showers, warm. 28-31 Heat wave, sunny.

Sept. 1991: Temp. 63° (2° above avg.); Precip. 2" (1" below avg.; 1.5" above west). 1-4 Cooling, showers. 5-9 Sunny, warm; sprinkles. 10-14 Showers, heavy west; milder. 15-17 Clear; hot. 18-21 Cloudy, cold snap. 22-24 Showers, warm. 25-28 Cloudy & cold. 29-30 Clear.

Oct. 1991: Temp 49.5° (1° below avg.); Precip. 2.5" (0.5" below avg.; 1.5" above west). 1-4 Sunny & very warm. 5-7 Rain, heavy west, snow mountains; cold. 8-11 Sunny, cool. 12-14 Heavy rain. 15-18 Cool, cloudy & rainy. 19-20 Clear & warm. 21-24 Heavy rain & snow, cold. 25-27 Sunny, seasonable. 28-31 Showers, then clear.

DOES 60 lbs. OF TOMATOES FROM ONE YIELD SOUND INCREDIBLE?
NOT IF YOU OWN THE *Amazing* TREE TOMATO

CAN BE TUB-GROWN INDOORS FOR YEAR-'ROUND TOMATO HARVESTS!

(Cyphomandra betacea)

— Wave After Wave Of Succulent Tree Tomatoes Grow As Quick As You Can Pick 'Em!

Plenty for your family, and to share with friends and neighbors. Your TREE TOMATO will arrive in temperate zones, plant it outdoors and enjoy its bountiful, exotic beauty in your garden. It also does very well as a tub-grown plant, or indoors as a houseplant. Nothing beats fresh produce, so why continue to pay high supermarket prices for inferior tomatoes, when you can grow your own TREE TOMATOES! And remember, WE SHIP MATURE PLANTS, NOT SEEDS. Full growing instructions included. ORDER YOUR TREE TOMATOES TODAY!

From Lakeland Nurseries comes the biggest garden sensation of the century... THE PERENNIAL TOMATO!

- Grow It Outdoors As A Tree—Indoors As A Houseplant —In Tubs On The Patio!
- Loads Of Luscious Red Fruits—Up To 60 Lbs. Per Plant Each Year!
- Heights To 8 Ft. Tall, Or Trim To Any Size—Produces Fruit Up To 7 Months A Year!

The TREE TOMATO ... a remarkable new horticultural concept from New Zealand ... unlike anything you've ever seen before! NOT a vine ... NOT a regular tomato plant ... the TREE TOMATO is a living, growing tree that BEARS FRUIT SEASON AFTER SEASON ... YEAR AFTER YEAR! Why settle for garden-fresh tomatoes a few short weeks of the year? Why buy hothouse tomatoes that taste like cardboard? Not when you can pick crop after crop of red, plump, juicy TREE TOMATOES up to 7 months a year (all year 'round when grown indoors!)

Thousands of Satisfied Customers!

Read what Mr. L.F.S. of Wisc. has to say: "Just a line to let you know the Tree Tomato is doing great ... about 5½ ft. tall ... you said leaves grew 12"... mine are 15" and 16"... It's just beautiful!"

Enjoy Tree Tomatoes So Many Delectable Ways!

The TREE TOMATO will thrive marvelously—indoors or out. And the mouth-watering flavor is out of this world ... It's hard to find a meatier, firmer, more bursting-with-goodness taste treat! Rich in vitamin C, ripe TREE TOMATOES are fabulous in salads, sandwiches, spaghetti sauce, and are absolutely fantastic just sliced up and popped in your mouth!

———— LAKELAND'S DOUBLE GUARANTEE ————

All plants must arrive in perfect condition. If you are not totally satisfied with any order, return within 10 days for a prompt replacement or refund of purchase price (except post. & hdlg.). And all plants must thrive after planting, or return anytime within 3 months for prompt replacement—no questions asked!

LAKELAND NURSERIES SALES® Hanover, PA 17333

For regional boundaries, see map page 133.

SUMMARY: Late fall and winter will average slightly warmer than normal with below-normal precipitation and snowfall in eastern sections, but slightly above in the west. After a mild and wet beginning in November, cold spells with snow will alternate with seasonable to mild periods from mid-November until the latter part of January. A severe cold wave is expected from the end of January into early February, followed by warm spells in the latter half of February and in March.

Spring is expected to be warmer than normal, with well above normal precipitation in the east, but slightly below normal in the west. Temperatures will be quite variable during April, with frequent but brief warm spells and several cool periods with heavy rains. May should be cool with frequent showers except for a warm spell at midmonth, while June's warm spells will outweigh the mild ones and the rainfall will be spread fairly uniformly over the month, but with greater intensity in the east.

The summer will be warmer and drier over the region, with brief hot spells in July and September, but with no heat waves except possibly for a week from the end of August to early September. Frequent showers are in the offing for July and early August, but then drier than normal conditions should prevail.

Several cold spells beginning at the end of September and during October make for a cool fall, while shower activity will be lighter in the west and heavier in the east.

Nov. 1990: Temp. 44° (Avg.); Precip. 2.5" (0.5" below avg.; 1" above east). 1-3 Heavy rain, cool. 4-6 Sunny. 7-9 Rain, heavy east. 10-12 Clearing & cold; snow east. 13-14 Sunny. 15-16 Snow. 17-18 Clear & cold. 19-20 Rain, snow north. 21-25 Clearing, mild. 26-30 Rain turning to snow, heavy east.

Dec. 1990: Temp. 35° (Avg.; 1° below east); Precip. 1.5" (1.5" below avg.). 1-3 Cold wave. 4-7 Severe cold, flurries east; then mild. 8-12 Rain, with snow north. 13-16 Cloudy, cold; flurries. 17-18 Clearing, milder. 19-21 Snowstorm. 22-25 Sunny & mild, 26-28 Flurries, seasonably cold. 29-31 Snow, cold.

Jan. 1991: Temp. 29° (1.5° below avg.; 2.5° below east); Precip. 2.5" (0.5" below avg.). 1-4 Clearing, mild. 5-9 Heavy rain turning to snow, seasonable. 10-15 Clearing, warm; snow east. 16-18 Snow. 19-21 Clear, cold nights; flurries east. 22-23 Cloudy & cold. 24-25 Clear, mild. 26-31 Severe cold wave, snow.

Feb. 1991: Temp. 33° (0.5° below avg.); Precip. 3" (0.5" above avg.; 0.5" below east). 1-3 Sunny, very cold. 4-7 Snow, then clear &

cold. 8-10 Snowstorm. 11-12 Sunny, cold nights. 13-15 Severe cold snap. 16-18 Heavy rain, snow north. 19-24 Clear, very mild. 25-26 Cold wave, snow. 27-28 Sunny & mild.

Mar. 1991: Temp. 48° (5° above avg.); Precip. 6" (2" above avg.; avg. east). 1-4 Rain, warm. 5-6 Cloudy, seasonable. 7-10 Rain turning to snow, then clear. 11-15 Sleet & snow, then cloudy. 16-18 Cold snap, snow. 19-20 Clear, warm. 21-29 Heavy rain, very warm, then cold. 30-31 Clear, warm; rain west.

Apr. 1991: Temp. 59° (4° above avg.); Precip. 5" (1" above avg.). 1-3 Rain then snow; cold. 4-5 Clear. 6-7 Rain, cold snap. 8-10 Sunny, warm. 11-13 Heavy rain, cool. 14-15 Clear, warm. 16-19 Heavy rain, cold. 20-24 Sunny, warm. 25-27 Showers. 28-30 Heat wave, showers east.

May 1991: Temp. 64° (Avg.); Precip. 3" (1" below avg.; 1" above east). 1-3 Cold wave; rain, heavy east. 4-5 Sunny, seasonable. 6-12 Rain, cool. 13-15 Sunny, very warm. 16-19 Rain, then clearing; cool. 20-22 Rain, heavy south. 23-27 Sunny & pleasant, few showers east. 28-29 Cloudy, mild. 30-31 Sunny & warm.

June 1991: Temp. 74° (1.5° above avg.); Precip. 2.5" (1.5" above avg.; 2" above east). 1-4 Warm, sprinkles. 5-9 Sunny, very warm. 10-13 Heavy rain, cool. 14-15 Clear, hot west. 16-17 Heavy rain. 18-21 Sunny, then showers & cooler. 22-23 Cloudy, warm west. 24-28 Showers, hot. 29-30 Rain, very warm.

July 1991: Temp. 78° (2° above avg.); Precip. 5" (1" above avg.; 0.5" below east). 1-2 Sunny & hot, showers west. 3-5 Rain, heavy west; mild. 6-10 Heat wave, showers. 11-12 Mild, few showers. 13-15 Clear, hot. 16-19 Heavy rain, then clearing. 20-22 Showers, warm. 23-24 Clear. 25-28 Rain. 29-31 Sunny, milder.

Aug. 1991: Temp. 77° (1° above avg.); Precip. 1.5" (2" below avg.; 0.5" below east). 1-4 Showers; clear & hot. 5-7 Sunny. 8-10 Showers, cool. 11-15 Sunny, showers; warm. 16-18 Showers. 19-21 Clear, warmer. 22-24 Showers, cloudy; mild. 25-31 Clear, record heat wave.

Sept. 1991: Temp. 71.5° (3° above avg.); Precip. 1.5" (1.5" below avg.). 1-2 Clear, hot. 3-5 Showers, warm. 6-9 Clear; light rain; sunny & warm east. 10-13 Rain, warm. 14-17 Clear & hot. 18-19 Cloudy. 20-23 Clear, heat wave. 24-26 Rain, turning cool. 27-30 Cloudy, cool.

Oct. 1991: Temp. 54.5° (2° below avg.); Precip. 2" (0.5" below avg.; 0.5" above east). 1-3 Sunny, pleasant. 4-6 Rain. 7-10 Cloudy, then rain; very cool. 11-16 Some rain, cool. 17-19 Clearing & warming. 20-22 Warm, heavy rain; then cold. 23-25 Clear & cold. 26-28 Sprinkles, seasonable. 29-31 Clearing & warm.

8. DEEP SOUTH

For regional boundaries, see map page 133.

SUMMARY: *Late fall and winter are expected to be colder and wetter than usual in northern sections, with above-normal snowfall, while southern sections will have close to normal temperatures, but above-average precipitation. November will be cold and very wet, with heavy rains at midmonth, but December should see warm spells early and late in the month, with a very cold, rainy period in between, with snow in the north. Following a mild and drier first half of January, a prolonged cold, wet, and snowy period is anticipated through mid-February; alternating warm and cold spells will occur through March, with frequent and heavy shower activity.*

Spring is anticipated to be warmer and drier than normal over most of the region, though northern sections will be wetter than normal. Except for cold and wet spells in early April and after midmonth, warmer and drier periods will prevail; May and June will be sunnier, warmer, and drier than normal except for heavy shower activity in early May and late June in northern sections.

Summer should be slightly cooler and considerably drier than normal in the north but slightly warmer and drier in the south. July will be quite warm and dry south but near normal north, while August may have a mild first half but then be very warm, with heavy rains south at midmonth. September will have alternating cool and warm spells, with showers confined to the first half.

Early fall is expected to be cooler than normal, due primarily to cold spells at the beginning of October and after midmonth; shower activity will be less than usual.

Nov. 1990: Temp. 55° (Avg.; 1° below north); Precip. 6" (2" above avg.). 1-3 Sunny, warm. 4-6 Rain, cool. 7-10 Sunny, showers; seasonable. 11-13 Rain then clearing. 14-15 Rain, cool. 16-17 Clear. 18-19 Heavy rain, mild. 20-27 Sun & rain; cold. 28-30 Clear.

Dec. 1990: Temp. 47.5° (1° below avg.); Precip. 3.5" (1" below avg.). 1-2 Sunny, rain north. 3-6 Clear & mild. 7-8 Rain, warm. 9-10 Sunny, warm. 11-15 Heavy rain then snow; cold. 16-18 Clearing, seasonable. 19-20 Heavy rain, snow north; cold. 21-26 Sunny & mild. 27-29 Cold, snow east. 30-31 Clear, mild.

Jan. 1991: Temp. 43.5° (2° below avg.); Precip. 4" (1" below avg.). 1-3 Sunny & warm. 4-6 Rain, heavy west; cold. 7-10 Seasonable, sunny; showers east. 11-14 Clear & warm. 15-17 Rain, heavy east, then snow. 18-20 Clear, cold nights. 21-23 Very cold, snow. 24-27 Showers, seasonable. 28-31 Cold, snowstorm.

Feb. 1991: Temp. 46° (3° below avg.); Precip. 6" (1.5" above avg.). 1-4 Continuing cold, snow. 5-7 Clear & cold. 8-10 Rain, snow east. 11-14 Cold snap, light snow. 15-18 Rain; milder. 19-23 Sunny, unseasonably warm. 24-26 Cold, snow. 27-28 Rain, milder.

Mar. 1991: Temp. 60° (4° above avg.; 2° above north); Precip. 6" (Avg.; 3" above north). 1-3 Rain, warm. 4-8 Sunny, warm; then rain. 9-10 Cloudy, cold. 11-12 Rain. 13-15 Sunny, some showers. 16-18 Cold. 19-23 Sunny, mild. 24-28 Cloudy, rain. 29-31 Sunny, warm.

Apr. 1991: Temp. 67° (2° above avg.); Precip. 5" (1" below avg.; avg. north). 1-4 Partly cloudy, showers; cool. 5-6 Heavy rain. 7-9 Sunny, warm. 10-12 Showers, very warm. 13-16 Cloudy, then sunny & warm. 17-19 Very heavy rain, cool. 20-27 Clear, increasing clouds; very warm. 28-30 Showers, seasonable.

May 1991: Temp. 73.5° (1° above avg.; 1° below north); Precip. 4.5" (0.5" below avg.). 1-2 Sunny, warm; showers west. 3-6 Seasonable, clear. 7-11 Rain, mild. 12-15 Clear, warm. 16-18 Showers, mild. 19-21 Sunny & warm; few showers. 22-27 Clear, hot. 28-31 Rain, mild.

June 1991: Temp. 81° (2° above avg.; avg. north); Precip. 2" (1" below avg.; 0.5" above north). 1-2 Showers. 3-6 Partly cloudy, seasonable. 7-9 Clear & hot. 10-12 Showers, milder. 13-17 Sunny, hot. 18-20 Showers, heat wave. 21-24 Thundershowers, milder. 25-27 Cloudy, showers. 28-30 Showers, heavy west.

July 1991: Temp. 84° (2° above avg.; avg. north); Precip. 2.5" (2" below avg.; avg. north). 1-5 Thundershowers, warm. 6-9 Sunny, very hot. 10-12 Sunny, showers west. 13-15 Clear. 16-19 Showers. 20-21 Sunny, hot. 22-24 Showers. 25-31 Showers, hot south.

Aug. 1991: Temp. 81° (Avg.; 2° below north); Precip. 6" (2" above avg.; 1" below north). 1-2 Showers, seasonable. 3-7 Sunny, rain north. 8-11 Sunny, mild. 12-15 Thundershowers, mild. 16-20 Sunny, some showers; hot south. 21-29 Clear & hot. 30-31 Showers, hot.

Sept. 1991: Temp. 76° (0.5° below avg.; 0.5° above north); Precip. 3" (1" below avg.; 2" below north). 1-4 Light showers, hot. 5-7 Clear & warm. 8-10 Rain, heavy south, mild. 11-12 Sunny, warm. 13-16 Cloudy, showers; milder. 17-19 Sunny, warm; rain south. 20-26 Clear & hot. 27-30 Cold wave, showers.

Oct. 1991: Temp. 63° (2° below avg.; 3° below north); Precip. 2" (0.5" below avg.). 1-4 Rain, cool. 5-9 Cloudy. 10-12 Rain, mild. 13-14 Sunny & warm. 15-16 Showers. 17-20 Sunny, warm. 21-23 Severe cold, rain. 24-26 Clear, warm. 27-31 Showers.

SUMMARY: Late fall and winter are expected to be cooler than normal, with above-normal precipitation in the west, but below in the east. Snowfall should be about normal in western sections, but below in eastern ones. November will be cold, wet, and snowy, with the period from mid-November through mid-December being particularly so. Mild weather is anticipated from mid-December to mid-January, but watch for a severe snowstorm in early January. Mid-January through mid-February will be cold, with light snow. Another cold period marks mid-February, while warm spells are in the offing in late February and March.

Spring is apt to be slightly cool with below-normal precipitation in the west, but above in the east. April brings frequent brief warm spells, along with storms crossing the region at regular intervals. Cooler than normal weather should prevail through May and June except for a sunny and warm period in late May to early June. May and June will have below-normal shower activity, with the exception of a very wet first half of May.

Summer is expected to be warm and dry with the arrival of a heat wave at the end of August, and warm spells through September. Shower activity will be less intense than usual.

Early fall is apt to be cool with frequent shower activity through October.

Nov. 1990: Temp. 39° (2° below avg.; avg. east). Precip. 2.5" (0.5" above avg.; 0.5" below east). 1-3 Rain, cold. 4-7 Cloudy. 8-11 Rain turning to snow, then clearing. 12-15 Snowstorm, cold. 16-18 Cloudy, flurries. 19-20 Snowstorm. 21-24 Sunny, cold. 25-27 Rain, snow north, then clearing. 28-30 Snowstorm, cold.

Dec. 1990: Temp. 27° (2° below avg.); Precip. 2" (0.5" below avg.). 1-2 Snowstorm. 3-6 Clear, very cold, then milder. 7-9 Snowstorm, rain south. 10-12 Rain turning to snow, cold. 13-17 Snow; cold. 18-21 Flurries then clear. 22-26 Some sun, flurries. 27-28 Cloudy, snow south. 29-31 Snow, heavy northeast, cold.

Jan. 1991: Temp. 20.5° (2° below avg.); Precip. 2" (Avg.). 1-3 Sunny, mild; flurries north. 4-6 Snowstorm, cold. 7-9 Snow abating, cloudy. 10-12 Sunny, mild. 13-16 Cloudy, snow; colder. 17-20 Cold, snow. 21-22 Cold wave. 23-25 Mild, snow. 26-31 Cold, snow.

Feb. 1991: Temp. 23° (4° above avg.); Precip. 0.5" (1" below avg.). 1-2 Clear, very cold. 3-6 Cloudy, flurries; milder. 7-10 Snow, cold. 11-15 Snow, milder; then clear, cold snap. 16-18 Snowstorm, heavy east; seasonable. 19-23 Clearing, unseasonably warm. 24-26 Cold snap, flurries north. 27-28 Sunny & mild.

Mar. 1991: Temp. 37.5° (0.5° above avg.); Precip. 5" (2" above avg.; 1" above east). 1-5 Heavy rain, snow north; mild. 6-10 Cold wave; snow, clearing. 11-13 Snow, milder. 14-16 Severe cold snap, snow south. 17-19 Clear, mild. 20-22 Cloudy & rainy. 23-24 Heavy rain, warm. 25-31 Sun & rain, warm.

Apr. 1991: Temp. 52.5° (3° above avg.); Precip. 2" (2" below avg.; avg. east). 1-2 Cold snap; heavy rain, snow north. 3-4 Sunny, cool. 5-7 Rain & snow. 8-9 Clear, pleasant. 10-12 Rain, heavy south; warm. 13-15 Cloudy, cold. 16-18 Heavy rain, cold. 19-23 Sunny, warm. 24-26 Showers. 27-30 Rain, very warm.

May 1991: Temp. 54.5° (4° below avg.; 2° below east); Precip. 5" (2" above avg.). 1-3 Heavy rain, cold. 4-7 Cloudy, rain south; milder. 8-11 Rain, turning heavy; warming. 12-13 Clear, cold. 14-17 Heavy rain. 18-21 Rain, seasonable. 22-26 Cool then clear & warm. 27-29 Cloudy & cool. 30-31 Clear & warm.

June 1991: Temp. 67.5° (3° below avg.; 1° below east); Precip. 3" (1" below avg.). 1-3 Cloudy, cool; showers north. 4-8 Sunny, very warm. 9-12 Rain, cool. 13-15 Sunny & warm. 16-18 Showers, cool. 19-21 Clear, warming; showers east. 22-25 Showers, cool. 26-28 Heavy rain, very warm. 29-30 Sunny, warm.

July 1991: Temp. 75° (Avg.; 1.5° above east); Precip. 4" (Avg.; 1" below east). 1-4 Heavy rain, cooler. 5-8 Sunny & hot; showers north. 9-11 Scattered showers, cooler. 12-14 Clear, very warm. 15-17 Showers, cooler. 18-24 Sunny & warm, scattered showers. 25-27 Heavy rain, cool. 28-31 Clear & warm, then showers.

Aug. 1991: Temp. 73° (1° below avg.; 1° above east); Precip. 2.5" (1" below avg.). 1-2 Showers, quite warm. 3-4 Rain, heavy north; milder. 5-9 Cloudy, cool, some rain. 10-14 Sunny, warm. 15-17 Rain, heavy north; cooler. 18-20 Sunny & warm. 21-23 Rain. 24-25 Clear & warmer. 26-31 Clear, severe heat wave.

Sept. 1991: Temp. 68.5° (2.5° above avg.); Precip. 2" (1" below avg.). 1-2 Sunny, hot; showers north. 3-6 Showers, warm. 7-10 Clear, hot; showers south. 11-13 Heavy showers, mild. 14-16 Sunny, very warm. 17-18 Cloudy. 19-23 Sunny, very warm; showers north. 24-26 Thundershowers, cool. 27-30 Sunny, mild.

Oct. 1991: Temp. 52.5° (2° below avg.); Precip. 1.5" (1" below avg.). 1-2 Clear & warm. 3-5 Rain, cooler. 6-10 Variable clouds, cool. 11-13 Rain, very cool. 14-16 Showers, cool. 17-19 Sunny & warm. 20-22 Rain, heavy south, snow north; cold wave. 23-28 Partly cloudy, cool; showers. 29-31 Clear & warm.

10. NORTHERN GREAT PLAINS-GREAT LAKES

For regional boundaries, see map page 133.

SUMMARY: *Late fall and winter are anticipated to be colder than normal with above-normal precipitation in the east, but below in the west; snowfall will be normal and above. November should be cold and very snowy, while December will see more mild spells, with below-normal precipitation but above-normal snowfall in the east and in the Black Hills. January will be quite dry with warm spells balanced by some cold snaps, while much of the early parts of February and March will be cold and snowy to contrast with mild and dry spells toward the ends of these months.*

Spring should be warmer than normal with above-normal precipitation in the west, but well below normal in the east. April will see variable temperatures with frequent warm spells and showers, with some flooding in the north. The first half of May will be showery and cool before ushering in a warm and dry latter half. That trend persists in the east through the first half of June. The end of June will be cool and wet, particularly in the west.

Summer will be much warmer than normal, and very dry in the east. A very warm and dry period up to mid-July will be relieved by a mild and wet latter half that should extend through much of August. Quite warm and dry spells dominate the balance of the season.

Early fall will be seasonable to cold through October except for brief warm and dry spells at the beginning and end of the month.

Nov. 1990: Temp. 30° (3° below avg.; 6° below west); Precip. 2.5" (1" above avg.). 1-2 Sunny, mild. 3-5 Rain. 6-7 Clear, mild. 8-11 Snowstorm, cold. 12-17 Sunny, cold; snow. 18-21 Snowstorm, cold. 22-25 Snow, heavy south; milder. 26-27 Clear, cold. 28-30 Snow, cold north.

Dec. 1990: Temp. 16° (3° below avg.; 1° above west); Precip. 1" (Avg.). 1-2 Snow, very cold. 3-5 Clear, seasonable. 6-7 Snowstorm. 8-12 Intermittent snow, cold. 13-16 Sunny, severe cold wave; snow east. 17-18 Clear, mild. 19-22 Snow, flurries south; cold. 23-28 Cloudy, mild. 29-31 Sunny, mild; snowstorm east.

Jan. 1991: Temp. 10° (1° below avg.; 1° above west); Precip. 0.3" (0.5" below avg.). 1-3 Cloudy, snow north; mild. 4-6 Severe cold snap. 7-8 Snow, heavy east; mild. 9-16 Sunny & mild, then snow. 17-19 Sunny, mild; very cold nights. 20-22 Severe cold. 23-24 Snow, milder. 25-27 Cloudy, very cold. 28-31 Snow.

Feb. 1991: Temp. 14.5° (3° below avg.); Precip. 0.3" (0.5" below avg.). 1-5 Increasing clouds; flurries. 6-9 Cold snap, snowstorm east. 10-12 Cold, snowstorm south. 13-16 Cloudy, severe cold. 17-19 Snow, sun; cold. 20-22 Sunny, mild. 23-24 Flurries, cold. 25-26 Sunny. 27-28 Snow.

Mar. 1991: Temp. 27° (2° below avg.); Precip. 2.5" (0.5" above avg.; 0.5" below west). 1-2 Sunny, mild. 3-5 Snowstorm, cold. 6-10 Snow abating, very cold. 11-13 Snowstorm. 14-16 Severe cold, clear. 17-20 Sunny, mild. 21-22 Light snow. 23-25 Rain, heavy east; mild. 26-29 Sunny, rain north. 30-31 Rain, very warm.

Apr. 1991: Temp. 50° (3.5° above avg.); Precip. 2" (Avg.). 1-3 Cloudy, cold; rain east. 4-6 Rain, snow north; cold. 7-10 Sunny & mild. 11-13 Rain, and snow north; cold. 14-15 Clear & warm. 16-17 Rain, snow west; cold. 18-19 Sunny, warm 20-22 Sunny, few showers. 23-25 Rain. 26-27 Clear & warm. 28-30 Rain.

May 1991: Temp. 59° (1° above avg.); Precip. 1.5" (2" below avg.). 1-3 Sunny & warm. 4-7 Rain, heavy west; sunny east. 8-11 Rain east, sun & showers west; cool. 12-15 Rain, heavy south; cold. 16-19 Sunny & warm. 20-21 Rain, locally heavy; cool. 22-26 Clear, hot spell. 27-28 Showers, mild. 29-31 Sunny & warm.

June 1991: Temp. 67° (1° below avg.); Precip. 3" (1" below avg,; 2" above west). 1-3 Showers, heavy west; cold. 4-7 Clear, warm. 8-12 Showers, locally heavy; mild. 13-18 Cloudy, showers; cooler. 19-21 Sunny, showers west; cool. 22-28 Rain, heavy south; cool. 29-30 Sunny, scattered showers; mild.

July 1991: Temp. 74° (1° above avg.); Precip. 2" (1.5" below avg.; 1" above west). 1-4 Rain, mild. 5-6 Clearing, hot, few showers. 7-14 Heat wave, clear. 15-17 Showers, milder. 18-22 Thundershowers, warm. 23-25 Sunny, warm; showers west. 26-28 Heavy thundershowers, sunny west. 29-31 Showers, seasonable.

Aug. 1991: Temp. 71.5° (1° above avg.; 0.5° below west); Precip. 3.5" (Avg.). 1-2 Sunny, warm; showers west. 3-5 Rain, heavy central; turning cool. 6-10 Showers. 11-15 Warming; thundershowers. 16-19 Sunny, showers west; warm. 20-22 Rain; clear & hot west. 23-26 Sunny. 27-31 Very hot, scattered showers.

Sept. 1991: Temp. 69° (6° above avg.); Precip. 1.5" (1" above avg.). 1-2 Showers, hot. 3-9 Clear & hot. 10-14 Rain, cool. 15-16 Clear & hot, showers east. 17-19 Sunny, very hot. 20-23 Scattered showers, gradual cooling. 24-26 Thundershowers, seasonable. 27-30 Clear, pleasantly warm; few showers west.

Oct. 1991: Temp. 50° (Avg.); Precip. 1" (1" below avg.). 1-3 Clear & warm. 4-6 Partly cloudy, showers east. 7-9 Sunny. 10-12 Rain, heavy central; cool. 13-15 Cloudy, cold. 16-19 Sunny; rain east. 20-22 Snow, cold snap. 23-26 Cloudy, mild. 27-31 Sunny & warm.

SUMMARY: *Late fall and winter are expected to be colder and wetter than normal, with slightly above normal snowfall except in the southwest. Following a mild and wet beginning, November is anticipated to be cold and wet, with considerable snow in the north. December through mid-January should see frequent warm spells, with the only significant cold spells occurring in early December and at the beginning and end of January. Despite warm spells at the end of February and the beginning and end of March, late winter will be dominated by cold and snow in mid-February and from early through mid-March.*

Spring will be much warmer than normal, with above-normal precipitation especially in eastern sections. April will be very warm with frequent but light precipitation turning heavier at the end of the month. Mild temperatures will prevail during the first half of May and last half of June with a warm and dry period in between.

Summer should be quite warm with above-normal rainfall except in the northwest, which will be drier than normal. Hot spells will be broken by periods of seasonable to mild weather, including a mild and wet period near mid-August.

Early fall will be cooler and drier than normal, with frequent cold snaps.

Nov. 1990: Temp. 35° (3° below avg.); Precip. 3" (1.5" above avg.). 1-2 Sunny, cool. 3-5 Heavy rain. 6-11 Cloudy then rain. 12-14 Cold wave; snow, heavy rain southeast. 15-17 Sunny, cold. 18-19 Snowstorm. 20-23 Flurries. 24-26 Rain, snow north; seasonable. 27-30 Cold snap, snow.

Dec. 1990: Temp. 27° (1° above avg.; 2° above south); Precip. 1" (Avg.; 1" below southeast). 1-5 Sunny, cold. 6-8 Rain, sleet, snow north; cold. 9-10 Sunny, milder. 11-14 Cold wave, snow. 15-18 Sunny, warming. 19-20 Cold; rain southeast. 21-25 Sunny, mild. 26-28 Cloudy & cold. 29-31 Clearing, warming.

Jan. 1991: Temp. 20° (1.5° above avg.); Precip. 0.5" (0.5" below avg.; 0.5" above south). 1-3 Clear & mild. 4-6 Blizzard. 7-9 Clearing, warming. 10-14 Sunny, mild. 15-17 Snowstorm, cold. 18-22 Clear, cold nights; flurries. 23-25 Sunny, milder. 26-31 Cold wave; snowstorm west, flurries east.

Feb. 1991: Temp. 22° (2.5° below avg.); Precip. 0.5" (0.5" below avg.). 1-2 Clearing west, snow southeast. 3-6 Snow, milder, then clearing. 7-11 Cold, flurries. 12-13 Partial clearing, cold.

14-17 Snowstorm. 18-23 Sunny, mild. 24-26 Cold snap, light snow. 27-28 Snow, seasonable.

Mar. 1991: Temp. 34° (1° below avg.; 4° below west); Precip. 4" (1.5" above avg.). 1-3 Rain, mild. 4-7 Cold wave; snow. 8-9 Clearing, cold. 10-11 Snow, heavy east. 12-16 Severe cold. 17-19 Clear, seasonable. 20-22 Rain & sleet. 23-26 Rain, mild. 27-30 Sunny; heavy rain south. 31 Rain & snow.

Apr. 1991: Temp. 54.5° (4° above avg.); Precip. 2" (1" below avg.). 1-2 Snow, cold. 3-6 Sunny; rain southeast. 7-8 Sunny, warm. 9-11 Warm, rain east. 12-14 Cloudy; cold north. 15-17 Cold; showers. 18-26 Sunny & warm, then cloudy & cool. 27-30 Rain, warm.

May 1991: Temp. 62° (Avg.; 1° above west); Precip. 2" (2" below avg.). 1-3 Cloudy, seasonable. 4-7 Rain, then clearing. 8-11 Rain, locally heavy; cool. 12-13 Sunny & warm. 14-16 Cold wave; rain. 17-26 Sunny, warm; few showers. 27-29 Showers; mild. 30-31 Sunny, warm.

June 1991: Temp. 71° (1° below avg.; 0.5° above south); Precip. 2" (2" below avg.; 2" above west). 1-4 Cold wave; rain. 5-9 Clear & warm. 10-12 Showers, warm. 13-15 Clear & hot. 16-18 Showers, heavy north; milder. 19-24 Sunny; showers south; mild. 25-30 Rain, seasonable.

July 1991: Temp. 76° (Avg.); Precip. 7" (4" above avg.; 1" below west). 1-3 Heavy rain; mild. 4-8 Sunny, seasonable. 9-11 Hot, showers. 12-16 Showers; milder. 17-22 Cooler, then showers. 23-27 Heavy rain, dry northwest; warm, then milder. 28-31 Sunny, showers east.

Aug. 1991: Temp. 74° (Avg.; 1° below west); Precip. 2" (2" below avg.; 2" above west). 1-3 Showers. 4-5 Sunny, seasonable. 6-11 Few showers; cool. 12-15 Clearing, warming. 16-20 Rain, heavy north; warm. 21-24 Clear & hot, few sprinkles. 25-28 Heat wave. 29-31 Showers, warm.

Sept. 1991: Temp. 70° (5° above avg.; 3° above south); Precip. 2" (1.5" below avg.). 1-4 Sunny & hot, showers northeast. 5-9 Showers, warm; then clearing. 10-12 Cold, rain. 13-14 Clearing, warming. 15-23 Sunny & hot. 24-26 Cold; rain north. 27-30 Clearing, mild.

Oct. 1991: Temp. 52° (2° below avg.); Precip. 1" (1" below avg.). 1-4 Clear, warm; rain southeast. 5-9 Cloudy, mild. 10-12 Heavy rain, cold wave. 13-15 Cold; showers west. 16-19 Sunny & warm. 20-21 Cold snap, showers. 22-27 Clear, cool; showers south. 28-31 Clear, warm.

For regional boundaries, see map page 133.

SUMMARY: *Late fall and winter are expected to be considerably colder than normal, with heavy precipitation in central and southern sections. November will start out warm and dry, but turn cold and wet during the latter half of the month. December and January will see warm spells alternating with cold ones, with heavy precipitation in early and mid-December and heavy snows in northern and central sections during January. Very cold periods with snow are anticipated for late January-early February and again at mid-March, with warm spells interspersed.*

Spring should be warm and wet in the north and warm and dry in the south, with April having brief hot spells through the month and little rainfall until the last few days. May will have mild periods with heavy rainfall at the middle and end of the month. The middle third of June will be quite hot. Heavy rain is expected in the northeast late in June.

Summer is anticipated to be warm in the south but cooler than normal in the north, with below-normal rainfall over much of the region. Seasonable to mild temperatures should prevail through July and early August before hot spells appear in mid and late August and late September. After showers in mid-July, central and southern sections will be quite dry until the south experiences heavy rains in the middle of September.

Early fall should be drier than normal with warm spells at the end of September and the middle part of October.

Nov. 1990: Temp. 54° (2° below avg.; 1° above south); Precip. 3" (0.5" above avg.; 0.5" below north). 1-3 Warm, showers east. 4-7 Mild, showers east. 8-10 Sunny, warm. 11-15 Cool then warming; rain east. 16-18 Cold wave, rain. 19-20 Clear, mild. 21-27 Cold; rain, heavy east. 28-30 Sunny, seasonable.

Dec. 1990: Temp. 47.5° (1° below avg.; 0.5° above east); Precip. 4" (2" above avg.; avg. east & west). 1-5 Clear & mild. 6-12 Heavy rain, some sun; cold. 13-17 Cold, snow north. 18-20 Heavy rain, sunny west; cold. 21-26 Clear & mild. 27-29 Cold. 30-31 Clear & warm.

Jan. 1991: Temp. 44° (1° below avg.); Precip. 2.5" (0.5" above avg.; avg. north). 1-2 Sunny & warm. 3-5 Rain, cold. 6-11 Clearing, mild. 12-15 Cloudy, showers east. 16-19 Cold, then clear & mild. 20-24 Cold, snow; rain south. 25-27 Clear & mild. 28-31 Snowstorm, severe cold.

Feb. 1991: Temp. 45.5° (4° below avg.); Precip. 1.5" (0.5" below avg.; 1" above south). 1-3 Snowstorm, light west. 4-6 Clear, cold. 7-10 Rain & snow; cold. 11-14 Cloudy & cold; flur-

ries. 15-17 Snow, very cold. 18-23 Clearing, warm. 24-28 Cold; snow, rain south.

Mar. 1991: Temp. 56° (1° below avg.; 2° above south); Precip. 4" (1" above avg.; avg. south & west). 1-3 Rain, light south; mild. 4-5 Sunny, seasonable. 6-7 Rain. 8-10 Cloudy, cold; snow north. 11-12 Sunny, cold. 13-17 Cold wave, snow. 18-23 Clearing, warm. 24-27 Rain, cooler. 28-31 Sunny, warm, few showers.

Apr. 1991: Temp. 69° (3° above avg.); Precip. 2.5" (2" below avg.). 1-4 Cold snap, then clear & warm. 5-8 Sunny, seasonable. 9-11 Cloudy, unseasonably warm. 12-13 Cloudy, showers east; milder. 14-16 Sunny, very warm; showers east. 17-24 Cloudy, seasonable, then very warm. 25-30 Showers, then heavy rain.

May 1991: Temp. 75° (1° above avg.; 2° above south); Precip. 6" (2" above avg.; 2" below north, 0.5" above south). 1-6 Sunny, very warm. 7-11 Cloudy, seasonable; showers east, then clearing. 12-16 Cloudy, heavy rain east; cool. 17-20 Sunny, very warm. 21-23 Showers. 24-27 Clear, hot. 28-31 Rain, cold wave.

June 1991: Temp. 83° (1° above avg.; avg. north); Precip. 3" (Avg.; 3" below south; 3" above north). 1-11 Clearing, warm; showers west. 12-15 Sunny, showers north; warm. 16-18 Clear & hot. 19-23 Cloudy, showers north; very hot west. 24-27 Cloudy, hot; heavy rain northeast. 28-30 Very heavy rain, light Gulf.

July 1991: Temp. 84° (1° below avg.; 0.5° above south); Precip. 4" (2" above avg.; 0.5" below west). 1-2 Rain ending, mild. 3-6 Sunny, rain Gulf. 7-9 Showers, mild. 10-16 Rain, heavy north. 17-19 Cloudy, hot. 20-24 Showers, heavy north & Gulf. 25-27 Sunny, showers north. 28-31 Cloudy, seasonable.

Aug. 1991: Temp. 87° (1° above avg.; 2° below north); Precip. 1" (1" below avg.; 2" above north). 1-3 Clear, seasonable. 4-7 Showers, milder. 8-11 Partly cloudy, mild. 12-19 Sunny, very hot; heavy rain northeast. 20-22 Seasonably hot, showers south. 23-27 Clear, very hot. 28-31 Cloudy, rain east; milder.

Sept. 1991: Temp. 79° (0.5° above avg.; 0.5° below south); Precip. 1" (3" below avg.; 3" above south Gulf). 1-4 Showers, rain Gulf; seasonable. 5-11 Sunny & hot. 12-15 Showers, heavy rain Gulf; mild. 16-20 Clear. 21-24 Rain south, sunny & hot north. 25-27 Clear & hot. 28-30 Sunny, milder; showers Gulf.

Oct. 1991: Temp. 65° (3° below avg.); Precip. 1.5" (2" below avg.). 1-6 Clear, seasonably warm. 7-11 Partly cloudy, showers north. 12-15 Scattered showers, cooler than normal. 16-20 Sunny, very warm. 21-25 Intermittent rain, cold wave. 26-31 Clear, seasonably warm.

For regional boundaries, see map page 133.

SUMMARY: *Late fall and winter are expected to be colder than normal with slightly below normal precipitation but above-normal snowfall. Following a mild opening, November will be very cold and stormy with above-normal snow, to be followed by a slightly mild and dry December despite a cold and snowy period at mid-month. January should be fairly mild after a cold and snowy beginning, quite dry in the south but wet in the north with above-normal snow. February and March will be quite cold with well above normal snowfall, especially in northern sections.*

Spring is anticipated to be warmer and drier than normal in southern sections but become slightly cooler and wetter than normal in northern ones. April and May will be quite variable, with brief warm spells alternating with cold ones and with frequent shower activity during April. June will be seasonable to warm except for a cold and wet final week, with frequent showers and some flooding in the north but considerably less in the south.

Summer is expected to be quite warm and dry in the south, but cooler than normal in the north with only slightly below normal precipitation. Other than a few brief hot spells during July, temperatures on through August should be seasonable to mild, while September will have alternating hot and cool periods. Only light shower activity is anticipated.

Early fall will see a continuation of warm and dry spells alternating with brief cold and wet ones,resulting in a generally warmer and drier than normal period.

Nov. 1990: Temp. 36° (3° below avg.); Precip. 2" (1" above avg.; avg. north; 0.5" below south). 1-3 Rain, seasonable. 4-5 Sunny & warm. 6-11 Cold wave; snow, heavy central. 12-16 Cold; snow, then clearing. 17-22 Continuing cold, some snow. 23-26 Colder, snowstorm south. 27-30 Clear, snowstorm north.

Dec. 1990: Temp. 31° (0.5° above avg.; 0.5° below south); Precip. 1" (0.5" below avg.). 1-3 Clear & mild. 4-6 Rain & snow, snow north. 7-10 Clearing north, snow south. 11-14 Cold, snowstorm. 15-17 Clear, very cold nights. 18-20 Normal cold, light snow. 21-24 Cloudy & cold, flurries; sunny south. 25-31 Clearing.

Jan. 1991: Temp. 31° (3° above avg.); Precip. 1" (0.5" below avg.). 1-5 Cold, snow. 6-12 Clear & mild south; warming north, with rain, sleet & snow. 13-15 Sunny, seasonable; light snow north. 16-20 Clear, cold. 21-25 Cold. 26-28 Milder, snow. 29-31 Cold.

Feb. 1991: Temp. 32° (2° below avg.); Precip. 1" (0.5" below avg.; 0.5" above north). 1-4 Clearing, warming. 5-8 Cloudy, cold; light snow. 9-11 Snow, sunny north. 12-13 Clear, seasonable. 14-16 Cold wave, snow. 17-19 Clear, seasonable. 20-23 Rain, snow mountains & north; mild. 24-28 Rain then snow; colder.

Mar. 1991: Temp. 37° (4° below avg.); Precip. 1.5" (Avg.). 1-2 Sunny , snow south. 3-7 Snow, cold. 8-11 Clearing, seasonable. 12-15 Cold, snow. 16-18 Sunny, warming. 19-22 Snowstorm. 23-26 Snowstorm, very cold. 27-29 Sunny & mild. 30-31 Rain & snow.

Apr. 1991: Temp. 49° (Avg.; 3° above south); Precip. 2" (Avg.; 1" below south). 1-4 Sunny, mild, then snowstorm. 5-6 Clearing, mild. 7-11 Rain turning to snow; colder. 12-13 Sunny, seasonable. 14-16 Rain, snow mountains; cold. 17-20 Sunny, very warm. 21-23 Rain, cool. 24-26 Clear & warm. 27-30 Cold & rainy.

May 1991: Temp. 59° (Avg.; 2° above south); Precip. 0.5" (1" below avg.; avg. north). 1-3 Clear, warm; showers north. 4-6 Showers, very cool. 7-11 Sunny, few showers; warm. 12-15 Rain, heavy north; cold. 16-18 Sunny, normal; showers north. 19-21 Clear & hot. 22-25 Showers, seasonable. 26-31 Sunny, very warm.

June 1991: Temp. 69° (0.5° above avg.); Precip. 2" (1" above avg.; avg. south). 1-3 Showers. 4-9 Sunny, warm; then showers, cooler. 10-14 Hot, showers. 15-18 Showers, some sun; warm. 19-23 Sunny & warm, rain north. 24-27 Cold, heavy rain. 28-30 Sunny & warm.

July 1991: Temp. 77° (0.5° below avg.; 2° below north); Precip. 0.5" (Avg.; 1" below south). 1-4 Sunny, hot; few showers. 5-7 Showers, milder. 8-12 Sunny, seasonable; rain north. 13-15 Clear & hot. 16-20 Showers, milder; clear & hot south. 21-22 Clear, hot. 23-29 Thundershowers, warm. 30-31 Clear, hot.

Aug. 1991: Temp. 74° (1° below avg.; 1° above south); Precip. 0.5" (0.5" below avg.). 1-2 Rain, cool. 3-7 Sunny, seasonable. 8-12 Showers, milder. 13-16 Hot, showers north. 17-22 Showers, then clearing & warm. 23-29 Showers, some sun & warm. 30-31 Clear, hot.

Sept. 1991: Temp. 67° (2° above avg.; 0.5° below north); Precip. 0.5" (0.5" below avg.). 1-7 Sunny, heat wave; few showers north. 8-12 Cold wave; cloudy & mild, showers. 13-19 Clear & hot. 20-24 Cloudy; rain, cool. 25-26 Clear. 27-30 Cold wave; rain, snow mountains.

Oct. 1991: Temp. 53° (Avg.; 1° above south); Precip. 0.5" (0.5" below avg.). 1-2 Showers, cold. 3-7 Clear, warm. 8-10 Cold snap; rain, snow mountains. 11-17 Sunny, Indian summer-like weather. 18-20 Light rain, cold. 21-24 Sunny, warming; showers south. 25-28 Clear & warm. 29-31 Turning cold, sprinkles.

For regional boundaries, see map page 133.

SUMMARY: *Late fall and winter are expected to be colder than normal, with below-normal precipitation in the west, but slightly above in the east. After a sunny and warm beginning, November will be generally cool with frequent showers, while December should be sunny and warm early and late in the month, with a cold, wet period in between. Except for a cold wave early in January, most of that month should be quite warm and dry; February and March will be generally cool with frequent showers, except for a warm and dry period at the end of February.*

Spring will be warmer and drier than usual, though eastern sections will have slightly above normal rainfall. After a few scattered showers in early April, sunny and seasonable weather is expected until the arrival of a heat wave late in the month. May should see frequent hot spells alternating with brief milder ones, with June being closer to normal except for showers in the east early in the month.

Summer will be warmer and drier than normal, although southern sections will have close to normal rainfall. Most of July will remain very hot and dry until the final week when rains, heavy in the south, are expected. Temperatures will be close to normal in August, with few showers except in the south and east, while the first half of September will be very hot and dry but then return to normal with a few showers.

Early fall will be sunny and slightly warmer than normal, with a cold front expected near the end of October.

Nov. 1990: Temp. 57° (4° below avg.; 1° below east); Precip. 0.5" (Avg.). 1-5 Cloudy then clear, warm. 6-9 Cloudy, cool. 10-12 Clear, cold nights. 13-17 Cold & rainy. 18-19 Sunny, cool. 20-24 Rain. 25-27 Few showers, cold. 28-30 Clear, cold nights.

Dec. 1990: Temp. 51° (2° below avg.); Precip. 0.3" (0.5" below avg.). 1-4 Clear, pleasantly warm. 5-7 Rain, locally heavy, cold. 8-9 Partial clearing, seasonable. 10-13 Rain, unseasonably cold. 14-20 Sunny, continuing cold; very cold nights. 21-26 Clear; mild days, cold nights. 27-31 Clear & warm.

Jan. 1991: Temp. 53° (0.5° above avg.); Precip. 0" (0.5" below avg.). 1-2 Sunny & warm. 3-5 Cold wave; rain, snow mountains. 6-8 Clearing & warming. 9-21 Clear; warm days, seasonable nights. 22-24 Cloudy, showers; seasonable. 25-29 Clear, turning warm. 30-31 Cold wave; showers, snow east.

Feb. 1991: Temp. 53° (3° below avg.); Precip. 0.3" (0.3" below avg.; 0.5" above south). 1-2 Cloudy, very cold; snow east. 3-6 Clear, very cold nights. 7-11 Cloudy, cold & rainy. 12-14 Clearing; cool. 15-19 Cold, rain. 20-26 Clear; warm days. 27-28 Cold wave, rain.

Mar. 1991: Temp. 57° (4° below avg.); Precip. 1.5" (0.5" above avg.; avg. east). 1-2 Rain, cool. 3-4 Sunny, mild. 5-8 Rain, heavy south; cool. 9-13 Sunny, cold nights. 14-16 Showers, snow east, then clearing. 17-20 Cloudy, seasonable; few sprinkles. 21-22 Sunny, cool nights. 23-26 Cold, rain. 27-31 Clear & warm.

Apr. 1991: Temp. 70° (2° above avg.); Precip. 0° (0.3" above avg.; avg. east). 1-2 Clear, cold nights. 3-5 Showers, cool. 6-11 Variable clouds, seasonably warm. 12-14 Clear, very warm. 15-17 Cloudy, seasonable. 18-21 Clear & hot. 22-25 Increasing clouds, very warm. 26-28 Cloudy, mild; showers east. 29-30 Clear.

May 1991: Temp. 77° (Avg.; 2° above south); Precip. 0" (0.1" below avg.). 1-3 Clear & hot. 4-7 Cloudy; cool nights. 8-11 Clear & hot. 12-15 Cloudy & warm; showers east. 16-21 Clear, hot. 22-23 Showers; mild, cool. 24-28 Clear, hot. 29-31 Cloudy, showers south.

June 1991: Temp. 85° (1.5° below avg.; avg. south); Precip. 0.1" (0.1" below avg.). 1-4 Gradual clearing, seasonable. 5-6 Cloudy, heavy rain east; milder. 7-9 Sunny, normal. 10-12 Showers, milder. 13-22 Clear, hotter than normal; showers east. 23-27 Cloudy, milder. 28-30 Partly cloudy, seasonable.

July 1991: Temp. 92° (Avg.; 0.5° above south); Precip. 1" (0.5" above avg.; 0.5" below east). 1-4 Clear, very hot. 5-7 Showers, seasonable. 8-10 Clearing. 11-14 Clear, very hot. 15-17 Cloudy, showers east. 18-20 Clear, hot. 21-27 Cloudy, showers; milder. 28-31 Showers.

Aug. 1991: Temp. 90.5° (0.5° above avg.); Precip. 0.5" (0.5" below avg.; 0.5" above east). 1-5 Clear & hot, milder nights. 6-11 Rain, seasonable. 12-15 Cloudy, hot. 16-18 Sprinkles. 19-22 Clear, hot. 23-26 Cloudy, showers. 27-31 Clear & hot, showers east.

Sept. 1991: Temp. 86° (1.5° above avg.; 2.5° above south); Precip. 0" (0.5" below avg.). 1-2 Clear, hot; showers south. 3-5 Cloudy, milder. 6-11 Sunny; very hot, then milder. 12-15 Partly cloudy, very warm; showers east, mild. 16-18 Sunny, very warm. 19-21 Showers, milder. 22-30 Sunny, seasonably warm.

Oct. 1991: Temp. 74° (0.5° above avg.); Precip. 0.3" (0.3" below avg.). 1-2 Showers, seasonable. 3-6 Clear & hot. 7-9 Partly cloudy, showers; warm. 10-12 Clear, hot. 13-17 Cloudy, milder; showers east. 18-20 Sunny & warm. 21-24 Showers, cool. 25-29 Clear, warm. 30-31 Cloudy, seasonable; showers.

For regional boundaries, see map page 133.

SUMMARY: Late fall and winter are expected to be warmer than usual, with below-normal precipitation and above-normal snow in the mountains. November and December will be wet, with more heavy precipitation the first half of January. It should then be drier than normal from mid-January through mid-February before the arrival of a wet period from the end of February through March. Cold spells alternate with warm ones from November through January except for a more prolonged warm period from mid-December to mid-January. Most of February and March see below-normal temperatures.

Spring may be much wetter than normal, with below-normal temperatures in the north and above in the south. The first half of May should see heavier than normal rainfall. Temperatures will be variable, with a sub-normal period in April and extended ones through the first half of May and the latter half of June, interspersed with warm spells.

Summer will be near normal except for a cooler and wetter period during late August. Warm spells in early and mid-July, early August, and mid-September will alternate with more extended subnormal temperatures over much of the rest of the season.

After a cold wave with heavy rains at the end of September, the early fall should see sunny and warm spells alternating with cold and rainy ones on through October.

Nov. 1990: Temp. 47° (1.5° above avg.; avg. north); Precip. 4.5" (0.5" below avg.). 1-4 Rain, seasonable. 5-8 Cold & rainy. 9-11 Rain, heavy north; milder. 12-16 Rain, locally heavy. 17-19 Heavy rain, colder north. 20-24 Cold wave; rain, snow mountains. 25-28 Sunny, warming. 29-30 Showers; rain north.

Dec. 1990: Temp. 44° (3° above avg.); Precip. 5" (1.5" below avg.; avg. north). 1-3 Sunny & mild. 4-7 Rain, heavy north; seasonable. 8-10 Some sun, cool. 11-16 Rain. 17-19 Heavy rain, milder. 20-24 Sunny then rain; milder than normal. 25-27 Rain, heavy north. 28-30 Sunny & mild. 31 Rain, heavy north; snow mountains.

Jan. 1991: Temp. 40° (1° below avg.); Precip. 6" (Avg.; 1" below north). 1-3 Rain then clearing; seasonable. 4-11 Cold waves; heavy rain, heavy snow mountains. 12-15 Rain, heavy north; milder. 16-19 Sunny & mild. 20-25 Cloudy, very cold. 26-28 Scattered showers, rain north; mild. 29-31 Clearing & mild.

Feb. 1991: Temp. 41° (2° below avg.); Precip. 4.5" (0.5" above avg.). 1-2 Clear, cold nights. 3-8 Cold; rain, snow mountains. 9-11 Cloudy, cold. 12-14 Heavy rain, snow mountains. 15-

17 Clear, very cold. 18-22 Heavy rain, mild. 23-26 Heavy rain, heavy snow mountains; cold. 27-28 Showers, mild.

Mar. 1991: Temp. 45° (1° below avg.); Precip. 4.5" (1" above avg.). 1-3 Heavy rain, snow mountains. 4-5 Sunny, seasonable. 6-7 Rain, snow mountains; cold. 8-9 Sunny, milder. 10-13 Rain, scattered north. 14-17 Cloudy, light showers. 18-24 Rain, snow mountains; cold. 25-27 Heavy rain; cold wave. 28-31 Rain.

Apr. 1991: Temp. 50° (Avg.; 1° below north); Precip. 1.5" (Avg.). 1-2 Clear & warm. 3-6 Light rain, seasonable. 7-11 Cold wave; rain, snow mountains. 12-13 Some sun, milder. 14-16 Cold & rainy. 17-19 Light showers, warmer. 20-22 Rain, cool. 23-25 Sunny & warm. 26-30 Rain, snow mountains; turning cold.

May 1991: Temp. 55° (1.5° below avg.); Precip. 3" (1" above avg.). 1-5 Sun, showers; cold. 6-12 Rain, locally heavy; cool. 13-15 Clearing & warm; rain north. 16-17 Rain, cool. 18-19 Sunny. 20-24 Showers, cold; clearing. 25-27 Cloudy, cool. 28-31 Sunny, warm.

June 1991: Temp. 64.5° (2° above avg.); Precip. 2" (0.5" above avg.). 1-3 Heavy rain, cold wave. 4-6 Clear & warm. 7-9 Cloudy, showers; cooler. 10-13 Clear, unseasonably warm. 14-18 Rain, locally heavy; cool. 19-20 Clear & pleasant. 21-25 Intermittent rain, turning cool. 26-30 Partly cloudy & mild.

July 1991: Temp. 68° (Avg.); Precip. 0.5" (Avg.; 1" above north). 1-4 Clear, warm. 5-8 Cloudy, mild. 9-11 Rain, cool. 12-13 Sunny, seasonable. 14-16 Sprinkles, cooler. 17-21 Clear, warm. 22-24 Showers, cool. 25-27 Sprinkles, mild. 28-31 Sunny, rain.

Aug. 1991: Temp. 66° (1.5° below avg.); Precip. 1.5" (0.5" below avg.; avg. north). 1-5 Rain ending; clear, very warm. 6-10 Cool; scattered showers. 11-16 Sunny, increasing clouds; cool. 17-22 Cool; rainy, heavy south. 23-25 Cloudy, warm; cool, rain north. 26-28 Rain, cool. 29-31 Clear, warm; showers north.

Sept. 1991: Temp. 62.5° (Avg.); Precip. 2.5" (1" above avg.; avg. north). 1-2 Sunny & warm. 3-9 Intermittent showers. 10-16 Clear & warm. 17-19 Rain, turning cool. 20-23 Sunny seasonable. 24-27 Rain, becoming heavy south; cold wave. 28-30 Heavy rain, partial clearing north; cold.

Oct. 1991: Temp. 53.5° (1° below avg.); Precip. 2.5" (0.5" below avg.). 1-3 Heavy rain, cool. 4-7 Sunny & warm. 8-12 Rain, locally heavy; cool. 13-14 Sunny & warm. 15-16 Rain, seasonably cool. 17-19 Partly cloudy, seasonable. 20-23 Clear & mild. 24-26 Cloudy, cooler. 27-31 Light showers, cold.

For regional boundaries, see map page 133.

SUMMARY: *Late fall and winter are expected to be warmer than normal in the north and slightly below average in the south. Precipitation may be well below normal with a continuation of drought conditions, while average snowfall is anticipated in the northern mountains but below average in the south. November will be cool and dry except for the north coast. Early December may see a winter storm hit Southern California and then the north should get one just before Christmas. January is anticipated to be very warm and dry, while February and the first half of March will be cooler, but continue drier than normal. The last half of March, though, should bring frequent storms and heavy snows to the mountains.*

Spring is apt to be cooler and wetter in the north, but warmer than normal with average rainfall in the south. A cool and rainy period prior to mid-April should be followed by warm, sunny spells later, and then warm spells alternate with cooler ones in May. June starts mild and showery, then sunny and warm.

The summer will be dry and cool in the north and warmer than normal in the south. A heat wave near mid-July and ones in early and mid-September are expected.

Early fall may see a cold wave at the end of September, but then clear and warm spells are expected during the first half of October and again at the end of the month.

Nov. 1990: Temp. 55° (Avg.; 2° below south & inland); Precip. 1.5" (1" below avg.). 1-3 Rain, showers south; cool. 4-5 Sunny, warm. 6-9 Partly cloudy, rain north; cool. 10-17 Sunny, seasonable; showers south. 18-20 Rain, few showers south; cool. 21-27 Partly cloudy, cool; sprinkles south. 28-30 Clear & warm.

Dec. 1990: Temp. 51° (2° above avg.); Precip. 2.5" (1" below avg.; avg. south). 1-2 Sunny, warm. 3-6 Mild; cloudy, rain south. 7-9 Rain, heavy south. 10-13 Showers, cool south. 14-20 Clear & warm. 21-23 Rain, heavy north; snow mountains. 24-26 Rain, light south; warm. 27-31 Drizzle; clear & warm south.

Jan. 1991: Temp. 52.5° (4° above avg.); Precip. 1" (3" below avg.). 1-3 Sprinkles, mild. 4-6 Rain, spotty inland; sunny south. 7-12 Rain, heavy north; sunny & warm south. 13-15 Sprinkles, mild; sunny & warm south. 16-21 Clear & warm. 22-28 Sunny; warm inland, seasonable south. 29-31 Sunny, showers south.

Feb. 1991: Temp. 51° (1° below avg.); Precip. 2" (1" below avg.). 1-7 Sunny, cold nights; drizzle coast. 8-10 Rain, snow mountains; cool. 11-14 Showers, cool; sunny south. 15-18 Clear & warm. 19-23 Showers, sunny south;

warm. 24-25 Sunny. 26-28 Cloudy, rain north.

Mar. 1991: Temp. 51° (1.5° below avg.; 2.5° below south); Precip. 3" (0.5" above avg.). 1-3 Warm, cloudy coast. 4-6 Rainstorm, cool. 7-12 Sunny, rain north. 13-15 Rain, cool; sunny south. 16-17 Clear & warm. 18-25 Heavy rain, snow mountains; cool. 26-27 Clear & warm. 28-31 Heavy rain, snow mountains; cold.

Apr. 1991: Temp. 55° (Avg.; 1° above south); Precip. 2" (Avg.). 1-3 Clear & warm, then rain, light south. 4-6 Partly cloudy. 7-9 Heavy rain, cool. 10-13 Showers, spotty south. 14-16 Heavy rain, sprinkles south; cool. 17-22 Sunny then rain, heavy north; clear & hot south. 23-26 Cloudy, sprinkles; cooler. 27-30 Rain; sunny & warm south.

May 1991: Temp. 56° (1.5° below avg.; 1° above south); Precip. 1" (0.5" above avg.). 1-4 Heavy rain, cool. 5-10 Sunny & warm; showers north. 11-13 Cloudy, mild. 14-16 Sunny, warm. 17-21 Clear & warm; hot inland. 22-25 Rain, cold wave; showers & cool south. 26-27 Clear & warm. 28-31 Partly cloudy, seasonable.

June 1991: Temp. 60° (1° below avg.; 0.5° above south); Precip. 0.2" (0.2" above avg.). 1-3 Rain, mild; showers south. 4-7 Heavy rain, warm. 8-10 Cloudy, sprinkles; mild. 11-13 Sunny, warm. 14-16 Cloudy, showers north. 17-23 Sunny & warm. 24-26 Cloudy, showers north. 27-30 Clear & hot; drizzle coast.

July 1991: Temp. 60° (2° below avg.; 1.5° above south); Precip. 0" (Avg.). 1-4 Clear & warm, hot inland. 5-8 Partly cloudy, milder inland; sunny south. 9-11 Few showers north, clear & hot south. 12-15 Clear & warm, very warm south. 16-21 Sunny, very hot inland. 22-31 Sunny, seasonable; few sprinkles.

Aug. 1991: Temp. 61° (2° below avg.; 0.5° above south); Precip. 0" (Avg.). 1-10 Sunny, warm; drizzle north coast. 11-16 Clear & warm, coastal fog. 17-22 Sunny, warm & dry. 23-25 Clear & hot. 26-28 Showers north; partly cloudy, milder. 29-31 Clear & warm.

Sept. 1991: Temp. 62° (2° below avg.; 1.5° above south); Precip. 0" (0.2" below avg.). 1-2 Clear, seasonably warm; hot inland. 3-7 Clear & hot. 8-11 Partly cloudy, drizzle north coast; seasonable. 12-19 Clear, very hot. 20-23 Cloudy, showers north coast; hot. 24-30 Cloudy; cold & light showers north.

Oct. 1991: Temp. 60.5° (Avg.; 0.5° above south); Precip. 0.5" (0.5" below avg.). 1-6 Clear & warm. 7-10 Rain north. 11-13 Clear & hot. 14-20 Cloudy, rain north, drizzle coast; mild. 21-23 Seasonable; rain south. 24-27 Clear, warm. 28-31 Cloudy, turning cool.

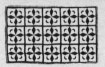

- Illustration by Sal Murdocca

William Dempster Hoard, Wisconsin journalist, politician, and crusader on behalf of the dairy industry, founded *Hoard's Dairyman* magazine in 1885 and ran for governor in 1888 as the "cow candidate." He reminded farmers of the virtue of their calling, posting in his own barn this notice: "Remember that this is the home of Mothers. Treat each cow as a Mother should be treated." In fact, Hoard said, "The Cow is the Foster Mother of the human race." With this in mind, we offer the following unhomogenized compendium of facts and lore about our foster mother, the dairy cow.

Facts and Stories About Our Foster Mother, the Dairy Cow

She gets up and down 14 times a day. She stands with her tail to the wind. She produces 15 tons of cow plops a year. And you'd be surprised how well she remembers!

BY SUSAN PEERY

WHERE COWS COME FROM AND WHAT THEY'RE CALLED

The genus name for cattle is *Bos,* hence the familiar call "Come, Bos" and pet name Bossie. All domestic cattle belong to species *Bos taurus* (European breeds such as shorthorn, Jersey, Holstein, and others) or *Bos indicus* (Brahman and others) or crosses of the two. The English word "cattle" is etymologically synonymous with "chattel," meaning property.

Egyptians domesticated cattle about 3500 B.C. Most cultures have used the males for draft and the females for supplying milk. (Raising catle for meat is a modern notion; some cultures still regard beef as unfit for human consumption.)

Gender terminology: A male is first a *bull calf,* then at puberty a *bull*; if castrated (before puberty), he becomes a *steer* and in two or three years is called an *ox*. Males castrated after sexual maturity (called *stags*) usually exhibit considerable sex drive. A female is first a *heifer calf*, then a *heifer*, and after breeding (usually at 1½ to two years) is called a *cow*. A *freemartin* is a sterile female born as a twin to a bull (only about one of 12 freemartins is fertile; for this reason, twinning is not considered a desirable trait to breed for). The term "freemartin" comes from an old English expression signifying a cow free to be fattened for slaughter at Martinmas (Saint Martin's Day) in November.

COW ANATOMY
(COURTESY OF RUBE GOLDBERG)

Like other ruminants, cows have a complex stomach with four divisions, the largest of which, called the *rumen* or paunch, has a capacity of as much as 30 gallons. The other three stomachs are the *reticulum* (which holds one gallon), the *omasum* (two gallons), and *abomasum* (or true stomach, holding two gallons). This design is responsible for frequent digestive disturbances, especially bloat and compaction. Perforation of the stomach caused by sharp objects in the feed is also common.

Because of the complicated design of her stomach, a cow cannot vomit. When she raises her cud from the first stomach to thoroughly grind it (having gulped her food the first time), she swallows it a second time. This time it goes automatically to the third stomach and finally to the fourth, then on to the bowels. (The second stomach, a reservoir of alkaline digestive juices, also collects foreign objects that wander down the cow's throat.)

A cow's intestines are as much as 170 feet long. Her liver weighs 10 to 12 pounds, the heart 5, and the kidneys average 20 pounds apiece.

A DAY IN THE LIFE OF A COW

Cows in a barn get up and down an average of 14 times in 24 hours.

Cows urinate between six and eight times a day and defecate from 13 to 16 times. This produces 30 pounds of urine and 65 pounds of feces (also known as cow plops, pies, or platters) per day per cow, or 15 tons a year. Cows tend to hump up to urinate, while bulls stand squarely on all fours.

Cows have keener senses of hearing and smell than humans. With the help of a stiff breeze, a cow can detect odors from six miles away.

The average cow belches up to 400 liters of methane a day, possibly contributing to global warming.

A line of cows following the leader toward the barn at milking time exhibits what veterinarians call allelomimetic behavior (a strong tendency to mimic) — the leader starts toward the barn, the others follow; because the others are following, the leader keeps going. (The leader is not necessarily the most dominant cow.)

Cows have good maternal instincts and exhibit great concern for newborns, licking them (to dry and "massage" them) and "talking" to them to encourage them to stand and nurse. A herd will often have five or six "secret" spots in the field where they like to have their calves, despite the farmer's best efforts to bring them into the barn. Cows often try to hide newborn calves and can become quite protective if the calf is threatened. However, most dairy calves are removed from their mothers at two to three days old and weaned onto milk replacement, severing the maternal bond to the distress of both parties.

Most cows will moo and get restless at any change in their routine. Dave and Lyndon Scott, whose family has farmed for nine generations in the Pioneer Valley at Whately, Massachusetts, once washed down their dairy barn only to find that their 50 cows, smelling a change, refused to go inside.

Cows remember: The Scotts moved their cows from an old barn into a new barn not far away. Two years later a storm blew open the doors of the old barn, and the cows found their way in. Each cow went unerringly to its original stanchion in the old barn.

Cows, like many other animals, become uneasy when a storm is approaching. During a storm they tend to face away from the wind and drift downwind. On breezy days they usually stand with their tails to the wind.

Some cows in a herd are more popular than others. Unpopular cows often are pushed and shoved by dominant cows. Every herd develops its pecking order, and cows usually keep the same relative position when new members are added. Sometimes conflict among dominant cows so disturbs the herd (hurting milk production) that the dominants are segregated; the rest of the herd generally settles into a new order, but within the limits of their feistiness. Usually the highest producers have the best temperaments.

Most cows like to be rubbed or scratched under the chin and behind the ears. Few cows like to have their faces rubbed. Many cows will enjoy having their backbones scratched with a long-handled brush.

Left to their own devices, cows live to about 18 or 20 years of age. In practice, dairy cows whose milk production has declined (perhaps at age ten or 12) become hamburger.

A calf whose tail nearly reaches the ground is more than a year old.

One rule of thumb is to castrate a calf when his testicles are the size of a squirrel's head.

How to Milk a Cow

The udder is not just an upside-down milk bottle waiting to be uncorked. It is a gland that secretes milk in response to the hormone oxytocin, which is released by the pituitary gland. Milk letdown occurs naturally when the calf nuzzles and begins to suck on the teat; letdown happens in the milking parlor when the udder is washed or sprayed with warm water, which has a massaging effect. Only then can a cow be milked.

Milking, the removal of milk from the udder, is accomplished most efficiently by a calf. Hand milking a cow is the next most efficient method. Cows are traditionally milked from the right. The advantage of hand milking is that the cow can be thoroughly milked out, which helps increase her milk supply. The last milk is the richest and contains a high percentage of butterfat.

It takes about 340 squirts to make a gallon of milk.

There is some evidence that cows respond best to a feminine hand. *Hoard's Dairyman* (1945) attributed this to "motherhood responding to motherly instincts."

What and How Cows Eat

Good pasture has a high content of protein (from green leafy legumes), minerals, and carotene. Necessary minerals include salt, calcium, phosphorus, iodine, and iron.

The greener the hay, the higher the carotene (which creates vitamin A), although hay stored for a long time may lose its carotene while retaining its color. Cows also need vitamin D (usually supplied by exposure to sunshine).

Some cows like to steal hay from the neighboring cow. Others will not eat hay that has another cow's saliva on it.

Cows spend about six hours a day eating and about eight hours chewing their cud. Cows chew about 50 times per minute.

Cows eat about 100 pounds of pasture grass a day. Cows fed in the barn usually eat about a bale of hay and 12 to 15 pounds of grain (a 20-percent-protein mix of corn, wheat, bran, and soy) each day.

A heavy milker may drink as much as 300 pounds of water a day.

A four-year-old cow has 32 permanent teeth, including 12 grinders upper and lower. Instead of upper front teeth there is a tough dental pad.

Some cows like to lap up a quart or two of fresh water, then dunk mouthfuls of hay in the rest of their water.

WOODEN TONGUE, LUMPY JAW, AND OTHER BOVINE DISEASES

Keeping a cow healthy is not always a simple matter. An entire lexicon of diseases is lurking out there, many of them preventable by good sanitation, proper handling, or vaccination; or curable by antibiotics. Good dairy farmers are quick to spot the first signs of such illnesses as foot-and-mouth disease, mastitis, brucellosis or Bang's disease, milk fever, Rinderpest, Johne's disease, blackleg, wooden tongue, lumpy jaw, cowpox, pink-eye, red nose, and yet others, many of which have alarming and even gruesome symptoms.

BYE-BYE, LOVE; HELLO, ARTIFICIAL INSEMINATION

The average dairy sire in A.I. stud is mated to about 2,000 cows annually. Bulls in natural service are mated to fewer than 50 cows annually.

Cows today are still being artificially bred to American Breeders Service's Holstein bull, Valiant, who died in 1984 but left plenty of seed. He already had 35,000 offspring worldwide at the time of his death (caused by old age, if not by exhaustion).

A FEW FARM AND PRODUCTION STATISTICS

Ninety-five percent of dairy farms are run by single families. Wisconsin has the most cows (1,795,000) and the most dairy farms (37,000) of any state.

In 1930 the size of the average dairy herd was 4.6 cows, and a dairy farmer spent an average of 147.1 hours a year milking each cow. The national herd numbered 21.9 million head.

In 1986 the size of the average dairy herd was 44 cows, and a dairy farmer spent an average of 20.7 hours a year milking each cow. The national herd numbered 10.5 million.

The 21.9 million cows in 1930 produced 116.6 billion pounds of milk.

The 10.5 million cows in 1986 produced 143.4 billion pounds of milk.

Milk is 87 percent water.

COW FOLKLORE

☞ A cow is more likely to give birth to a heifer if her head is to the north and tail to the south when she is bred.

☞ Heavy thunder will sour the milk.

☞ Never geld a bull when the Moon is waning.

☞ Use a mixture of hot milk and pepper to cure colds; use sour cream to heal boils. To cure tuberculosis, eat butter made from the milk of cows that have grazed in a churchyard.

☞ It's good luck for cows to lie down on Christmas Day.

☞ Cows may lie down and refuse to graze when a storm is approaching.

OUR FAVORITE MILK RECIPE

Take a stack of homemade chocolate chip cookies. Pour a large glass of fresh cold milk. Carefully balancing the cookies and milk, take them to your screened porch on a hot summer day. Sit in the porch swing. Eat the cookies; wash them down with cold milk. If possible, do this while gazing at a herd of Holsteins in a green pasture, preferably with a few daisies in the foreground. Perfect. □□

- Illustration by Sara Mintz Zwicker

Following the Lilac's Lead

*To establish which spring frost is the last one, the best ways,
new studies now indicate, are the old ways. . . .*

BY JON VARA

"Sow seed after all danger of frost has passed." That familiar gardening dictum isn't intended to draw laughs, but it is suspiciously similar to the old joke about the train traveler who, unsure of his stop, asks the passenger in the next seat for directions.

"Nothing to it," the man replies. "Just watch me, and get off one stop before I do."

Establishing which frost is the last one is an ancient problem, and it is not surprising that farmers and gardeners through the ages have relied on a variety of natural indicators to aid in making that decision — a practice known as *phenology,* from the Greek for "the science of appearances."

Some phenological lore is based on the habits of wildlife. In the first century B.C., for example, the Roman poet Virgil suggested that grape growers refrain from putting out their frost-tender young vines until the springtime return of the white cranes. The Seneca Indians — of what is now New York State —

used human physiology as a model. Not until a naked person could comfortably sit on the bare ground, they believed, was it safe to plant corn. The Indians of southern New England kept tabs on the advancing season by watching the trees. Early New England farmers, following the Indian custom, planted corn when elm leaves were the size of a squirrel's ear or when oak leaves were the size of a mouse's ear.

The last-mentioned approach — in which hardy trees or shrubs are used to track evolving weather conditions — is generally the most accurate. That is because plant growth is not determined by any single factor, but by a host of them — everything from daytime temperature highs and nighttime lows to soil moisture, day length, and other influences too subtle for the gardener to recognize, let alone quantify. Plants, moreover, respond to conditions at the site where they are grown, not those at the nearest weather station. If the oak tree in your yard tells you one thing, and the little color-coded zone map on the back of the seed packet tells you something else, listen to the oak.

In fact, plant phenology has shown itself to be so useful as a forecasting tool that it has drawn the attention of agricultural researchers, who hope that it may — among other things — someday result in more detailed and accurate climatic zone maps than those available today. But even the newest USDA zone map (see accompanying box, page 166) can't account for circumstances in your own backyard.

One of the first systematic efforts to collect phenological data in this country began in the mid-1960s, when the late Dr. Richard Hopp, a plant and soil scientist at the University of Vermont, organized a statewide network of volunteer observers who regularly recorded the dates of five growth stages in the lilac cultivar Red Rothomagensis.

"The lilacs are playing the odds," Dr. Perry says, "just like any weather forecaster."

The earliest stage, "first leaf," occurs when the widest parts of the first emergent leaves extend beyond the enclosing bud scales. It is succeeded by "full leaf," at which at least 95 percent of the leaves have unfurled. "First bloom" is defined as the point at which at least 50 percent of the flower clusters have one or more open flowers; it is followed by "full bloom," when all of the flowers are open on at least 95 percent of the flower clusters. The fifth and final stage, "end of bloom," is reached when at least 95 percent of the flowers have withered.

The original study has now grown into a much more extensive project, with observers in 25 states and six Canadian provinces. According to Dr. Leonard Perry, who has succeeded Dr. Hopp at UVM, the data compiled in Vermont so far suggests that cold-tolerant vegetables, such as lettuce, peas, and spinach, can safely be planted when the lilacs are at first leaf. Corn, beans, squash, tomatoes, and other frost-sensitive crops, however, should wait for the lilac's full-bloom stage.

Those indicators are generally reliable, Dr. Perry says, but he is quick to point out that they are not infallible. The lilac blossoms themselves, after all, occasionally fall victim to unseasonably late frosts.

"The lilacs play the odds," he says, "just like any weather forecaster."

That is because the lilac's schedule — like that of many spring-flowering perennials — represents a carefully calculated risk. An individual plant that flowers late enough to be certain of missing the latest possible spring frost would accept a much larger risk of losing its developing seeds to any *early* frost at the other end of the growing season. And since those are the same variables that human gardeners must contend with in planting corn, following the lilac's lead is simply a way of tapping into the species' long years of evolutionary trial and error.

The UVM phenology study chose the lilac as its indicator species for a number of reasons. Lilacs thrive on a variety of soils and over a wide climatic range. They are subject to few diseases or insect pests. And because all of the individual lilac plants in the data pool are genetically identical — the Red Rothomagensis lilacs are propagated from cuttings — observed variations in leaf and blossom development can be attributed to environmental conditions rather than to any biological differences in the plants themselves.

In other words, lilacs are an excellent indicator species for a wide-ranging, long-term study because the findings can easily be compared and cross-referenced. But in a smaller area — in your yard, say — that is probably not an important consideration. Forsythia, honeysuckle, shadbush, and many other perennials can be used as indicator species, as well. According to Dr. Perry, practical home phenology is simply a matter of noting the stage of development of the indicator at the time you plant — and, if the results are satisfactory, planting on the same "phenological date" the following year. A garden diary will make it easier to keep track of things; the longer you keep records, the more meaningful the results will become.

Folklore and common sense are reinforced by results of the lilac study. The data agree fairly closely with the old New England adage that spring advances at the rate of about 100 miles a week. This concept itself was expressed in scientific terms in 1918 by researcher A. D. Hopkins of the U.S. Department of Agriculture. Hopkins proposed a bioclimatic law of latitude, longitude, and elevation for temperate North America. His rule of thumb was that spring varies four days for each one degree of latitude, five degrees of longitude, and 400 feet of elevation (later northward, eastward, and upward in the spring; autumn is the reverse). Surely Mr. Hopkins would be gratified by the purple tide of Red Rothomagensis lilacs creeping northward, eastward, and upward each spring, attended carefully by phenological observers with notebooks.

Using phenology as a guide to spring planting dates, however, is just a beginning. Data from the UVM project, for example, have enabled McIntosh apple growers in the Northeast to predict the full-bloom stage in their orchards with nearly pinpoint accuracy. That knowledge, in turn, enables them to move hives of bees into the orchard in time to achieve maximum pollination, leading to heavier crops in the fall.

Phenology can help keep other insects *out* of the crops. Agronomists at the New York Experimental Station in Geneva, New York, have found that cabbage growers can use the flowering of yellow rocket — a common field weed — to predict the initial springtime hatch of the destructive cabbage maggot. Successive summer and fall hatches are forecast by the blossoming of the common day lily, the Canada thistle, and the pale lavender variety of wild aster. (On Long Island, New York, the spring arrival of adult cabbage maggots comes when forsythia blooms.) With that sort of information in hand, growers can apply pesticides only when they are needed, holding expenses down and minimizing the use of toxic sprays.

The science of phenology is as old as agriculture itself. Only recently, however, has its potential value been recognized. Farmers and gardeners are beginning to reap some of the benefits of its first flowers; its full-bloom phase — yet to come — will no doubt provide many more. □□

NEW PLANT HARDINESS ZONE MAP

FOR CANADA, THE UNITED STATES, AND MEXICO

In response to changing climatic and environmental conditions in the last 20 years, the U.S. Department of Agriculture issued in January 1990 a new edition of its popular Plant Hardiness Zone Map. The map, based on data collected over the last two decades from 8,000 weather stations in North America, is a refinement of the 1965 edition of the map, which appears in many gardening catalogs and books. The new map reflects the extremes in weather that we've seen in recent years, especially killing frosts in some areas of Florida and California. In general, there are large regional changes to cooler temperatures in many zones. The map also subdivides zones to show little "heat islands" (urban areas) and cool spots (usually a function of altitude). However, gardeners will still need to know what's happening in their own backyards. For that, remember to follow the lilac's lead.

☞ TO ORDER THE NEW MAP: Send a check for $6.50 to Superintendent of Documents, Government Printing Office, Washington, DC 20402. Request Item #1475, "USDA Plant Hardiness Zone Map."

GESTATION AND MATING TABLE

	Proper age for first mating	Period of fertility, in years	No. of females for one male	Period of gestation in days	
				Range	Average
Ewe	90 lbs. or 1 yr.	6		142-154	147 151[8]
Ram	12-14 mos., well matured	7	50-75[2] 35-40[3]		
Mare	3 yrs.	10-12		310-370	336
Stallion	3 yrs.	12-15	40-45[4] Record 252[5]		
Cow	15-18 mos.[1]	10-14		279-290[6] 262-300[7]	283
Bull	1 yr., well matured	10-12	50[4] Thousands[5]		
Sow	5-6 mos. or 250 lbs.	6		110-120	115
Boar	250-300 lbs.	6	50[2] 35-40[3]		
Doe goat	10 mos. or 85-90 lbs.	6		145-155	150
Buck goat	Well matured	5	30		
Bitch	16-18 mos.	8		58-67	63
Male dog	12-16 mos.	8			
She cat	12 mos.	6		60-68	63
Doe rabbit	6 mos.	5-6		30-32	31
Buck rabbit	6 mos.	5-6	30		

[1]Holstein & Beef: 750 lbs. Jersey: 500 lbs. [2]Handmated. [3]Pasture. [4]Natural. [5]Artificial. [6]Beef; 8-10 days shorter for Angus. [7]Dairy. [8]For fine wool breeds.

BIRD AND POULTRY INCUBATION PERIODS, IN DAYS

Chicken.... 21 Goose.... 30-34 Guinea ... 26-28
Turkey..... 28 Swan .... 42 Canary 14-15
Duck ... 26-32 Pheasant 22-24 Parakeet .. 18-20

GESTATION PERIODS, WILD ANIMALS, IN DAYS

Black bear............... 210 Seal 330
Hippo .... 225-250 Squirrel, gray 44
Moose............... 240-250 Whale, sperm...... 480
Otter............... 270-300 Wolf 60-63
Reindeer 210-240

MAXIMUM LIFE SPANS OF ANIMALS IN CAPTIVITY, IN YEARS

Box Turtle   Elephant.............. 84   Oyster
 (Eastern) .... 138 Giant Tortoise.. 190   (Freshwater)..... 80
Bullfrog.............. 16 Giraffe .... 28 Pig 10
Camel................. 25 Goat .... 17 Polar Bear.......... 41
Cat (Domestic) ... 23 Gorilla.................. 33 Rabbit 13
Cheetah .... 16 Grizzly Bear....... 31 Rattlesnake........ 20
Chicken .... 14 Horse   Reindeer 15
Chimpanzee 37   (Domestic) .... 50 Sea Lion 28
Cow .... 20 Kangaroo........... 16 Sheep 20
Dog (Domestic).. 22 Lion.................... 30 Tiger 25
Dolphin .... 30 Moose .... 20 Timber Wolf...... 15
Eagle .... 55 Owl..................... 68 Toad.................... 36
                                                       Zebra 25

REPRODUCTIVE CYCLE IN FARM ANIMALS

	Recurs if not bred	Estrual Cycle incl. heat period (days)		In heat for		Usual time of ovulation
	Days	Average	Range	Average	Range	
Mare	21	21	10-37	5-6 days	2-11 days	24-48 hours before end of estrus
Sow	21	21	18-24	2-3 days	1-5 days	30-36 hours after start of estrus
Ewe	16½	16½	14-19	30 hours	24-32 hours	12-24 hours before end of estrus
Goat	21	21	18-24	2-3 days	1-4 days	Near end of estrus
Cow	21	21	18-24	18 hours	10-24 hours	10-12 hours after end of estrus
Bitch	pseudo-pregnancy	24		7 days	5-9 days	1-3 days after first acceptance
Cat	pseudo-pregnancy		15-21	3-4 if mated	9-10 days in absence of male	24-56 hours after coitus

How to Grow the

TASTIEST
Tomatoes

You already know about watering, weeding, and feeding. Here's the real secret to superior taste.

BY ROGER A. KLINE

Any vegetable gardening book worth its salt will describe the technique of growing tomatoes. Choose rich soil, but not too rich in nitrogen or fresh manure. Plant after the last frost; choose a sunny location. Water, weed, feed, water, weed, and harvest. Pick them green if a frost threatens. In their haste to instruct you and move you on to the next vegetable, most garden books fail to explain some of the principles of flavor in tomatoes. It is important for gardeners to understand how a tomato can become the quintessence of a fine garden.

The tomato begins with its genetic potential for flavor as well as for other characteristics. The Microtom will always be a dwarf basket type no matter what environmental conditions it encounters. Grown under the same conditions, Better Boy has a stronger vine characteristic than Sun Coast, and Walter, Supersonic, and Mountain Pride all have better flavor than Early Girl.

Flavor in tomatoes is a balance between sugars and acids. Individual taste will prefer the balance shifting one way or the other. Added to this are the

"volatiles" — subtle chemical compounds that are very important for that full tomato flavor. Volatiles that have an off taste or aftertaste can ruin the perceived flavor. From the garden we will accept rough or misshapen or even ugly fruit as long as a rich, appealing tomato flavor is offered.

A major factor in the development of tomato flavor is the amount of leaf area that is exposed to the sun and the amount of sunlight that radiates upon the plant. Consequently, small plant types with heavy fruit loads offer less flavor. Seasons that are rainy and overcast produce poor flavor compared with the same plants grown under sunny conditions. Think of the leaves as warehouses that supply flavor compounds. The leaves are dependent on sunlight to manufacture these compounds; the leaves then distribute the compounds to the fruit. Therefore, the more leaves present, the more flavor compounds produced and supplied to the tomatoes. Or, the fewer tomatoes on the plant with the same total leaf area, the more flavor distributed to each individual tomato.

During a rainy season the fruit set on any variety will be the same as if it were a sunny season. But because sunlight is needed to produce flavor compounds, those compounds are reduced during a cloudy season, and the same number of tomatoes must divide up fewer flavor units. The result is less flavor and quality.

There's not much you can do to increase the amount of sunlight in a growing season. But certain cultural practices affect the flavor of your tomatoes. The effect of severe pruning, which some gardeners do when tomato plants are staked with a single main stem, is to drastically reduce the leaf tissue area, the site of manufacture of sugars and other compounds. This denies flavor units to the existing fruit load on a plant.

However, *light* pruning can increase the size of fruit on the plant because of the redistribution of compounds away from meristems (the technical term for certain formative tissues, or growing points) and to the fruit. Not only will the tomatoes be larger, but they will mature earlier. Pruning does have certain drawbacks, sometimes causing problems with wilt, cracking, and blossom end rot, but research has shown that light pruning is a good practice especially in large plant types with luxurious foliage.

Early types of tomatoes usually set fruit when the plant is young and small. These plants have less leaf area per tomato and do not have the time to accumulate sugars. Therefore, early tomato types tend to have less flavor than late-season varieties.

Tomatoes enjoy warm weather, but it is said that in the South they grow too fast to develop the sugars, acids, and beneficial volatiles needed for best flavor.

Lifting plants up off the ground is a good way to avoid bruising and rotting, which can more easily occur if the fruit is in contact with the soil. Caging the plants without pruning them is a safe alternative to staking and trimming tomatoes. The cage should be large enough so leaves are not pressed together, but can intercept the sun as much as possible.

A tomato is not considered mature until it has developed gelatinous material around its seeds; the flavor compounds as well as the vitamin C are concentrated in this gel. Development of the gel occurs at temperatures above 60° F as the tomato begins to turn red. Supermarket tomatoes bred for shipping are picked before the gel develops and usually receive complaints for lack of flavor.

A tomato can even vary in flavor from one end to the other. Color change usually begins at the blossom end and proceeds toward the stem end. If you are very observant, you may see ripening occurring over the septa (inner walls) and then moving to the locule (open inner space containing the gel).

If you bite into a tomato and nothing oozes out, chances are the tomato lacks good flavor. At the other end of the spectrum, Beefsteak tomatoes grown and ripened in the garden are embarrassingly sloppy to eat, but have the best of all flavors. Those tomatoes that are large and soft and runny, those for which we must wear a bib, those we must eat in the privacy of our own home are the greatest reward for the home gardener. □ □

· illustration courtesy of Roger Kline

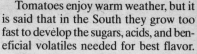

Winning Recipes in the 1990 Recipe Contest

DRIED BEANS AND PEAS

First Prize

CURRIED CASSOULET

3 cups white beans, soaked overnight
½ pound ham, cubed
½ pound salt pork, scored
2 pounds lean lamb, cubed
2 large onions, chopped
1 cup celery, chopped
4 tablespoons olive oil
pinch thyme
salt and pepper to taste
2 tablespoons curry powder or to taste

Drain beans and place in kettle. Cover with water. Add ham and salt pork. Bring to a boil. Simmer for 1½ hours or until beans begin to get tender. Keep adding water as it cooks down.

Meanwhile, in a large frying pan, brown the lamb, onions, and celery in olive oil. Pour off excess fat. Add 1 cup of the bean soup, and simmer. Add seasonings and combine with the rest of the beans when they are tender, removing the salt pork. Continue to simmer and correct the seasonings.

Serve with fluffy rice and condiments such as chutney, coconut, toasted walnuts, bananas, raisins, and pickles. This cassoulet may be prepared in advance and reheated. Serves 8 to 10.

Helen M. Marty
Phoenix, Arizona

Second Prize

SPINACH GREENS AND NORTHERN BEANS

1 pound Great Northern beans
2 cloves of garlic, minced
2 scallions, chopped
1 teaspoon paprika
5 tablespoons olive oil
10-ounce bag of fresh spinach, washed
and chopped
½ teaspoon Tabasco
¼ teaspoon cayenne pepper
salt to taste
optional:
1 cup chopped smoked ham,
½ cup chopped green olives

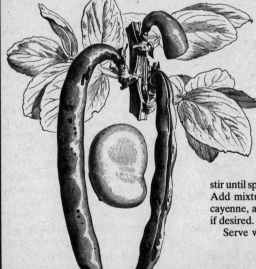

Cook beans as indicated on the package. (Start early! This is a lengthy process.) Sauté garlic, scallions, and paprika in olive oil until garlic is light brown. Reduce heat and add spinach. Stir. Add approximately ½ cup juice from the beans, and stir until spinach is cooked (about 5 minutes). Add mixture to beans and stir in Tabasco, cayenne, and salt. Add optional ingredients if desired. Serves 6.

Serve with or over crusty Italian bread.

Andrea Moriniti
DeWitt, New York
(submitted by Christopher Hall)

BUTTER BEAN SPREAD

½ cup dried lima or butter beans
2 cups water
1 clove of garlic, minced
4 ounces cream cheese
4 ounces smoked ham, chopped fine
3 to 4 drops Tabasco sauce
salt and pepper to taste

Cook beans in water until very soft, adding water as necessary. Drain. Place beans, garlic, and cream cheese in a food processor or blender and mix until smooth. Add ham and Tabasco. Add salt and pepper to taste. Chill and serve with crackers. Makes 1½ to 2 cups.

Ann L. Combs
New Hampton, New Hampshire

1991 Recipe Contest

RECIPES USING APPLES

For 1991, prizes (first prize, $50; second, $25; third, $15) will be awarded for the best original recipes using apples. All entries become the property of Yankee Publishing Incorporated, which reserves all rights to the materials submitted. Winners will be announced in the 1992 edition of *The Old Farmer's Almanac.* Deadline is March 1, 1991. Address: Recipe Contest, *The Old Farmer's Almanac,* Dublin, NH 03444.

THE OLD FARMER'S ALMANAC COOKBOOK CONTEST

Readers of *The Old Farmer's Almanac* are invited to submit as many as five of their favorite recipes in any category for possible inclusion in the upcoming *Old Farmer's Almanac Cookbook.* All entries become the property of Yankee Publishing Incorporated; readers whose recipes are chosen for inclusion in the book will be compensated. Address: Cookbook Contest, *The Old Farmer's Almanac,* Dublin, NH 03444.

Winning Essays in the 1990 Essay Contest

"MY MOST UNFORGETTABLE JOB"

First Prize

Because of circumstances, this job was short-lived. One morning I found a large safety pin on the ground and got an ingenious idea. I went door to door asking people if I could clean the cracks in their sidewalks for a penny. I was making good money for a little girl of five in 1945. If you spent your money wisely, you could get three or four candies for a penny then.

Well, I was almost finished with my fourth customer when all of a sudden sirens sounded and women came running from their houses singing, laughing, crying, and dancing in the streets. They were hugging each other and acting very strangely. I ran to my mother, and she told me my uncle was coming home. We danced around in the street, tears falling from her face.

I might have been the richest little entrepreneur in San Jose, but I lost the tool of my trade in all the excitement. I gladly gave it up for the end of World War II. I've had other jobs since, but there's nothing like being your own boss, making good money, and pleasing others all at the same time.

Lorraine Thomas
San Jose, California

Second Prize

At the tender age of 16, while salivating over the thought of owning my first automobile, a 1953 Mercury, I took a seasonal job with the local canning factory. My job as "thistle picker" began at 6 A.M., 12 hours per day, six days a week. Armed with burlap bags and one heavy leather glove, I roamed the pea fields in search of thistles, plucking them from existence. We thistle pickers rid the fields of those thorny plants bearing fruit in the form of buds that the unwitting pea combine could not distinguish from the legume it was designed to harvest. We kept those hard little thistle balls from reaching the dinner table. What a proud group we were with muddy jeans, green shoes, prickled arms, and one overworked, mushy leather glove. During that summer of 1959, I managed to save over $400, with little time to spend it. This was more than the asking price of my soon-to-be auto.

I was heartbroken to find it had been sold a few days prior to my arrival with pay in pocket, but I'll never forget my thistle pickin' days, dreaming about my shiny red Mercury two-door hardtop.

Rod R. Lukes
Dodgeville, Wisconsin

Third Prize

In order to bring in extra money one summer, I decided to put an ad in a local newspaper to take in typing jobs. When the ad appeared, it read "Tying down in my home" instead of "Typing done in my home."

The first call came from a woman who wanted to learn tie-dying. She made it sound so interesting that I, too, wanted to learn it. The second call came from a distraught woman who told me that she was at the end of her rope. Her mother-in-law was living with her family and was giving them all a hard time. The woman said she really thought her mother-in-law belonged in a mental institution or a home for the aged, where personnel were trained to take care of such people.

"Then," she said, "I saw your honest ad. Would you really be willing to tie my mother-in-law down in your home?"

Alexis Rotella
Mountain Lakes, New Jersey

Your home workshop can
PAY OFF BIG!

This One Low-Cost Power Tool
SAWS to desired Width...
PLANES to desired Thickness...
MOLDS all popular Patterns...
All at once or separately... All By Power Feed!

30 DAY FREE TRIAL OFFER

Only 3-in-1-Workshop Tool Of Its Kind!
From the Day It Arrives... Your Planer will make and save you money. With shortages and inflation driving lumber prices sky-high, this versatile power tool easily pays for itself by quickly converting low-cost rough lumber into high value finished stock. In just one pass turn out your own quarter-round, door and window stop, casing, tongue-and-groove... all popular patterns. Other Foley-Belsaw operators are making cases for grandfather clocks, furniture, picture frames, fencing, bee hives, bed slats, surveying stakes... all kinds of millwork.

Built For Pros... Priced for the Home Craftsmen
... it is engineered and built to industrial standards, but factory-direct selling keeps the price low. Handles tough oak and walnut as easily as pine, and so simple to operate even beginners with no experience can use it.

Start Your Own Business... Earn Extra Income Right at Home
With just this one low cost power-feed machine in a corner of your garage or basement, you can set up a profitable business by supplying lumberyards, cabinetmakers, carpenters, remodelers, contractors and hobbyists in your area with custom-planed lumber, trim, molding... ALL of their millwork requirements. Supply picture molding to art shops, hardware and department stores, or sell direct to framing shops. All standard patterns in stock... custom knives ground to your design or sample.

FREE BOOKLET!
Get FREE Book with facts and full details... RUSH COUPON TODAY!

If coupon has been removed, just send postcard with name and address to:
Foley-Belsaw Co.
6301 Equitable Rd., Dept. 91571
Kansas City, Mo. 64120

NO RISK 100%
Guarantee of Satisfaction
"Try the Foley-Belsaw in your own shop for a full 30-Days and put it to work for you. Give it a thorough test and make it prove that it can do everything we say it will... use it as much as you want. Then if you are not completely satisfied, just send it back and we'll return every penny sent with your order. And YOU are the sole judge. There are no questions asked... there are no fine print 'use' charges. Our flat guarantee is that YOU must be 100% satisfied or you get your money back."

Does The Foley-Belsaw Pay? YOU BET!
READ WHAT OTHER FOLEY-BELSAW OWNERS SAY:
A Good Investment: "I believe that the Planer is the best investment I ever made. I've been a planer man for years and am now retired. The Foley-Belsaw has earned me over $60,000 extra income in the past eleven years."
Robert Sawyer, Roseburg, Oregon

... And Foley-Belsaw Is The Choice of Professionals: "I recommend Foley-Belsaw's Planer-Molder-Saw as the most useful shop tool that any craftsman could own. We use ours everyday in the WORKBENCH model shop, and couldn't get along without it."
JAY HEDDEN — Editor of WORKBENCH Magazine

NO OBLIGATION and NO SALESMAN Calls!

Send for your copy Today!

FOLEY BELSAW
Foley-Belsaw Co.
6301 Equitable Rd.
Dept. 91571
Kansas City, Mo. 64120

☐ **YES**, please send me the FREE Booklet that gives me complete facts about your Planer-Molder-Saw and full details on how I can qualify for a 30-Day Free Trial right in my own shop. I understand there is No Obligation and that No Salesman will call.

NAME_____

ADDRESS_____

CITY_____

STATE_____ ZIP_____

My friend John, who was raised in rural North Carolina, had a childhood friend locally famous for his marksmanship and great strength. John's friend could shoot a bumblebee on the wing with a .22 rifle, he lifted the back end of a mired Ford pickup once, and like many Appalachian farm children in lean times, John's friend grew up on bulldog gravy. It's the common opinion among Appalachian Mountain communities that if it weren't for bulldog gravy, a lot of little babies would have died of malnutrition.

Southerners raised outside certain parts of Appalachia may not recognize it by that name, though a good many of them eat bulldog gravy with each meal every day of their lives. Bulldog gravy also goes by "white gravy" and "milk gravy." In some high-toned Southern cookbooks it's called "country gravy," but in most places it's simply "gravy," as in "biscuits and gravy," as common and taken-for-granted on rural Southern dinner tables as salt and pepper.

The ingredients are modest and easily come by on a farm: meat drippings thickened with flour, then milk beaten in to gravy consistency, seasoned with salt and plenty of pepper. Bacon and sausage drippings (or lard if no drippings are handy) are most common for breakfast biscuits and gravy, but bulldog gravy does service for dinner and supper as well. You use steak drippings for gravy served with chicken-fried steak — that's a slice of round steak breaded and fried like fried chicken — and many Southerners also serve bulldog gravy with fried chicken itself. A woman I know in northern Arkansas, locally famous for her fried chicken and gravy, confided that she adds a pinch of sugar for seasoning.

Of course you can add anything you want to bulldog gravy, and crumbled sausage meat is popular. Bill Neal (author of *Bill Neal's Southern Cooking*, Chapel Hill) suggests adding raw country ham (salt cured, not smoked) in julienne strips. In a recent dinner-table conversation on the subject of bulldog gravy, a friend volunteered that she knew a woman who added chocolate syrup to her gravy, served over biscuits, because she had nothing else in the house that day to start her boy off to school. Since that conversation, I've talked to two other Southerners who take their bulldog gravy with chocolate flavoring or make it with chocolate milk.

Though no one I spoke to can say for sure, it's a matter of agreement, and makes some sense, that bulldog gravy originated in areas of rural poverty. It is documented, however, that during the

On Behalf of Bulldog Gravy

Some call it white gravy or milk gravy. And, sure, it's simple to make. But if you want to do it right, you have to know a few tricks.

BY DEBORAH NAVAS

1930s striking miners in coal mining areas around Kentucky subsisted on beans and bulldog gravy alone. "[It's] the single contribution to world cuisine of the highland South," Ben Kimpel, a noted University of Arkansas scholar, put it. The highland South Kimpel referred to are the Cumberlands, the Blue Ridge Mountains, the southern Appalachian Mountains, and the Ozarks, but bulldog gravy long since made its way down to the more affluent flatlands, the southern coast, and at least as far west as Texas and Oklahoma. There are few breakfast counters anywhere in the South that don't feature biscuits and gravy on their breakfast menus, and that includes McDonald's, whose southern franchises serve more biscuits with gravy than Egg McMuffins.

"To get that certain flavor, the roux has to brown . . . almost to the burning point."

Because people have become wary of saturated fats, most public eating places now make their bulldog gravy with a vegetable oil or shortening base. Jerry's Restaurant in Fayetteville, Arkansas, has been serving biscuits and gravy for over ten years, and according to Doris, Jerry's wife, people come into Fayetteville from as far away as Little Rock and Fort Smith asking for Jerry's biscuits and gravy. They use a margarine and flour roux as the gravy's base, Doris said (for professional reasons she didn't go into the specifics of preparation).

Though the ingredients are simple, making a very good bulldog gravy requires experience. The *White Trash Cooking* cookbook advises: "Always keep reminding yourself that it takes years of practice to make a good gravy. Nobody's perfect right at the very first." Sue McKay, who makes gravy for the University of Arkansas Food Services,

agreed. Sue's gravy is reported to be absolutely first-rate, and she starts in at five o'clock every morning to make gravy at Brough Commons, a dining hall that serves students, faculty, university employees, and anyone willing to pay 65¢ for a serving of one fresh-baked baking powder biscuit topped with as much gravy as he or she wants.

The real trick to good gravy, according to Sue, is browning the roux. In an electric skillet, Sue melts about one-third the amount of margarine she'll use, gets it real hot, and with a whip beats in flour ("I measure by guess and by God," she said). "To get that certain flavor, the roux has to brown real good, almost to the burning point." Sue can tell when it's right by the color, "a little darker than caramel." Then she adds the skillet roux to a somewhat larger amount of margarine and flour mixture that she's already prepared in a five-gallon steamer (the margarine and flour in this pot have been beaten together over low heat but not browned). Sue stirs it all together, then adds salt and pepper and beats in the whole milk. When the gravy's ready, she divides it into two pots and adds cooked crumbled sausage to one pot.

"The sausage gravy's most popular," Sue said, "but they love the plain, too. The kids love it, it's cheap and filling, and I've had instructors tell me it's the best in town." (Sue makes her gravy in volume, but if you want to try her method for a batch of gravy that will serve four, use 2 tablespoons shortening, 2 tablespoons flour, 1½ cups milk, ½ teaspoon salt, ¼ teaspoon pepper.)

Sue came by her expertise naturally — she's an Arkansas native, born in Chula, "a little town that's nowhere on the map." When I asked her if she had grown up eating biscuits and gravy, she said, "Well sure, didn't everybody?"

If the demand at the University of Arkansas Food Services is any indication, everybody — at least south of the Mason-Dixon line — still does. □□

★ ★ Pot pie will never be labeled as "nouvelle cuisine." Savory main-dish pies have been gracing the dinner tables of England since the Norman invasion. But it was here in the New World that meat pies came into their own. Thrifty colonists used a deeper dish than their forebears across the sea and called the result a "pot pie." Filled with a variety of game or seafood, main-dish pies were satisfying ways to stretch scarce ingredients.

America's Love Affair with ★ ★ Pot Pie ★ ★

It started 200 years ago with chicken pot pie, whose variations – from pasties to tamales – have become a kind of soul food.

BY VICTORIA DOUDERA

- illustrated by Sheila Gilligan

The settlers of America's eastern shoreline turned to the sea for many a pie filling, from the plentiful cod, a mainstay of the New Englander's diet, to clams, oysters, crab, haddock, and lobster. Inland, cooks used freshwater fillings such as trout, salmon, and pike.

In the Midwest, cooks adapted an old English favorite, Cornish pasties, and made them a regional specialty. These individual meat pies, usually beef, potatoes, and onions wrapped in a leakproof crust, were a staple of the miner's lunch pail. Settlers farther west in the mountains and Northern Plains became adept at using buffalo, moose, bear, and venison in their meat pies, a variation that remains popular.

Meat pies from the Southwest reflect a centuries-long history shared with Mexico. Ingredients like peppers, garlic, cheese, beans, tomatoes, cornmeal, and cumin, common in Mexican cooking, actually date back to the American Indians. The recipe for spicy Tamale Pie that follows uses cornmeal rather than real tamales and originated in Texas.

Chicken pot pie, probably the most popular savory pie, was first lauded in the press around 1792 and boasts as many variations as there are regions in the United States. Purists insist on using only three components: chicken, gravy, and pastry. Peas and carrots have become predictable additions, and other vegetables, such as celery and bell peppers, figure in many blue-ribbon recipes. One old Mississippi version calls for the extravagance of asparagus tips.

Chicken pot pie can be made using an entire chicken, cooked and boned, or leftover pieces of baked or roasted chicken. Southern cooks use the first method, often pricking a special code in the pastry to indicate the location of the light and dark meat.

Toppings can vary too. Pastry may be used either to top the pie or to encase it top and bottom. Some recipes substitute biscuits, bread, or cornbread. One South Carolina recipe specified that the baking dish be lined with an inch or so of cooked, buttered rice. At the church-sponsored chicken-pie suppers I remember attending with my grandparents in Vermont, steaming hot chicken and peas in a rich sauce were ladled over warm individual biscuits.

The pot pie, easily assembled from leftover meat and a few vegetables, will perfume the kitchen while it's baking and, like soup, is easily reheated and even tastier the second day. Chicken and other meat pies also welcome experimentation, accommodating themselves to substitutions and seasonings. The pot pie may not be "nouvelle," but who cares — it's delicious!

CHICKEN POT PIE WITH VEGETABLES

1 3-pound chicken with giblets, cut up
1 medium onion, quartered
1 stalk celery, cut in half
3 sprigs fresh parsley
5 whole peppercorns
1 bay leaf
1 teaspoon salt
2 cups water
1½ cups carrot strips, 2" long
5 small onions, quartered
1 cup fresh or frozen peas
1 cup chopped fresh mushrooms
½ teaspoon poultry seasoning
salt and pepper to taste
⅓ cup flour
½ cup milk
pastry for a single-crust 9" pie
1 egg yolk, beaten with 1 tablespoon water

Place chicken, medium onion, celery, parsley, peppercorns, bay leaf, 1 teaspoon salt, and 2 cups water in a 4-quart Dutch oven. Bring to a boil over high heat, then reduce heat to low, cover, and simmer for 1 hour or until chicken is tender. Strain broth (discard vegetables) and return to Dutch oven. Cool chicken and giblets, remove meat from bones, and cut into large chunks. Discard skin and bones.

Add carrots and 5 small onions to broth; cook, covered, until tender. Remove vegetables, reserving broth. Add enough water to broth to make 2½ cups liquid, and return to Dutch oven. Stir in peas, mushrooms, poultry seasoning, salt and pepper, chicken, giblets, carrots, and onion. Combine flour and milk

in a jar; cover and shake until blended. Stir flour mixture into broth and cook over medium heat, stirring constantly, until mixture boils and thickens. Pour hot mixture into 2-quart casserole.

Roll out pastry to fit top of casserole. Cut slits in top. Place crust over chicken mixture and trim edge, leaving enough to fold under and form a ridge. Flute edge and brush with egg wash. Bake at 400° F for 30 to 35 minutes, until crust is golden and filling is bubbly. Makes 6 servings.

TEXAS TAMALE PIE

1 onion, chopped
1 green pepper, diced
1 tablespoon butter
¾ pound ground beef
2 cups (16 ounces) tomato sauce
12 ounces canned or frozen whole-kernel corn
½ cup ripe olives, chopped
1 clove garlic, minced
1 tablespoon sugar
1 teaspoon salt
½ teaspoon pepper
1½ teaspoons chili powder
1 cup shredded Monterey Jack cheese

Topping:

¾ cup cornmeal
½ teaspoon salt
2 cups cold water
1 tablespoon butter

In a large skillet sauté onion and green pepper in butter until tender. Add meat and brown. Stir in tomato sauce, corn, olives, garlic, sugar, salt, pepper, and chili powder. Simmer for 20 minutes. Add cheese and stir until melted. Pour into a greased 8"x8" or 10"x6" baking dish and set aside.

In a medium saucepan stir cornmeal and salt into water. Cook over medium heat, stirring, until thickened. Stir in butter. Spoon over meat mixture in strips. Bake at 375° F for about 40 minutes. Makes 6 to 8 servings.

NEW ENGLAND LOBSTER PIE

10 tablespoons butter, divided
½ cup good-quality sherry

2 cups lobster meat (picked from
    4 small or 2 large lobsters)
2 tablespoons flour
1½ cups half-and-half
4 egg yolks, beaten

Topping:

½ cup cracker meal
2 tablespoons crushed potato chips
½ teaspoon paprika
2 tablespoons Parmesan cheese
4 tablespoons melted butter

Melt 4 tablespoons of the butter, add sherry, and boil for 1 minute. Add lobster and remove from heat. In a medium saucepan, melt the remaining butter. Add flour and cook, stirring, until mixture bubbles. Remove from heat. Drain the sherry from the lobster meat and add it and the cream into flour mixture. Stir slowly until thoroughly blended. Return to heat and cook, stirring constantly, until sauce is smooth and thick. Remove from heat.

Spoon 4 tablespoons of the sauce into a small bowl and add beaten egg yolks a tablespoon at a time, stirring well. Return egg mixture to sauce and mix well. Stir over low heat for about 3 minutes, but do not allow to boil. Remove from heat and add lobster. Turn into 4 individual ramekins or a small, deep pie plate.

Combine topping ingredients and blend well. Sprinkle over pie(s). Bake at 325° F for 10 minutes to heat through. Makes 4 servings.

DAKOTA BUFFALO AND BEER PIE

2 pounds commercially raised buffalo
    meat, cut into 1" cubes
2 teaspoons salt
½ teaspoon freshly ground pepper
1 teaspoon sage
⅓ cup flour
¼ cup oil
1 large onion, chopped
1 carrot, chopped
1 stalk celery, diced
1 large potato, cubed
2 cups beef broth
¼ cup tomato puree
1 cup beer
1 clove garlic, crushed
1 bay leaf
3 sprigs parsley
1 whole clove
½ teaspoon thyme
pastry for a single-crust 9" pie

Season the meat cubes with salt, pepper, and sage and dredge in ¼ cup of the flour. Heat oil in a large skillet and brown the meat on all sides. Using a slotted spoon, transfer meat to a heavy Dutch oven. In the remaining oil in the skillet sauté onion, carrot, celery, and potato until lightly browned. Using a slotted spoon, add vegetables to meat in Dutch oven. Sprinkle remaining flour over drippings in skillet and cook, stirring, until lightly browned. Stir in the broth, tomato puree, beer, garlic, bay leaf, parsley, clove, and thyme. Pour over meat and vegetables.

Bring to a boil, cover, and simmer until meat is tender, about 1½ hours. Pour into a deep 9" pie dish and let cool. Preheat oven to 425° F. When meat is cool, roll out pastry and cover dish. Cut steam vents in crust and bake for 30 to 35 minutes, until pastry is browned. Makes 6 servings.

MIDWESTERN CORNISH PASTIES

1¼ pounds beef round or chuck, minced
1 cup diced peeled potatoes
¼ cup chopped onion
1 tablespoon finely chopped beef suet
½ teaspoon salt
⅛ teaspoon pepper

Pastry:

4 cups sifted flour
2 teaspoons salt
1½ cups lard
2 eggs, beaten
¼ cup ice water
1 egg yolk, beaten with 1 tablespoon
    water

Combine beef, potatoes, onion, suet, salt, and pepper in a bowl. Mix thoroughly. In another bowl combine flour and salt; cut in lard to form coarse crumbs. Blend eggs and ice water in a small bowl and sprinkle over flour mixture a bit at a time, tossing with a fork until dough forms. Press dough firmly into a ball.

Divide pastry into 6 portions. Roll each portion on a floured surface into a 7" circle. Place 1/6 of the meat mixture on half of each circle; fold other half over meat, pressing edges together to seal. Cut slits in top and place on ungreased baking sheets. Brush with egg wash.

Bake at 400° F for 15 minutes, then reduce temperature to 350° F and bake 30 to 35 minutes longer, until crust is golden. Makes 6 servings. □□

OUTDOOR PLANTING TABLE, 1991

The best time to plant flowers and vegetables that bear crops above the ground is during the LIGHT of the Moon; that is, between the day the Moon is new to the day it is full. Flowering bulbs and vegetables that bear crops below ground should be planted during the DARK of the Moon; that is, from the day after it is full to the day before it is new again. These Moon days for 1991 are given in the "Moon Favorable" columns below. See pages 48-74 for the exact times and days of the new and full Moons.

The three columns below give planting dates for the Weather Regions listed. (See Map p. 133.) Consult page 84 for dates of killing frosts and length of growing season. Weather Regions 5 and the southern half of 16 are practically frost free.

- Illustration by Virginia Peck

Above Ground Crops Marked(*)	Weather Regions 1, 6, 9, 10, North 13		Weather Regions 2, 3, 7, 11, South 13, 15		Weather Regions 4, 8, 12, 14, 16	
E means Early L means Late	Planting Dates	Moon Favorable	Planting Dates	Moon Favorable	Planting Dates	Moon Favorable
*Barley	5/15-6/21	5/15-28, 6/12-21	3/15-4/7	3/16-30	2/15-3/7	2/15-28
*Beans (E)	5/7-6/21	5/13-28, 6/12-21	4/15-30	4/15-28	3/15-4/7	3/16-30
(L)	6/15-7/15	6/15-26, 7/11-15	7/1-21	7/11-21	8/7-31	8/9-25
Beets (E)	5/1-15	5/1-12	3/15-4/3	3/15, 3/31-4/3	2/7-28	2/7-13
(L)	7/15-8/15	7/27-8/8	8/15-31	8/26-31	9/1-30	9/1-7, 24-30
*Broccoli (E)	5/15-31	5/15-28	3/7-31	3/16-30	2/15-3/15	2/15-28
Plants (L)	6/15-7/7	6/15-26	8/1-20	8/9-20	9/7-30	9/8-23
*Brussels Sprouts	5/15-31	5/15-28	3/7-4/15	3/16-30, 4/14-15	2/11-3/20	2/14-28, 3/16-20
*Cabbage Plants	5/15-31	5/15-28	3/7-4/15	3/16-30, 4/14-15	2/11-3/20	2/14-28, 3/16-20
Carrots (E)	5/15-31	5/29-31	3/7-31	3/7-15, 31	2/15-3/7	3/1-7
(L)	6/15-7/21	6/27-7/10	7/7-31	7/7-10, 27-31	8/1-9/7	8/1-8, 8/26-9/7
*Cauliflower (E)	5/15-31	5/15-28	3/15-4/7	3/16-30	2/15-3/7	2/15-28
Plants (L)	6/15-7/21	6/15-26, 7/11-21	7/1-8/7	7/11-26	8/7-31	8/9-25
*Celery Plants (E)	5/15-6/30	5/15-28, 6/12-26	3/7-31	3/16-30	2/15-28	2/15-28
(L)	7/15-8/15	7/15-26, 8/9-15	8/15-9/7	8/15-25	9/15-30	9/15-23
*Corn, Sweet (E)	5/10-6/15	5/13-28, 6/12-15	4/1-15	4/14-15	3/15-31	3/16-30
(L)	6/15-30	6/15-26	7/7-21	7/11-21	8/7-31	8/9-25
*Cucumber	5/7-6/20	5/13-28, 6/12-20	4/7-5/15	4/14-28, 5/13-15	3/7-4/15	3/16-30, 4/14-15
*Eggplant Plants	6/1-30	6/12-26	4/7-5/15	4/14-28, 5/13-15	3/7-4/15	3/16-30, 4/14-15
*Endive (E)	5/15-31	5/15-28	4/7-5/15	4/14-28, 5/13-15	3/15-3/20	2/15-28, 3/16-20
(L)	6/7-30	6/12-26	7/15-8/15	7/15-26, 8/9-15	8/15-9/7	8/15-25
*Flowers (All)	5/7-6/21	5/13-28, 6/12-21	4/15-30	4/15-28	3/15-4/7	3/16-30
*Kale (E)	5/15-31	5/15-28	3/7-4/7	3/16-30	2/11-3/20	2/14-28, 3/16-20
(L)	7/1-8/7	7/11-26	8/15-31	8/15-25	9/7-30	9/8-23
Leek Plants	5/15-31	5/29-31	3/7-4/7	3/7-15, 3/31-4/7	2/15-4/15	3/1-15, 3/31-4/13
*Lettuce	5/15-6/30	5/15-28, 6/12-26	3/1-31	3/16-30	2/15-30	2/15-28
*Muskmelon	5/15-6/30	5/15-28, 6/12-26	4/15-5/7	4/15-28	3/15-4/7	3/16-30
Onion Sets	5/15-6/7	5/29-6/7	3/1-31	3/1-15, 31	2/1-28	2/1-13
*Parsley	5/15-31	5/15-28	3/1-31	3/16-30	2/20-3/15	2/20-28
Parsnips	4/1-30	4/1-13, 29-30	3/7-31	3/7-15, 31	1/15-2/4	1/31-2/4
*Peas (E)	4/15-5/7	4/15-28	3/7-31	3/16-30	1/15-2/7	1/15-30
(L)	7/15-31	7/15-26	8/7-31	8/9-25	9/15-30	9/15-23
*Pepper Plants	5/15-6/30	5/15-28, 6/12-26	4/1-30	4/14-28	3/1-20	3/16-20
Potato	5/1-31	5/1-12, 29-31	4/1-30	4/1-13, 29-30	2/10-28	2/10-13
*Pumpkin	5/15-31	5/15-28	4/23-5/15	4/23-28, 5/13-15	3/7-20	3/16-20
Radish (E)	4/15-30	4/29-30	3/7-31	3/7-15, 31	1/21-3/1	1/31-2/13, 3/1
(L)	8/15-31	8/26-31	9/7-30	9/7, 24-30	10/1-21	10/1-6
*Spinach (E)	5/15-31	5/15-28	3/15-4/20	3/16-30, 4/14-20	2/7-3/15	2/14-28
(L)	7/15-9/7	7/15-26, 8/9-25	8/1-9/15	8/9-25, 9/8-15	10/1-21	10/7-21
*Squash	5/15-6/15	5/15-28, 6/12-15	4/15-30	4/15-28	3/15-4/15	3/16-30, 4/14-15
*Swiss Chard	5/1-31	5/13-28	3/15-4/15	3/16-30, 4/14-15	2/7-3/15	2/14-28
*Tomato Plants	5/15-31	5/15-28	4/7-30	4/14-28	3/7-20	3/16-20
Turnips (E)	4/7-30	4/7-13, 29-30	3/15-31	3/15, 31	1/20-2/15	1/31-2/13
(L)	7/1-8/15	7/1-10, 7/27-8/8	8/1-20	8/1-8	9/1-10/15	9/1-7, 9/24-10/6
*Wheat, Winter	8/11-9/15	8/11-25, 9/8-15	9/15-10/20	9/15-23, 10/7-20	10/15-12/7	10/15-23, 11/6-20, 12/5-7
Spring	4/7-30	4/14-28	3/1-20	3/16-20	2/15-28	2/15-28

GARDENING BY THE MOON'S SIGN

The Outdoor Planting Table (opposite) shows how the phases of the Moon can be used as a guide. Gardeners who use the Moon's *astrological* sign listed below (not astronomical place as on pages 48-74) follow these rules: 1) When the Moon is between new and first quarter (see Left-Hand Calendar Pages 48-74 for Moon phases), plant or transplant above-ground crops that produce seeds on the outside (i.e. strawberries, corn, leafy and "bolting" vegetables), and cucumbers, when the Moon is in Taurus, Cancer, Scorpio, Capricorn, or Pisces. 2) When the Moon is between first quarter and full, plant or transplant above-ground crops bearing seeds inside the fruit (i.e. tomatoes, squash, peas, beans) when the Moon is in Taurus, Cancer, Scorpio, Capricorn, or Pisces. 3) When the Moon is between full and last quarter, plant below-ground crops when the Moon is in Taurus, Cancer, Scorpio, Capricorn, or Pisces. 4) When the Moon is between last quarter and new, do not plant; use for destroying weeds, brush, pests, and for cultivating and plowing when the Moon is in Aries, Gemini, Leo, Virgo, Libra, Sagittarius, or Aquarius.

Prune to encourage growth when the Moon is in Cancer, Scorpio, or Capricorn; to discourage growth when the Moon is in Aries or Sagittarius. Wean animals when the Moon is in Taurus, Cancer, or Pisces.

MOON'S PLACE IN THE ZODIAC

	Nov. 90	Dec. 90	Jan. 91	Feb. 91	Mar. 91	Apr. 91	May 91	June 91	July 91	Aug. 91	Sept. 91	Oct. 91	Nov. 91	Dec. 91
1	ARI	TAU	CAN	VIR	VIR	SCO	SAG	CAP	PSC	ARI	GEM	CAN	VIR	LIB
2	TAU	GEM	LEO	VIR	LIB	SCO	SAG	AQU	PSC	TAU	GEM	LEO	VIR	SCO
3	TAU	GEM	LEO	LIB	LIB	SAG	CAP	AQU	PSC	TAU	CAN	LEO	LIB	SCO
4	GEM	CAN	VIR	LIB	SCO	SAG	CAP	PSC	ARI	TAU	CAN	VIR	LIB	SCO
5	GEM	CAN	VIR	SCO	SCO	SAG	AQU	PSC	ARI	GEM	LEO	VIR	SCO	SAG
6	CAN	LEO	LIB	SCO	SCO	CAP	AQU	PSC	TAU	GEM	LEO	VIR	SCO	SAG
7	CAN	LEO	LIB	SAG	SAG	CAP	AQU	ARI	TAU	CAN	VIR	LIB	SAG	CAP
8	LEO	VIR	LIB	SAG	SAG	AQU	PSC	ARI	GEM	CAN	VIR	LIB	SAG	CAP
9	LEO	VIR	SCO	SAG	CAP	AQU	PSC	TAU	GEM	LEO	LIB	SCO	SAG	CAP
10	VIR	LIB	SCO	CAP	CAP	PSC	ARI	TAU	CAN	LEO	LIB	SCO	CAP	AQU
11	VIR	LIB	SAG	CAP	CAP	PSC	ARI	GEM	CAN	VIR	SCO	SAG	CAP	AQU
12	VIR	SCO	SAG	AQU	AQU	PSC	TAU	GEM	LEO	VIR	SCO	SAG	AQU	PSC
13	LIB	SCO	SAG	AQU	AQU	ARI	TAU	CAN	LEO	LIB	SCO	SAG	AQU	PSC
14	LIB	SCO	CAP	AQU	PSC	ARI	GEM	CAN	VIR	LIB	SAG	CAP	AQU	PSC
15	SCO	SAG	CAP	PSC	PSC	TAU	GEM	LEO	VIR	SCO	SAG	CAP	PSC	ARI
16	SCO	SAG	AQU	PSC	ARI	TAU	CAN	LEO	LIB	SCO	CAP	AQU	PSC	ARI
17	SCO	CAP	AQU	ARI	ARI	GEM	CAN	VIR	LIB	SAG	CAP	AQU	ARI	TAU
18	SAG	CAP	PSC	ARI	ARI	GEM	LEO	VIR	LIB	SAG	CAP	AQU	ARI	TAU
19	SAG	CAP	PSC	TAU	TAU	CAN	LEO	LIB	SCO	SAG	AQU	PSC	ARI	GEM
20	CAP	AQU	PSC	TAU	TAU	CAN	LEO	LIB	SCO	CAP	AQU	PSC	TAU	GEM
21	CAP	AQU	ARI	GEM	GEM	LEO	VIR	SCO	SAG	CAP	PSC	ARI	TAU	CAN
22	CAP	PSC	ARI	GEM	GEM	LEO	VIR	SCO	SAG	AQU	PSC	ARI	GEM	CAN
23	AQU	PSC	TAU	GEM	CAN	VIR	LIB	SCO	SAG	AQU	PSC	TAU	GEM	LEO
24	AQU	PSC	TAU	CAN	CAN	VIR	LIB	SAG	CAP	AQU	ARI	TAU	CAN	LEO
25	PSC	ARI	GEM	CAN	LEO	VIR	SCO	SAG	CAP	PSC	ARI	GEM	CAN	VIR
26	PSC	ARI	GEM	LEO	LEO	LIB	SCO	CAP	AQU	PSC	TAU	GEM	LEO	VIR
27	ARI	TAU	GEM	CAN	VIR	LIB	SCO	CAP	AQU	ARI	TAU	CAN	LEO	LIB
28	ARI	TAU	CAN	VIR	VIR	SCO	SAG	CAP	AQU	ARI	GEM	CAN	VIR	LIB
29	TAU	GEM	LEO	—	LIB	SCO	CAP	AQU	PSC	ARI	GEM	CAN	VIR	LIB
30	TAU	GEM	LEO	—	LIB	SAG	CAP	AQU	PSC	TAU	CAN	LEO	LIB	SCO
31	—	CAN	VIR	—	LIB	—	CAP	—	ARI	TAU	—	LEO	—	SCO

"We're looking for people

"Writing for children is the perfect way to begin," says the author of 53 children's books. "Your ideas come right out of your own experience. And while it's still a challenge, it's the straightest possible line between you and publication —if you're qualified to seek the success this rewarding field offers."

By Alvin Tresselt, *Dean of Faculty*

IF you want to write and get published, I can't think of a better way to do it than writing books and stories for children and teenagers. Ideas flow naturally right out of your own life experience. While it's still a challenge, the odds of getting that first unforgettable check from a juvenile publisher are better than they are from just about any other kind of publisher I know.

Later on, you may get checks from other publishers. But right now, the object is to begin—to break into print—to learn the feeling of writing and selling your work and seeing your name in type. After that, you can decide if you want your writing to take another direction.

But after 40 years of editing, publishing, and teaching—and 53 books of my own—I can tell you this: you'll go a long way before you discover anything as rewarding as writing for young readers.

An incomparable experience

Your words will never sound as sweet as they do from the lips of a child reading your books and stories. And the joy of creating books and stories that reach young people is an experience you'll never have anywhere else.

Alvin Tresselt, Dean of Faculty, was Executive Editor of Parents' Magazine Press, the first editor of *Humpty Dumpty's Magazine*, and a board member of the Author's Guild. His 53 books for young readers have sold over two million copies.

But, that's not all. The financial rewards go far beyond most people's expectations because there's a surprisingly big market out there for writers who are trained to tap it. Over $1 *billion* worth of children's books are purchased annually—some 4,000 different titles—many by new authors.

And over 400 children's magazines rely on freelancers to fill each issue. You can imagine how much writing *that* takes!

Yet two big questions bedevil nearly every would-be writer: "Am I really qualified?" and "How can I get started?"

"Am I really qualified?"

This is our definition of a "qualified person": it's someone with an aptitude for writing who can take constructive criticism, learn from it, and turn it into a professional performance. That's the only kind of person we're looking for at the Institute of Children's Literature® The reasons are simple: our reputation is built on success, and if prospective students don't have the aptitude, we probably can't help them. And we tell them so. It's only fair to both of us.

To help us spot potential authors, we've developed a revealing test for writing aptitude. It's free, and we don't charge for our evaluation. But no one gets into the Institute without passing it. Those who pass receive our promise:

> *You will complete at least one manuscript ready to submit to a publisher by the time you finish the course.*

One-on-one training with your own instructor

I've learned a lot about writing for children and I love it. Now I'm passing my knowledge on to my students so they can profit from it. When I'm not writing my own books I spend my time at the Institute, a workshop for writers that does one thing and does it better than any other educational institution I know of: it trains qualified people to write for the young reader.

This is the way I work with my students, and my fellow instructors—all of whom are experienced writers or editors —work more or less the same way.

The testimonials in this ad were provided voluntarily, without remuneration, by the Institute's students between 1985 and 1990.

to write children's books"

When you're ready —at your own time and your own pace—you send your assignment to me and I read it and I reread it to get everything out of it you've put into it. Then I edit your assignment with a well-tempered pencil, just the way a publishing house editor would—if he had the time. I return it along with a detailed letter explaining my comments. I tell you what your strong points are, what your weaknesses are, and just what you can do to improve. It's a matter of push and pull with each assignment. You push and I pull and between us both, you learn to write.

The home of the Institute of Children's Literature, founded in 1969.

The proof of the pudding

This method really works. I wouldn't spend five minutes at it if it didn't. The proof of the pudding is that many students break into print even before they finish the course.

"My how-to article that sold to *4H* Magazine for $75 was my rewrite of a course assignment," says Jeanne Shoemaker, Birmingham, AL. "My beloved instructor has made this course one of the highlights of my adult life!"

"—my dream come true!"

"The thing that gives me the most satisfaction," writes Brandy S. Wells, Greensboro, MD, "is the idea that my story will be read by 150,000 Sunday school children—my dream come true."

"Most importantly, the course has allowed me to explore my creative writing skills without committing myself to a strict classroom environment with immediate deadlines and meeting schedules," reports Jeanne Nickerson, Washington, DC. "I needed the flexibility, which a correspondence course provided, and I have enjoyed dealing on a one-on-one basis with my instructor."

To find qualified men and women with an aptitude for writing, we have prepared an intriguing Aptitude Test. It is offered free and will be professionally evaluated at no cost to you by our staff.

Free Writing Aptitude Test

Just mail the coupon below to receive your free test and 28-page illustrated brochure describing the Institute, our course and faculty, and the current market for children's literature. If you demonstrate a true aptitude for writing, you will be eligible to enroll. But that's up to you.

There is no obligation.

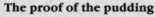

Get both FREE

Institute of Children's Literature
93 Long Ridge Road
West Redding, CT 06896-0812

Yes, I'm interested in your program to help new writers get started. Please send me your free Writing Aptitude Test and 28-page brochure. I understand I am under no obligation whatever and no salesman will visit me.

Please circle one and print name clearly:

Mr.   Mrs.   Ms.   Miss   **JY5**

_____
Name

_____
Street

_____
City

_____
State   Zip

Founded in 1969 • APPROVED BY THE
CONNECTICUT COMMISSIONER OF EDUCATION

COPYRIGHT © ICL, 1990, A DIVISION OF THE INSTITUTE, INC.

Praise the Lard and Pass the Flaky Pie Crust

The "forgotten shortening" is making a comeback – and some people, particularly in the Midwest, need no convincing.

– Illustrated by Margo Letourneau

BY SUSAN PEERY

Once upon a time and long ago B.C. (Before Cholesterol), when pigs were plump and pie crusts were short, lard was the fat of choice for many people. Often there was no choice — where butter was dear, manufactured products were nonexistent, and pigs were plentiful, lard was the only shortening used for pastry making, baking, and frying. "Lard bucket" was no term of opprobrium; it simply meant the useful tin pail in which lard was sold and stored.

Lard is a valuable by-product of hog slaughtering, a no-waste process that allowed frugal farmers to boast that they used everything but the squeal. Lard is made by the simple process of heating, or rendering, the natural hog fat (mostly back fat and "leaf" fat, the internal fat around the abdomen) to separate it from the fine connective tissues (which, after rendering, are known as cracklings). Connective tissue cells hold a plastic mixture of fats much the way a honeycomb holds honey. The melted fat, which turns creamy white when chilled, needs no further refining. It is lard.

During the early years of settlement in the Midwest and Great Plains, pigs were often left outdoors to forage. The skinny, half-wild creatures finally rounded up for slaughter were referred to scornfully as "prairie racers" by one Wisconsin farmer. By 1900, thanks to better husbandry and feed, the average pig was more than 15 percent lard, and production boomed. A hog that dressed out at 165 pounds yielded about 35 pounds of lard and 127 pounds of meat (the squeal apparently accounted for the rest).

Lard met its first serious competition in 1911, when Procter & Gamble patented a hydrogenation process that led to the introduction of Crisco, a solidified vegetable shortening. Although Crisco and its imitators, which could be stored at room temperature without becoming rancid, cut into lard sales, they also provided a point of comparison. Good cooks insisted that lard had superior shortening power to other fats, was easily workable over a wide range of temperature, gave excellent results when used for deep-fat frying, and was more digestible.

During the Depression declining exports of lard (especially to the German market) and desperation slaughtering of hogs by Dust Bowl farmers who couldn't afford to buy feed glutted the market with lard. The extension services at several major land-grant universities in the Midwest swung into action with research and consumer campaigns designed to convince cooks to buy lard. They argued on the basis of economy (lard cost only one-third as much as competing shortenings) and performance in cooking. They tested shortening power, measuring the force needed to break a cracker or pie crust (the lower the amount of force, the greater the shortening value and therefore the flakier the pastry), and rated lard on top. The University of Nebraska College of Agriculture even commissioned a study to convert a standard recipe for butter cake to one that used lard. (Lard cake never quite caught on.) Lard, because of its high fatty-acid content, was also proposed as a cure for eczema.

The extension researchers made some converts. More important, they gave scientific backbone to what cooks already knew by intuition: for certain uses, particularly in pie crusts, biscuits, crackers, and deep-frying, lard has advantages not met by other shortenings. Because of its rough crystalline structure (under a microscope the crystals look like rough balls), lard mixes unevenly with flour, leaving unincorporated bits of fat to provide flakiness. (Other shortenings form needlelike crystals that incorporate more smoothly with liquids to create light, even-textured cakes and icings.) In deep frying, lard imparts an attractive golden crust and may be heated as high as 425° F without smoking.

Although as late as 1978 the National Live Stock and Meat Board in Chicago was promoting lard in its pamphlet "Lard Makes It Better," the trend since World War II in this country has been away from lard. Let's face it, lard became déclassé. As dieticians urged folks to eat less animal fat, the pork industry worked on breeding hogs down from 15 percent lard to less than 5 percent — back to the prairie racers! The National Pork Producers Council likes to describe pork as white meat (read "low fat") and no longer promotes the use of lard. The Council probably wishes we would all forget that lard and pigs have any connection at all.

Some people have never forgotten. Cooks in fancy restaurants and farm kitchens alike know that judicious use of lard in such products as pie crusts and biscuits produces a superior product. Jasper White, chef at the esteemed Boston restaurant, Jasper's, makes his pie crusts using shortening in a ratio of two-thirds lard to one-third butter. Diana Kennedy, in her book *The Art of Mexican Cooking* (Bantam, 1989), reports on the extensive lard use in traditional Mexican cooking and calls lard "absolutely indispensable" for making *tamales* and in frying beans. "The flavor of homemade lard is incomparable," she writes, "and what's more, you're not getting any preservatives." A Wisconsin grandmother swears by her recipe for Cherry Cobbler, which uses biscuits shortened with lard to "cobble" the cherries.

The recipes that follow capitalize on lard's fine shortening power and show its versatility. If you have a favorite biscuit, doughnut, or pie crust recipe using butter or another shortening and you wish to convert it to lard, remember this rule of thumb: use four-fifths as much lard as butter; use only three-fourths as much lard as solid vegetable shortening. Count the calories saved as another plus for lard. *Spend* those calories on your second piece of pie!

TENDER FLAKY PASTRY

2 cups flour
½ teaspoon salt
⅔ cup lard
about 6 tablespoons ice water

Place flour and salt in bowl and whisk to blend. Cut in lard, using a pastry blender, two knives, or your fingers, until particles are the size of peas. Add ice water a tablespoonful at a time until dough just holds together. Form dough into 2 balls, one slightly larger, and flatten to about 1" high. Wrap well in plastic and chill for at least 1 hour. Roll out on a lightly floured board, using the larger portion for the bottom crust. Do not stretch dough. Fill as desired. Makes 1 double crust for an 8" or 9" pie. (Recipe may be halved to make a single pie shell.)

HOMEMADE BISCUIT MIX

8 cups flour
¼ cup baking powder
2 teaspoons salt
1 cup lard

Sift flour, baking powder, and salt together. Cut lard into flour with a pastry blender until the mixture has a fine, even crumb. Cover and store in refrigerator until ready to use. This mixture will keep for at least a month. Makes 10 cups of biscuit mix.

To make biscuits: Add ½ cup milk to 2 cups Homemade Biscuit Mix and toss until combined. Turn onto a lightly floured surface and knead gently for about 20 seconds. Pat or roll to ½" thickness and cut with a medium-sized (about 2") biscuit cutter. Bake in a preheated 450° F oven for 12 to 15 minutes, until golden. Serve hot. Makes 10 to 12 biscuits.

RED CHERRY COBBLER

1 can (16 ounces) tart red cherries
⅓ cup brown sugar
3 tablespoons cornstarch
½ cup orange juice
2 tablespoons butter
⅛ teaspoon salt
½ teaspoon almond extract
1½ cups Homemade Biscuit Mix (see recipe above)
⅓ cup sugar
¼ teaspoon freshly grated nutmeg
1 egg
¼ cup milk

Drain cherries, reserving juice. Combine brown sugar and cornstarch in saucepan. Stir in cherry juice, orange juice, butter, and salt; cook, stirring constantly, until thickened. Stir in cherries and almond extract.

For biscuit topping, combine Homemade Biscuit Mix, sugar, and nutmeg. Beat egg and milk and stir into biscuit mixture until combined. Heat cherry mixture to boiling and pour into a low 1-quart baking dish. Drop batter by spoonfuls (about 6) on top of hot cherry mixture and bake at 350° F for 35 to 40 minutes, until biscuits are golden. Serve warm. Makes 6 servings.

SOUR MILK DOUGHNUTS

3½ cups sifted flour
½ teaspoon salt
1 teaspoon baking soda
½ teaspoon baking powder
1 teaspoon freshly grated nutmeg
½ teaspoon ginger
¾ cup sugar
2 tablespoons lard
2 eggs
1 cup sour milk or buttermilk
lard to melt for deep-frying

Sift dry ingredients (except sugar) three times. Cream sugar and lard well, add the eggs, and beat with an electric mixer. Add milk to egg mixture and beat well. Add sifted dry ingredients all at once and mix well. Cover and chill for 1 hour. Divide dough into two parts and roll on a floured board to ½" thick; cut with doughnut cutter. Melt lard in deep fryer and heat to 375° F. Fry doughnuts quickly, turning as soon as they come to the top (do not crowd kettle). Cook to golden brown. Roll in granulated sugar while still hot if desired. Makes about 2 dozen.

Lard may be strained, covered, stored in the refrigerator, and used again for frying.

CREAM OF TARTAR BISCUITS

2 cups flour
4 teaspoons cream of tartar
1 teaspoon baking soda
½ teaspoon salt
¼ cup lard
¾ cup cold milk

Sift flour, cream of tartar, baking soda, and salt into a medium bowl. Cut in lard using a pastry blender. Add milk all at once and toss with fork. Knead 5 or 6 times on a lightly floured board and roll or pat to ½" or ¾" thickness. Cut with a biscuit cutter and top each biscuit with a bit of butter. Bake in a preheated 475° F oven for 5 minutes. Turn off heat and leave in the oven for 5 to 10 minutes longer, until golden. Serve hot. Makes 8 to 10 biscuits. □ □

GET IN ON THE PROFITS OF SMALL ENGINE SERVICE AND REPAIR

START YOUR OWN MONEY MAKING BUSINESS & BEAT INFLATION!

You get all this Professional equipment with your course, PLUS 4 H.P. Engine... ALL YOURS TO KEEP... All at NO EXTRA COST.

Work part time, full time right at home. In just a short time, you can be ready to join one of the fastest growing industries in America... an industry where qualified men are making from **$25.00 to $30.00 per hour**. Because the small engine industry has grown so quickly, an acute shortage of qualified Small Engine Professionals exists throughout the country. When you see how many small engines are in use today, it's easy to understand why qualified men command such high prices — as much as $49.95 for a simple tune-up that takes less than an hour.

65-million small engines are in service today!

That's right — there are over sixty-five million 2-cycle and 4-cycle small engines in service across the U.S.A.! With fully accredited and approved Foley-Belsaw training, you can soon have the skill and knowledge to make top money servicing these engines. Homeowners and businessmen will seek you out and pay you well to service and repair their lawn mowers, tillers, edgers, power rakes, garden tractors, chain saws, mini-bikes, go-carts, snowmobiles... the list is almost endless.

No experience necessary.

We guide you every step of the way, including tested and proven instructions on how to get business, what to charge, how to get free advertising, where to get supplies wholesale... all the 'tricks of the trade'... all the inside facts you need to assure success right from the start.

Send today for FREE facts!

You risk nothing by accepting this offer to find out how Foley-Belsaw training can give you the skills you need to increase your income in a high-profit, recession-proof business of your own.

Just fill in and mail coupon below (or send postcard) to receive full information and details by return mail. DO IT TODAY!

FOLEY-BELSAW INSTITUTE
6301 Equitable Rd., Dept. 51849
Kansas City, Mo. 64120

NO OBLIGATION... NO SALESMAN WILL CALL

RUSH COUPON TODAY FOR THIS FACT-FILLED FREE BOOKLET!

Tells how you quickly train to be your own boss in a profitable Spare time or Full time business of your own PLUS complete details on our 30 DAY NO RISK Trial Offer!

FOLEY-BELSAW INSTITUTE
6301 EQUITABLE RD., DEPT. 51849
KANSAS CITY, MO. 64120

☐ YES, please send me the FREE booklet that gives full details about starting my own business in Small Engine Repair. I understand there is no obligation and that no salesman will call.

NAME _____

ADDRESS _____

CITY _____

STATE _____ ZIP _____

Catching the Bass of a Lifetime

BY MEL R. ALLEN

F ishing is anticipation and waiting, hope and dreams. Sometimes months, even years pass by before the fisherman's skill and luck intersect the hunger and curiosity of a great fish. It seems to matter little if the fish of a lifetime was caught a year ago or 20 years past. Ask about the first pull of the fish against line, and the scene once again erupts with life. The record-setting bass described below were caught in home waters whose ledges, currents, depths, and moods were as familiar as a neighborhood to the anglers. When a record fish comes from local waters, everyone who fishes there shares the pride and excitement, as if a hometown child has gone on to glory. Here are the stories, in the fishermen's own words.

"I NEVER SAW SO MUCH COMMOTION OVER A FISH"

The story of the world record **Smallmouth Bass** *(Micropterus dolomieui), 11 pounds, 15 ounces; caught by David L. Hayes of Leitchfield, Kentucky, July 9, 1955, at Dale Hollow Lake on the Kentucky-Tennessee border using a pearl-colored "bomber."*

☞ "If people know anything about smallmouth bass, they know Dale Hollow Lake. It's a beautiful lake right on the line between Tennessee and Kentucky. In the 1950s the lake was at its peak, and I kept a boat docked there. I did a lot of trolling on that lake. The day I caught the fish, we left the house at daybreak, and we started fishing about 8 o'clock. The wife and my six-year-old son were sleepy and just crawled into the bed on the cruiser and went to sleep.

"I had on 20-pound test line so I wouldn't get hung up on anything. It happened at a spot called Shale Point. He hit the line so hard that I thought I was hung up. Nobody was there to see me catch that fish but me — until I went to land it.

"He battled me for maybe 20 minutes, so he was pretty well wore out, but you know how smallmouth is; it come alive when it found there was danger in sight. He still had the smallmouth will. I had to get the wife up; I had to have somebody to hold the rod for me. I set the drag loose on the reel and positioned my wife so I could hand her the rod at the right time, and I told her to hold the tip up if he made a run. I put the net down underneath of him and scooped him up.

"When I got to the dock, I called one of the fellas. I said, 'Look here, Red, you want to see a nice smallmouth?' He said, 'Golly. Let me have that fish!' He went and weighed it. Next day I received a phone call. It was a world record. I caught this fish pretty close to the Tennessee-Kentucky line. Tennessee takes its fishing seriously, so does Kentucky, so I just let both states claim it. My little son said, 'I never saw so much commotion over a fish in all my life, Daddy.' "

"THE ONLY FRESHWATER WORLD RECORD ACTUALLY FILMED LIVE"

The story of the world record Suwannee Bass (Micropterus notius), 3 pounds, 14 ounces; caught March 2, 1985, by Ronnie Everett of Gainesville, Florida, on the Suwannee River, Florida, using a black skirt-tail spinner bait.

☞ "Do you want to know the real story? Or do you want to know the lie? I can make you think I'm the greatest fisherman in the world. Or I can tell you the truth.

"The truth is I wasn't even really fishing that morning. My real love is bow hunting, and I wanted to scout for turkeys. It was just daylight, and I was floating with the current down a tributary of the Suwannee River in my bass boat with a buddy. We had a video camera with us, and when the first turkey gobbled, we were going to ease over to the bank and my buddy was going to sit 50 yards or so behind me and film me calling in a turkey.

"So I picked up my rod and reel. I had a black skirt-tail spinner bait on, and I was just casting it up to the bank, letting it sink and bringing it back while my buddy got the lighting right. And to my surprise on the second cast a fish jumped on my lure.

"I was just playing him for the camera, letting him jump, and about the third jump I realized then this was a Suwannee River bass. I realized I had something special on, so I got it into the boat. For the length of her she could not have been any fatter.

"At the dock I asked an old country boy to take a look at it. They call the Suwannee bass 'redeyes' down here and he said he'd been fishing that river all his life, and that was the biggest old redeye he'd ever seen. Two pounds is considered to be a large one. So that fired me up so, I called the game and fish commission and had it weighed on certified scales, and the rest is history. It will take a monster to beat this fish. Believe it or not, this is the only freshwater world record actually filmed live. And that's the truth. If you want a lie, I can make it a helluva story!"

"I TOLD THEM WE COULD TAKE ONE MORE CAST"

The story of the world record Guadalupe Bass (Micropterus treculi), 3 pounds, 11 ounces; caught September 25, 1983, by Allen M. Christenson, Jr., of Austin, Texas, on Lake Travis in Austin, using a three-inch grub with silver glitter.

☞ "I remember the day well. I'm a professional guide on Lake Travis, and that morning I was guiding an attorney and his wife from Houston. We were mainly catching fish on surface plugs. I just held the boat with a trolling motor and let them cast top water lures, and they each caught a couple of nice bass. Then the ac-

tion slowed, and I was fixing to take them to the next point down just a few hundred yards. I had a rod rigged up with a three-inch plastic grub, smoky clear with silver glitter. I was using six-pound test. "I told them we could take one more cast. And I threw the grub out as an afterthought and let it sink about seven or eight foot off this point, and I was just going to jig it once. Occasionally I was getting some fish doing that underneath the top water action. That's when this fish hit.

"We had a tremendous fight. Guadalupe bass are native to central Texas — it's the only black bass that's found only in Texas and is the official state fish — and if you get one over two or three pounds, you've got the fighting equivalent of a four- or five-pound largemouth. When I finally got it near the boat, I could see it was the biggest Guadalupe bass I had ever seen. And I catch a lot of them every day.

"When I got it up to the boat, we had some real excitement. I was playing it real easy. I was just going to reach down and lift it into the boat. But the woman grabbed the landing net and took a swipe at it when it came near the boat, and she almost hit my line with the net. I thought I was going to lose it. So I had to do some quick coaching. I said just keep the net in the water. I said let me lead the fish into the net. Just lift up. I finally got her to stop chasing the fish with it. When we got it weighed, it was nearly a pound heavier than the previous record."

"HE COME TO THE TOP OF THE WATER AND SHOOK HIS OLD HEAD"

*The story of the world record **Redeye Bass** (Micropterus coosae), 8 pounds, 3 ounces; caught October 23, 1977, by David A. Hubbard of Williamson, Georgia, on the Flint River, Georgia, using a large black-and-white spotted salamander.*

☞ "The redeye is found in only three bodies of water — the Chattahoochee River and the Flint River in Georgia and the Coosa River in Alabama. They're raised in the freshwater shoals, and they grow really strong from swimming in the shoals. I tell you, a two-pound redeye fights as hard as a five-pound largemouth.

"When we got up that morning, there was a frost and it looked just like it had snowed. My friend and I went down to the Flint River below Thomaston, Georgia. The days were getting short and we were trying to fish all the holes, so we waded down to what we call the bottom hole. We were using live black-and-white spotted salamanders. Down here we call them 'ground dogs.' My buddy had already waded across that hole and I come down behind him.

"The river there is narrow and full of weeds. I threw that ground dog upstream and let it come downstream and wash past the weed beds into the hole. Right off I caught one, so I put another one of those lizards on and threw it back in. A fish bucked it, and I figured it was another one of those little bass. I let him run with it a little, and then he stopped. I could feel him just pecking at it. And I said, 'Well, he's just chewing that lizard up,' so I tightened the line up and set the hook in.

"Well, sir, I guarantee you all Hades broke loose. He come up to the top of the water and shook his old head. He

made two or three runs back and forth and come on top of the water again. He made several more runs, and I started backing up, getting toward the edge of a little eddy by the bank. I backed as far as I could, right up against a rock. I kept a tight line on him, and everytime he come to me, I brought him in a little bit more. Finally I got him to the eddy and reached in and grabbed him by the mouth. He was history."

"IF IT WASN'T FOR TOMMY TODD, I'D HAVE EATEN THAT FISH FOR SUPPER"

*The story of the world record **Yellow Bass** (Morone mississippiensis), 2 pounds, 4 ounces; caught March 27, 1977, by Donald L. Stalker of Bedford, Indiana, on Lake Monroe in Indiana. ("I'm not going to give you the bait; I won't do that.")*

☞ "It was early evening and pouring down rain. We thought there'd be a bass laying around the logs so we just kept beating the bank all day. My neighbor, Tommy Todd, was with me. We try to fish about three or four days a week. Mostly for bass, mostly on Lake Monroe, right near Bloomington.

"We were just fishing for fish to eat. When I caught that fish, I told Tommy, 'I'm going to eat that for supper.' He told me to hold on. We thought it was a white bass, but we didn't think there was any white bass in Lake Monroe. So we took it up to a fishing shed near Bloomington to have it weighed. The man who ran it wasn't there, but his wife told us to leave it. So I did.

"The next day I got a call. I had me a world record yellow bass. And I almost ate that fish. It's a real tasty fish to eat. If it wasn't for Tommy Todd, I probably would have. Now I don't think that record will be broken; not too many yellow bass left in that lake today." □□

BEST FISHING DAYS, 1991
(and other fishing lore from the files of *The Old Farmer's Almanac*)

Probably the best fishing time is when the ocean tides are restless before their turn and in the first hour of ebbing. All fish in all waters — salt or fresh — feed most heavily at that time.

Best temperatures for fish species vary widely, of course, and are chiefly important if you are going to have your own fish pond. Best temperatures for brook trout are 45° to 65° F. Brown trout and rainbows are more tolerant of higher temperatures. Smallmouth black bass do best in cool water. Horned pout take what they find.

Most of us go fishing when we can get off, not because it is the best time. But there are best times:

- One hour before and one hour after high tide, and one hour before and one hour after low tide. (The times of high tides are given on pages 48-74 and corrected for your locality on pages 86-87. Inland, the times for high tides would correspond with the times the Moon is due south. Low tides are halfway between high tides.)
- "The morning rise" — after sunup for a spell — and "the evening rise" — just before sundown and the hour or so after.
- Still water or a ripple is better than a wind at both times.
- When there is a hatch of flies — caddis or mayflies, commonly. (The fisherman will have to match the hatching flies with *his* fly — or go fishless.)
- When the breeze is from a westerly quarter rather than north or east.
- When the barometer is steady or on the rise. (But, of course, even in a three-day driving northeaster the fish isn't going to give up feeding. His hunger clock keeps right on working, and the smart fisherman will find something he wants.)
- When the Moon is between new and full.

MOON BETWEEN NEW & FULL

Jan. 15-30	July 11-26
Feb. 14-28	Aug. 9-25
Mar. 16-30	Sept. 8-23
Apr. 14-28	Oct. 7-23
May 13-28	Nov. 6-21
June 12-26	Dec. 5-21

"DO YOU KNOW THESE LITTLE KNOWN NATURAL HEALTH TIPS AND CURES?"

AN AMAZING TREASURE TROVE OF 230 CURES AND HEALTH TIPS

(By Frank K. Wood)

FC&A, a Peachtree City, Georgia, publisher, announced today the release of a new book for the general public, *"Natural Healing Encyclopedia"*.

—"We're so positive that one of these health secrets will work for you that we'll send you a free gift just for trying them."

LOOK AT SOME OF THE SECRETS REVEALED IN THIS NEW BOOK

- ▶ Alzheimer's Disease from your cookware? Check your pots and pans.
- ▶ Lose weight without eating less. When you eat can help you lose weight.
- ▶ Inner ear noises could be from a lack of these vitamins in your diet.
- ▶ High blood pressure? Natural, drug-free ways to bring it down.
- ▶ Feeling tired? This remedy helps many.
- ▶ Breast lumps? Is that morning cup of coffee responsible?
- ▶ Cut your heart attack risk by adding this trace mineral to your diet.
- ▶ Severe headaches? The cause may be in your refrigerator.
- ▶ See how a tennis ball can keep your mate from snoring.
- ▶ A quick fix for canker sores.
- ▶ Hangover? The U.S. Government's official remedy.
- ▶ Bladder control problems? How this simple technique can save you from embarrassment.
- ▶ PMS relief.
- ▶ How being "lady-like" can cause this disease.
- ▶ Why sucking a cough drop may be the worst thing you can do for a cold.
- ▶ 2 minerals that can help many diabetics.
- ▶ Body odor? Use this little-known bathing method to avoid offending people.
- ▶ A Q-tip® may actually help you get rid of the hiccups.
- ▶ Dressing differently can help ease angina pain. Here's how.
- ▶ Ways to keep calm when feeling stressed.
- ▶ A nutritional supplement to help poor memory.
- ▶ Back pain? A $10 piece of wood can end it for many.
- ▶ Vitamins and minerals that may actually slow down aging.
- ▶ Strokes are totally unrelated to heart disease. Right? Wrong.
- ▶ Hemorrhoids? Here's quick, natural relief.
- ▶ Kidney stones? This helps many.
- ▶ Sleeplessness. Causes and common-sense remedies.
- ▶ Eat this and cut in half your chances of getting certain cancers.
- ▶ How to get rid of corns and calluses — for good.
- ▶ Chest congestion? A readily available natural beverage brings quick relief.
- ▶ How your breath can warn you about a serious disease before it's too late.
- ▶ Arthritis? There's nothing "fishy" about this treatment from the deep, blue sea.

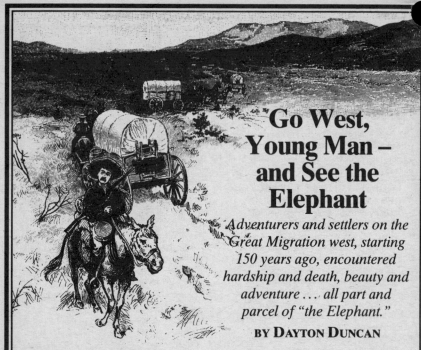

Go West, Young Man – and See the Elephant

Adventurers and settlers on the Great Migration west, starting 150 years ago, encountered hardship and death, beauty and adventure . . . all part and parcel of "the Elephant."

BY DAYTON DUNCAN

W e are told that the Elephant is in waiting, ready to receive us . . . if he shows fight or attempts to stop us on our progress to the golden land, we shall attack him with sword and spear." So wrote James D. Lyon in his diary in 1849. Lyon was not in Africa; he was in Wyoming, on his way to the California goldfields. And he was not referring to a real beast, but to an imaginary one.

For reasons still unknown, to the people who heeded Horace Greeley's much-publicized advice to go west in the mid-19th century, "the Elephant" was the universal symbol of their journey, implying both romantic adventure and great danger. Wagon covers were festooned with elephant images. Diary entries constantly mention the mythic beast, as in James Abbey's notation that a particularly violent prairie storm was "a brush of the elephant's tail." The most common password on the trail was, "Have you seen the elephant?"

Kind of a trick question. Following are ten more (with their answers) about the Great Migration.

☞ *Which were the main trails west?*

During the Great Migration — for about 25 years starting in 1841 — emigrants could choose from a variety of routes. Some went by the southwestern overland trails (the Santa Fe, Spanish, and Gila trails). Others went by sea, either entirely by ship around Cape Horn, or by ship to Nicaragua and Panama and then by land over the isthmus to meet another ship for the final leg to the West Coast.

But the most popular trails were the ones that started at Missouri River "jumping off" towns such as Independence and St. Joseph, followed the Platte River Valley west across Nebraska, and then veered northwest along the North Platte and Sweetwater rivers to South Pass in Wyoming, where they crossed the Continental Divide. West of South Pass the trails diverged to Salt Lake City (the Mormon Trail), to the goldfields of California (the California Trail), and to the Willamette River Valley in Oregon (the Oregon Trail).

☞ *How many people emigrated over those three trails?*

Precise statistics don't exist, but the best estimates — based on sources such as travelers' diaries and records at the few army forts along the way — suggest some 350,000 people traveled the Oregon, California, and Mormon trails during the Great Migration. About two-thirds of them were California bound; Utah and Oregon split the remainder. At least 50,000 people crowded through South Pass in the summer of 1850 alone, almost all of them on their way to the California goldfields.

☞ *Why did they go?*

The overwhelming motivation for most overlanders was the hope of bettering themselves economically. From 1850 until the passage of the Homestead Act of 1862, Oregon was the only place where the government offered free land to people willing to travel 2,000 miles to claim it. Midwestern farmers comprised the bulk of those who were drawn by that offer. The discovery of gold in California in 1848 touched off the biggest rush west. People from all backgrounds and regions set off to strike it rich, and the growing communities of farmers and miners attracted entrepreneurs from gamblers to merchants who saw opportunity over the western horizon.

Other reasons for going west included health (the drier air of the West was considered therapeutic for malaria and consumption), patriotism (orators proclaimed the United States' "manifest destiny" to expand to the Pacific), and religion (missionaries to Indian tribes were among the first to go to Oregon). The Mormons fled religious persecution in the Midwest and saw Utah as a remote place where they could be left alone to pray and prosper.

☞ *How many died along the way?*

Again, exact numbers aren't available. Respected estimates, however, place the fatality rate at between four and six percent or somewhere between 14,000 and 20,000 deaths. One historian, calculating that there were ten burial sites for every mile of the route to California, called graves the "highway markers" of the trail.

The most popular trails west ran parallel as far as South Pass in Wyoming, then split off for California, Oregon, and Salt Lake City.

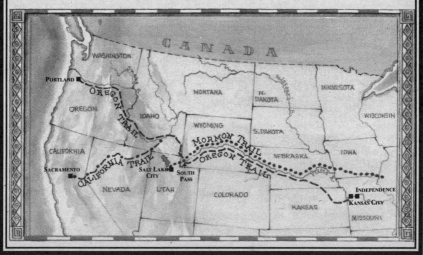

- illustrated map by Margo Letourneau

cause of death. Drownings at river crossings led this category, followed closely by accidents with firearms (most commonly a mishandled gun going off and killing its owner). A prankster in one wagon train thought it would be a good joke to sneak up on the encampment wearing a buffalo robe. His fellow travelers opened fire. Deaths by drowning and by gun accidents each outnumbered deaths at the hands of Indians.

Because of the rocky soil, a lack of spades, and the general haste wagon trains felt in pushing forward, most graves were very shallow and thus easily disturbed by the weather and predators such as wolves. Later caravans often encountered grave sites in which body parts — feet, hands, skulls — were exposed to view.

☞ *Were the Indians the main cause of death and injury?*

No, quite the contrary. Many emigrant diaries recount instances of Indian bands assisting travelers with directions or trading food for manufactured goods. Annoying instances of begging and horse theft were not uncommon, but the notion of circled wagon trains under constant Indian attack is the result of Hollywood's imagination: the wagons were, indeed, circled every night, but the people usually slept and cooked *outside* the ring while the animals were corralled inside.

☞ *So what caused most of the deaths?*

By far, the number-one threat along the trail was disease, contributing to about 90 percent of the fatalities. Asiatic cholera, which broke out in 1849, 1850, and 1852, was the most fearsome killer, followed distantly by mountain fever and scurvy.

Accidents were the second leading

Other accident-related fatalities included children falling off wagons and being crushed by the wheels or people being trampled during stampedes of the train's livestock. At least six people are known to have been killed by lightning. No cases of fatal snakebite are recorded. Murders — generally prompted by jealousy or frayed nerves rather than robbery — were fairly uncommon, although diaries record at least a dozen summary trials and hangings for murders along the trail.

☞ *How long did the journey take?*

The trip to Oregon from the jumping-off towns (Independence, Westport, Leavenworth, and St. Joseph, Missouri, and Council Bluffs, Iowa), about 2,000 miles, averaged 135 days (or less than 15 miles per day). The trip to California was about two weeks shorter. Ideally, wagons would leave in mid-April, when there was sufficient grass for the animals on the prairie, cross South Pass over the Fourth of July, and be over the western-most mountains before snow started falling in late September.

☞ *How much did it cost?*

Costs varied widely. Some farm families, already possessing oxen, wagons, and other necessary items, made the trip without spending any extra cash. Others had to save for five years before departing. Some city dwellers spent as much as $1,500 per person in getting to the "jumping off" town, outfitting themselves for the journey, and making the trip west. Guidebook writers of the day advised travelers to expect a range of $100 to $200 per person for outfitting a trip, plus another $50 to $200 along the way. As a point of comparison, consider that a skilled worker in 1860, toward the end of the Great Migration, earned about $1,000 a year.

☞ How did people travel?

They normally grouped themselves in wagon trains of about 15 to 25 wagons, with up to a hundred or more people. The wagons were not the huge, boat-shaped Conestogas (used by freighting companies along the Santa Fe Trail), but smaller and lighter versions with a straight bed. A heavy canvas top was stretched over bows to protect the belongings packed in the wagon. Being more compliant, hardier, and less likely to be stolen by Indians, oxen were used more often than mules and horses to pull the wagons.

After a shakedown journey of about a hundred miles, most groups elected their leaders for the remainder of the trip. Quarreling and bickering were so commonplace among emigrants, however, that most groups splintered into smaller trains well before South Pass. Many broke over disagreements on whether to observe the Sabbath by resting every Sunday. Even more fell apart in arguments over what and whose items to discard once it became clear — as it eventually did to virtually all of the overlanders — that they had packed too much weight into the wagons.

Out on the High Plains, wood for fires vanished. Buffalo "chips" were used for fueling cooking fires in long trenches; two to three bushels of the dried droppings were needed to cook a meal. Bread, bacon, and coffee were staples unless game (increasingly scarce in later years) could be shot or unless a family had brought along a milch cow. There were few fresh springs along the way; most drinking water came from the muddy rivers.

Virtually all of the married women had small children accompanying them; an estimated 20 percent of the women were in some stage of pregnancy during the trek. Women's diaries reveal that, on the whole, most women had not wanted to make the journey and uproot themselves from their homes. They came because it was the only way to keep the family intact. Women were also more likely to record the human costs of the Great Migration, as Lodisa Frizzell's entry near South Pass testifies: "The heart has a thousand misgivings & the mind is tortured with anxiety & often as I passed the fresh made graves, I have glanced at the side boards of the wagon, not knowing how soon it might serve as a coffin for some one of us."

Violent storms, strong and constant winds, broilingly hot days, mosquitoes, gnats, and lice, and worries about health, food, fresh water, and getting across the mountains in time — these were constant companions of the emigrants in the Great Migration.

☞ Given all the trouble, why didn't people turn back?

Some did, especially during the cholera scares. The turnarounds, as they were called, had "seen enough of the elephant," according to diarists' accounts. But most persevered, evidently feeling much the same as William Wells, a forty-niner, who wrote to his wife on his way to California: "Tell Green McDowell TO THANK his God hourly that he did not start on this trip — if he had he would have wished himself in HELL, at home or any where else but here ten thousand times . . . But never mind, Gold is ahead." □□

MATHEMATICAL·PUZZLES

BLANTON C. WIGGIN, PUZZLE EDITOR

Here are 15 classical, original, and timely puzzles for 1991 from our readers. There should be something to interest everyone, and we hope they are challenging. Everyday common sense and a little agility are all you'll need; you won't need calculus, computers, alertness to tricks, or specialized knowledge, though sometimes they may be helpful. Some puzzles may require information from your local library.

We will award one prize of $50 for the best set of solutions to puzzles 12 through 15 received before February 1, 1991. The answers to these four are omitted here.

We use a point system to judge the prize set. A basic unadorned, correct answer is 20 points. For a thorough analysis, an elegant or novel answer, up to 5 points extra. Numerical errors lose only 2 or 3 points, if it is clear that the method is understood.

Explanations and Prize-Set Answers will be sent after June 15 to anyone sending $1 and a self-addressed stamped envelope to "Puzzle Answers," *The Old Farmer's Almanac,* Dublin, New Hampshire 03444. Copies of prize-set puzzles and answers for previous years (1973 to the present) may be obtained from *The Old Farmer's Almanac* for $1 and a one-ounce stamp for each year requested; a self-addressed envelope should be included.

We will also pay $15 for any original puzzles we use in *The Old Farmer's Almanac* for 1992. Closing date for submissions is February 1, 1991. Entries become the property of Yankee Publishing Incorporated and cannot be acknowledged or returned.

Last year's contest was won by Tina Virzi of Plattsburgh, New York, frequent runner-up, with well worked out answers and a new way of constructing the chessboard; 91 points. Bob Symons of Waterloo, Ontario, 1987 winner, was runner-up. Nice work.

Have fun with these 1991 puzzles, and send your answers early for puzzles 12-15. Please use a separate sheet for each puzzle or answer. Be sure to put your name and address on each sheet. Good luck!

Answers appear on page 120.

1. FIGURE-OF-8 OR TREFOIL?

Difficulty: 1

☞ Are these the same or different? In other words, can one be pulled and

pushed into the other without cutting?

Eliza Gettel
Merrimack, New Hampshire

2. TIC-TAC-TOE

Difficulty: 1

☞ In tic-tac-toe, how many opening moves are there? And how many replies, or pairs of opening moves, are possible?

How often can the second player win?

Walter Vengren
Dracut, Massachusetts

3. TELEPATHIC MATH

Difficulty: 2

☞ Ask a friend to think of any two-digit

number and keep it secret, but to tell you the difference between the two digits. Now have him

a.) transpose the digits to form a second two-digit number, and

b.) subtract the smaller two-digit number from the larger, but *not* tell you.

Can you tell *him* what this difference is?

Ernest Frank
West Palm Beach, Florida

4. OVERLAPPING DATES

Difficulty: 2

☞ Will any one of the millions of people to be born in the nineties be older than any one of the millions born in the eighties?

Sidney Kravitz
Dover, New Jersey

5. SWIM MEETS

Difficulty: 2

☞ It is obvious that when John and Jan start simultaneously from opposite ends of a pool and swim laps at the same speed, they will always meet and pass in the middle.

Suppose, though, that they started together from the same end of a 50-meter pool, that John swam 5% faster than Jan, and that both made their turns at their swimming speeds.

Now, what is the pattern of their meetings, and how many times will they meet or pass before John completes 1,500 meters?

Kenny Wright
Holly Hill, Florida

6. TOUR D'ALMANAC

Difficulty: 3

☞ Greg will start cycling from San Diego at sunset the first day of spring, 1991, and will arrive in Halifax, Nova Scotia, at moonset, the third Sunday after Easter, covering 4,352 miles. He averages 8 hours riding per day, counting only those days having at least 6 hours of ride-time available.

a.) What is his average speed?

b.) What is his elapsed time for the transcontinental trip?

Davis Phinney
Glastonbury, Connecticut

7. THIRD FOLD

Difficulty: 3

☞ When you fold an ordinary 8½"x11" sheet of paper into a #9 envelope, you want to be sure you are folding into nearly exact

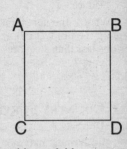

thirds. How would you fold a *square* sheet to find exactly ⅓ of a side? No rulers or rolling creases, please.

Ted P. Abraham
Auburndale, Massachusetts

8. ALMANAC OLDIE

Difficulty: 3

☞ While Gresham's Law was removing silver coins from circulation in the mid-sixties, many people separated rolls of silver from the new cheaper coins. One sorter accidentally mixed a roll of cheap 9-gram coins with 9 rolls of 10-gram.

Using only a *scale*, not a balance, how did he identify the roll of 9-gram coins in only one weighing?

OFA 1982

9. CANNIBALOGIC

Difficulty: 4

☞ An interesting variant on a classic:

A single shipwrecked sailor floats up to a small island and is greeted by three natives. Knowing that cannibals always lie, and noncannibals always tell the truth, he asks each in turn, "Are you a cannibal?"

The first man's answer is inaudible.

The second man's: "The first man said he is not a cannibal. He is not; neither am I."

The third reply: "Both those men are

lying. They're both cannibals. I'm not."
What is each man?

Al Milchen
Nashua, New Hampshire

10. INTEGRATED SERIES
Difficulty: 4

☞ What is the next number in this series, if the product of any two numbers is one less than a square?

1, 3, 8, ?

Nancy Knapp
Geneva, Switzerland

11. COUNTRY SURVEY
Difficulty: 4

☞ Old farmers may not have studied

Euclid, but some knew geometry instinctively; for example, how to find the exact shortest distance from a point to a straight road. Using only a length of rope and a few sticks for markers, construct a perpendicular to extend AB, from P. No cut-and-trying, fitting, knots, or estimating tangent points, please.

Art Kesten
Westport, Connecticut

12. GOLDBACH REVISITED
Difficulty: 5

☞ How many consecutive even numbers can you make using the sum of any 2 prime numbers, employing any prime not more than 7 times in the series?

Larry Ream
Wayne, New Jersey

13. TETRA-TILING
Difficulty: 5

☞ What is the smallest rectangle or square you can construct, filling it in completely using only square pieces, each piece being a different integer-multiple of the smallest piece?

David Edgar
Hartford, Connecticut

14. ARCH NUMBERS
Difficulty: 5

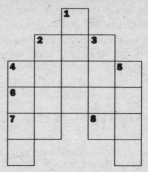

☞ The year of last year's *OFA* is the only composite number in this puzzle.

Each digit is used exactly twice — no leading zeros, of course.

Four of the digits in 4 across are also in 6 across.

Bob Lodge
Seattle, Washington

15. QUADICE
Difficulty: 5

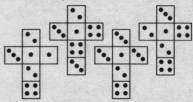

☞ Each of these 4 crosses is an "unfolded" 6-sided special die. Mark up or make 4 equal blocks with these 4 patterns of numbers and arrange them touching in a row, as shown, so that all four numbers appear on each of the 4 long sides of the group.

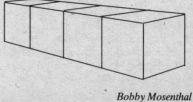

Bobby Mosenthal
Corinth, Vermont

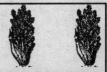

SECRETS OF THE ZODIAC

FAMOUS DEBOWELLED MAN OF THE SIGNS

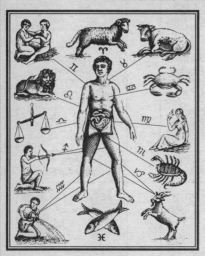

Ancient astrologers associated each of the signs with a part of the body over which they felt the sign held some influence. The first sign of the zodiac — Aries — was attributed to the head, with the rest of the signs moving down the body, ending with Pisces at the feet.

♈ Aries, head. ARI Mar. 21-Apr. 20
♉ Taurus, neck. TAU Apr. 21-May 20
♊ Gemini, arms. GEM May 21-June 20
♋ Cancer, breast. CAN June 21-July 22
♌ Leo, heart. LEO July 23-Aug. 22
♍ Virgo, belly. VIR Aug. 23-Sept. 22
♎ Libra, reins. LIB Sept. 23-Oct. 22
♏ Scorpio, secrets. SCO Oct. 23-Nov. 22
♐ Sagittarius, thighs. SAG Nov. 23-Dec. 21
♑ Capricorn, knees. CAP Dec. 22-Jan. 19
♒ Aquarius, legs. AQU Jan. 20-Feb. 19
♓ Pisces, feet. PSC Feb. 20-Mar. 20

ASTROLOGY AND ASTRONOMY

☞ It was the early astrologers who first made the connection between celestial movements and the physical changes that took place here on Earth. Eventually the science of astronomy became the charting of the actual placement of the planets and the constellations, and astrology became the study of how those placements affected aspects of human behavior. Astrology as we know it today is simply a tool we use to time events according to the placement of the two luminaries (the Sun and the Moon) and the eight known planets (Mercury, Venus, Mars, Jupiter, Saturn, Uranus, Neptune, and Pluto) in the 12 signs of the zodiac. Only a qualified astrologer can give a complete interpretation, but Sun signs can aid us in recognizing and understanding some of our abilities and personal timetables.

Astrologers observed that the Sun appeared to move through each of the 12 constellations (or signs) systematically, always starting out in the sign Aries. On the first day of spring (approximately March 21) the Sun crossed over the equator and began moving north, bringing with it warmer weather and the growth of new plants. The Moon, too, had a cycle all its own (approximately every 29½ days), going from a new Moon to a full Moon and back again. On the nights of the full Moon people and animals appeared to be much more active than normal. Many astrologers consider surgery ill-advised during full Moon days (three days before and after) because of excessive bleeding.

SUN SIGNS AND MOON SIGNS

☞What is the difference between Sun signs and Moon signs? Sun signs tell us in what sign the Sun was on our day of birth; they are easy to find by turning to page 204. There are 12 signs; each one rules a specific time of year, certain characteristics, qualities, and abilities. The Moon sign is more complicated to find because it changes every few days. It tells us where the Moon was at the hour of our birth. Astrologically speaking, the Sun represents our goals and the opportunities we will be offered. The Moon represents our instincts and reactions to the world.

Many readers have asked us which signs are best suited for various activities. Astrologers use Moon signs for this determination, and a month-by-month chart showing appropriate times for certain activities is provided on the next page. (To find the astrological place of the Moon in the zodiac, as well as detailed gardening information, see page 181.) Do not confuse this with the astronomical position of the Moon, as listed on the left-hand pages (48-74); because of precession and other factors the astrological and astronomical zodiacs do not agree.

A Month-by-Month Astrological Timetable for 1991

Herewith we provide the following yearlong chart, based on the Moon signs, showing the appropriate times each month for certain activities. BY JOANNE H. LEMIEUX

	Jan.	Feb.	Mar.	Apr.	May	June	July	Aug.	Sept.	Oct.	Nov.	Dec.
Give up smoking	15	14	16	14	13	12	11	9	8	7	6	5
Begin diet to lose weight	30	7-9	7-8	3-5 30	1-2 10-11	7-8	4-5 31	1 27-29	5-6 24-25	2-3 30-31	26-27	23-24
Begin diet to gain weight	23-24 27-28	19-20 24-25	19-20 23-24	15-16 19-20	13 16-17	13-14	11	none	none	none	20	17-18
Buy clothes	23-24	19-20	19-20	15-16 26-27	13 23-24	19-20	16-17	13-14	9-10	7-8	20	17-18
Seek favors	2-3 29-30	26-27	25-26	21-22	18-20	15-16	12-13	9-10	5-6	2-3 30-31	26-27	23-24
Dental care	4-5 14-15	10-11	9-11	23-25	3-4 21-22	17-18	14-15	11-12 19-20	7-8 16-18	4-6 14-15	10-11 28-29	7-9 25-26
End old projects	30	28	30	28	28	26	26	25	23	23	21	21
Hair care	23-24 27-28	19-20 24-25	19-20 23-24	15-16 19-20	16-17 25-27	13-14 21-23	19-20	15-16	11-13	9-10	20	17-18
Seek pleasures	2-3 29-30	26-27	25-26	21-22	18-20	15-16	12-13	9-10	5-6	2-3 30-31	26-27	23-24
Start a new project	16	15	17	15	14	13	12	10	9	8	7	6
Fishing	9-10	5-6	4-6 14-15	1-2 11-12 29	8-9	5-6	1-3 10	7-8 29-30	30	1 27-29	24-25	2-4 22 30-31
Breed	18-20 23-24	15-16 19-20	19-20	15-16	13	none	none	none	21-22	19-20	16-17	12-14 17-18
Destroy pests/ weeds	none	12-13	12-13	8-9 13	6-7 10-11	7-8 11	4-5 8-9	5-6	1-2 5-6	2-3 30-31	1-2 28-29	none
Graft or pollinate	15 27-28	24-25	23-24	19-20	16-17	13-14	11 24-25	20-21	16-18	14-15	10-11	7-9
Harvest above-ground crops	2-3 11-13 30	7-9 12-13	7-8 30	3-5 8-9 10-11	1-2 6-7 29-30	2-3 7-8 31	4-5	1 27-29 24-25	5-6 30-31	2-3	26-27	23-24
Harvest root crops	none	12-13	12-13	8-9	5-7	2-3 29-30	8-9 27-28	5-6	12 28-29	25-26	22-23	none
Begin logging	2-3 11-13	8-9	7-9	3-5 13 30	1-2 10-11 29	7-8	4-5 31	1 27-29	5-6 24-25	2-3 30-31	26-27	23-24
Prune or cut hay	11-13	8-9	7-8	4-5 13	1-2 10-12	7-9	4-5 31	1 27-28	24-25	none	none	none
Seed grain	6-8	3-4	2-3	26-27	23-24	19-20	17-18	13-14	9-10	7-8	3-4 30	1 27-29
Set posts or pour concrete	2-3 30	12-14	12-13	8-9	6-7 12	2-3 29-30	6-7 27-28	2-4 30-31	5-6 26-27	3-4 30-31	26-27	23-24
Slaughter	none	1-2	2-3	1-2 30	1-2 31	29-30	29-30	28-29	26-27	26	24-25	25-26
Wean	1	none	14-15	11-12	8-9 11	5-6 9-10	1-3 29-30	2-4 7-8 30-31	26-27	24 28-29	24-25	22
Castrate animals	14	10-11	10-11	6-7	3-4 31	1	6-7	2-4 30-31	26-27	none	none	none

ARIES MARCH 21-APRIL 20

Symbol: ♈ The Ram. *Ruling planet*: Mars.
Element: Fire. *Quality*: Assertive. *Ability*: To lead.

Governs: Explorers, pioneers, beginnings, and innovations. *Colors that draw luck*: Shades of red. *Best time of year for*: Personal luck — Mar. 21-Apr. 20; love and recreation — July 23-Aug. 22; travel, meeting new people, and fun — Nov. 23-Dec. 21. *Compatible with*: Fire signs (Leo and Sagittarius) and Air Signs (Gem-

ini, Libra, and Aquarius). *Places that offer new opportunities*: Saudi Arabia, Costa Rica, and Idaho.

TAURUS APRIL 21-MAY 20

Symbol: ♉ The Bull. *Ruling planet*: Venus.
Element: Earth. *Quality*: Materialistic.
Ability: To follow through.

Governs: Builders, farmers, hard work, and possessions. *Colors that draw luck*: Shades of pink. *Best time of year for*: Personal luck — Apr. 21-May 20; love and recreation — Aug. 23-Sept. 22; travel, meeting new people, and fun — Dec. 22-Jan. 19. *Compatible with*: Earth signs (Virgo and Capricorn) and Water signs (Cancer, Scorpio, and Pisces). *Places that offer new opportunities*: Holland, Panama, and Vancouver.

GEMINI MAY 21-JUNE 20

Symbol: ♊ The Twins. *Ruling planet*: Mercury.
Element: Air. *Quality*: Intellectual.
Ability: To communicate.

Governs: Writers, siblings, neighborhoods, and ideas. *Colors that draw luck*: Shades of yellow. *Best time of year for*: Personal luck — May 21-June 20; love and recreation — Sept. 23-Oct. 22; travel, meeting new people, and fun — Jan. 20-Feb. 19. *Compatible with*: Air signs (Libra and Aquarius) and Fire signs (Aries, Leo, and Sagittarius). *Places that offer new opportunities*: Bali, Montserrat, and Detroit.

CANCER JUNE 21-JULY 22

Symbol: ♋ The Crab. *Ruling planet*: Moon.
Element: Water. *Quality*: Compassionate.
Ability: To understand.

Governs: Mothers, elders, endings, and home. *Colors that draw luck*: Shades of sea green. *Best time of year for*: Personal luck — June 21-July 22; love and recreation — Oct. 23-Nov. 22; travel, meeting new people, and fun — Feb. 20-Mar. 20. *Compatible with*: Water signs (Scorpio and Pisces) and Earth signs (Taurus, Virgo, and Capricorn). *Places that offer new opportunities*: Georgia, U.S.S.R.; Egypt; and Salt Lake City.

LEO JULY 23-AUGUST 22

Symbol: ♌ The Lion. *Ruling planet*: Sun.
Element: Fire. *Quality*: Forceful.
Ability: To supervise.

Governs: Rulers, leaders, children, and creations. *Colors that draw luck*: Shades of gold and orange. *Best time of year for*: Personal luck — July 23-Aug. 22; love and recreation — Nov. 23-Dec. 21; travel, meeting new people, and fun — Mar. 21-Apr. 20. *Compatible with*: Fire signs (Aries and Sagittarius) and Air signs (Gemini, Libra, and Aquarius). *Places that offer new opportunities:* Kenya, Hawaii, and Argentina.

VIRGO AUGUST 23-SEPTEMBER 22

Symbol: ♍ The Virgin. *Ruling planet*: Mercury.
Element: Earth. *Quality*: Curious.
Ability: To organize.

Governs: Bankers, accountants, health, and place of work. *Colors that draw luck*: Shades of brown. *Best time of year for*: Personal luck — Aug. 23-Sept. 22; love and recreation — Dec. 22-Jan. 19; travel, meeting new people, and fun — Apr. 21-May 20. *Compatible with*: Earth signs (Taurus and Capricorn) and Water signs (Cancer, Scorpio, and Pisces). *Places that offer new opportunities*: Australia, Tahiti, and Quebec.

LIBRA SEPTEMBER 23-OCTOBER 22

Symbol: ♎ The Scales. *Ruling planet*: Venus. *Element*: Air. *Quality*: Idealistic. *Ability*: To relate.

Governs: Diplomats, lawyers, relationships, partners, and politics. *Colors that draw luck*: Shades of blue. *Best time of year for*: Personal luck — Sept. 23-Oct. 22; love and recreation — Jan. 20-Feb. 19; travel, meeting new people, and fun — May 21-June 20. *Compatible with*: Air signs (Gemini and Aquarius) and Fire signs (Aries, Leo, and Sagittarius). *Places that offer new opportunities*: Scotland; Sheboygan, Wisconsin; and Madagascar.

SCORPIO OCTOBER 23-NOVEMBER 22

Symbol: ♏ The Scorpion. *Ruling planet*: Pluto. *Element*: Water. *Quality*: Powerful. *Ability*: To concentrate.

Governs: Detectives, researchers, secrets, and passions. *Colors that draw luck*: Shades of dark red. *Best time of year for*: Personal luck — Oct. 23-Nov. 22; love and recreation — Feb. 20-Mar. 20; travel, meeting new people, and fun — June 21-July 22. *Compatible with*: Water signs (Cancer and Pisces) and Earth signs (Taurus, Virgo, and Capricorn). *Places that offer new opportunities*: Istanbul, Spain, and Prince Edward Island.

SAGITTARIUS NOVEMBER 23-DECEMBER 21

Symbol: ♐ The Hunter. *Ruling planet*: Jupiter. *Element*: Fire. *Quality*: Expansive. *Ability*: To be versatile.

Governs: Hunters, scholars, travel, and religion. *Colors that draw luck*: Shades of purple. *Best time of year for*: Personal luck — Nov. 23-Dec. 21; love and recreation — Mar. 21-Apr. 20; travel, meeting new people, and fun — July 23-Aug. 22. *Compatible with*: Fire signs (Aries and Leo) and Air signs (Gemini, Libra, and Aquarius). *Places that offer new opportunities*: Guatemala, Maine, New Zealand, and Albuquerque.

CAPRICORN DECEMBER 22-JANUARY 19

Symbol: ♑ The Mountain Goat. *Ruling planet*: Saturn. *Element*: Earth. *Quality*: Trustworthy. *Ability*: To be disciplined.

Governs: Authoritarian figures, fathers, time, and status. *Colors that draw luck*: Shades of gray and black. *Best time of year for*: Personal luck — Dec. 22-Jan. 19; love and recreation — Apr. 21-May 20; travel, meeting new people, and fun — Aug. 23-Sept. 22.

Compatible with: Earth signs (Taurus and Virgo) and Water signs (Cancer, Scorpio, and Pisces). *Places that offer new opportunities*: Italy, Kashmir, and New Orleans.

AQUARIUS JANUARY 20-FEBRUARY 19

Symbol: ♒ The Water Bearer. *Ruling planet*: Uranus. *Element*: Air. *Quality*: Independent. *Ability*: To be inventive.

Governs: Scientists, astronomers, changes, and television. *Colors that draw luck*: Electric blue and indigo. *Best time of year for*: Personal luck — Jan. 20-Feb. 19; love and recreation — May 21-June 20; travel, meeting new people, and fun — Sept. 23-Oct. 22. *Compatible with*: Air signs (Gemini and Libra) and Fire signs (Aries, Leo, and Sagittarius). *Places that offer new opportunities*: Samoa, Ceylon, and Montreal.

PISCES FEBRUARY 20-MARCH 20

Symbol: ♓ The Fish. *Ruling planet*: Neptune. *Element*: Water. *Quality*: Imaginative. *Ability*: To be psychic.

Governs: Fishermen, poets, dreams, and inspirations. *Colors that draw luck*: Shades of white. *Best time of year for*: Personal luck — Feb. 20-Mar. 20; love and recreation —

June 21-July 22; travel, meeting new people, and fun — Oct. 23-Nov. 22. *Compatible with*: Water signs (Cancer and Scorpio) and Earth signs (Taurus, Virgo, and Capricorn). *Places that offer new opportunities*: Oslo; Block Island, Rhode Island; and Baden-Baden.

The Birth of Basketball

It happened one December afternoon 100 years ago. And the very first game was played in bed! BY **CHRISTINE SCHULTZ**

L ate one cold December afternoon 100 years ago, a disheartened young instructor climbed the narrow steps to his office and slumped into a chair. For two weeks James Naismith had struggled to engage his class members at the International YMCA Training School in Springfield, Massachusetts, in some competitive indoor sport — long ball, prisoners' base, indoor lacrosse — but had failed so far to capture their interest. Naismith, a graduate of Presbyterian Theological College in Montreal, was convinced that he could teach clean living better through sports than from the pulpit. The following day he would have to report to the faculty and admit that, despite all his theories, he had done no better than the instructors before him. Had he given up that day, one of the most exciting chapters in sports history would never have been written.

Late into the night he wrestled with the problem. His class was bored with the usual calisthenics, yet indoor versions of football and soccer resulted only in bruises. His mind drifted to his younger days at Bennie's Corners in the lumbering region of northern Ontario. As a lad orphaned at age eight, he had been forced to use his own initiative, making ice skates one winter from the only materials available to him — two old files fastened firmly into strips of hickory wood. Now, years later, the inventive lad, grown to 30, was faced again with the challenge of devising a sport for winter play.

Naismith snapped his fingers. He had an idea at last. He slept fitfully and dreamed. "I believe that I am the first person who ever played basketball," he wrote, "and although I used the bed for a court, I certainly played a hard game." That night, with his work still before him, Naismith had no way of knowing that his new game would soon spread across the country as the first major sport of strictly U.S. origin.

In the morning, the game still on his mind, Naismith arrived early at the school (later called Springfield College). He met the janitor, Pop Stebbins, in the hall and asked him for two 18-inch-square boxes for goals. "No, I haven't any boxes," Pop replied, then thought for a moment. "But I'll tell you what I do have — two old

James Naismith dreamed up basketball to teach clean living through sports.

- courtesy Basketball Hall of Fame

peach baskets down in the storeroom, if they'll do you any good."

They were good enough; had they not been, we might have inherited a game called "boxball." The baskets were tacked to the balcony, and Naismith set to penciling 13 rules (12 of which still apply today) on a scratch pad. Then, in another unknowingly historic moment, Naismith looked at the two balls on the floor of his office — a football and a soccer ball — and chose the latter. He hurried into the gym a bit nervously to face the contentious class. "I was sure in my own mind that the game was good," Naismith wrote in his book on the game's origin, "but it needed a real test. I felt that the success or failure depended largely on the way the class received it."

By 11:30 A.M. the students, dressed in gym costumes of black long-sleeved woolen jerseys and gray trousers and sporting the handlebar mustaches of the day, stood listening somewhat dubiously to the rules. Naismith divided the boys nine to a side with three forwards, centers, and backs. He threw the first ball into play December 21, 1891. "It was the start of the first basketball game and the finish of the trouble with that class."

Naismith had thought out many of the game's details, but failed to consider cutting the bottom from the basket, so when a basket was scored, the game stopped while someone climbed a ladder to fetch it. Perhaps it was just as well that on that first day only one basket went in. The players had yet to master the skills, and they looked comical in Naismith's estimation. "If we could see the game today as it was played then, we would laugh," Naismith once noted. Oftentimes a player would receive the ball and hold it over his head, poised to shoot at the basket. At that moment another player would reach from behind and steal the ball. No matter how often this happened, the slighted player would look about with a startled expression, not at first realizing where the ball had gone.

As a means of getting around a close guard, some players tried to roll the ball. Other bright fellows realized they could maintain more control by bouncing it. Naismith had not incorporated dribbling into the rules, but the idea caught on and became a feature that distinguished the sport from any other. As early as 1896 Yale and other teams were playing what was known as the dribble game.

To keep spectators from being injured or from throwing things at the players, wire fences were often built around the court.

Basketball quickly became popular at YMCAs across the country where students had tired of calisthenics and Indian clubs. People passing the Springfield gym heard the commotion and filled in the galleries to watch Naismith's new game. There were no backboards at that time and overzealous onlookers often leaned from the gallery to help the ball in or deflect it. One spectator, Miss Maude E. Sherman, became a member of the first women's basketball team. She was a fan not only of the game, but of its inventor as well. She married Naismith three years later.

As basketball grew in popularity, it took on a life of its own. Despite Naismith's attempts to keep the game clean, in its early stages the sport was often brutal. Injuries were common as players slammed into each other, making padded pants, knee guards, and elbow pads necessary. "The center tap was murderous," one early star noted. "I saw guys get crippled." To keep spectators from being injured or from throwing things at the players, wire fences were often built around the court, and thus basketball players came to be known as "cagers."

Signs of the game's widespread acceptance were everywhere — an old hoop hung deep in the Wisconsin woods or on a weather-beaten shed in the South or in a deserted workman's camp in Colorado — and Naismith derived great pleasure from seeing the hoops hung in out-of-the-way places.

Despite widespread enthusiasm about the game, certain elements did not catch on — the overhead dribble, the one-point field goal, and the rule that an out-of-bounds ball was up for grabs to the first man to touch it. Other elements evolved that the inventor had not foreseen — the backboard, the open net basket, and the five-man team. But Naismith considered them only minor modifications to his original game. He proudly acknowledged that the only true change was in the skill of the players. As young players spent more time shooting baskets, scores shifted to the double digits.

Baskets didn't become bottomless until 1906.

In 1919 the United States team scored an amazing 93 points against France's eight in the Inter-Allied Games. The tournament, considered the first international basketball competition, paved the way for world championships and Olympic recognition.

In 1936 the National Association of Basketball Coaches (NABC) headed a nationwide drive for money to send "the father of basketball" to Berlin. There the game was played for the first time in the Olympics. The teams from each nation filed in behind their flags, and Naismith addressed the assembled players. That day he would cheer the American team to a 19-8 victory over Canada outdoors in the rain. It was the happiest day of his life, he said.

Upon his return from Berlin, the NABC initiated a campaign to raise money for a basketball hall of fame, but it wasn't until 1968 that the hall opened on the Springfield College campus, where the game had begun. In June 1985 the exhibits were moved to a modern, $11.5 million, three-level building between the Connecticut River and Interstate 91 in Springfield. The hall was named in Naismith's honor, and he was among the first to be enshrined there.

Though Naismith didn't live to see the hall, he maintained remarkable stamina into old age. He walked briskly and erect with the carriage of a young athlete, taught football at Kansas University for 39 years, and continued to practice fencing. But he was known best for basketball. When he died at age 78 on November 28, 1939, in Kansas, his eulogizer remarked that "His contribution to the athletic world of the game of basketball will leave a mark that even time cannot erase. Dr. Naismith gave to youth basketball, a game that takes the youngster to maturity. The youth of the world will arise and call him blessed."

Both young and old will honor him in January 1991, when Springfield begins a year-long celebration of the 100th anniversary of the sport. The town hopes to host representatives from 160 nations with contests at all levels — an NBA game, NCAA teams, foreign teams, women's teams, and championship high school teams.

Most agree that Naismith deserves all the hoopla for his promotion of basketball, but some dispute his claim to have been the first to conceive the idea. In neighboring Holyoke, Massachusetts, Clara Gabler insists that her late father, George Gabler, a college buddy of Naismith's, first showed him the game. Former Holyoke alderman Thomas Kennedy supports her claim saying, "My research shows that the game was being played two years earlier in Holyoke." There have been stirrings, too, in Herkimer, New York, to erect a shrine in support of the claim that a local YMCA director first introduced basketball on February 7, 1891, ten months before Naismith.

But right or wrong, it is Naismith's version of the story that has been passed down to us over the years. The game that he worried might not capture the interest of his YMCA class has, in the end, fascinated people of all ages and backgrounds for 100 years. That's why 41,000 spectators crowded into the Hoosier Dome in Indiana to watch a high school tournament in March 1990, why close to 66,000 people watched Louisiana State upset Georgetown in January 1989, and why some 62,000 fans turned out for a regular season game between the Boston Celtics and the Detroit Pistons. Basketball has become the favorite team game in the world, more popular, in fact, than football and baseball combined. It is played by millions of athletes and watched by millions more. To Naismith that would have been the biggest tribute of all. □□

THE EVOLUTION OF BASKETBALL

March 11, 1892 — The first public contest took place at the School for Christian Workers, Springfield, Massachusetts, with the students beating the instructors 5-1 before a crowd of 200.

March 22, 1893 — The first women's game was played at Smith College, Northampton, Massachusetts. The female players wore bloomers, so no male spectators were allowed to watch.

1894 — Soccer balls were replaced by laced basketballs manufactured at the Overman Wheel Company in Chicopee Falls, Massachusetts. Also that year, the first backboards were erected to keep spectators from interfering from the balconies.

1897 — Five-man teams became accepted after games with up to 50 players on a team became unmanageable.

1899 — Players were allowed to alternate hands while dribbling. (Previously a player could switch only once.)

1901-1908 — Players could not shoot for the goal after dribbling, but had to pass to a stationary teammate.

1903 — Court boundaries were required to be straight. (Some early courts jogged around pillars, stairways, and other obstructions.)

1906 — After years of climbing up to remove the ball from the peach basket and after trying a contraption to eject the ball, the bottom of the basket was finally removed.

1907-08 season — Buffalo Germans began a string of 111 straight wins.

1921 — Basket ball became one word: basketball.

1923-24 — "Designated foul shooter" was eliminated; person fouled had to take the foul shot.

January 7, 1927 — Harlem Globetrotters, organized by Abe Saperstein, played their first exhibition game in Hinckley, Illinois.

1929 — The "cage" was eliminated; use of rope or chicken wire around the court was discontinued.

1932 — The center jump after each score was eliminated; ten-second rule (for advancing ball past midcourt) went into effect.

1944-45 — Goal-tending declared illegal.

1956 — The foul lane was widened from six to 12 feet.

1960 — The Minneapolis Lakers moved to Los Angeles, California, giving professional basketball coast-to-coast coverage for the first time.

1971 — Size of women's teams was reduced from six to five players.

1974 — Moses Malone signed with the Utah Stars of the American Basketball Association to become the first professional basketball player to go directly from high school to the pro ranks.

January 5, 1986 — Game called because of rain. (A leaking roof in the Seattle Coliseum forced an NBA game to be cancelled.)

March 1, 1987 — Boston Celtics became the first NBA team to win 2,000 regular season games.

1989 — President Ronald Reagan sent $10,000 worth of basketball equipment to Burundi.

March 24, 1990 — 41,046 fans attended the Indiana High School Championship in the Hoosier Dome.

CLASSIFIED ADVERTISING

ASTROLOGY/OCCULT

ASTROLOGY. Personalized, comprehensive Natal Chart ($9). Progressed chart for current year ($9). Both ($12). Send name, birth date, birth time, birthplace. Cycles, Dept. FAA, 2251 Berkley Ave., Schenectady NY 12309

BIORHYTHMS. Your physical, emotional, intellectual cycles charted in color. Interpretation guide. Six months ($9). Twelve months ($12). Send name, birth date. Cycles, Dept. FAB, 2251 Berkley Ave., Schenectady NY 12309

SPELLS PERFORMED Immediately! Tell me what you want, and I will use my Mystical Powers to cast a spell in your favor. Free details. Send self-addressed, stamped envelope. Florentine, Box 5387-R, High Point NC 27262

FREE LUCKY NUMBERS. Send birth date, self-addressed envelope. Mystic, Box 2009-R, Jamestown NC 27282

ANCIENT WITCHCRAFT POWERS bring success, protection, love. World's foremost occult school now accepting students. Free information. Box 1366, Nashua NH 03061. 603-880-7237

LEARN WITCHCRAFT for protection, success, and serenity. Gavin and Yvonne Frost, world's foremost witches, now accepting students. Box 1502-0, New Bern NC 28563

VOODOO, oldest organization. Catalog $7.50. Ritual work by request. TOTS, Suite 310, 1317 North San Fernando Blvd., Burbank CA 91504, Dept. OFA

MOTHER CHRISTIAN, Spiritual Healer. Do you need help on all problems in life? Call 404-382-1858.

SEX AND THE ZODIAC. Astrology-for-Yourself Books. Details free. Betty, Box 80717-F, Las Vegas NV 89180

MRS. RITA. Spiritual Psychic. Astrologer. Helper of all problems. Reunites separated lovers. Send $2, self-addressed stamped envelope: 16450 N.E. 6th Ave., North Miami Beach FL 33162. Phone 305-944-6182.

OCCULT CATALOG: Complete Spiritual & Magical Needs. Herbs, oils, incenses, jewelry, books & more. Large, informative. $2 Handling. Joan Teresa Power Products, Box 442-F, Mars Hill NC 28754

PYRAMID POWER! Change your life forever! Money, Love, Health. Use the power! $10 for pyramid and inst. **SRG,** 6033 W. Century Blvd., Los Angeles CA 90045

BEER & WINE MAKING

BEGINNERS ONLY! Make beer, wine. Pop-build a still! Complete details, $2 (refundable). Home Brew International, 1126 South Federal Highway, Suite F182, Ft. Lauderdale FL 33316

WINEMAKERS — BEERMAKERS - Free Illustrated Catalog. Fast Service, large selection. Kraus, Box 7850-YB, Independence MO 64053

HOMEBREWERS! Free Catalog. Best prices, selection. Case discounts. Draft systems. Mid-South Malts, 2537 Broad, Memphis TN 38112

BOAT KITS & PLANS

BOAT KITS & PLANS. Boatbuilding supplies. 250 Designs. Catalog $3. Clarkcraft, 16-29 Aqualane, Tonawanda NY 14150

BOOKS/MAGAZINES

350 FASCINATING INDIAN BOOKS! Catalog by first class mail $1. Indians, Box 3300, Rapid City SD 57709

BEES for Fun and Profit. Informative booklet, $3.95. Hummingbird Press, P.O. Box 656, New Albany OH 43054

PUBLISH YOUR BOOK! Join our successful authors. All subjects invited. Publicity, advertising, beautiful books. Send for fact-filled booklet and free manuscript report. Carlton Press, Dept. OA 11, West 32 St., New York 10001

CHRIST RETURNS 1996? Biblical U.S.A.? World government, religion? Trinity? Immortality? Free. P.O. Box 7700, Pasadena TX 77508

MANUSCRIPTS WANTED, all types. Publisher with 70-year tradition. Free examination "Guide to Publication." 1-800-695-9599

DID A BROTHER OR SISTER DIE? The internationally acclaimed book, *It's OK,* is a survival kit for grieving sisters and brothers of all ages. $8 (includes P&H). Floridians add 49¢ tax. Keystone Press, Box 6163, Bradenton FL 34281

CATALOG OF BOOKS. 50-page catalog describes over 300 titles. Books on survival and dozens of other subjects! Send $1 to: Paladin Press, P.O. Box 1307-1AZ, Boulder CO 80306.

GOLD IN MAINE. History. Adventure. Where to pan. Free details. John Wade, Box 303, Phillips ME 04966

WILDERNESS SURVIVAL, homesteading, self-defense, gardening, food, hunting, medical, more. Free catalog. Aspen Cabin, 5038-C 6th Ave., Kenosha WI 53140

WORLD NEWS. Hear all about it first with world band radio. Free report tells how. PIF News, Box 232, L.d.R., Laval, Quebec, Canada H7N 4Z9

EASY CREDIT OR LAYAWAY! Thousands of items! Catalogs: $5. GMM Homeshopping, Box 295, Rome GA 30162-0295

BUSINESS OPPORTUNITY

RECONDITION BATTERIES! High profits, small investment, proven method. Free Details. Battery, Dept 14, Box 1433, Hallandale FL 33008

AMAZING! EASY WORK at Home! $100 to $500 possible per week. Assembly, sewing, recording videotapes, electronics, and more. Free recording reveals complete information. Call 205-822-0986, Ext. 100.

EARN BIG PROFITS! Free Information! Profitable home business opportunities! Iron-clad guarantee. Write: SMC Marketing services, 1460 W. Foothill Blvd. #H-101, Upland CA 91786.

STUFF ENVELOPES for $140/100. Send address label to: Associates, 5117 Folsom #603, Sacramento CA 95819.

EARN $1,000s/week at home. No experience. Send SASE to: PEN, Box 1886-L, Temple City CA 91780.

NEW BEST-SELLER BOOK LIST, including secrets of millionaires. $2 to: Greenbacks, 1500 Forest (221), Richmond VA 23229.

$2000 FROM ¼ ACRE! Grow Ginseng. Sell $60/pound. Free information. 5712-FA Cooper Road, Indianapolis IN 46208

EARN $100 PER DAY. Plan Plus six formulas. Send $1. Robross, Box 8768F, Boston MA 02114

MAKE MONEY! SAVE MONEY! 3,000 items below wholesale. Free sample offer. Lindbloom, 3636-FA Peterson, Chicago IL 60659

INVENTIONS/NEW PRODUCTS/IDEAS WANTED: Call TLCI for free information. 1-800-468-7200. 24 hours/day, USA/Canada.

MAKE $100 AN HOUR imprinting advertising specialties. We supply imprint machine, supplies, 1001 products for imprinting. Spectacular new home business opportunity. Free details and sample. BASCO, 9351 De Soto Ave., Dept. B358-106, Chatsworth CA 91311-4948

SPARE TIME Businesses that can make you rich. Free details. Bell's, Dept. F, P.O. Box 6, Clarendon TX 79226

EARN $1000s processing mail. No experience needed. Send SASE. Downtown Marketing, P.O. Box 434-G, Muncie IN 47303

LET THE GOVERNMENT FINANCE your small business. Grants/loans to $500,000 yearly. Free recorded message: 707-448-0270. (KEI)

$24,000 IN BACKYARD! Grow new specialty plants. Start with $60. Free information. Growers, Box 988-OFA, Friday Harbor WA 98250

HOME ASSEMBLY WORK Available! Guaranteed easy money! Free details! Homework-FA, Box 520, Danville NH 03819

GARAGE/YARD SALE? Extra customers guaranteed! Free details. Don Ling, Box 309C, Butterfield MN 56120

CARNIVOROUS PLANTS

CATALOGS

CRAFTS

DO IT YOURSELF

EDUCATION / INSTRUCTION

FLAGS

FOR THE HOME

GARDENING/PLANTS/NURSERY

TWO RED INDIAN CLING PEACH TREES $14. Postpaid price list — free. Ponzer Nursery, HCR 33 Box 18, Rolla MO 65401

GREENHOUSE PLASTIC. Superstrong, ripstop woven polyethylene. Resists windstorms, yellowing. Sample: Bob's Greenhouses, Box 42FA, Neche ND 58265. 204-327-5540

GINSENG AND HERBS

GINSENG! GOLDENSEAL! Profitable, good demand. Have seeds, roots. Comfrey. Free information. William Collins, Viola IA 52350

GINSENG, GOLDENSEAL Growing Information $1. First-year ginseng roots $15/100. Seed $10/oz. Ginseng (OFA), Flagpond TN 37657

WILD HERBS AND ROOTS WANTED! Free 1990 price list, write: Wilcox Natural Products, P.O. Box 37, Eolia MO 63344. 314-485-2400

GOVERNMENT SURPLUS

NARCOTICS RAID SEIZURES! Autos, vans, boats, airplanes. Millions surplus bargains. Many 1% original cost! Nationwide Directory, $3. DISPOSAL, Box 19107-JM, Washington DC 20036

JEEPS, trucks from $52.50. Low as 2¢ on dollar. Money-back guarantee. 400,000 bargains. Buy in your area. Surplus Directory $3. Surplus, Box 1409-OFA, Holland MI 49422

HEALTH/BEAUTY

ASTHMA/HAYFEVER SUFFERERS. Free information. Nephron Corporation, Dept. NCFA, P.O. Box 1974, Tacoma WA 98401

DISCOUNT PRESCRIPTIONS AND VITAMINS. Thousands of money-saving health-care products. Free postage. Satisfaction guaranteed. Call toll-free 1-800-TEL-DRUG (835-3784) for free catalog.

LIVE LONGER! Secret report tells how you can remain healthy and mentally alert at 80, 90, even 100 years of age! Only $4. O'Malley's M.O., Department A, 7870 Locher Way #21, Citrus Heights CA 95610

FREE HERBS & HOME REMEDIES BROCHURE. Stamped envelope. Pharmacist Champion, Box 26363-FA, Memphis TN 38126

AT LAST! Lose and keep weight off naturally. Guaranteed. Stoffa House, 933 Winchester, Lincoln Park MI 48146

"NEW, PROVEN REMEDIES for children/adult bladder control problems." To own this manual, send $9.95 to: Valucenter, POB 1253C, Elmira NY 14902.

"OVERCOMING INSOMNIA Without Medication." To own this manual, send $4.95 to: Valucenter, P.O. Box 1253N, Elmira NY 14902.

PILES (HEMORRHOIDS)? Stop bleeding! End discomfort! For homecare information write to: Careguide Services, Box 110B, 55 McCaul, Toronto, Ont., M5T 2W7, Canada.

HEARING AIDS

HEARING AID. Free hearing-aid catalog. Save ½ by mail. Write: Money-Saver, 36658FA Apache Plume Drive, Palmdale CA 93550.

HELP WANTED

AUSTRALIA WANTS YOU! Big Pay! Transportation! New Employment Handbook, $3. International, Box 19107-JM, Washington DC 20036

$100 TO $1,000 DAILY. Overseas! Stateside! Free list. Zincs 113, Box 13110, Las Vegas NV 89112

OVERSEAS EMPLOYMENT OPPORTUNITIES! All occupations! $35,000-$75,000+. Free Report! Employment International, Box 19760-JM, Indianapolis IN 46219

JOBS. Any state, any occupation, including government, state, public. Also cruiseships, tugs, ships, riverboats, oil rigs. Women & men. Work a month, home a month. USA plus overseas. Information $5. Nationwide Employment, B235, Central IN 47110

HOUSING/HOME BUILDING

YOU CAN SAVE TO 50% by building your own home. New book shows how. Free details. Triangle Publishing, P.O. Box 163-61, Rose Hill KS 67133

INVENTIONS/PATENTS

INVENTORS: If you have an invention for sale or license, write for free booklet explaining how we can help you. Kessler Sales Corp., C-42, Fremont OH 43420

INVENTORS. Confused? Need Help? Call IMPAC for free information package. In U.S./Canada 1-800-225-5800

LOANS BY MAIL/FINANCIAL

LOW INTEREST LOANS Source List, 5% to 7% interest, 100% financing. Long-term repayment. Below bank rate loans. Details: $3/SASE. Credit Information, B2000FA, Central IN 47110

MONEY AVAILABLE! 1st and 2nd mortgages, business and personal loans, credit cards. Grants regardless of past credit history. Check us out with the Better Business Bureau, Lancaster, Pa. We want your business. 717-531-1025, Ext. 500

FREE MONEY! $300,000,000 Giveaway. Grants. Never repay. Information $1. (Refundable). Jakla, Box 3066-FAO-1, Seminole FL 34642

MISCELLANEOUS

"JUST MARRIED" bumper stickers for decorating newlyweds' cars. One for $2, two for $3 ppd. U.S. funds only. 1776 Enterprises, Box 374OFB, Sudbury MA 01776

DIRECT FROM MANUFACTURER. Special to Almanac readers — EVIN specialty down-filled or poly-filled work parkas with exclusive "telescopic sleeve" for freedom of movement. Write or call for free brochure. 514-288-6233 or EVIN Industries Ltd., 3575 St. Lawrence Blvd., Suite 201, Montreal, Quebec. H2X 2T7

INVENTIONS, IDEAS, new products! Presentation to industry and exhibition at national innovation exposition. Call 1-800-288-IDEA.

FAMILY-TREE RESEARCH, census 1790-1910, every county, every state. Details: Long stamped envelope. Walter White, Room 16-C, 340 N. Main Street, Columbia City IN 46725

COATS-OF-ARMS.
Hand-painted. Researched. 37th year. Brochure $2, refundable. Vernon Nickerson, Box 1776F, North Chatham MA 02650

SATELLITE TV. Free Details. Install it yourself! Complete systems, upgrades. Orbitek Satellite Communications, Box 264A, Bohemia NY 11716-0264. 516-589-1292

EASILY MADE BIRDBATHS, benches, statues, etc. Illustrated manual for making molds and products: $10. MoldCraft, Box 991-FO, Alexander City AL 35010

QUALITY PLAYING CARDS. Sample deck $3 (2/$5.00). Products Unique, 210 Fifth Ave., New York NY 10010

CASH FOR OLD RECORDS! Illustrated 72-page catalog, including thousands of specific prices we pay for 78s on common labels (Columbia, Decca, Victor, etc.), information about scarce labels, shipping instructions, etc. Send $2 (refundable). Discollector, Box 691035 (FA), San Antonio TX 78269

METAL DETECTORS. World's best brands. All discounted! 1-800-876-FIND. Kansas/ Texas Detectors, Box 17015-A, Ft. Worth TX 76102-0015

OWN A FOREST HOMESITE for $53.85 per month. Own, control, and protect five acres of hardwood forest. Mountains, rivers, lakes. Environmental Protection. Choose from hundreds of acreages. Nothing down, 9% interest. Free Catalogs. Woods & Waters, Box One-FA, Willow Springs MO 65793. 417-469-3187

FIGHT BACK! Learn how to complain and get results. Easy instructions. $4. Box 3150, Boulder CO 80307-3150

RETIRING BROKE? Here's how to find out now what your Social Security payments will be. Easy instructions. $5. Box 3150, Boulder CO 80307-3150

WHAT ARE THEY SAYING about you in your credit report? Here's how to find out now. $4.95/SASE. Box 3150, Boulder CO 80307-3150

TREASURE. Locate quarter mile away with ultrasonic locator. Brochure free. Research Products, Box 270270-TTC, Tampa FL 33688

SEND YOUR MONEY TO: R. Prihoda Pheasant Farm. Save the pheasants. 10759 W. 8 Mile Road, Franksville WI 53126

MUSIC/RECORDS/TAPES

ENJOY MAKING MUSIC! Instructions: Fiddle, banjo, guitar, other instruments, tunebooks, videos, recordings. Free catalog. Captain Fiddle, 4 Elm Court, Newmarket NH 03857. 603-659-2658.

SPIRITUAL, RELIGIOUS POEMS wanted for musical setting recording. $1,000 for best song. Chapel Recording (FA), Box 112, Wollaston MA 02170 (Talent Co.)

LYRICS, POEMS for musical setting and recording. $1,000 for best poem. Satisfaction guaranteed. Talent, Box 31 (FA), Quincy MA 02169

ACCORDIONS, BUTTON BOXES, concertinas, electronic organ accordions. New, used, trade, repair. Credit cards, catalogs. Castiglione, Box 40, Warren MI 48090-0040. 313-755-6050

OF INTEREST TO ALL

BEAUTIFUL LACE BABY BLANKET. Perfect for: gifts, religious ceremonies, discreet nursing, protection from sun or insects. Washable. $38 ppd. World Enterprise, P.O. 8473, Cedar Rapids IA 52408

FORGET-ME-NOT CROSSES. Attractive markers for hard-to-find-graves, tragedy sites, etc. Several styles and wood types. Send for brochure, $2 (refundable). Crosses, 4250 DaVinci Ave., Jacksonville FL 32210

CASH LOANS! 98% approval. Unsecured charge card! Details: Visa/Mastercard. MLS, Box 271447-FA, Tampa FL 33688

WWIII: UNDERSTAND, SURVIVE & WIN. Revealed path to how begins here. Now send $2 & SASE to: HEBEGB, POB 193004-R4, San Francisco CA 94119-3004

HAVE SOME FUN! Introductions. Confessions. Jokes. Advice. 1-900-FUN-1990. 95¢ minute.

I EARNED $5,000 on ¼ acre growing Oriental vegetables. So can you. Growing/marketing/seed source. Booklet $4. Scherer, Box 250, Ewing VA 24248

WORLD'S LARGEST OCCULT, mystic arts, witchcraft, voodoo. Thousands of unusual curios. 3 fascinating 1991 catalogs, $1. By airmail, $2. Worldwide Curio House, Box 17095-A, Minneapolis MN 55417

FREE! World's most unusual novelty catalog. 1,800 things you never knew existed. Johnson-Smith, F410, Bradenton FL 34206

FUR COATS! LARGE! PETITE! Custom manufactured! Undersell stores nationwide! Mail order N.Y.C. showroom. 516-379-6421. (Fox vests — $395.)

LUCKY NUMBERS — C.O.D. or Cash. 24 numbers: 3-digit, 4-digit lottery or 2-digit lotto numbers by psychic. We say way and date. Send $10 and birth date. Psychic Authority, Box 47110-L803, Jacksonville FL 32247. Rush C.O.D. Toll-free 24 Hrs. 1-800-888-1744

GOLFERS: GET TO PUTT like the pros. Send for the device. $5. PAVO Enterprises, P.O. Box 246B, Morgan Hill CA 95038

OF INTEREST TO WOMEN

EARN $400 A MONTH at home, spare time, doing only two $1.0 invisible reweaving/reknitting jobs a day. Good money paid for making cuts, tears disappear from fabrics. Details free. Fabricon, 2051 Montrose, Chicago IL 60618

AT LAST! Be beautiful, fashionable for pennies. Satisfaction guaranteed. Free information. Margean, Box 3003, Kingman AZ 86401

LINGERIE. Feel sexier whatever your size. We offer two lingerie catalogs. Sizes S, M, L and 1X-3X. Send $3 and specify which catalog you want; $3 will be credited on your first order. We pay all shipping costs. Hamilton House, 440 Nichols Drive (FA), Suwanee GA 30174

ORGANIZATIONS

BOOK COLLECTORS! Join the National Book Collectors Society! Free information: NBCS, 65 High Ridge Road #349, Stamford CT 06905

PERSONALS

ARE YOU HAVING PROBLEMS In luck, love, health, money? Depressed or confused? Call Carol for help, 615-726-2882. 2801 Nolensville Rd., Nashville TN 37211

LATIN-ORIENTAL LADIES seek friendship, marriage. Free photos, details. "Latins," Box 1716-FR, Chula Vista CA 92012

LONELY? SINGLE? NEEDING LOVE? Marriage minded? Guaranteed results. (Special services.) Marriage Bureau, Box 4773-OFA, Jackson MS 39296-4773

NANCY CLARK. Love Psychic. Specializes in reuniting soul mates. Mental telepathy. Aura readings and karma and Tarot readings available. Serious calls only. 404-335-6382. 252 Homer St., Commerce GA 30529

EVANGELIST ADAMS, Spiritual Healer and Advisor. Will solve all life's problems. Love, marriage, health, business, bad luck. 8287 Spanishfort Blvd., Spanishfort AL 36527. 205-626-7997

BEAUTIFUL OVERSEAS LADIES seek marriage. Free videos, photos. Devotion, Box 549-FA, Dublin VA 24084-0549. 703-674-4475

FIND THAT OLD-FASHIONED GIRL! Free details. Enclose six 25¢ stamps. Anticipations, Box 2307-FZ, Makati, Philippines.

MEET CHRISTIAN SINGLES the sensible way! Local. Worldwide. Phone/mail introductions text. Love. Dating. Marriage. Meaningful companionship can change your life today! Free brochure. Samples: 1-800-323-8113, Ext. 433

MEET USA SINGLES by phone/mail. Low fee. M. Fischer Club, Box 2152-FA, Loves Park IL 61130

CASH GRANTS AVAILABLE from nonprofit foundations! Never repay! 401 sources/application instructions, $3. FundSearch, Box 19107-JM, Washington DC 20036

MEET CHRISTIAN SINGLES: 18-80. Free info. U.S. Christian Singles, P.O. Box 715-FH, Wayzata MN 55391

NICE SINGLES with Christian values wish to meet others. Free magazine. Send age, interests. Singles, P.O. Box 310-OFA, Allardt TN 38504

BORROW $50,000 OVERNIGHT. Any purpose. Keep indefinitely! Free Report! Success Research, Box 19749-JM, Indianapolis IN 46219

SPIRITUAL PSYCHIC Sister Mary. 30 years experience in removing bad luck, sickness, pain and sorrow. Tells past, present, future. I can and will help in marriage, love, nature, money, job, lawsuits, drugs, and alcohol problems. For fast help and free reading, call: Sister Mary, 6019 South U.S. 1, Ft. Pierce FL 34982. 407-466-0589.

UNMARRIED CATHOLICS. Nationwide, huge membership, unlimited choice. Founded 1980. Sparks Services, Box 872-FA, Troy NY 12181

FAITHFUL ASIAN WIVES! Attractive photos/details free! AWC, Box 1026-FA, Delano CA 93216-1026. 805-725-0364

REVEREND PASTOR LEWIS, reader and advisor on all problems. Love, business, health, marriage, lost nature. Will help solve your problems in your home. Send $5 with SASE to: 1214 Gordon St., Atlanta GA 30310. 404-755-1301

MOTHER DOROTHY, Reader and Advisor. Advice on all problems — love, marriage, health, business, and nature. Gifted healer, she will remove your sickness, sorrow, pain, bad luck. ESP. Results in 3 days. Write or call about your problems. 404-755-1301. 1214 Gordon St., S.W., Atlanta Ga 30310

SISTER HOPE Solves All Problems. Are you sick? Have bad luck? Bothered by evil spells? Has your loved one left you? Call today 404-548-8598 or 803-583-1926. P.O. Box 221, Bogart GA 30622

POULTRY

GOSLINGS, DUCKLINGS, CHICKS, TURKEYS, GUINEAS. Illustrated catalog, book list $1, deductible. Visa/MC. Pilgrim Goose Hatchery, OF-91, Williamsfield OH 44093

GOSLINGS, DUCKLINGS, CHICKS, TURKEYS, GUINEAS, gamebirds, bantams, swans, peafowl. Books, equipment. Hoffman Hatchery, Gratz PA 17030

RAISE BANTAMS, CHICKENS, Turkeys, Ducks, Guineas, Geese for hobby, food and profit. Send 50¢ for big picture catalog showing all kinds of fancy poultry. Clinton Chicks, Box 548-FA, Clinton MO 64735

MINIATURE BANTAM CHICKS. Exotic and standard breed chicks. Over 75 breeds. Shipped safely to your local post office. Incubators, books, medications, hatching eggs, equipment. Send 50¢ for colorful catalog. Crow Poultry, Box 106-18, Windsor MO 65360

FREE: BEAUTIFUL POULTRY CATALOG with pictures in color. Interesting ideas for presents. Country's largest selection. Over 100 varieties. Baby chicks, bantams, ducklings, goslings, turkeys, guineas, pheasants, partridge, quail, peacocks, hatching eggs, medications, incubators, books, equipment. 74 years supplying large, small, and hobby flocks for eggs, meat, and exhibition. Safe shipment entire U.S., Canada, and overseas. Special 4-H, FFA offers. Surprise gift and special bargains for early orders. Write or call. Murray McMurray Hatchery, C 101, Webster City IA 50595. Phone: 515-832-3280.

REAL ESTATE

ARKANSAS — FREE CATALOG. Natural beauty. Low taxes. The good life for families and retirement. Fitzgerald-Olsen Realtors, P.O. Box 237-A, Booneville AR 72927. Call toll-free 800-432-4595, Ext. 641A.

ARKANSAS LAND — FREE LISTS! Farms, ranches, homes, recreational acreages. Gatlin Farm Agency, Box G, Waldron AR 72958. 1-800-562-9078 XOFA, 501-637-3281

GOVERNMENT LANDS from $10. Repossessed homes, $1. Drug/tax seizures. Surplus recreational, agricultural, commercial properties. Nationwide Directory, $3. Lands, Box 19107-JM, Washington DC 20036

FREE REAL ESTATE CATALOG. Farms, country homes, businesses & more. Top buys nationwide from America's Leader in Rural Real Estate. Call or write today! United National Real Estate, 4700-BYF Belleview, Kansas City MO 64112. Phone toll-free: 1-800-999-1020.

480,000 ACRES valuable government land. Now available low as $6.80 per acre. Campsites, farms, homesites. Fabulous business opportunities. Latest report $2. Satisfaction guaranteed. American Land Disposal, Box 1409-OFA, Holland MI 49422

RECIPES

POTATO CANDY. Delicious, economical, no-bake. $3. Stuff's, "All Kinds of Good Stuff," Box 20907, Louisville KY 40250-0907

FIREHOUSE RECIPES. Assorted favorites from L.A. City firefighter. $5. Firehouse Favorites, P.O. Box 7464, Fox Hills CA 90233-7464

FREE DETAILS! Beautifully illustrated, write-your-own cookbook. 264 "blank" recipe pages. Browse 'n' Buy, Box 504-AL, Bohemia NY 11716-0504

"PEANUT DELIGHT RECIPES" Cookbook. 94 Delicious recipes. $3 + $1 P&H. Lawler, 76 Wesley Ave., Atlantic Highlands NJ 07716

DELICIOUS SUGAR-FREE, Honey-Free Cakes. Carrot. Pineapple Upside Down. Others. $4, LSASE. Lura, 813 Marias, St. Louis MO 63137

COOKIE RECIPES from my grandmother's 1904 cookbook. Five for $3.75, LSASE. JKE, Box 1685, Forney TX 75126

RELIGION

BIBLE FACTS helpful everyday. Expect revealing information. 32 pages. Free. Hopebooks-O, Box 15324, San Diego CA 92115

52 BIBLE VERSE WORD-FIND Puzzles, $1.75. Send to BSWF, POB 512, Lisbon OH 44432

BECOME AN ORDAINED MINISTER. Free ministerial credentials legalize your right to the title "Reverend." Write: Ministry of Salvation Church, 659-D Third Ave., Chula Vista CA 92010

CHRIST'S NAME IS YASU. Why was it changed? (Acts 4:12). KMB, POB 16105, Columbus OH 43216

WHY DOES GOD PERMIT EVIL? Write for free booklet to: Pastoral Bible Institute, 4454 S. 14th St., Milwaukee WI 53221-2357

TODAY'S WORLD CHANGES! Where do these fit into God's Plan? Write for free booklet to: Pastoral Bible Institute, 4454 S. 14th St., Milwaukee WI 53221-2357

FREE BIBLE COURSE. Zion Faith College, P.O. Box 804, Caldwell ID 83606-0804

WORK CLOTHES

OSHKOSH B'GOSH! FREE CATALOG! Men's Work to Size 66! Youth Coveralls! Children's, Women's Basic Denim Fashions! Phone: 414-326-3533. Write: Bohlings, Z159 Stark, Randolph WI 53956

WORK CLOTHES. Save 80%. Shirts, pants, coveralls. Free folder. Write: Galco, 4004 East 71st St., Dept. OF-7, Cleveland OH 44105

FREE CATALOG Women's work gloves that finally fit! Great for gardening, building, etc. Womanswork, Dept. 111, P.O. Box 2547, Kennebunkport ME 04046

WANTED

AUTOGRAPHS, LETTERS, SIGNED PHOTOS of famous people wanted. Herb Gray, P.O. Box 5084, Cochituate MA 01778. 508-877-5254

SLOT MACHINES, any condition, or related parts. Also Wurlitzer jukeboxes and Nickelodeons. Paying cash. 708-985-2742

OLD BASEBALL CARDS, 1885-1975. Wanted by private collector. Fair prices, no hassles, any quantity. Include phone number for reply. Stan, Box 1269, Framingham MA 01701 or 617-492-7730

The Chemistry of Music

When a Japanese geneticist was recently researching the chemical origins of life in the genes of a mouse, he was startled to find not only rhythms – but also a melody.

BY GUY MURCHIE

Is there such a thing as chemistry in music? All atoms vibrate and have been discovered to exhibit detectable rhythms. Indeed, during the past two centuries in which ancient alchemy has steadily evolved into modern chemistry, all the known atoms have been painstakingly classified into what is now universally accepted as the periodic table of elements. It is a table that spans seven octaves, more or less comparable to a piano keyboard.

The harmonic basis of chemistry, however, is not as simple as the music of a harp or a piano, where each note is produced by the vibrations of a string of similar material but of different length or thickness. For each element is actually made of a unique kind of atom, and the atoms range progressively in size and weight up the scale, octave by octave, totaling only a few more than the 88 keys of a piano.

When a distinguished Japanese geneticist named Susumu Ohno was recently searching for the chemical origins of life in a research institute in California, he was startled to find more than rhythm in the genes of a mouse. He found also a melody. While studying the complex helical structures of DNA (or deoxyribonucleic acid), he discovered patterns that repeated themselves. He noticed the flowing, repetitious nature of the DNA genes, which made him think of music. Ohno reflected, "A melody becomes a melody only when it is repeated." Thus looking for music in mouse genes is something like looking for a Rosetta stone among ancient scriptures in forgotten languages — you seek the most frequently recurring set of symbols and the patterns they create. In this case the recurring symbols are the four basic nucleic acids: adenine, guanine, cytosine, and thymine. Because there are eight notes to an octave of music, Dr. Ohno assigned two consecutive notes to each chemical, resulting in twice as many notes as nucleic acids for each gene he translated into music. This is how he was able to compose what might be called gene music.

He did not find, as he might have hoped, any very close resemblance between mouse genes and melodies in Johann Strauss Jr.'s opera *Die Fledermaus*, perhaps because that work of 1874 was inspired by a bat, not a mouse. But he did discover a lively waltz that was a dead ringer for passages in Frederic Chopin's Nocturne, opus 55, no. 1. Moreover, he had half expected it and was far from totally surprised. As Dr. Ohno explained, "Art imitates life more than any of us had fully realized. This is not surprising. Nature follows certain physical laws. The universe obeys them, as does the process of life. Music follows the same patterns. . . ."

Ohno went so far as to suggest that this genetic similarity of genes and music may explain the origins of music in both man and nature. Although man had long been familiar with music in bird song, the human voice, the howling of wolves, the moaning of the wind, and other natural phenomena, he had no idea until recent millenniums what music really was or how to measure it. It may have been a mere 70,000 years ago that man first realized that music had to do with vibrations. That was about when the bow and arrow were invented (as evidenced in cave paintings), and it was very probably long enough ago to have coincided with the beginning of all stringed music. Certainly the twang of a bowstring made a strikingly different sound than the long familiar crash of a tree falling in the forest or the well-known and periodic rhythm of hoofbeats upon gravel. Indeed, the bow twang produced a single musical note of the simplest kind that, when first heard, must have seemed like purest magic.

To make sure its basic nature is clearly understood, may I explain that waving one's finger once in the air will send a slight shock wave of air pressure out in all directions at a fifth of a mile a second. But this is neither sound nor music, and it makes no sensation in the ear, which cannot detect

a single ordinary sound wave. Even shaking the finger back and forth as fast as is humanly possible will not break the silence. But if one could wave it 50 times a second, a faint deep humming note would begin to permeate the air, something like that made by a hummingbird's wings, rising in pitch with any increase in the waving rate.

That actually is what pitch is — and all that it is. Pitch is sound-wave frequency. It is to sound what color is to light. Run a stick along a picket fence, slowly at first, then faster, and you will notice the same thing: the accelerating taps of the stick will blend into a rising tattoo that becomes a musical tone. Pour liquid out of a jug and you can hear its gurgling melody descending the tonal scale as the incoming air takes longer and longer to reflect its pressure waves back and forth across the expanding cavity within, thus lowering their frequency — the principle of the bagpipes, trombone, oboe, and other wind instruments. And the humming string of the bow or the harp is not different in essence: waving back and forth, it hits the air each time, sending out regular impulses of pressure that collectively amount to a musical note of steady pitch.

No doubt the string was particularly inspiring to Pythagoras because it is so easy to observe in action,

In Chopin's Nocturne, opus 55, no. 1, Susumu Ohno found remarkable correspondence between mouse genes and music. The letters A, G, C, and T refer to the four basic nucleic acids, which are matched up with Chopin's notation and can be played on the piano.

so simple and amenable to handling and experimenting, and perhaps also because it is so close to the border (if there is one) between the concrete and the abstract. The latter consideration, which Pythagoras seems to have felt intuitively, has since been made much clearer in a modern laboratory by fixing a needle to a vibrating tuning fork (similar in principle to a string) so that it continuously scratches a wavy line on a long piece of smoked glass passing steadily under it — revealing the beautiful sine curve of "simple harmonic" sound.

By such experiments it was discovered that the note called "middle C" on the piano consists of about 262 pressure waves a second, that any sort of regular vibrations at the rate of 262 per second, whether they come from a vacuum cleaner's motor or a bumblebee's wings, will play middle C, showing that middle C, like every note, is not made of any particular kind of sound, but is purely a *rate* of impulses, a *number* — in other words, an *abstraction*.

The modern general theory of vibrations shows that all materials oscillate in somewhat the same way that celestial bodies swing around their orbits: not necessarily describing complete ellipses, however, but commonly alternating their directions in some partial orbit or folded ellipse like a pendulum, or perhaps in the subtle rocking motion of a moon. This happens, generally speaking, because every material possesses at least one position in which it can theoretically remain at rest — otherwise it would be a "perpetual motion" machine. And if or when it is in such a position of equilibrium, all the forces influencing each particle of it must (by definition) be exactly balanced. But of course, any little disturbance such as a whisper or a ray of light arriving from outside will move the structure at least a little out of equilibrium into some new and unstable position in which each particle of it will feel a "restoring force" trying to return it to balance again. By the time this force succeeds in getting it back to equilibrium, however, the structure is virtually certain to have picked up such momentum that it will overshoot the position and coast beyond it until another (and opposite) restoring force reverses it once more. Thus an oscillation is set up: the natural harmonic motion called vibration when its path is short, but which, on the larger scale, keeps clocks on time, holds stars to their courses, and is inextricably involved in the genetic origins of life.

Dr. Ohno was delighted with the implications of this now well-proved theory that he surmised reached into the genes of all life and could throw light on why certain melodies seem happy and others sad. The melody within a cancer-causing oncogene, for instance, sounds funereal, while the gene that gives transparency to the lens of the eye produces mainly airy trills and arpeggios of light.

When Ohno reversed the process, converting music to chemistry, he was intrigued to find that Chopin's funeral march contained entire passages that were identical to melodies in a cancer gene found in humans, possibly including Chopin's own genes, though the composer died early, before genes were known. Ohno theorizes that there is a principle of periodicity at work here that moves the universe from chaos to order and back to chaos, and that "the same patterns that govern the movement of planets and galaxies also appear in genes and music." He has found similar patterns in the genes from a chicken's eye, from slime mold, brewer's yeast, a rainbow trout, and the human brain. And one of his compositions, derived from an enzyme that metabolizes sugar, is regularly played at naptime in Japanese kindergarten classes because "it always puts the children to sleep." Some people say it is really a lullaby. □□

Guy Murchie's book, The Seven Mysteries of Life, *is available from Houghton Mifflin Co., 2 Park St., Boston, MA 02108.*

PLEASANTRIES

A motley collection of amazing (if sometimes useless) facts, strange stories, and questionable advice kindly sent to us during 1990 by readers of this 199-year-old publication.

CAN SQUIRRELS REALLY REMEMBER WHERE THEIR NUTS ARE BURIED?

At last, the answer to the question that's puzzled us all for centuries.

Can squirrels remember where they have buried their acorns? Or do they simply rely on a hit-or-miss scent-detection method of locating caches of nuts? Biologists and animal behaviorists have long puzzled over this question. For the most part it had been considered unsolvable; after all, it is very difficult to determine whether a squirrel has located an acorn by scent or by memory. And that was that. At least until biologist Lucia Jacobs of the University of Pittsburgh recently decided to investigate the nut-burying habits of squirrels for her doctoral dissertation.

Jacobs released several tame squirrels into an outdoor arena along with ten hazelnuts. All the squirrels participated in burying the nuts. That done, each squirrel was removed for a two- to ten-day period before being turned loose once again into the arena to have a go at nut detection. But unbeknownst to the squirrels, Jacobs had removed their buried nuts and substituted an identical number of different ones in the same holes, thus eliminating the smell of "their" nuts. She'd also added nuts in locations *not* originally chosen by the squirrels. "In this way," she explained, "I hoped to simulate the situation faced under natural conditions where a squirrel has a choice of two types of nuts — its own and its neighbors'."

As a result, despite the fact that the squirrels had buried the nuts as long as a week and a half earlier, and despite the confusing array of similar-smelling nuts Jacobs had scattered about, "each squirrel retrieved significantly more nuts from the hiding places it had chosen in the first place . . ." thus indicating quite conclusively that, instead of relying on smell, squirrels rely on remembering where their nuts are buried.

Finally, after all this time and speculation, we know. Thanks, Dr. Jacobs.

Courtesy of Mark Sunlin

NINE GOOD WAYS TO GET SICK

Follow these simple directions for food spoilage and you won't have to lie when you call in sick to work.

1. Leave food in a slightly warm oven for several hours waiting for someone who is late getting home for dinner. This will encourage bacteria to grow and multiply — and bacteria growth can, and often does, cause various forms of food poisoning.

2. Defrost meat or poultry on the kitchen counter all day while you are at work. The bacteria in these raw foods will grow rapidly when kept at room temperature.

3. Cut vegetables for salad with the same knife and cutting board with which you recently finished cutting up raw chicken. The knife and board will pass the bacteria from the raw poultry to the salad.

4. Make a salad from meat and vegetables left uncovered and unrefrigerated on a salad bar in a store or restaurant all day. More than two hours at room temperature can make cooked meats very dangerous.

5. Pack meat sandwiches for a picnic or work and leave them sitting in a car for a couple of hours before eating them. A warm car offers a perfect environment for bacterial growth.

6. Stop off at a friend's house to chat for an hour or so after doing the grocery shopping. This will offer time for your groceries to begin to spoil rapidly.

7. Leave a pot of stew on the kitchen counter to cool off for a few hours before you put it in the refrigerator. The next time you serve it, it will pack a powerful punch.

8. Make everyone's favorite custard pie for the church supper and leave it on the counter while dinner is served and eaten. Makes everyone sick. (Don't limit the benefits of poisoning only to yourself.)

9. Leave leftovers on the table after dinner while you watch your favorite TV program. Spoilage time accumulates. Preparation time plus serving time plus eating time plus time on the table adds up to plenty of time for bacterial growth.

If you want to be sure of food poisoning, remember to keep food in the temperature range of 40° to 140° F for at least two hours. This is the best range for bacterial growth.

Courtesy of Carol D. Courser, RD
Extension Specialist, Nutrition
University of New
Hampshire

A Startling Fact About Sex and the Dark

Sunlight increases sexual desire by stimulating the pituitary gland, which regulates the ovaries and testes. Darkness signals the pineal gland to produce melatonin, which inhibits sperm production, ovulation, and sexual desires.

Courtesy of Marc McCutcheon and
"Fascinating Facts About Humans"
(January 15, 1990, Bottom Line)

Why You May Not Want to Brush Your Teeth in Durham, North Carolina

Hint: It has to do with a report on recent accidents in this country . . .

The U. S. Consumer Product Safety Commission keeps track of injuries "requiring medical attention or resulting in limitation of normal activity." In 1980, for example, baseball was responsible for more "recreational accidents" (478,000) than football (470,000). More people were hurt dancing (26,000) than were injured practicing the martial arts (19,000). Around the house there were more accidents involving lawn mowers (68,000) than guns (60,000), and pencils, pens, and desk supplies maimed more (45,000) than fireworks (10,000). Also 6,000

Americans reported injuries involving musical instruments.

One of the safest activities in our daily lives is brushing our teeth. Researchers who have recently scrutinized medical literature have found only 31 cases in all recorded history of people who swallowed their toothbrushes. Strangely enough, four of these cases occurred in Durham, North Carolina.

The other toothbrush swallowing occurrences in this country are isolated to one each in California, Tennessee, and Louisiana. The remainder of the 31 are scattered about the world.

Being blown up by an air mattress is not a common accident either. However, in just this past year a Tampa, Florida, man, one Marty Deane, was in the process of blowing up his $39 air mattress with a hair dryer when it, in turn, blew him up. The explosion knocked out windows and a sliding glass door, broke heating pipes, and stove in a bedroom door. In all, $6,000 worth of damage. As to Marty Deane, he was lucky to escape with only slight injuries to his eyes and shoulder.

Just Who Put the First Bathtub in the White House?

If you're truly anxious to know, then skip over this item.

No, it was not Millard Fillmore. His supposed White House bathtub was part of a fictitious story made up by H. L. Mencken in 1917 and, to this day, believed by many to be true.

Actually, just who put the first bathtub in the White House may be anyone's guess. Some say Dolley Madison had bathtubs installed on request from her husband, James. President Monroe, according to some authorities, bought a $20 tin bathtub, presumably portable, for the mansion. Andrew Jackson is said to have had running water, both hot and

cold, as well as a shower bath, while he was president.

Another story gives President Van Buren credit for installing a White House bathtub. But Stuart, Bret & Co., a firm of New York specialists in waterworks securities, as recently as 1932 issued a report claiming that the first permanent bathtub was installed in the White House during the presidency of Abraham Lincoln.

In Wheatland, the home of President James Buchanan in Lancaster, Pennsylvania, is an old-fashioned metal-lined tub that was installed shortly after Mr. Buchanan retired from the presidency in 1861. It is said to be an exact copy of a bathtub that Buchanan used in the White House, installed there, the story goes, just before he became president in 1857. The president who preceded Buchanan was Franklin Pierce. So what do you think?

Courtesy of John Menaugh and the New England Progress *Magazine*

Three Reasons to Worry

1. Old Faithful Isn't

Yellowstone National Park's "Old Faithful" apparently isn't as faithful as it used to be. Recently, the intervals between eruptions have lengthened by about 14 minutes. When the geyser was discovered in 1870, the average interval between eruptions was 65 minutes. Two years ago it was 78.9 minutes. Uh oh.

2. Waves Getting Bigger

According to a study by the Institute

of Oceanographic Sciences in England, waves in the northeastern Atlantic Ocean are getting bigger. The average wave height in the 1960s was about seven feet. Now the average is nine to ten feet high. Uh oh.

3. ... AND A SCARY STATISTIC

From 1980 to 1982 there were no reports of innocent bystanders being shot to death in Los Angeles, California. From 1986 to 1988, however, 105 innocent bystanders were shot to death in Los Angeles, California. Uh oh.

THREE REASONS NOT TO WORRY

1. LOTS OF SUNSHINE LEFT

Yale astronomers concluded last year that our sun is younger than we thought — by some 200 million years. So now we don't need to be concerned about it dying out for another 5 billion years.

2. SPRING FEVER IS OK

"Spring fever," according to Connecticut Health Center doctors, is not laziness. Instead, it is the same sort of thing that prompts bears to emerge from hibernation and birds to mate. Seems the increase in sunlight triggers the pineal gland at the base of the brain to release hormones that give us all that so-called "restless feeling." Perfectly normal.

3. ... AND MORE LOBSTERS FOR US ALL

Despite the fact that 90 percent of female lobsters who achieve legal size end up on the dinner table, including many who've never laid eggs, the lobster population seems to be surviving. Why? Well, it's sort of a mystery. According to Bruce Ballenger and *The Lobster Almanac* (The Globe Pequot Press), it might be because the big deep-water lobsters that aren't fished for are the "parental stock" of the smaller, heavily fished coastal lobsters. Whatever.

ANOTHER OF LIFE'S LITTLE PUZZLES

No need to think about this. Just know that it works every time.

☞ Take your age and multiply it by two; add five; multiply by 50; subtract 365; add the loose change in your pocket (under one dollar); then add 115.

The first two figures in the answer will be your age, and the last two figures will be the change in your pocket.

Courtesy of Thomas E. Oetzel

"JINGLE BELLS": A YE OLDE YANKEE SONG? OR A Y'ALL SOUTHERN SONG?

Here's an important historical controversy that will surely go on forever . . .

Both the North and the South agree that one James Pierpont of Medford, Massachusetts, wrote "Jingle Bells" sometime during the 1850s. But Northerners say he wrote it *in* Medford in 1850 and that it is, therefore, a Yankee song. Southerners say he wrote it in Savannah, Georgia, in 1857 and that it is, therefore, a Southern song. And both sides have documentation to support their cases.

THE UNION ARGUMENT: James Pierpont, an organist for various churches and the son of famous abolitionist Rev.

John Pierpont, lived not far from a boardinghouse in Medford owned by a Mrs. Otis Waterman. In the boardinghouse was the community's only piano, which James Pierpont often borrowed in order to practice and compose songs. Back then, sleigh races between Medford and neighboring Malden were popular, and one winter day in 1850 when the sleighs were racing by Mrs. Waterman's boardinghouse windows, James Pierpont was inspired to peck out "Jingle Bells," which he immediately played for Mrs. Waterman. She loved it.

According to Rev. Carl Seaburg, information director for the Medford Unitarian-Universalist Church, the song was "first sung in public at Simpson's Tavern in Medford not long after Pierpont wrote it."

THE SOUTHERN ARGUMENT: As both sides agree, James Pierpont moved to Savannah, Georgia, about 1852 for health reasons. (During the Civil War he would change his name to Pierrepont and compose a bunch of Confederate battle songs.) In Savannah he was the organist for a small Unitarian church at which his brother, John Jr., was minister. But it was then and there, say the Confederates, that James Pierpont wrote "Jingle Bells" — either for his brother's children or simply because he was homesick for New England Christmases.

THE ULTIMATE EXAMPLE OF YANKEE INGENUITY

You're flying a Cessna with your nine-year-old daughter when the hydraulic fluid to activate the landing gear leaks out. What do you do?

It happened on a flight from Orlando, Florida, to Athens, Georgia. Piloting the Cessna was Alan Frankel of West Virginia. His passenger was his nine-year-old daughter, Alexis. About 15 minutes out of Orlando, Frankel discovered there was no hydraulic fluid in the landing system. That meant the wheels couldn't go down.

First thing Frankel did was show his daughter how to keep the plane level while he crawled to the rear and poured some milk from a milk carton they happened to have with them into the plane's drained hydraulic line. But it wasn't enough to lower the wheels.

Alexis, meanwhile, said later she had just one thing on her mind: "Help!"

Frankel was about resigned to a crash landing when he suddenly thought of something else. He decided to pee into the hydraulic line. Well, actually he filled the milk carton with urine, poured it in, and then had Alexis do the same. They took turns — and finally, miracle of miracles, it was enough to lower the front wheels!

But, alas, the rear wheel didn't budge. So they eventually made a successful emergency belly landing in the Gainesville, Florida, Regional Airport. Neither was hurt.

Alexis said afterwards she wasn't sure she'd ever fly again. We don't know what her father said — but we'd guess that from now on he'll probably always be inclined to have that extra cup of coffee before climbing into the cockpit. You just never know. . . .

Supporting the Southern case is the fact that the song was copyrighted on September 16, 1857 — long after James had left Medford and was living in the South. But supporters of the Union argument still say he wrote it years earlier in Medford and simply didn't go to the expense of copyrighting until he realized its potential market value.

Well, dandy little song, anyway.

Courtesy of Dick O'Donnell

ODD ENDINGS

by Chuck Shepherd

With apologies to everyone involved, we present here a few recent demises that, unfortunately, could conceivably have elicited an inadvertent giggle before the appropriate tears . . .

☞ Reuters News Service reported that a poodle named Cachi caused the deaths of three people in Buenos Aires in October 1988. The dog fell from a 13th-floor balcony and hit Maria Espina, 75, on the head, killing her. As a crowd gathered around Espina, onlooker Edith Sola, 46, was hit by a bus and killed. Then a man who witnessed both incidents had a heart attack and died in an ambulance on the way to the hospital.

☞ Several years ago South Carolina prison inmate Michael Godwin successfully fought to have his electric-chair sentence for murder changed to life imprisonment. In March of 1989, while sitting naked on a metal prison toilet, attempting to fix a television set, the 28-year-old Godwin bit into a wire and was electrocuted.

☞ Robin Morrell, 12, was killed when a huge snowball he made on a hill near the village of Longtown in England in February 1989 rolled over on him.

☞ Mario Morby, 12, a cancer patient in remission in Streetly, England, who had amassed a Guinness-book record two million postcards of get-well support from around the world, was found suffocated in December 1988 after a pile of an estimated 500,000 cards fell over on him.

☞ Experienced parachutist Ivan Lester McGuire, 35, sky-dove to his death in April 1988 near Louisburg, North Carolina. He had loaded up with portable video equipment to record his dive, but apparently forgot to pack his parachute. Tape of the dive was recovered, showing McGuire flailing his arms upon discovery of his omission.

☞ In May of 1989, moments after giving a speech to the Florida Toastmasters Club in Johannesburg, South Africa, in which he encouraged listeners to "enjoy life while you can" because death could come at any moment, businessman Danie du Toit, 49, collapsed and choked to death on a peppermint.

☞ Roh Ki Hwa of Seoul hanged herself recently in front of 70 people at a company picnic because of embarrassment when she returned too late from a hike to prepare her husband's lunch. She was an hour late because of the country's shift that day to daylight saving time (the first time in 26 years that South Korea had changed over). □ □

Chuck Shepherd's weekly column, "News of the Weird," distributed by Universal Press Syndicate, appears in over 35 daily and weekly newspapers. He is the coauthor, with John J. Kohut and Roland Sweet, of *News of the Weird*, a (November) 1989 paperback published by Plume Books (New American Library).

Buying by the Pound

For instance, 75-watt light bulbs are much more expensive than a new two-door Chevy . . .

BY JON VARA

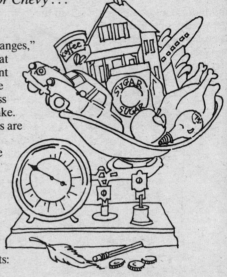

- Illustration by Linda Wielblad

That's mixing apples and oranges," we say of a comparison that fails to account for different units of measurement. The implication is that only a thoughtless consumer would make such a mistake. In reality, though, the world's apples are so thoroughly commingled with its oranges that it's virtually impossible to keep them separate. Perhaps that's just as well; a straight apples-to-apples comparison of some common household goods yields some surprising — not to say bewildering — results. Here's how much you could expect to pay for one pound of the following products:

PRODUCT	COST PER POUND (Spring 1990)
Firewood, hard maple, dry	$.02
Oxygen, compressed	.24
Nutshell, English walnut, crushed (for industrial use)	.27
Sugar, refined white	.42
House, wood-framed, two-story, full basement	.52
Oranges, navel	.70
Apples, McIntosh	.89
Turkey, frozen	1.25
Turkey, fresh	1.50
Walnuts, English, in shell	1.70
Lincoln-head penny	1.79
Bacon, sliced	2.40
Chevrolet Cavalier, two-door	3.28
Coffee, ground-roasted	3.75

PRODUCT	COST PER POUND (Spring 1990)
Walnuts, English, shelled	4.40
Pencils, #2, with erasers, unsharpened	10.00
Light bulbs, 75-watt	14.30
Aspirin, generic	14.50
Feathers, turkey wing, bleached	15.00
Eisenhower silver dollar (face value)	18.22
Roosevelt dime	19.75
Shoelaces, dress, 27"	140.00
Condoms, latex	150.00
Needles, hand-sewing, #7	250.00
Razor blades, double-edged	320.00
Jetliner, Boeing 747	375.00
Gold	6,000.00